MW00782904

Longevity

*The Tao of
Eating and Healing*

Aileen Yeoh

TIMES EDITIONS

© 2004 Marshall Cavendish International (Asia) Private Limited

First published in 1989

Photographs: Yim Chee Peng, Culinary Studios
Cover photograph: Dex Images
Illustrations: NS Chen

Published by Times Editions – Marshall Cavendish
An imprint of Marshall Cavendish International (Asia) Private Limited
A member of Times Publishing Limited
Times Centre, 1 New Industrial Road, Singapore 536196
Tel: (65) 6213 9288 Fax: (65) 6285 4871
E-mail:te@sg.marshallcavendish.com
Online Bookstore: Http//www.timesone.com.sg/te

Malaysian Office:
Federal Publications Sdn Bhd (General & Reference Publishing) (3024-D)
Times Subang
Lot 46, Persiaran Teknologi Subang
Subang Hi-Tech Industrial Park
Batu Tiga, 40000 Shah Alam
Selangor Darul Ehsan, Malaysia
Tel: (603) 5635 2191 Fax: (603) 5635 2706
E-mail: cchong@tpg.com.my

National Library Board (Singapore) Cataloguing in Publication Data

Yeoh, Aileen.
Longevity : The Tao of eating and healing / Aileen Yeoh. – Singapore : Times Editions, c2004.
p. cm.
First published in 1989.
Includes bibliographical references and index.
ISBN : 981-232-828-9

1. Diet therapy. 2. Diet in disease. 3. Longevity – Nutritional aspects.
I. Title.

RA784
613.2— dc21   SLS2004008254

Printed in Malaysia.

To my parents, relatives, friends,
teachers, patients and
Singapore Straits Times readers

Contents

Preface *6*

Acknowledgements *9*

Introduction *11*

Part One: The Tao of Eating

1 Basic Ingredients *24*

2 Whole Cereal Grains *28*

3 Legumes and Pulses *47*

4 Seeds and Nuts *71*

5 Seaweeds *79*

6 Vegetables *86*

7 Herbs and Spices *112*

8 Dried Ingredients *126*

9 Eggs *135*

10 Fish and Other Seafoods *141*

11 Chicken *154*

12 Fruits *164*

13 Beverages *177*

14 The Importance of Cooking in the Tao Diet *186*

15 Meals and Menu-Planning *189*

Part Two: The Tao of Healing

16 Introduction *214*

17 Constipation *227*

18 Colds and 'Flus *236*

19 Sinusitis and Hay Fever *242*

20 Asthma *248*

21 Headaches and Migraines *260*

22 Pains of Joints, Muscles and Nerves *276*

23 Cystitis, Prostate Gland Problems and Prostatitis *289*

24 Acne *294*

25 Adult Onset Diabetes *299*

26 High Blood Pressure and High Blood Cholesterol *305*

27 Psoriasis *314*

28 Multiple Sclerosis *319*

29 Failing Eyesight *326*

30 Balding *330*

31 Brain Nourishment and Poor Memory *334*

32 Women's Problems *341*

33 Cancer *355*

Appendices

A. Classification of Foods *367*

B: Charts for Feet Reflexology *373*

C: Acupuncture Points for Acupressure, Moxibustion and Aromatherapy *376*

Bibliography *382*

Further Reading *384*

Useful Addresses *385*

Index *386*

Preface

The twentieth century is an age of ultra advancement. In modern medicine, powerful drugs, radiation and even lasers are now being used to treat disease. In the food industry, food is super-cleaned, prepacked, freeze-dried, frozen, canned or microwaved.

With these supposedly advanced methods in practice, how come most of us are not as healthy or happy as we want to be? Why are we no healthier or happier than people of past ages when medical care was appalling and food sanitation atrocious?

Health-conscious people who have given up convenience foods for more natural, wholesome foods, or those who have become vegetarians, vegans, fruitarians or raw food converts fare better. However, they may still be victims of hay fever, sinusitis, arthritis, rheumatism, multiple sclerosis, high blood pressure, high blood cholesterol, diabetes, gallstones, kidney stones, overweight, water retention, dandruff, leucorrhoea, cystitis, prostatitis, leukaemia, cancer, depression, anxiety, and more. Why? Perhaps:

- the new diet does not follow the laws of Tao
- the person's lifestyle is not a healthy one

- the person is not spiritually aware of his body and does not appreciate those around him.

In order to be healthy and happy there must be peace of mind, body and spirit. You cannot have one without the others. They are all closely connected and yet separate.

This book does not aim to replace Western doctors, surgeons or Western medical care. And it is not to be used alone to heal yourself, but rather as an introduction to numerous books of my teachers from which you can gain further knowledge and insight. This book has been written in the hope that people will use it to become aware of their bodies and learn to be more responsible for their health and happiness. My advice is appropriate for those who seek good health and happiness, as well as for those who are already ill.

As this is a guide to only the Tao way of eating and living, you may find it too Eastern in its approach. This is only natural, as I am Chinese and look to my ancestors for wisdom. Please feel free to adapt the Tao way to suit your ancestry once you have understood the basic principles in this book.

Health, happiness and peace of mind must be earned through discipline, organisation, perseverance, positive thinking and appre-

ciation for being alive, i.e. the food we eat, the air we breathe and the people and nature around us.

I know this only too well. May 1978 was the turning point of my life. I have not looked back since. My health, happiness and spiritual awareness have improved by leaps and bounds since that time, although I am still learning from my patients, readers, books, teachers and life in general.

My parents brought me up on a diet of meat, fruits, white rice and vegetables. As a child, my father, a doctor of Western medicine, always encouraged me to eat meat and fruits. My Cantonese mother believes that all foods are classified according to properties of cooling, heating, irritating, etc. Even though she taught me which foods were good or bad for my chronic childhood cough, her well-meaning advice was chucked away as soon as my cough cleared (in my early teens) and I longed for all the forbidden foods.

When I came to the United Kingdom to further my studies, I chose to read biochemistry because I wanted to discover what made a person tick, the mysteries of life itself.

Years of university and research did not give me the answer I was seeking. Then on 1 May 1978 I read a book called Macrobiotics, the astonishing oriental food plan for total health, vitality, and longevity by Sakurazawa Nyoiti (written by George Oshawa with an English version by William Duffy). The book made a great deal of sense, and helped clarify my mother's classification of foods.

At this time I was on a vegetarian diet consisting of eggs, cheese, bread, vegetables and lots of vitamin and mineral supplements. My change in diet came about because I had learned at university that chickens, pigs and cows were fed hormones and antibiotics to fatten them for the table and to decrease infections due to intensive breeding. I also learned that traces of insecticides, pesticides, and fungicides sprayed on grasses for cows can still be found in milk, cream, cheese and butter. (This is because the chemicals are oil-soluble and concentrate in butter.)

At the university too I became aware of the numerous carcinogens added to foods for taste, preservative and cosmetic reasons. My salary as a biochemist's technician in a research laboratory was too low, I decided, to be wasted on foods that would eventually lead me to a slow death from cancer! At about that time also, two of my aunts passed away from cancer and my own father had the disease. I had nothing to lose by trying the macrobiotic diet.

On 1 May 1978 I went to the Body, Mind and Spirit Exhibition in London and bought myself a packet each of brown rice, aduki beans and sesame seeds, as well as more books on macrobiotics. Out went the sugar, honey, eggs, cheese, bread, vitamins and minerals.

Within three months, my health slowly improved. By the time one year had passed I no longer suffered from migraine headaches, premenstrual tension, leucorrhoea, constipation, dandruff, frequent urination, frequent coughs, colds and 'flu, lumps below my armpits, painful breasts, and low blood sugar. (I used to faint if I did not eat every two hours; and I'd eat a chocolate bar for energy.)

I left my job as a research technician in May 1980 because I could see that the answer to life's mysteries did not lie at the end of a microscope, but in the macrocosm in which I lived!

During the past eight years, my studies have led me into the wonderful world of macrobiotics, *shiatsu*, chanting, reflexology, acupuncture, and Tao meditation. My life is now one of learning and fulfilment and I am getting nearer my quest for the secret of life.

In these past years I have treated patients through acupuncture and reflexology, and encouraged them to follow the Chang Ming Diet. Their disorders have included: constipation, colitis, diverticulitis, stomach ulcers, Meniere's disease, psoriasis, eczema, incontinence, arthritis, rheumatism, sciatica, lower back pain, varicose veins, leucorrhoea, pelvic inflammation, sinusitis, hay fever, asthma, chronic cough, water retention, piles, prostatitis, cystitis, heart palpitations, gallstones, brain damage, tunnel vision due to radiation, chronic leukaemia, and diabetes.

The success of my treatment depends entirely on the patient's perseverance in self-help, positive thinking and gratefulness for just being. It is difficult to gauge my success as it is really the patient's success. I am only the guide.

The Tao Longevity or Chang Ming Diet is essentially the same as the macrobiotic diet: 50 per cent of the diet is comprised of wholegrains, 25 per cent of fresh, seasonal and local vegetables, 15 per cent of legumes or pulses, 5 per cent of seeds, and 5 per cent of *miso*. The difference is that the foods are not classified according to just *yin* and *yang*, but according to the principles of cooling, heating, irritating, etc. Herbs and spices are also used for taste and for their medicinal properties.

My dream is that after you have read this book you will learn to take good care of yourself and slowly, by your example, others will ask for your secret to health, happiness and peace of mind. Please show them the Tao way, but realise that it is important not to preach about your newfound freedom. Just be patient, and you will see how many people will approach you.

This was also the late George Oshawa's dream. He said,

'One grain. A thousand grains.'

In Peace and Health,
Aileen Yeoh

Acknowledgements

I am truly indebted to my friend, Heather Henderson, a registered medical herbalist, for going through every single chapter before I sent them off for editing, and later going through the proofs. Her comments and suggestions were most invaluable for the chapters on Herbs, Beverages and Women's Problems. I am also indebted to Robert Henderson for reading the chapters thoroughly to spot spelling errors!

Thanks and sincere appreciation to Jane Kohen Winter, my editor, for helping me throughout the book. Jane made some very useful remarks and helped to shape the book for readers of East and West. When she returned to Chicago, Goh Sui Noi, another Times Books International editor, took over. Many thanks also to Yim Chee Peng and his assistant, Judy, for arranging and displaying the wholefoods in the best possible light for photography.

I would like to thank the following for their help: Nature's Best, wholesaler of macrobiotic products in Singapore, and Pulse Wholefoods of the United Kingdom, both for providing ingredients for colour photographs.

Introduction

Chang Ming means longevity. The Chinese word Tao means way or path. Tao refers to the way of nature, how the daylight hours are followed by nightfall, and how the dark night slowly changes back to daylight again. We see this happening with the seasons too: the dead, cold winter slowly comes to life in the spring. In spring, things grow quickly into the summer. After the summer peak, growth slows down and decay sets in for autumn, which leads to death in winter and to rebirth again the next spring.

In tropical countries, there are roughly two seasons: the *yin*, wet, monsoon days and the very *yang*, dry, hot days. In hilly areas, we can see how a small spring at the top of the mountain trickles into life, becomes an active gurgling brook further down the mountain, and may eventually change into rapids or waterfalls. As this river approaches the lowland areas, it begins to slow down and meander in a snake-like fashion until it reaches the sea.

The small spring does not end at the sea. Every droplet of water evaporates from the sea's surface to form clouds. These clouds empty themselves in the form of rain. The rain pours down the mountain, collects in the earth and continues to feed the trickling spring.

Tao teaches us the laws of spiralic change.

Day follows night, night follows day; small becomes big, big becomes small; slow changes to fast, fast slackens to slow; what goes up comes down and vice versa. The Taoist symbol illustrates the law of spiralic change.

As you can see, there is a white dot in the black space and a black dot in the white space. This illustrates the point that there is no such thing as absolute *yin* or *yang* if there is to be equilibrium. In any *yin* phenomenon there is a little *yang*; in every *yang* phenomenon there is a little *yin*. In other words, the *yin* night is never completely dark because there is always some *yang* light (from the moon, stars, fireflies, street lights, etc.). And the *yang* day has some darkness (shadows, for instance).

This symbol also shows how the *yin* darkness at its very peak slowly turns to the *yang* light, or how the *yang* light at its peak changes back to *yin* darkness. This goes on indefinitely. It also shows how one becomes two, i.e. that *yin* and *yang* are opposite and separate yet complementary. This is known as the Tao law of dual monoism.

In human life, the active *yang* sperm from the male swims toward the passive *yin* egg of the female to fuse and form one egg, the embryo. This cell divides into two, these two cells each divide into two, and so on, to form

a multicellular foetus. The foetus grows in the mother's womb until it is born. The child grows up, becomes an adult, and eventually dies. According to the Taoists, when a human dies he simply leaves the material world for the vibrational world where he waits to appear on the earth again. So human life (*yang*) and death (*yin*) are opposite and separate, yet part of one cycle that goes on and on.

Tao as explained here has been in existence since the very creation of the cosmos. Tao as a philosophy did not become a human concept until man appeared on the earth. According to some sources, spiritual beings came to earth and imparted their knowledge to a chosen few. They taught them all aspects of life from simple crafts like farming, pottery, metal-work, spinning, weaving, and glass-making to medicine and spiritual awareness. At that time, man did not know how to write, so his knowledge was passed down by word of mouth.

The discoveries of the legendary Shen Nong, the god of husbandry who lived about 2700 B.C., were passed down this way. It was not until about A.D. 450 that someone wrote down Shen Nong's *Book of Herbs* (*Shen Nong Ben Cao*) which was supposed to have listed the medicinal properties of 365 Chinese herbs according to the Taoist principles of *yin* and *yang*. Most of these herbs are still in use today.

The legendary Yellow Emperor's *Classic of Internal Medicine, Nei Jing*, was also passed down by word of mouth. It was not until about A.D. 200 that several people began compiling this knowledge into a book, which deals with acupuncture, moxibustion, massage, herbal medicine and surgery. (This work may not have been written by the Yellow Emperor. The Chinese are fond of using the names of famous people to lend authenticity to their works.)

About 500 B.C., Lao Tzu wrote down his Taoist teachings before leaving his troubled city to seek solace in the mountains. His poems, in two volumes, help awaken man's spiritual consciousness. They have been translated several times and in several languages by people seeking spiritual well-being, and will no doubt continue to be read for centuries to come.

More recently, Li Shi Zhen (1518-1596), who was regarded as the greatest herbalist in Chinese medicine, wrote *Ben Cao Gang Mu* or *Herbal Systematics*. It consists of 52 volumes describing 1,892 herbs and is still consulted by traditional Chinese herbalists and modern researchers of Chinese medicine.

TAO IN DAILY LIFE

Historically, the Chinese have believed that everything is classified according to whether it is more *yin* or more *yang*. A thing is *yin* when it has more *yin* qualities, and *yang* when it has more *yang* qualities. Things that are neither too *yin* nor too *yang* are considered more or less balanced. The following table classifies some common characteristics and qualities according to *yin* and *yang*.

Yin	Yang
black	white
dark	bright
heavy	light
sinking	floating
cold	hot
winter	summer
watery	dry
weak	strong
soft	hard
long and narrow	short and broad
material	immaterial
substance	energy
internal	external
passive	active
plants	animals

All things are *yin* and *yang* relative to each other. In other words, seaweeds, for example, are *yin* because they are passive plants that grow in the sea. Fish might also be considered *yin* because they live in the sea, but compared to seaweed, they are classified as *yang* because they are active animals.

YIN AND *YANG* CONSTITUTIONS

Our constitutions are determined largely by the health of our parents at the time of conception. Our mother's diet and her emotional and spiritual states throughout our nine months in the womb can alter the constitution. If her physical and spiritual states were sound we will be blessed with good qualities in addition to our predestined constitutional make-up. However, if her diet, emotional and spiritual states were unsound, we will have a constitution slightly below what was predestined.

The father's physical and emotional conditions are important too because he affects the mother who, in turn, affects the unborn child. All couples wishing to have healthy, happy children must harmonise their own bodies, minds and spirits before embarking on the creation of new lives.

People with *yin* constitutions have a lack of vitality. Although they can be fat or thin, they are generally on the thin and weak side and have weak bone structure. They succumb easily to diseases and adverse weather conditions and have a passive nature.

People with *yang* constitutions are full of vitality. Although they can be fat or thin, they are generally on the stout side. They have strong bone structures, and diseases and adverse weather conditions do not harm them. They tend to be happy too, because they are full of life.

BLOOD SYSTEMS

The term 'blood system' should not be confused with constitution. Unlike the constitution, the blood system can be altered from day to day or from season to season, depending on diet and climatic conditions. If warming or hot energy foods are eaten to the exclusion of cooling or cold energy foods and herbs, the blood system may get overheated. The opposite can also occur, the result of which is a cooled blood system.

It is much easier to cool an overheated blood system than to warm a cooled blood system. People with *yang* constitutions tend toward overheated blood systems if they indulge in warming or hot energy foods. Such people should eat more neutral and cooling foods and drink cooling herbal teas to restore balance.

People with *yin* constitutions should avoid eating too many cold or cooling energy foods because their systems are already cool. They should eat more neutral and warming energy foods and, once in a while, they should drink warming or tonifying herbal brews to give them strength, warmth and vitality.

WHAT IS THE NATURE OF YOUR BLOOD?

Tongue Diagnosis
Look at your tongue first thing in the morning before eating, drinking or brushing your teeth. If your blood system is neutral, the body of the tongue will be a lovely pink with a very fine film-like fur. If the blood system is overheated, the body of the tongue will be red, the tongue coating will be yellow and may have a dry, sticky or damp appearance. A dry fur indicates a lot of dry heat in the body. If the fur is sticky or damp, the body has a lot of damp heat. (Smokers tend to have yellow fur on their tongues because smoke creates dry heat in the body. People who take drugs may also have yellow, brown or black fur on their tongues. Do not confuse these with the natural yellow fur caused by heat in the body.)

If the blood system is cooled, the body of the tongue will be very pale pink or, sometimes, lilac. The fur is usually white and moist.

Urine Diagnosis
The first urine of the day will be a pale golden colour if your blood system is balanced. If your system is overheated, the first urine of the day will be deep yellow, yellow-brown or reddish. The volume may be scanty and it will often have an unpleasant odour. (If you are taking drugs, your urine may also change colour. Do not confuse this with your natural urine colour.) If the first urine of the day is as clear as water or very pale yellow, your blood system is on the cool side. The volume may also be copious.

Stool Diagnosis
If you have a normal blood system, your stools will be well formed, neither too hard nor too soft and moist. The odour will not be unpleasant. If your blood system is overheated, the stools will be hard and dry and the odour will be unpleasant. Sometimes, the stools may be small and pebbly. According to traditional Chinese medicine, this occurs when the heat of the body has burnt out the *yin* fluids, leaving the intestines dry.

If you have a cooled blood system, stools are not well formed and tend to be soft. Sometimes, there is undigested food in them. According to traditional Chinese medicine, this indicates that there is insufficient *yang* heat in the body to digest and absorb food.

Other symptoms and signs of an overheated blood system include: red complexion, red or yellow in the whites of the eyes, red lips, pimples or acne on the face or body, bad breath, frequent sore throats, a constant feeling of warmth, difficulty in

bearing hot weather, preference for cold liquids and foods, fairly active nature. You may have a cooled blood system if you experience these symptoms: pale face, pale lips, easily tired, dislike of the cold, preference for hot foods and drinks and curling up in bed beneath lots of warm bedclothes.

It is possible to have a cooled blood system one day, and an overheated one the next, especially when you have indulged in too many warming or hot energy foods. When you first begin the Chang Ming Diet, you should monitor your body closely every day until you determine your natural blood system, and then you should eat accordingly.

CLASSIFICATION OF FOODS

Foods are also classified according to their nature. Classifications range from cold, cooling and neutral to warming and hot. In general, foods which grow or live in ponds, lakes, streams, rivers, seas and oceans are colder or more cooling than those which grow on the land. Watercress, seaweeds, fish and all kinds of seafood, for example, have cold or cooling natures, while carrots, leeks, eggs, chicken and red meats have warm or hot natures. The natures of all foods can be changed by the way they are cooked. If watercress is stir-fried, for instance, it is less cooling than when it is boiled in a soup. And if chicken is steamed it is less heating than when it is grilled.

Cereal grains and pulses, which comprise 50 per cent and 15 per cent respectively of the Chang Ming Diet, tend to be neutral. Leafy greens and root vegetables are more cooling than cereal grains and pulses. And those grown in fresh water or the sea are even more cooling than land plants. Fruits are more cooling than vegetables and flesh foods are more warming than cereal grains and pulses. Of course, land animals are more warming than fish and other seafoods.

Cereal grains, pulses, vegetables, fruits and flesh foods can be further divided into cooling, neutral and warming as shown in Appendix A.

Some of the foods listed in the appendix are said to create 'internal wind' when eaten in excess. This does not only mean flatulence, but pain, aches or skin rashes that move from place to place, as well as muscle spasms, convulsions, tremblings and epilepsy. Some of these foods include: spinach, all types of mushrooms, rhubarb, rooster's head, seafood, soyabean milk, sweet glutinous rice, coconut water and coconut milk. Eating too many cold energy foods can also bring about internal wind.

The following foods are said to create damp heat in the body: white or brown sugar, sweet glutinous rice, baked flour products, almonds, peanuts, dried milk, skim-milk or full cream milk, hard cheeses, pork, oranges, mandarins, tangerines, clementines, rambutans, *bacang* and pineapples.

Some foods tend to cause irritations in an existing wound, skin disease or insect bite. At such times it is advisable to avoid: celery, duck, goose, yam, taro, all seafood, yellow fish, fish roe, fish sauce, shrimp paste, tomatoes, potatoes, aubergines, sweet bell peppers, chillies, fresh bamboo shoots, cheeses, chocolate, pineapple, mangoes, *bacang* and *langsat* (Malaysian fruits).

FOODS TO AVOID

If you wish to follow the Chang Ming Diet for health, vitality and spiritual awareness, it is advisable to avoid the following foods. It will be very difficult to give up these foods straight away if you have eaten them all your life. Try to wean yourself from them gradually.

Sugar

Avoid: granulated white sugar, white castor sugar, icing sugar, rock sugar, demerara, soft light or medium brown sugar, Barbados sugar, muscovado sugar, molasses sugar, *gula melaka*, syrup, treacle, honey, sweets, toffee, fudge, chocolate.

Caution! There is hidden sugar in: breakfast cereals, alcoholic and soft drinks, biscuits, cakes, pastries, ice-cream, tomato ketchup, chilli sauce and soyasauces, tinned and frozen foods, convenience foods.

Sugar is bad for the body because it is an unnatural and highly refined food. The body needs lots of B vitamins and minerals to digest it and, in doing so, robs itself of precious nutrients needed for the growth and repair of nerves and other cells. It is not surprising to find a high rate of nervous disorders like nervous tension, depression, anxiety and frustration in a population that consumes a great deal of sugar.

Honey should not be eaten regularly but taken from time to time for medicinal purposes.

Dairy Products

Avoid: fresh milk, powdered milk, condensed milk, skim-milk, sterilised milk, homogenised milk, cream, butter, ghee, ice-cream, cheese, cottage cheese, curd cheese, whey cheese, cream cheese, yogurt, kefir, quark, buttermilk, and sourmilk.

Humans are the only animals that continue to drink milk products into adulthood! What is more, cows are given hormones to increase milk production and antibiotics to keep them disease-free. The grasses on which they feed are sprayed with chemical fertilisers, insecticides and pesticides. Furthermore, these chemicals are oil-soluble so that they are not washed away when it rains. It is very likely that there are traces of these harmful chemicals in the milk we drink.

Even though dairy products from organically-bred goats and sheep are free from hormones and chemicals, I do not take them because I do not believe in robbing other species of their young's milk. Besides, the ancient Chinese believed that if you gave a child cow's milk, he would grow up stupid, and if you gave him goat's milk he would grow up stubborn!

It is now scientifically proven that dairy products are also rich in saturated fats which increase the body's serum cholesterol. In countries where people have cut down on dairy products, the incidence of heart problems has decreased dramatically.

Coconut Products

> *Avoid:* coconut milk, coconut cream, coconut oil, coconut flakes, desiccated coconut, sweets, biscuits, cakes, pastries, *kuih-muih,* and curries made with coconut products.

Coconut products are very rich in saturated fats which are very difficult to digest. Although it is harmful to eat coconut products daily, it is acceptable to have curry cooked with coconut products every now and then.

Red Meat

> *Avoid:* veal, beef, lamb, mutton, pork, bacon, gammon, ham, sausages, haggis, black puddings, meat burgers, meat paté, minced meat and organ meats (like liver, kidney, heart, tongue, brain, sweetbread, head, feet, tail, tripe, cheek and bone marrow), duck, goose and Chinese wind-dried meats (like sausages and duck).

Red meat, however lean it is, is finely marbled with saturated fats. If animals have been fed on grasses sprayed with chemicals, their meat will contain traces of chemicals too. Calves, cows, lambs and pigs are often fed chemicals (and probably hormones) to increase their weight. Liver organs, especially, should be avoided because the liver is the first site for detoxification in the body.

Chinese wind-dried meats, especially sausages, are generously marbled with saturated fat.

Animal Fat

> *Avoid:* beef dripping, mutton dripping, pork lard, animal suet, fat in veal, lamb, mutton, pork, duck, goose and chicken.

These foods are made up of lumps of saturated fat and, if the animals were fed on sprayed grasses, it is likely that they contain traces of harmful chemicals.

Deep-fried Foods

> *Avoid:* deep-fried chips, crisps, crackers (prawn, etc.), peanuts, cashews, fish, shallots, garlic, bananas, and *tofu.*

Even the healthier polyunsaturated oils can be unsafe when they are subjected to high heat – as in deep-frying. The heat changes them to something like the harmful saturated fats.

Eggs

Eggs from battery hens are very harmful because they are fed on antibiotics, hormones and other chemicals. The antibiotics are used to prevent infections due to intensive breeding and the hormones speed up laying capacities. These poor creatures live under intense stress all the time, so it would not be surprising if stressful vibrations were passed on to their eggs. If you were to consume these 'stressful' eggs daily for a long time, you might pick up the stressful vibrations and become prone to frustration, depression, and nervous tension.

White Flour Products

> *Avoid:* bread, *chapati, nan, roti,* biscuits, cakes, pastries, *kuih-muih,* pasta, noodles and dumplings made from white flour.

White flour products are highly refined foods that contain few nutrients. They lack fibre, which helps the body regulate the bowels, and they lack vitamins and minerals for cell growth and repair. They are nothing more than calorie-laden foods that sit in the body, causing obesity and other health problems.

Breakfast Cereals

> *Avoid:* cornflakes, Puffa-Puffa Rice, Rice-Krispies, All Bran, Bran Flakes, packaged muesli, instant porridge oats, Readybreak and Nestum, etc.

Breakfast cereals are often highly processed and laden with sugar. Read the labels before buying!

Beverages

> *Avoid:* tea, coffee, Milo, Ovaltine, Horlicks, cocoa, chocolate, all soft and aerated drinks, and those with artificial flavourings and colourings.

Tea and coffee are stimulants. Prolonged consumption on a daily basis may lead to weakening of the central nervous system which may manifest itself in the following symptoms: nervous tension, anxiety, depression, frustration and headaches. The other beverages are often laden with sugar and chemicals.

Chemicals

> *Avoid:* saccharine, sorbitol, other artificial sweeteners, monosodium glutamate, preservatives, colourings, flavourings, and other additives.

These chemicals are most unnatural! Some may even be carcinogenic if taken in small doses on a daily basis for prolonged periods.

Vegetables

> *Avoid:* tomatoes, potatoes, aubergines (eggplants or brinjals), sweet bell peppers (capsicums), cayenne, tabasco and chillies.

All these vegetables belong to the Deadly Nightshade or *Solanaceae* family. My macrobiotics teachers explained that they are all very *yin* vegetables and contain the same poison (solanin) as the Deadly Nightshade but in very minute amounts. However, after several years on a daily diet of potatoes and tomatoes this minute amount of solanin will accumulate to quite a substantial amount. We do not know what the specific effects of the accumulated solanin will do to the body system except it will make a person very *yin,* i.e. passive and lethargic.

According to traditional Chinese medicine, potatoes, tomatoes, aubergines and sweet bell peppers have cooling energies. These foods are not meant for daily use especially by people with cooled blood systems. They cool their blood systems further still to cause lethargy, oedema, loose stools, diarrhoea, undigested food in the stools or frequent bowel movements.

Here are some examples of the effects of

these foods on some of my patients and friends. One patient with a cooled blood system used to live on onions, potatoes, tomatoes, sweet peppers, aubergines and cheese because she is a vegetarian. She could not get rid of water retention in her legs and abdomen even after several months of weekly reflexology treatment. I advised her to stop eating the above foods and start on a diet of brown rice, brown lentils, black-eyed beans, chick-peas, marrowfat peas, carrots, pumpkin, cabbages, leeks, onions, garlic and ginger. She said that within a week of her new diet, her water retention was much improved.

Several patients with arthritis or rheumatism have mentioned that they cannot eat tomatoes because their aches and pains would worsen. However, potatoes, tomatoes and aubergines can be used by people with overheated blood systems. They must be taken in small amounts about two to three times a week and not more. Please see Chapter 26 on High Blood Pressure.

Potatoes, tomatoes, aubergines and sweet bell peppers are used by the Chinese to cook with warming red meats like beef and lamb to make them less warming. Therefore if you are a vegan or vegetarian you must avoid these vegetables because you do not have any warming meats in your diet to counteract them.

Cayenne peppers, tabasco peppers and chillies have hot energies. They must not be eaten by anyone with an overheated blood system. The likely effects are high blood pressure, migraine, conjunctivitis, psoriasis, eczema, pimples, spots, boils, stomach ulcers, ulcerative colitis, gall bladder inflammation, cystitis, prostatitis and other diseases caused by too much heat in the blood.

My grandmother advised us not to eat chillies because she said they are bad for the eyes. To confirm this, my mother noticed that among her elderly relatives and friends those who *must* have chillies with every meal tend to develop cataracts compared to those who never touched chillies in their lives.

Cayenne peppers, tabasco peppers and chillies can be used in tiny amounts with other foods to drive away the cold and damp from the body. You will read about this in the chapter on Arthritis and Rheumatism.

> *Note:* I would not advise you to combine potatoes, tomatoes, aubergines or sweet bell peppers with cayenne, tabasco or chillies, even though the cooling and heating natures of the vegetables balance each other. There will be too much solanin in such a dish.

Citrus Fruit

> *Avoid:* oranges, grapefruit, tangerines, mandarins, clementines, satsumas, limes, ugli (tangelo), kumquat and ortanique.

These fruits are not harmful if picked ripe and eaten in the country in which they are grown. This is because the acids in the fruits have been allowed to change naturally into sugars. Citrus fruits for export are picked when still green and allowed to ripen either naturally or by chemical means during transport, so they contain acids which may be harmful.

Surprisingly, citrus fruits do not contain as much vitamin C as home-grown parsley, chives, Welsh onion or window-sill-grown alfalfa seed sprouts. In the East, guavas are the best source of vitamin C, not oranges.

Limes were once used as a source of vitamin C for sailors because they can be

stored for long periods. If you have a garden or window-sill with plenty of sunlight, it is better to grow your own sources of vitamin C.

Alcohol

> *Avoid:* beer, lager, shandy, cider, wine and hard spirits.

Do you know how much sugar and how many chemicals are involved in the making of alcoholic beverages? Sugar is used to encourage the growth of yeast, but not all of it is converted, especially in sweet drinks. It is common knowledge that large quantities of alcohol can damage the liver (although the occasional drink for healthy people at celebrations is fine).

Convenience Foods

> *Avoid:* cartonned, tinned, frozen and freeze-dried foods.

Convenience foods usually contain sugar, artificial colourings and flavourings, and preservatives. Plastic, paper and other manmade containers are not healthy either because they are chemically treated to withstand the acidity or alkalinity of the food they hold.

WHAT IS LEFT TO EAT?

After this long list of forbidden foods, you may be wondering which foods you *can* eat. Do not despair. There are numerous wholesome foods available. The following chapters aim to introduce you to them. They include whole cereal grains, legumes, pulses, seeds, nuts, seaweeds, vegetables, some common Western and Eastern herbs, dried Chinese ingredients with medicinal properties, free-range eggs, fish and other seafoods, free-range chickens, fruits and beverages.

All these wholesome foods are classified according to cooling, neutral and warming energies. This is because in the Chang Ming Diet you choose foods to suit your blood system, to maintain a neutral blood system. For example, if you have an overheated blood system you should eat mainly neutral and cooling energy foods to cool you down. If you have a neutral blood system, you can have cooling, neutral and warming energy foods in equal proportions. If you have a cooled blood system, you should eat mainly neutral and warming energy foods to warm you up.

Remember, the most constant thing is change. Therefore, when your overheated blood system or cooled blood system has reached a balanced neutral system, you can have foods with cooling, neutral and warming energies to maintain this balance.

HOW TO USE THIS BOOK

This book is written for people from the West and East. So if you come across unfamiliar foods, please do not be alarmed. You are not meant to eat them. Ideally, you should eat foods grown in your own locality. Such an ideal is not always possible so you can eat foods imported from other countries within the same latitude as your own. For example, temperate countries should import from temperate countries and the tropics from the tropics. Temperate countries should not

import foods from the tropics and vice versa.

The best way to use Part I of the book is to quickly browse through all the chapters to get an idea what it is all about before re-reading them again. This is because many foods will be unfamiliar to you. Secondly, Part I was written as a reference for the second half of the book.

Cooking Tao Recipes

Chapter 14 explains the importance of cooking in the Tao or Chang Ming Diet. Chapter 15 gives you some ideas about how to plan menus for different blood systems.

This is not a cookery book in which the recipes are always mouth-watering. I have tried my best to include palatable and interesting recipes here and there only to show you how to use these unfamiliar foods according to Taoist principles. Sometimes I only give suggestions on how to combine foods to create a neutral balance between cooling, neutral and warming energy foods.

In Chapters 1 to 13, I have categorised the foods into cooling, neutral and warming energies. There is an appendix – Appendix A – right at the end for easy reference. Please use this often to help you choose the appropriate foods for your blood system.

Measures

The recipes are mostly for one person because not everyone in the family suffers from the same problem. It is easy to increase proportions of ingredients for two or more. However, you do not double or add more of sea-salt, *tamari*, *shoyu*, *miso*, unrefined cold-pressed oils, herbs and spices. I leave it to you to judge the amount of condiments required.

Measurements are given in metric and imperial standards. For convenience, I have used teaspoons, tablespoons and British cups.

Hanyu Pinyin and Chinese Characters

As this book is for people of all nationalities, I have included, where appropriate, Hanyu Pinyin for Mandarin-educated individuals, Chinese characters for the dialect users, and Malay names for the people of Indonesia, Malaysia and Singapore who know many ingredients by their Malay names.

Sometimes the spelling of Chinese names has not been according to Hanyu Pinyin, for example, Tao has been used in preference to Dao. It has been difficult to decide which spelling (and pronunciation) to use in some cases. My decision was influenced always by the familiarity of the name to as many readers as possible.

I wish you many hours of happy reading and experimenting in your search for health, vitality and tranquillity.

The Tao of Eating

1 Basic Ingredients

This chapter deals with many of the basic ingredients featured in the recipes in the chapters that follow. It is advisable to become familiar with them now, as they will be mentioned again and again in the text.

SEA-SALT

Many health and diet experts discourage the use of any type of salt. In my opinion, only pure, refined table salt (sodium chloride) is unhealthy. The body cannot cope with its unnatural, highly refined pureness. In addition, most table salt is sold with additives to maintain its free-flowing consistency.

Sea-salt, on the other hand, contains traces of other elements which are not present in land plants. These elements, such as iodine, are found in seaweeds. If you cannot take seaweeds, for example because you have a weak constitution or a cooled blood system, then sea-salt can help make up the minerals not found in land plants.

In addition, sea-salt in *small doses* is essential in the digestion of food. A small amount of salt promotes the secretion of saliva, which is necessary for the digestion of food in the mouth prior to digestion in the alimentary canal. Sea-salt, therefore, is very important in a vegan, vegetarian or macrobiotic diet because wholefoods require lots of chewing and saliva for predigestion. Tiny pinches of sea-salt should be added to wholegrains, legumes, pulses, seeds, nuts, dried fruits and vegetables during cooking. It should not be sprinkled at the table.

The Chinese believe sea-salt in small doses is good but too much can harm the kidneys and heart. People suffering from water retention, oedema, kidney problems and heart problems should use one of the salt substitutes sold in health food shops.

If you are prone to mouth ulcers or sore throats, a daily gargle with some sea-salt water will prevent recurrence. Diluted sea-salt solution can also be used to bathe certain types of skin diseases.

Note: Crystal or rock salt can be used instead of sea-salt.

COOKING OILS

The best cooking oils are unrefined, cold-pressed oils. Health food stores stock oils made from: sesame, sunflower, safflower, corn, wheatgerm, olive, almond, walnut, grape, etc. I prefer sesame oil, so this oil is used in my recipes. If you prefer other oils please use them by all means, instead of sesame oil.

Unrefined, cold-pressed oils are not extracted by heat or chemical solvents, like highly processed oils. They are produced by crushing the seeds, nuts, wheatgerm, grain or olive until the oil oozes out. Often bits of sediment like crushed seeds, nuts, etc. will settle at the bottom of the bottle. Cold-pressed oils are more expensive than other oils, but you do not need much – only enough to coat the bottom of the wok, pan or pot to prevent burning.

Pure Roasted Sesame Seed Oil

Unlike unrefined, cold-pressed sesame oil, which is pale gold with a subtle aroma and taste, pure roasted sesame oil is more viscous, reddish brown, very aromatic and strongly flavoured. The Chinese use it in fish and chicken dishes. It has warming properties and is used as a marinade, sauce or dressing. It does not need to be cooked because it is extracted from roasted seeds. Because of its warming nature, roasted sesame oil is good for those with weak constitutions and cooled blood systems or with tendencies toward

them. It should be used infrequently by those with overheated blood systems or tendencies toward them.

SUGAR SUBSTITUTES

Sugar is very unhealthy. According to Chinese medicine, overconsumption of sugar creates body dampness which manifests as water retention, fatty tissue, catarrh, mucus, phlegm or sputum. Try to avoid sugar in all its forms, including hidden sugar in processed foods.

Sugar substitutes are healthier than sugar, but they should not be eaten liberally. If you have a sweet tooth, it may be because you eat too much salt. If you reduce your sea-salt intake you may find it easier to cut down on sugar and cravings for sweet things.

Below is a table of sugar-free substitutes classified according to cooling, neutral and warming energies. Choose those that are appropriate for your needs.

Cooling	Neutral	Warming
Bananas (dried)	Apple juice (concentrated)	Chinese black and red dates
Figs (dried)	Barley malt extract	Hunza apricots
Pear juice (concentrated)	Currants	Longans
Pure honey	Dates	Nectarines (dried)
	Prunes	Peaches (dried)
	Raisins	
	Rice malt extract	
	Sultanas	

Note: Make sure all dried foods are free of sugar, glucose, sulphur dioxide, mineral oil and additives.

Cooking Utensils

The best cooking utensils are good quality enamel, stainless steel or cast-iron pots and pans. They last longer than glass, clay, terracotta or earthenware.

Cast-iron pots and pans ensure even cooking and minimum fuel. Food stays warm longer in cast-iron pots and they can be used on the stove top or in the oven. Unfortunately, they are heavy and expensive, and great care must be taken not to chip or scratch them with metal implements or scouring pads.

Stainless steel pots and pans are lighter and less expensive. Enamel pots and pans tend to get chipped easily so you must look for good quality and take great care of them. Aluminium pots and pans are not recommended. Aluminium is not an inert metal, so every time you cook, bits of it go into the food, especially when cooking highly acidic vegetables or fruit. Have you noticed how pitted old aluminium pots and pans look? The pits indicate places where bits of aluminium have gone into the food over the years. Sometimes the pitted spots are where the cooking utensils have been battered by cooking implements.

Is the Wok Essential for Stir-frying?
You can stir-fry in any deep-sided pan with a wide diameter. I often use pots for stir-frying. The typical Western frying pan has very low sides, and is unsuitable for quick stir-frying.

Fuel and Cooking Methods

You have a choice of wood, charcoal, oil or gas.

What you are about to read may sound like nonsense. I write to point out what dangers there can be in electric and microwave cooking. I leave it to my readers to decide for themselves what is best for them.

Smoke from wood or charcoal fires may be dirty but it is not more carcinogenic than cigarette or cigar smoke or other carcinogens found in food and air. This form of cooking fuel has been in use since man discovered fire. If it were carcinogenic man would not have survived for so long. Of course if you eat too much charcoal-burnt food you are more likely to develop cancer: modern research says charred foods are carcinogenic.

Electricity is not recommended, especially if you are a cancer patient. Macrobiotic teachers believe that the energy from electricity is chaotic. Cancer is a result of chaos, therefore cancer patients who use electricity to cook may make their cancer worse. Similarly people suffering from nerves, irritability, depression and frustration should try not to cook with electricity as their bodies are in a way in chaos and out of tune with nature. Food should be cooked with a less chaotic energy, for example, gas, oil, coal, charcoal or wood.

Microwave cooking, in my opinion, is worse than chaotic electrical energy. It is explosive. Food is cooked in seconds. On top of that, even when the microwave oven is brand new and the model has passed all safety requirements, I believe you are still subjected to microwave leakage every time you use it. This daily minute dose will gradually accumulate in your system over the years and injure you at your weakest moment and weakest bodily parts.

Slow Cookers or Crockpots
A slow cooker that uses very little electricity

is ideal for stewing wholegrains, legumes, pulses, root vegetables and chicken. Boil legumes and pulses in a separate pot on top of the stove for at least 15 minutes to break down the 'poisonous' bean proteins before adding them to the slow cooker or crockpot. It is also a good idea to lightly brown a chicken before putting it into the slow cooker to prevent *Salmonella* poisoning. Any of the recipes in this book that require long hours of cooking can be done in a slow cooker. Some slow cookers have a high or low temperature setting so you may have to experiment a bit to determine which setting is best for which ingredients.

Note: Slow cookers or crockpots are only ideal for busy career women. If you can organise your life so that you do not need them, so much the better.

Pressure cookers

Pressure cookers can also be used to cook wholegrains, root vegetables and chicken if you are in a hurry. This is because pressure cooking cuts down the cooking time by half. However, be sure to buy a stainless steel pressure cooker and not an aluminium one.

Legumes or pulses should not be cooked in a pressure cooker because you will be trapping the noxious gases, thus causing too much flatulence. If you must, bring the legumes or pulses to a boil first with the lid off for 15 to 20 minutes, to allow all the noxious gases to escape before closing the lid.

Solid Fuel Cookers

Solid fuel cookers can be run on wood, coal, oil or gas. Their cool ovens are ideal for slow cooking.

2 Whole Cereal Grains

What are whole cereal grains? They include brown rice, pot barley, whole wheat grains, oat groats, rye, millet and sweet corn. Buckwheat is the seed of a herbaceous plant, not a cereal grain, but we will include it under whole cereal grains because it is used as such.

Whole cereal grains are vital to the Chang Ming Diet because they provide an ample supply of good quality complex carbohydrates, small amounts of protein and polyunsaturated fats, plenty of vitamins B and E, some minerals and trace elements, and lots of dietary fibre called bran.

Complex carbohydrates are broken down slowly to give you constant energy and stamina. Do not confuse complex carbohydrates with simple carbohydrates like white sugar which is broken down quickly, giving you a short, unsustained burst of energy. Eating lots of simple carbohydrates, like white sugar, can lead to obesity, whereas moderate amounts of complex carbohydrates, in the form of whole cereal grains, can give you constant energy and stamina with no weight gain.

Vitamin B complex strengthens and nourishes the nerves so you do not feel tense, edgy, irritable or restless. It is required for cell growth and repair, and is good for the skin and hair. Vitamin E, housed in the wholegrain germ, is essential for vitality, blood circulation, and cell growth and repair. It is also good for the skin and hair.

Minerals and trace elements are also necessary for cell growth and repair, and are good for the skin, hair, nails, teeth and bones. Bran is a valuable dietary fibre. It helps keep the bowels (the large intestines) working regularly to prevent constipation, piles and even diarrhoea.

A Whole Cereal Grain

Grain germ containing Vitamins B and E, minerals, trace elements, proteins and polyunsaturated fats

Bran containing dietary fibre

Endosperm containing complex carbohydrates

As you can see, nature has packed a great deal of goodness into little parcels of whole cereal grains. One grain, if given the right germinating and growing conditions, will grow into a healthy plant. Even our teeth have been designed for grinding whole cereal grains. We have 20 molars for grinding, eight incisors for cutting vegetables and only four canine teeth for eating animal foods.

It is much better to eat cereal grains in their unrefined, unprocessed state than as

processed flakes, meals or flours. Once a whole cereal grain is processed, its vitality is lost.

The ancient Taoists saw the potential of wholegrains and advised people to use them as a staple food to harness vital energy. Metaphysically, the Taoists believed that grains, which grow upright, were a connection between the forces of heaven and earth. By eating them, the Taoists believed that man could strengthen his connection with heaven and earth, and discover the secrets of health, vitality, longevity and tranquillity.

CHOOSING WHOLE CEREAL GRAINS

The vitality of the grain depends on the grain germ. When selecting whole cereal grains, make sure each germ is intact. You should also look for the bran covering each grain. If it is over-polished, the bran or germ will be wholly or partially missing. Fresh grains smell nice too. When they have a musty odour, they have been kept too long.

Refer to the drawing of whole cereal grain.

STORING

Whole cereal grains can keep indefinitely in a cool, dry place if they are stored in airtight containers. In tropical countries, add a bay leaf and a dried hot chilli to prevent bugs, or store the airtight container in the refrigerator. The older the wholegrain, the longer it takes to cook. Processed germs, flakes, meals and flours do not keep for long.

CHANG MING DIET

In the Chang Ming Diet, grains make up 50 per cent of your daily food intake. A variety of wholegrains should be eaten. This chapter, like the others in Part I of the book, contains descriptions of each kind of wholegrain and recipes using each type. The recipes are subject to countless variations. Have fun experimenting.

BARLEY
(Hordeum vulgare)
properties: cooling, low in gluten

Pot barley is barley with its bran and germ intact. Pearl barley has lost its bran and germ, so it is no longer nutritious.

According to the *Nei Jing*, pot barley harmonises the stomach; it aids digestion, is good for the intestines, promotes urination, and is helpful in treating people with cystitis (pain on urination) and diabetics who tend to have overheated blood systems.

Unlike brown rice, pot barley is not tasty on its own. It is best cooked in a vegetable soup, stew or casserole. Because it has cooling properties, pot barley is an excellent food for those who tend to have overheated blood systems. For weak people or those with cooled blood systems, pot barley should be cooked with ginger to make it less cooling. All health food shops and wholefood shops stock pot barley. (Wholefood shops sell natural, wholesome foods in bulk. The products they sell are often reasonably priced and of the highest quality.)

Pot Barley and Brown Rice

This is an excellent dish for people suffering from diabetes, acute and chronic cystitis, prostatitis and other diseases that result from having an overheated blood system.

$^3/_8$ cup brown rice
$^1/_8$ cup pot barley
1 cup water
pinch sea-salt

Wash the grains and cook them as you would brown rice (see page 37).

Pot Barley Water

This drink has helped many of my patients with cystitis. According to traditional Chinese medicine, cystitis is due to too much damp heat in the body, so a cooling drink like pot barley water helps. It can also help relieve prostatitis. People with overheated blood systems should drink pot barley water once or twice a week, especially during the hot, dry seasons. As a child in Penang, Malaysia, my mother would give me this drink twice a week.

1 cup pot barley
7 cups water
pinch sea-salt
barley malt extract (to taste)

1   Wash the pot barley and put it in a large pot with the water and sea-salt.
2   Bring to a fast rolling boil for 15 minutes, then gently simmer until the grains are soft.
3   Sweeten with a little barley malt extract and serve strained or with the barley.

Note: Do not discard the cooked pot barley. Either eat it on its own, sweetened with barley malt extract, or mix it with some vegetables for lunch or dinner. In an acute attack of cystitis, drink pot barley water throughout the day instead of tea, coffee or other liquids, and see your doctor. In cases of chronic cystitis, drink barley water daily until the condition clears.

BUCKWHEAT
(Fagopyrum esculentum)
properties: cooling, gluten-free

This herbaceous seed is rich in iron, B vitamins, rutin (which is good for circulatory complaints), and other minerals and trace elements. Buckwheat has a cooling nature so it is best dry-roasted. Those people who tend to have cooled blood systems or those with weak constitutions should cook roasted buckwheat with ginger or other warming vegetables, herbs and spices.

Kasha

This breakfast cereal is very popular in Poland and Russia.

$^1/_4$ cup buckwheat
$^1/_2$ cup water
1 thin slice ginger (optional)
pinch sea-salt
spring onions
gomasio

1   Wash the buckwheat and drain thoroughly. Dry-roast in a heavy-based stainless steel or cast-iron pan on top of the stove. Stir frequently until fragrant or

until it has a slight golden hue.

2 Meanwhile, bring the water to a boil with the ginger (optional) and sea-salt.

3 Cool the buckwheat a little to prevent spitting and add it to the boiling water.

4 Simmer gently for 20 minutes until all the water has been absorbed.

5 Serve with chopped spring onions and *gomasio*.

Buckwheat and Leeks

¹/₂ cup buckwheat
1 thin slice ginger (optional)
1 medium leek
cold-pressed sesame oil
pinch sea-salt
1 cup water
parsley
gomasio

1 Wash and drain buckwheat.

2 Finely mince the ginger, if used, and slice the leek diagonally.

3 Heat a pot. When hot, add enough oil to coat the bottom. When the oil is hot, add ginger, if used, and stir 1 minute. Add leek and sea-salt and stir until limp. Add buckwheat. Stir for 2 to 3 minutes.

4 Add the water, bring to a boil, then simmer for 20 minutes until all the water has been absorbed.

5 Garnish with chopped parsley and *gomasio*.

Variations:

1 Substitute onions for leeks.

2 Use herbs with warming energies (like garlic, basil or fennel) with the onions to balance the cold energies of the buckwheat.

Buckwheat Noodles

Use buckwheat noodles as you would wholewheat spaghetti (see page 36). Those who are allergic to wholewheat flour and gluten should note that buckwheat noodles are made with buckwheat flour and wholewheat flour.

MILLET

(Panicum miliaceum)
properties: cooling, gluten-free

Nutritionally, millet is one of the richest grains. It is an excellent source of iron and B vitamins. According to the *Nei Jing*, millet is good for the spleen, pancreas, stomach and kidneys. It is also good for diabetics who tend to have overheated blood systems. Because millet is one of the most alkaline grains, it is helpful for people suffering from too much acidity, for example, those with stomach ulcers, acidosis, bad breath and chronic indigestion from too much heat in the stomach.

Millet is as versatile as brown rice. It takes only 20 to 30 minutes to cook and can be used in savoury as well as sweet dishes. (The *Nei Jing* warns us that the consumption of millet with apricot seed can lead to vomiting and diarrhoea.)

Those with cooled blood systems or those who are weak should always cook millet with ginger and other warming vegetables, herbs, or spices to make it less cooling. Millet's cooling nature makes it most appropriate for the summer months. Unfortunately, it does take some time to acquire a taste for it.

Millet

$^1/_4$ cup millet
$^3/_4$ cup water
pinch sea-salt
gomasio
spring onions

1 Wash the millet and drain as thoroughly as possible.
2 Dry-roast it in a heavy-based, cast-iron skillet or stainless steel pan on top of the stove, stirring frequently until fragrant or until it becomes slightly golden. No oil is required.
3 Bring the water and pinch of sea-salt to a boil.
4 Cool the roasted millet slightly, then add it to the hot water to prevent too much spitting.
5 Simmer for 15 to 20 minutes or until all the water has been absorbed.
6 Garnish with *gomasio* and finely chopped spring onions.

Note: Those with cooled blood systems or weak constitutions must add ginger.

Millet and Brown Rice

This recipe is ideal for those who are having trouble acquiring a taste for millet.

$^3/_8$ cup brown rice
$^1/_8$ cup millet
1 cup water
pinch sea-salt

Cook the same way you would brown rice (see page 37).

Note: Again, add ginger if you have a cooled blood system or a weak constitution.

Autumn Millet

$^1/_4$ cup millet
110 g (4 oz) pumpkin
110 g (4 oz) string beans
1 clove garlic
1 thin slice ginger
cold-pressed sesame oil
pinch sea-salt
gomasio

1 Wash and drain the millet.
2 Dice the pumpkin into 5 mm ($^1/_4$ in) cubes.
3 Slice the string beans diagonally into 5 mm ($^1/_4$ in) diamonds.
4 Finely mince the garlic and ginger.
5 Heat a pot. When hot, add enough oil to coat the bottom. When the oil is hot, add the garlic and ginger and stir for 1 minute. Add the string beans and stir for 2 minutes. Add the pumpkin and stir for 2 minutes. Add the millet and stir for 2 minutes, then add $1^1/_2$ cups water and the sea-salt.
6 Bring to a boil and gently simmer for 20 to 30 minutes until all the water has been absorbed.
7 Sprinkle with *gomasio* and serve with a bean dish to complement the grains.

Variations:
1 In autumn, use onion, pumpkin and French beans.
2 In summer, use baby carrots and fresh tender garden peas or just spring onions or chives.
3 In winter, use leeks or onions and carrots.

Millet Flakes

Millet flakes can be used like millet grains for people with stomach ulcers who find millet too harsh for their delicate stomach linings. Those who have no digestive problems should eat whole millet grains for vitality.

Millet Slice *(serves 8)*

3 cups water
1 cup sultanas
$^1/_4$ tsp ground cinnamon
pinch sea-salt
1 cup millet flakes
roasted sesame seeds

1 Bring water, sultanas, ground cinnamon and sea-salt to a boil.
2 Meanwhile, dry-roast the millet flakes and cool slightly.
3 Add the roasted millet to the boiling water a little at a time. Stir thoroughly to break up lumps and simmer for 20 minutes.
4 Pour the hot mixture into a rinsed 20 cm (8 in) loose-bottom quiche tin.
5 Sprinkle with roasted sesame seeds and leave to set for 1 to 2 hours, depending on the weather.

Variations:
1 Use raisins instead of sultanas.
2 Use caraway seeds instead of cinnamon.
3 Use peanuts instead of sesame seeds.

WHEAT
(Triticum vulgare)
properties: cooling, rich in gluten

Wheat grows in all temperate zones, but is rarely eaten in its natural form – whole wheat grains. We eat it as white flour in its highly refined form, in bread, *nan, chapatis, roti,* pasta, noodles, etc.

According to the *Nei Jing,* whole wheat grains nourish the heart, benefit the kidneys, cool the blood system and relieve thirst. Diabetics eat them to cure thirst, as do those with mental depression due to too much heat in the body.

Whole wheat grains take a long time to cook and, like barley, should be eaten with other foods such as brown rice.

Whole Wheat Grains and Brown Rice

$^3/_8$ cup brown rice
$^1/_8$ cup whole wheat grains
1 cup water
pinch sea-salt

Wash grains and cook them as you would brown rice (see page 37).

Whole Wheat Grain Water

This drink is good for mental depression caused by too much heat in the blood system. Without the barley malt extract, this is an excellent thirst quencher for diabetics.

1 cup whole wheat grains
7 cups water
pinch sea-salt
barley or rice malt extract (to taste)

Prepare the same way as pot barley water (see page 30).

Frumenty

Years ago in Britain it was customary to serve frumenty for breakfast on Christmas morning. Traditional frumenty consists of whole wheat

grains, milk, sultanas, raisins, honey, nutmeg, cinnamon, brandy and double cream. This is a less expensive, simpler version which can be eaten on a cold wintry morning. The nutmeg and cinnamon have warming energies and the 12 hours of slow, gentle simmering add even more warmth and strength.

¹/₄ cup whole wheat grains
¹/₄ cup raisins
¹/₈ tsp ground cinnamon
a few gratings of nutmeg
pinch sea-salt
water

1 Wash the whole wheat grains and raisins and place them in a small ovenproof pot.
2 Add the spices and sea-salt and enough water to cover.
3 Simmer very gently for 12 hours on the cooker top or bring the mixture to a boil for 15 minutes before simmering for 12 hours in a cool oven set at 125°C or 250°F. If you have a solid fuel cooker, put the pot in the coolest corner of the cool oven overnight, making sure you have enough water to prevent it from burning. The finished product is a deep, rich, brown, deliciously sweet cereal with a wonderful aroma. It is on the moist side and each grain is nice and plump.

Note: You can shorten the cooking time to only 1 to 2 hours by presoaking the grains overnight.

Gandum

The traditional version of this Malaysian whole wheat grain dessert is sweetened with white sugar, thickened with coconut milk and flavoured with *pandan* (screwpine) leaves. My healthier version uses raisins instead of sugar and leaves out the coconut milk altogether. This is an excellent dessert for people with constipation due to an overheated blood system.

¹/₄ cup whole wheat grains
¹/₄ cup raisins
pinch sea-salt
water
1 pandan leaf (optional)

1 Wash the whole wheat grains and raisins and place them in a pot.
2 Add sea-salt and enough water to cover.
3 Bring to a boil, wash and add the *pandan* leaf and gently simmer for 12 hours.

Note: You can shorten the cooking time to 1 to 2 hours by presoaking the grains overnight.

Bulgar

Bulgar is a wheat product made from whole wheat grains that have been cracked, hulled, steamed and roasted. Since bulgar is precooked, it is much easier to prepare compared to whole wheat grains. Although bulgar should be taken every now and then for quick meals, it should not be eaten daily because it has been processed and much of its vitality has been lost. Ideally, bulgar should be eaten in the summer because it has a slightly cooling nature and requires little cooking. It is not as cooling as whole wheat grains, however, because it has been steamed and roasted.

1 cup water
pinch sea-salt
$^1/_3$ cup coarse bulgar

1 Bring the water to a boil with a pinch of sea-salt.
2 When the water is boiling vigorously, add the bulgar and simmer gently for 15 to 20 minutes or until all the water has been absorbed. Serve.

Note: To make fine bulgar, use 2 parts water to 1 part bulgar, i.e. $^2/_3$ cup water to $^1/_3$ cup fine bulgar.

Fried Bulgar
Fry bulgar as you would brown rice (see page 38). First prepare the bulgar as above and, while it is cooking, prepare the other ingredients in the fried brown rice recipe; then fry accordingly.

Couscous
Couscous is fine semolina grain coated with flour. The semolina is produced from the endosperm, the starchy part of the grain, and is processed more than bulgar. For this reason, have couscous only occasionally, as a dessert.

Banana Couscous

$^1/_8$ cup couscous
pinch sea-salt
pinch ground cinnamon
$^1/_4$ cup water
2 ripe bananas

1 Place the couscous, sea-salt and cinnamon in a heatproof dish about 10-13 cm (4-5 in) in diameter, and about 4-5 cm (1$^1/_2$-2 in) deep. Add the cold water and leave to soak

for 30 minutes.
2 Mash 1$^1/_2$ peeled bananas and add to the couscous. Cut the remaining $^1/_2$ banana diagonally and place on top. (Do this quickly or the bananas will discolour.)
3 Steam for 10 minutes and serve hot or cold.

Variations:
1 In Southeast Asia use *pisang raja* for the sweetest, most aromatic flavour and use *pandan* leaves instead of cinnamon. Cut the *pandan* leaves into 2$^1/_2$ cm (1 in) lengths and rest the banana slices on top.
2 Use other warming spices such as allspice, cloves or nutmeg instead of cinnamon.
3 Use pre-soaked raisins, sultanas or Hunza apricots instead of bananas.

Wholewheat Pasta
Wholewheat pasta is much easier to digest than hard-baked wholewheat bread, so it is ideal for people with poor digestive systems. But since it is processed, it should not be eaten daily. Eating it two or three times a week to break the monotony of wholegrains is about right. In autumn and winter, it is much better to eat a dish of hot wholewheat pasta than a cold sandwich.

Wholewheat Macaroni with Egg

pinch sea-salt
1 thin slice ginger
2 cups water
2 medium onions, diced
75 g (3 oz) wholewheat macaroni
1 free-range egg
spring onions
shoyu or tamari

1 Add sea-salt and ginger to the water and bring to a vigorous boil.
2 Add the diced onions and cook uncovered.
3 When the onions begin to turn glassy, add the macaroni and cook until it is *al dente* (or firm to the teeth). If all the water has been absorbed, add a little more to prevent the pasta from burning.
4 Break an egg into the pasta and stir rapidly. Serve with freshly chopped spring onions and a dash of *shoyu* or *tamari*.

Variations:
1 For Western vegans, add a small carrot and some small Brussels sprouts, and substitute *tofu* for the egg.
2 For Asian vegans, add a carrot and long beans, French beans or snow peas, and substitute *tofu* for the egg.
3 In winter, vegetarians can add spinach and a few gratings of nutmeg.
4 In summer, vegetarians can add tender fresh garden peas or snowpeas.
5 Substitute all types of wholewheat pasta for the macaroni.

Wholewheat Spaghetti with Mushrooms and *Miso* Sauce

75 g (3 oz) wholewheat spaghetti
2 cups water
1 clove garlic
1 small onion
110 g (4 oz) field mushrooms
1 tsp mugi miso
cold-pressed sesame oil
$^1/_4$ tsp dried thyme or fresh thyme, if available
pinch sea-salt
parsley

1 Cook the spaghetti in the water until *al dente*. Drain and save the cooking water. Rinse the spaghetti in cold water.
2 Finely mince the garlic, finely slice the onion and mushrooms.
3 Thin out the *miso* with a little warm spaghetti water.
4 Heat a wok. When hot, add enough oil to coat the bottom. When the oil is hot, add the garlic and stir 1 minute. Add the onion, thyme and a pinch of sea-salt and stir 2-3 minutes. Add the mushrooms and stir until soft. Add a little spaghetti water and simmer the vegetables for 1 minute. Add the thinned *miso* and simmer gently for 5 minutes. Then add the drained spaghetti and mix thoroughly until heated through.
5 Garnish with some chopped parsley.

Variations:
1 Use other wholewheat pastas.
2 Use marjoram, sage or fresh coriander leaves instead of thyme.
3 Use *genmai miso* instead of *mugi miso*.
4 If you find the mushrooms too cooling, add minced ginger.

RICE
(Oryza sativa)
properties: neutral, gluten-free

Brown rice comes in three different sizes – short, medium or long. Short- and medium-grain brown rice grow in temperate zones while long-grain varieties grow in the tropics. The shorter the grain, the more concentrated the goodness. People living in temperate zones should eat short-grain brown rice in

autumn and winter, and medium-grain in summer. Those living in the tropics should eat long-grain brown rice all year round. Each type of brown rice contains seven layers of bran, so it is an excellent food for those suffering from constipation.

According to the *Nei Jing*, brown rice is good for strengthening the spleen and pancreas, harmonising the stomach, nourishing the body's vital energy and relieving mental depression.

All types of brown rice are available from health food shops and wholefood shops around the world. In some Southeast Asian countries, for example Thailand and Singapore, the 'brown rice' refers to a mixture of brown and red rice. You can use this for both brown and red rice recipes.

Brown Rice

$1/_2$ *cup brown rice*
1 cup water
tiny pinch sea-salt

1 Wash the brown rice once or twice in a sieve with plenty of water. (If you wash it too much you will wash away all the goodness.)
2 Place the rice in a small pot that has a tight-fitting lid.
3 Add the water and sea-salt.
4 Bring to a fast, rolling boil.
5 Remove the lid for 5 minutes to release steam.
6 Replace the lid and simmer till grains are cooked (about 45-60 minutes). When cooked, the surface of the rice will have little craters where the steam has escaped,

each grain will pop open and all the water will be absorbed.
7 Serve with beans, peas, lentils, fish or chicken and plenty of vegetables. (See chapters 3-11 for recipes.)

Note: The success of cooking brown rice depends on the size of the pot and the amount of rice cooked. If you are cooking a small amount (such as $1/_2$ cup), you should use a small pot with a narrow bottom, high sides and a tight-fitting lid. The high sides prevent the water from boiling over. The tight-fitting lid allows the brown rice to cook in its own steam, in as little water as possible, to concentrate its goodness. *Never boil brown rice in water and drain away excess liquid!* This will wash away all the precious B vitamins. You can also cook brown rice in a claypot or a rice cooker.

When cooking with gas fires: a flame spreader is very useful at the simmering stage to ensure that the entire pot is evenly heated. When using a solid fuel cooker like an Aga, a Rayburn, a wood-burning stove, an oil-fired cooker: remove the lid after you have brought the rice to a rolling boil on the hottest plate, to let as much water evaporate as possible. Then, when the water level is just above the rice level, replace the lid and move the pot to the hottest corner of the cool oven to finish the cooking.

Fried Brown Rice

It is best to make fried brown rice with leftover cooked brown rice. I normally cook a double portion of brown rice for lunch so I have another portion left for fried rice at night. Freshly cooked brown rice is too soggy to use for fried rice.

Vegan Fried Brown Rice

150 g (5 oz) tofu
1 tsp genmai miso
pinch sea-salt
1 portion leftover cooked brown rice
1 small leek
1 thin slice ginger
1 small carrot
cold-pressed sesame oil
dash shoyu or tamari
dry-roasted sunflower seeds

1 The night before, or at lunch-time, dice the *tofu* into 5 mm ($^1/_4$ in) cubes. Thin out the *miso* in a little warm water until it has a creamy consistency.
2 Combine *tofu* cubes, *miso* cream and sea-salt. Coat *tofu* with the *miso* cream and leave to marinate for 5 hours.
3 Just before the meal, loosen the leftover brown rice so it does not clump together.
4 Wash the leek and slice diagonally into 5 mm ($^1/_4$ in) sections. Finely mince the ginger.
5 Cut the carrot into 5 mm ($^1/_4$ in) diamonds by cutting it into 3 long slices, then cutting each slice into 3 narrow strips, and each of those strips diagonally into diamond shapes.
6 Heat a wok. When hot, add enough oil to coat the bottom. When the oil is hot, add the minced ginger and stir for 1 minute. Add the leek and stir until just limp. Add marinated *tofu* and stir for 2 to 3 minutes. Add the carrot and stir for 2 minutes.
7 Add just enough water to cover the bottom of the wok and cook, covered, for 2 minutes. (Besides allowing the aromas of the ingredients to blend, covering the wok helps the leek and carrot to finish cooking.

If you prefer the leek and carrot well-cooked, cover for more than 2 minutes.)
8 Lower heat and add brown rice. Stir thoroughly. Add a dash of *shoyu* or *tamari* to taste.
9 Sprinkle some dry-roasted sunflower seeds to complement the *tofu* and grain proteins.

Variations:
1 In summer, use baby carrots and finely chopped baby carrot tops instead of carrots and leeks, which are appropriate for winter.
2 In autumn, use pumpkin and spring onions or chives.

Vegetarian Fried Brown Rice

1 small leek
110 g (4 oz) button mushrooms
1 thin slice ginger
1 free-range egg
2 pinches sea-salt
1 portion leftover brown rice
cold-pressed sesame oil
dash shoyu or tamari
small bunch fresh parsley

1 Wash the leek and slice into 5 mm ($^1/_4$ in) sections.
2 Wash the mushrooms and dice into 5 mm ($^1/_4$ in) cubes.
3 Finely mince the ginger.
4 Beat the egg with a pinch of sea-salt.
5 Loosen the leftover brown rice so the grains do not clump together.
6 Heat a wok. When hot, add enough oil to cover the bottom. When the oil is hot, add the minced ginger and stir for 1 minute. Add the leek and another pinch of sea-salt and stir until just limp. Add the

mushrooms and stir until just cooked. Then add enough water to cover the bottom of the wok and cook, covered, for 2 minutes.

7   Lower heat, add brown rice and stir thoroughly. Then stir in the beaten egg and keep stirring until it is cooked. (This fried rice is moist and creamy. If you prefer drier rice, make paper-thin omelettes with the beaten egg at the beginning, and cut them into fine strips to garnish the rice.)

8   Add a dash of *shoyu* or *tamari* to taste and garnish with some chopped parsley.

> **Variations:**
>
> 1   If it is a very cold winter and you cannot seem to get warm, even by the fire, add some freshly ground black pepper to the beaten egg. (In summer, pepper is not necessary.)
>
> 2   For vegans, substitute *tofu* for the egg and use freshly ground black pepper to balance the cooling button mushrooms and *tofu*.
>
> 3   In summer, substitute spring onions or chives for the leek.

Asian Vegetarian Fried Brown Rice

110 g (4 oz) tofu
tamari
3 dried Shiitake mushrooms
roasted sesame oil
5 tender long beans
1 small carrot
1 clove garlic
cold-pressed sesame oil
pinch sea-salt
1 portion leftover brown rice
dry-roasted peanuts

1   At lunch-time or at least 5 hours before you wish to eat, dice the *tofu* into 5 mm ($^1/_4$ in) cubes and coat with *tamari* to marinate.

2   Wash the dried Shiitake mushrooms and soak them in hot water for 20 minutes. Save the soaking water. When soft, cut the mushroom caps into 5 mm ($^1/_4$ in) cubes. Cook the hard stalks with brown rice.

3   Place the diced mushrooms in a small saucer. Add a dash of roasted sesame oil and enough *tamari* to coat the mushroom pieces. Mix well and place the saucer inside the pot on top of the brown rice to steam.

4   Just before the meal, cut the long beans diagonally into 5 mm ($^1/_4$ in) lengths. Cut the carrot into 5 mm ($^1/_4$ in) diamonds. Finely mince the garlic.

5   Heat a wok. When hot, add enough oil to coat the bottom. When the oil is hot, add the garlic and stir until fragrant. Add the *tofu*, mushrooms and sea-salt and stir for 2 to 3 minutes. Add the long beans and stir for 3 minutes. Add the carrot and stir for 1 minute.

6   Add the water you soaked the mushrooms in earlier and top it up with tap water to just cover the bottom of the wok. Cover for 2 minutes or until the beans are just cooked.

7   Lower the heat and stir in the brown rice and sea-salt. Mix thoroughly.

8   Add a dash of *tamari* and serve with some dry-roasted peanuts.

> **Variations:**
>
> 1   Use pumpkin instead of carrot.
>
> 2   Use French beans or string beans instead of long beans.
>
> 3   In the West, in summer, use fresh tender garden peas instead of long beans.

4 Add additional minced garlic and minced ginger if you find the *tofu* and mushrooms too cooling.

Brown Rice Congee

Brown rice congee is a very nourishing breakfast cereal for those living in the tropics and those who tend to have overheated blood systems. This is a cooling dish with many medicinal properties, for example it clears damp heat and indigestion.

Traditionally, the village people of China have brown rice congee for three consecutive mornings after the Chinese New Year celebrations. This is to counteract the damp heat created by the heavy, greasy, spicy foods and alcohol taken during the holiday. Of course, brown rice congee helps negate the ill effects of heavy feasting after Christmas, Easter and other festivities too!

Brown rice congee can be cooked to a thick or thin consistency depending on the amount of water added. A thick congee is less cooling for the elderly. A thin, watery congee served with some raw shredded lettuce is more cooling for the young and active. The tangerine peel helps relieve indigestion and has warming properties.

$^1/_4$ cup brown rice
2 cups water
$2^1/_2$ cm (1 in) piece dried tangerine peel
pinch sea-salt

1 Wash the brown rice.
2 Place it in a small pot with high sides and add the water, tangerine peel and sea-salt.
3 Bring it to a rolling boil for at least 20 minutes with the lid off.
4 Replace the lid and simmer for several hours until the grains are soft.

Miso Soup with Brown Rice Flakes

Brown rice flakes are neither as wholesome nor as sustaining as brown rice, so it is best to use them only as a substitute for brown rice when you are in a hurry. They can also be used as a thickener in soups or as a substitute for whole grain brown rice in congee.

1 cup water
1 medium onion
1 heaping tsp miso
$^1/_3$ cup brown rice flakes
small bunch fresh parsley

1 Bring the water to a boil. Dice the onion, add it to the boiling water and cook uncovered.
2 Thin out the *miso* in a little onion stock. Set aside.
3 When the onion is cooked, add the rice flakes. Reduce heat to a simmer and add the thinned *miso*. Mix thoroughly and simmer for another 10 minutes.
4 Sprinkle with chopped parsley and serve.

Note: If you prefer a thinner soup, add more water.

Savoury Biscuits with Brown Rice Flakes (*makes 4-5 biscuits*)

$^1/_2$ cup brown rice flakes
$^1/_8$ tsp sea-salt
$^1/_4$ cup cold water
1 tsp cold-pressed sesame oil
1 heaped tsp gomasio
fresh spring onions, chopped

1 Mix the brown rice flakes, sea-salt and cold water together and leave to soak for 1 hour.

2 Preheat the oven to the highest baking temperature.

3 Add sesame oil to the flake mixture. Slowly add more cold water and mix thoroughly until you obtain a soft, doughy consistency.

4 Add *gomasio* and spring onions and mix thoroughly.

5 Grease a baking tray with unrefined, cold-pressed sesame oil. Drop teaspoonfuls of the mixture onto the tray, making them as thin as possible, about 5-7 cm (2-3 in) in diameter.

6 Bake for about 15 minutes until crisp.

Variations: Substitute freshly chopped parsley or coriander leaves for spring onions.

Red Rice

For nutrition, red rice is supposed to be even better than brown rice. It is especially nourishing for the elderly. Unfortunately, it is not readily available outside China, Hong Kong, Thailand and Singapore. In Hong Kong, you can usually buy red rice from September onward. Availability of red rice depends on the year's harvest in China.

Use red rice as you would brown rice. The consistency will be chewier than brown rice. If you prefer a smoother texture, add more water and cook longer than 1 hour.

RYE

(Secale cereale)
properties: neutral, low in gluten

Rye is a popular grain in northern and eastern Europe and parts of Russia. It is often made into bread, but seldom used in its wholegrain form. This is a pity because rye is a good source of vitamins B_2 and B_3 and valuable minerals such as potassium and magnesium. It also contains a substance called rutin which is good for circulatory problems like varicose veins and heart ailments.

Like barley and wheat, rye grains are difficult to eat on their own, so I recommend cooking them with brown rice.

Rye and Brown Rice

$^3/_8$ *cup brown rice*
$^1/_8$ *cup whole rye grains*
1 cup water
pinch sea-salt

Wash the grains and cook them as you would brown rice (see page 37).

SWEET CORN

(Zea mays)
properties: neutral, gluten-free

According to the *Nei Jing*, sweet corn is a very nutritious food. It can stimulate the appetite, promote urination and prevent heart disease. The *Nei Jing* cautions that people with digestive disorders may find it difficult to digest sweet corn and are advised to chew the kernels well before swallowing, and not to eat too much at one sitting. The same advice applies to children, who tend to eat too fast.

Sweet Corn

The simplest and most delicious way to cook sweet corn is to steam the whole ears. Remove the husks and lightly brush the ears with a pinch of sea-salt. Place them in the pot on top of the steaming brown rice during its last 15 to 20 minutes of cooking. They will be ready

when the brown rice is done. Sprinkle with freshly chopped parsley, chives or spring onion before serving.

Sweet Corn and Brown Rice Congee
This is a very nourishing congee for children and the elderly. It is good for the spleen, pancreas and stomach and it aids digestion.

$^1/_4$ cup brown rice
1 ear sweet corn
6 cups water
pinch sea-salt
1 thin slice ginger (leave out for children)
chives or spring onions
gomasio

1   Wash the brown rice and place it in a pot. Remove the raw sweet corn kernels with your thumb and add to brown rice. (Do not use a knife to remove kernels.)
2   Add water, sea-salt and ginger. Bring to a rolling boil for 15 to 20 minutes, then simmer until the grains of brown rice are soft. Add more water if necessary, and cook to the desired consistency.
3   Serve with finely chopped chives or spring onions, and *gomasio*.

Popcorn
This is a delicious snack for children and more nutritious than sweets. It is very heating, however, because the corn kernels are popped under great heat, and should be eaten only on cold autumn and winter days. This recipe uses barley malt extract as a sweetener and cooling agent to counteract the heating effects of the corn.

corn oil
popping corn
pinch sea-salt
barley malt extract

1   Heat a pot. When hot, add enough oil to coat the bottom.
2   Add enough popcorn to just cover half the bottom of the pot so the kernels have plenty of room to expand.
3   Add a pinch of sea-salt and place the pot on a high flame. Shake the pot frequently to prevent burning.
4   Meanwhile, pour some barley malt extract into a large bowl. When popcorn is done, discard the burnt bits, mix the rest thoroughly with the malt and serve.

Cornmeal Polenta
Cornmeal can be used when fresh sweet corn is not available. It should only be used occasionally for quick soups, because it has little nutritional value. People who cannot tolerate gluten should use cornmeal to thicken their soups (and polenta and beans instead of wholewheat pastas).

pinch sea-salt
$2^3/_4$ cups water
$^1/_3$ cup cornmeal

1   Put the sea-salt, water and cornmeal in a pot, and bring to a boil on medium heat, stirring constantly to prevent lumps.
2   Simmer gently for 20 minutes until the polenta has a thick and creamy consistency.
3   Leave polenta to set until it cools completely. Serve with a bean dish which

has a tasty sauce to flavour and moisten the polenta.

Cornmeal and *Tofu* Soup

This soup is a meal in itself. If you prefer a thinner consistency, add more water.

1 clove garlic
1 thin slice ginger
1 medium leek
1 small carrot
150 g (5 oz) tofu
cold-pressed sesame oil
pinch sea-salt
$^1/_4$ cup cornmeal
2 cups water
parsley
gomasio

1 Finely mince the garlic and ginger.
2 Wash the leek and slice diagonally into 5 mm ($^1/_4$ in) sections.
3 Wash the carrot and dice into 5 mm ($^1/_4$ in) diamonds.
4 Dice the *tofu* into 5 mm ($^1/_4$ in) cubes.
5 Heat a pot. When hot, add enough oil to coat the bottom. When the oil is hot, add the minced garlic and ginger and stir for 1 minute. Add the leek and the sea-salt and stir until limp. Add the *tofu* and stir for 2 to 3 minutes. Add the carrot and stir for 1 minute. Add the cornmeal and stir for 2 minutes.
6 Now add the water, stirring constantly to prevent lumps. Bring to a boil, then reduce heat and simmer 20 minutes, stirring occasionally.
7 Garnish with finely chopped parsley and a sprinkling of *gomasio*.

Variations:
1 Use 110 g (4 oz) mushrooms instead of the carrot.
2 Try carrot with onions and thyme.
3 Garnish with pumpkin seeds, caraway seeds or dry-roasted nuts.

OAT GROATS
(Avena sativa)
properties: warming, low in gluten

This wholegrain probably originated in northern Europe and is still very popular in Scotland. Now, more and more people in the West are eating oats for breakfast in the form of muesli.

Oats are a rich source of B vitamins, so they are good for nervous people or those under great stress. Medical researchers have recently discovered that the gummy substance found in oats lowers blood cholesterol and helps diabetics regulate their blood sugar levels. People with bowel and gall bladder problems have found oat groats a great help too.

Although oat groats are higher in protein and fats than other grains they are good for dieters or those who wish to maintain their weight. This is because they contain minerals and trace elements like iron and iodine. Iron nourishes the blood and iodine is used by the thyroid gland to regulate body metabolism and weight.

Oat groats are especially good for cold autumn and winter mornings. They keep the body warm, nourish the nerves, regulate body metabolism and prevent dieters from eating between meals. They are also a very good

substitute for cream or milk in the preparation of creamy soups. Soups made with oat groats are nourishing for the old, the weak, or those recovering from a long illness.

> *Note:* Eat oats infrequently if you suffer from catarrh, sinusitis, and phlegm. They are mucus-forming.

Oat Groats

$^1/_4$ cup oat groats
$1^1/_2$ cups water
pinch sea-salt

1 Put the oat groats, water and sea-salt in a pot and bring to a boil.
2 Simmer for 15 minutes.
3 Turn off the cooker, cover the pot and leave the oats to cook in their own heat overnight.
4 Next morning, bring the oats to a boil and simmer for 20 minutes.

> *Note:* Use a stainless steel or enamel pot instead of an aluminium pot. If you have a solid fuel cooker, leave the oats in the cool oven to cook overnight after simmering for 15 minutes on the cooler hot plate.

Oat Groats Muesli

Muesli sold in boxes is usually laden with sugar so read the labels before buying. Muesli sold in wholefood and health food shops is usually sugar-free, but ask before buying. Store-bought muesli contains a mixture of four cereal grain flakes (oats, barley, wheat and rye) with dried fruits like raisins and sultanas, and nuts and seeds like sesame seeds, sunflower seeds, hazelnuts, peanuts and Brazil nuts.

Traditionally, the Swiss mix the muesli with fresh milk the night before so the cereal flakes and dried fruits are well soaked and softened for easy digestion. However, nowadays most people pour cold milk over their muesli and eat it right away, and this causes intestinal pain and flatulence. The dry cereal flakes are left undigested and swell up each time liquids are taken, and the dried fruits begin to ferment. It is this mixture that causes the flatulence, and it is worse for those with weak digestive systems. I would advise everyone to cook muesli the way they cook porridge (with water, in the morning). And, if you have a weak digestive system, make your own muesli with only one kind of cereal flake, one kind of dried fruit, one kind of seed and one kind of nut.

$^1/_4$ cup oat groats
$1^1/_2$ cups water
a handful of raisins
5 walnut halves
1 heaped tsp linseed
pinch sea-salt

Cook the ingredients as you would plain oat groats (see left column).

> *Variations:*
> 1 Use any combination of different dried fruits, nuts and seeds.
> 2 On very cold days, add a pinch of cinnamon, nutmeg or cloves to give extra warmth.

Creamy Mushroom Soup

$1/_4$ cup oat groats
1 clove garlic
1 thin slice ginger
1 small onion
115 g (4 oz) fresh mushrooms
cold-pressed sesame oil
pinch sea-salt
parsley

1 Wash and drain the oats.
2 Finely mince the garlic and ginger.
3 Dice the onion and mushrooms into 5 mm ($1/_4$ in) cubes.
4 Heat a pot. When hot, add enough oil to coat the bottom. When the oil is hot, add the garlic and ginger and stir for 1 minute. Add the onion and a pinch of sea-salt and stir until the onion begins to brown. Add the mushrooms and stir until cooked. Add the oats and stir for 1 minute.
5 Add 2 to 3 cups of water, bring to a rolling boil and simmer until the grains are cooked. The longer it cooks (about 3 to 4 hours is ideal), the more delicious it is. The amount of water you add determines the soup's consistency. You can also liquidise the soup to make it smoother and lighter.
6 Garnish with some chopped parsley.

Variations:
1 Use leeks or carrots instead of mushrooms.
2 Use a combination of leeks and mushrooms or spinach and nutmeg.

Jumbo Oats Muesli

Jumbo oats appear to be the least processed of all oat products. They cook faster compared to oat groats and are an ideal breakfast food for people in a hurry.

$1/_4$ cup jumbo oats
a handful of sultanas
6 hazelnuts
1 heaped tsp sesame seeds
$3/_4$ cup water
pinch sea-salt

Place all the ingredients in a pot, bring to a boil and simmer gently for 20 minutes.

Variations:
1 Add more water if you prefer a thinner consistency.
2 Use combinations of different dried fruits, nuts and seeds.
3 On very cold days, add a pinch of cinnamon, nutmeg or cloves to give extra warmth.

Savoury Jumbo Oats

This very warming breakfast is ideal for the coldest winter mornings. The ginger and spring onions warm the body as well as aid the digestion of the oats and egg. And the egg nourishes and warms the body.

$1/_4$ cup jumbo oats
1 thin slice ginger
spring onions
1 cup water
pinch sea-salt
1 free-range egg
dash of shoyu or tamari

1 Place jumbo oats in a pot with finely shredded ginger and the whites of the spring onions, finely shredded.
2 Add water and a pinch of sea-salt.
3 Bring to a rolling boil and then simmer gently for 20 to 30 minutes.
4 Just before serving, beat the egg and blend thoroughly into the porridge.

5 Garnish with finely chopped spring onion greens and a dash of *shoyu* or *tamari*.

> *Note:* This porridge is rather thick. Add more water if you prefer a thinner consistency.

WHOLEGRAIN MILKS FOR BABIES AND INFANTS

Wholegrain milks are excellent for babies and infants. They are rich in B vitamins that can improve the nerves, skin, hair and general growth and development. And they are very good supplements to mother's milk.

Wholegrain milks can be made from a variety of wholegrains. Brown rice has neutral energies and should be taken more often than the others. Oat groats have warming energies so they are good during winter for weak babies or those who have pale or sallow complexions. Pot barley has cooling energies, so it is an excellent summer drink for babies who suffer from heat rashes or those who cry during hot or humid weather.

Wholegrain Milk

As the baby grows older and the mother's milk thins and decreases, it is a good idea to mix some warm wholegrain milk with mother's milk to wean the baby onto wholegrains. At first, give the child thin grain milks. Later, he or she can take thicker mixtures. This way, by the time the child is old enough to eat solid foods, he can have thick grain milks mashed up with fresh fruits and vegetables.

1 tbsp wholegrains
2 cups water

1 Wash the wholegrains thoroughly.
2 Bring grains to a boil, then simmer very gently for 1 to 2 hours, or until they are soft and their liquid is thin and milky. Add more water if necessary.
3 Strain and cool milk before serving to babies. Save the thick residue at the bottom of the pot for the mother, to give extra carbohydrates to produce milk.

> *Note:* Wholegrain milks must never be given instead of mother's milk. They must be prepared fresh each time to prevent internal wind. Milk made from oat groats is mucus-forming, and must not be given to babies who suffer from catarrh, mucus or phlegm.

3 Legumes and Pulses

Most people are more familiar with legumes and pulses – beans, peas, and lentils – than they are with whole cereal grains. They are a nourishing source of vegetable protein, they cost very little and can be stored easily in airtight containers.

All over the world, people use beans, peas and lentils as part of their daily diet. In the Far East, the soyabean is an inexpensive source of vegetable protein. In India and the Middle Eastern countries, lentils and chick-peas are more popular. Europeans eat marrowfat peas, yellow and green split peas, butter-beans and haricot beans. Red kidney-beans seem to stand out in most people's minds as the bean of the Mexican people. In the West Indies, black-eyed beans are very popular as are red and black kidney-beans.

Beans, peas and lentils contain complex carbohydrates, polyunsaturated fats, proteins, minerals, trace elements, vitamins B and E and dietary fibre. The proteins in legumes and pulses are incomplete, so they are classified as second class proteins (after animal proteins). However, if you combine whole cereal grains, which contain different proteins, with beans, peas and lentils, you will have the full protein complement. This is a fact that all vegans, vegetarians and macrobiotics must be aware of if they want to ensure adequate nutrition in their diet.

The Chang Ming Diet, which dictates that each meal should be comprised of 50 per cent whole cereal grains and 15 per cent beans, peas or lentils, has taken this vital fact into account. This chapter aims to introduce you to a different aspect of beans, peas and lentils. Not many people know that legumes and pulses have healing powers, and are inexpensive, tasty sources of vegetable protein.

If you have a particular medical problem, eat the recommended dish often. If not, try to vary your choices as much as possible.

TWO BASIC RECIPES

Beans, peas and lentils are difficult to digest if not cooked properly, which is why they cause flatulence. Here is a good way of making them more digestible.

Aduki Beans, Black-eyed Beans, Butter-beans, Haricot Beans, Kidney-beans, Lentils

25 g (1 oz) dried beans or lentils
1 thin slice ginger
1 medium onion or 1eek (optional), sliced
pinch sea-salt
shoyu or miso
fresh parsley or spring onion

1 Soak the beans or lentils overnight in water at room temperature. (Do not use hot water or the beans will never cook.) About 25 g (1 oz) of dried beans or lentils is enough for one person per meal; too much will cause flatulence.

2 The next day, boil beans or lentils in the soaking water with the slice of ginger. (The ginger will aid digestion.)

3 When the water is boiling vigorously, remove the lid for 10 minutes. (This is to allow noxious gases from the beans or lentils to escape so you avoid flatulence.) At this stage, add the onion or leek, if desired, and allow it to release its noxious gases. Replace the lid when the onion or leek is just cooked and continue to boil the mixture for another 10 minutes. (If you wish to add other vegetables – such as carrot, celeriac, beetroot, pumpkin or white cabbage – add them before replacing the lid.)

4 Simmer until the beans or lentils are cooked, add a pinch of sea-salt and simmer for another 15 minutes. (Do not add sea-salt at the beginning or the beans will never cook.) Add more water if necessary.

5 Add *shoyu* (to give a light meaty taste) or add *miso* (for a hearty beefy taste) and simmer very gently for another 15 minutes. *Shoyu* and *miso* contain beneficial enzymes that will be destroyed if cooked vigorously.

6 Garnish with freshly chopped parsley or spring onion.

Note: Black-eyed beans tend to cook in about 30 minutes while the others take between 45 to 60 minutes.

Chick-Peas, Marrowfat Peas and Split Peas

25 g (1 oz) dried peas
1 thin slice ginger
pinch sea-salt

1 Soak peas in plenty of cold water overnight.

2 The next day, drain and rinse the peas to rid them of noxious gases.

3 Add water and a thin slice of ginger to the peas and cook them as you would beans or lentils.

FERMENTED BLACK SOYABEANS
property: cooling

When fermented, black soyabeans have cooling energies. They promote perspiration to sweat out fevers caused by chills or 'flus. They are delicious when cooked with garlic and ginger.

Tofu with Fermented Black Soyabeans

150 g (5 oz) tofu
pinch sea-salt
1 tsp fermented black soyabeans
1 clove garlic
1 thin slice ginger
some fresh coriander leaves
cold-pressed sesame oil
shoyu or tamari

1 Dice the *tofu* into 5 mm ($^1/_4$ in) cubes and marinate the cubes in a pinch of sea-salt for 1 hour.

2 Mince the fermented black soyabeans, garlic and ginger.

3 Roughly chop up the coriander leaves.

4 Heat a wok. When hot, add enough oil to just coat the bottom. When the oil is hot, add the minced mixture and stir for 1 minute or until aromatic. Add the marinated *tofu* and stir for 2 to 3 minutes. Then add the coriander leaves and stir for 1 minute. Add a dash of *shoyu* or *tamari* before serving.

> *Note:* If you prefer a dish with warming energies, add some water and simmer for 2 minutes before adding a dash of *shoyu* or *tamari*.
>
> If you prefer a cooling dish, use silken or watery *tofu* and steam it on its own. Meanwhile, stir-fry the minced mixture until aromatic, then add the fresh coriander leaves and stir for 1 minute. Add a dash of *shoyu* or *tamari*, pour mixture over the steamed *tofu* and steam for another minute before serving.
>
> *Variations:* Use spring onions, chives or leeks instead of coriander leaves.

FERMENTED SOYABEAN CHEESE
property: cooling

There are three varieties of fermented soyabean cheese: the white variety, with chillies (neutral) and without chillies, and the red kind (cooling), fermented with salt and red rice wine. A product of China, these cheeses are often used in Chinese home-cooking. They are available from Chinese supermarkets.

Long Beans in White Fermented Soyabean Cheese

1 cube white fermented soyabean cheese
7 long beans
1 clove garlic
cold-pressed sesame oil

1 Thin out the cheese with a little warm water.

2 Wash, top and tail the beans and cut them into $2^1/_2$ cm (1 in) lengths. Mince the garlic.

3 Heat a wok. When hot, add just enough oil to coat the bottom. When the oil is hot, add the garlic and stir for 1 minute. Add the long beans and stir for 2 to 3 minutes. Add just enough water to cover the bottom of the wok, cover and steam until beans are just cooked. Then add the thinned out cheese and very gently simmer for 5 minutes. Serve.

> *Variations:*
> 1 Use *miso* instead of soyabean cheese.
> 2 Use onion instead of garlic.
> 3 Use French beans instead of long beans.

MISO
property: cooling

To the Japanese, *miso* is a gift from God.

I believe they are quite right. *Miso* is made from pure soyabeans (or soyabeans and wholegrains), sea-salt, well or mountain water, and a special mould called *koji* in Japanese. During *miso*'s 18 months of fermentation, the *koji* produces enzymes that break down the complex carbohydrates, oils

and proteins of the soyabeans and whole-grains into easily assimilated and digested simple sugars, alcohols, esters, fatty acids and amino acids. The high concentration of sea-salt gives added minerals. The fermentation process also produces vitamin B_{12} which is necessary for the formation of red blood cells.

Miso is excellent for people with weak digestive systems. It is also good for those on a course of antibiotics, which can destroy the helpful bacterial culture in the intestines. *Miso* repopulates this helpful bacterial culture to prevent side-effects and guards the body against infections.

Scientists have shown that *miso* also has the ability to attract, absorb and discharge radioactive elements such as Strontium 90 from the body. In the past, when the Japanese used to smoke pipes, *miso* soup was used to clean tar out of the pipes. Maybe *miso* soup can keep our bodies clean in a similar way!

Because *miso* is alkaline, it has the ability to neutralise the acidity in the stomach and help prevent morning sickness or nausea. Packets of instant *miso* soups without seaweeds are ideal during the first few months of pregnancy. Just half a bowl will do the trick. I have also discovered, by chance, that daily consumption of *miso* in winter can help prevent dry, cracked lips.

Today *miso* is sold all over the world in Japanese food shops and health food shops. Make sure you buy naturally-fermented *miso* with no added sugar, preservatives or alcohol. In the West, there are four main varieties of *miso* available in health food shops: *hatcho miso* made from soyabeans; *mugi miso* made from soyabeans and barley; *kome miso* made from soyabeans and white rice; and *genmai miso* made from soyabeans and brown rice.

Instant packet *miso* soup is sold in health food shops in two varieties: with or without seaweeds. These packets are very handy for hikers or travellers, especially those who get motion sickness.

Miso is a live food and cannot be overheated or its medicinal properties and enzymes will be destroyed. Very gentle simmering for 10 to 15 minutes is sufficient.

While the recipes here are for *miso* soups, *miso* can also be cooked with vegetables, *tofu*, *fu zhou*, legumes, pulses, grains, fish and squids. I have made sauces with it too. Refer to the various food chapters for suggestions on how to use *miso* in daily home-cooking.

Miso is made with lots of sea-salt and should be used with care by people suffering from high blood pressure, water retention and other kidney problems. Food made with *miso* should not taste salty; it should only have a hint of saltiness. You have used too much if you need to drink right after a meal.

Miso is best kept in a cool place, like the refrigerator, in a glass jar.

Tofu and Spinach *Mugi Miso* Soup (for overheated blood systems)

$1^1/_2$ cups water
tiny pinch sea-salt
1 medium onion
1 handful tender spinach leaves
110 g (4 oz) soft tofu
1 tsp mugi miso
1 small red radish

1 Bring the water to a rolling boil with a tiny pinch of sea-salt.
2 Meanwhile, finely dice the onion and add to the boiling water. Leave the lid off to let the onion vapours escape and prevent flatulence. When the onion looks cooked,

replace the lid and boil the liquid down to 1 cup.

3 Wash the spinach leaves. Wash and drain the *tofu* and dice into 1 cm ($^1/_2$ in) cubes.

4 Thin out the *mugi miso* with some of the onion stock.

5 Add the spinach leaves and *tofu* to the boiling onion stock when it has been reduced to 1 cup.

6 After 2 minutes reduce to a very gentle simmer, add the thinned out *miso* and simmer for 10 to 15 minutes.

7 Garnish with rounds of finely sliced red radish before serving.

Variations:

1 Use watercress instead of spinach.

2 Omit the *tofu*.

3 Use a carrot or leek stock instead of onion.

4 For a complete meal, add cooked brown rice.

Leek and Carrot *Genmai Miso* Soup
(for neutral blood systems)

This *miso* soup is excellent in winter to help prevent colds and 'flus.

1 thin slice ginger
1 small leek
1 small carrot
cold-pressed sesame seed oil
tiny pinch sea-salt
1$^1/_2$ cups water
1 tsp genmai miso

1 Finely shred the ginger. Slice the leek and carrot diagonally into 5 mm ($^1/_4$ in) sections.

2 Heat a pot. When hot, add enough oil to just coat the bottom. When the oil is hot,

add the ginger and stir for 1 minute. Add the leek and a tiny pinch of sea-salt and stir until the leek is limp. Then add the carrot and stir for 1 minute.

3 Add the water and bring the contents to a rolling boil. Then reduce the heat and boil until 1 cup of liquid is left.

4 Meanwhile, thin out the *genmai miso* with a little vegetable stock. Add the *miso* to the pot when it has been reduced to 1 cup. Simmer very gently for 10 to 15 minutes to reactivate the enzymes. Serve.

Variations:

1 Use garlic, onions or spring onion instead of leek.

2 Use pumpkin instead of carrot.

3 Add another vegetable such as white cabbage, broccoli, Brussels sprouts, garland chrysanthemum, baby sweet corn, sweet corn kernels, long beans, French beans or snow peas.

4 For a complete meal, add cooked brown rice and cooked black-eyed beans.

Fish *Genmai Miso* Soup
(for cooled blood systems)

1 small mackerel
1 clove garlic
1 thin slice ginger
1 small leek
cold-pressed sesame seed oil
sea-salt
3 black peppercorns
1$^1/_2$ cups water
ground black pepper
1 tsp genmai miso

1 Fillet the fish but save the head and bones. Wash off the blood and drain.

2 Finely mince the garlic, finely slice the ginger and finely shred the leek.

3 Heat a pot. When hot, add enough oil to just coat the bottom. When the oil is hot, add the garlic and ginger and stir for 1 minute. Add the leek and a tiny pinch of sea-salt and stir until soft. Add the fish head and bones and stir for 1 minute.

4 Next, add the black peppercorns and water and bring to a fast rolling boil. Reduce heat and simmer until 1 cup of stock is left.

5 Meanwhile, slice the fish fillet thinly and marinate it with a tiny pinch of sea-salt and a dash of ground black pepper. Thin out the *genmai miso* with some of the fish stock.

6 When the stock has been reduced to 1 cup, remove the head and bones, reduce heat to a very gentle simmer and add the *miso*.

7 After 10 minutes, add the fish slices and simmer for another 5 minutes. Serve.

Variations:

1 Use white fish instead of herring or mackerel.

2 Use onion or spring onions instead of leek.

3 Add other vegetables such as carrots, white cabbage, broccoli, Chinese flowering cabbage, baby sweet corn, long beans, French beans or snow peas.

4 For a complete meal, add cooked brown rice.

SHOYU AND TAMARI
property: cooling

Shoyu and *tamari* are the Japanese names for soyasauce: *shoyu* is a thinner sauce, while *tamari* is more full bodied. I have used the Japanese names because I prefer the naturally-fermented Japanese soyasauces. (Before you buy them, make sure no sugar, monosodium glutamate or preservatives have been added.)

Shoyu and *tamari* are both by-products of *miso*. I use them to give dishes a richer taste. Because they contain sea-salt, you must use them with care, especially if you have high blood pressure, water retention or kidney problems.

MUNG BEANS
(Phaseolus aureus)
property: cooling

Mung beans are not found in the Chinese diet as much as aduki beans because the Chinese prefer not to eat cooling energy foods. They are used more for medicinal purposes than as a daily food. Indians, however, eat mung beans often. They cook them with a lot of hot spices to counteract their cooling properties.

According to the *Nei Jing*, mung beans can be used to cool down the heart and stomach when they become overheated. They also promote diuresis and counteract the effects of hot energy herbs.

In China and Hong Kong, mung beans are often eaten during the hot summer seasons to keep the body cool. The beans are also appropriate for people who live in countries with a hot, dry season.

Recently, researchers have shown that mung beans have the ability to lower excessive fat in the blood of animals. If this is the case, then mung beans may be able to prevent and treat heart disease in humans.

According to a famous Hong Kong herbalist, the husks of mung beans are an ideal pillow stuffing for people with high blood pressure. The husks, he says, have

cooling energies that can help cool the head. People with high blood pressure tend to have too much heat in the head, he says, which can be aggravated by sleeping on a pillow stuffed with feathers, cotton or *kapok*. Babies and young children with high fevers should sleep on pillows of mung bean husks to soothe their feverish heads.

The recipes for cooling sweet soups that follow are appropriate for anyone with a strong constitution who has an overheated blood system.

Those with weak constitutions and temporarily overheated blood systems should boil a small portion of mung beans with a thin slice of ginger and eat them as a side-dish. The beans should be quite dry in this case because the more liquid they have the more cooling they will be.

People with too much fat in their blood (i.e., triglycerides) should boil mung beans with garlic or onions and eat them as a side-dish once or twice a week.

Sweet Soup with Mung Beans and Job's Tears

This sweet soup is traditionally given to Chinese children during the hot summer months when they suffer from sunburn, sores and boils. It is also good for adults with acne caused by the sun.

25 g (1 oz) mung beans
25 g (1 oz) Job's tears
tiny pinch sea-salt
barley malt extract

1 Wash the beans and soak them overnight.
2 The next day, wash Job's tears, add them and plenty of water to the mung beans and boil until the beans are soft.

3 Add a pinch of sea-salt and simmer for another 15 minutes.
4 Sweeten the soup with barley malt extract and serve.

Note: Thinner soup is cooler than thicker soup.

Sweet Soup with Mung Beans and Fresh Lotus Leaf

This sweet soup is good for children and adults with prickly heat or heat rash.

25 g (1 oz) mung beans
1 fresh lotus leaf
pinch sea-salt
barley malt extract

1 Wash the beans and soak them overnight.
2 The next day, boil them in their soaking water with the lotus leaf until the beans are soft.
3 Add a pinch of sea-salt and simmer for another 15 minutes.
4 Sweeten with barley malt extract and serve.

Note: If fresh lotus leaf is not available, use dried lotus leaf or dried lotus petals (available from a Chinese herbalist).

SOYABEANS
(Glycine max)
property: cooling

Soyabeans are very rich in protein but difficult to digest in their whole forms. The Chinese have known about this for centuries and, therefore, rarely cook with the whole bean. They prefer soyabean products such as *tofu*, soyabean milk, dried soyabean sticks, fresh

and dried soyabean sheets and fermented products such as *tempeh*, *miso*, fermented soyabean cheese, *shoyu* and *tamari*.

Tofu has become very popular among vegans, vegetarians, macrobiotics and wholefooders in the West. Generally, freshly made *tofu* can be bought from Chinese or Japanese supermarkets. Vacuum packed *tofu* is sold in health food and wholefood shops. *Tofu* can be hard and crumbly, rubbery and smooth, or soft, silken and watery.

Soyabeans on their own have cooling energies. When they are made into *tofu* they become even more cooling because of the water and the cooling calcium sulphate (gypsum, a salt), used to coagulate the milk. People with overheated blood systems should eat *tofu* often to balance their systems. People with cooled blood systems can still eat *tofu* if it is stir-fried, grilled or baked with warm energy vegetables, herbs and spices.

Tofu Soup (cooling)

This is a nice summer soup. Those with cooled blood systems can either stir-fry the onions before boiling, or add a thin slice of ginger.

150 g (5 oz) tofu
1 medium onion
2 cups water
pinch sea-salt
10-20 fresh garden peas

1 Dice the *tofu* into 5 mm ($^1/_4$ in) cubes.
2 Finely mince the onion and boil it in the water with a pinch of sea-salt.
3 Reduce the water down to 1 cup then add the diced *tofu* and the peas.
4 Simmer until the peas are cooked.

Variations:
1 Use *tofu*, onion and carrot.
2 Use *tofu*, onion and Shiitake mushrooms.
3 Use *tofu*, onion, carrot and Shiitake mushrooms.
4 Use *tofu*, leeks and carrots.
5 Use *tempeh*, soyabean sticks or soyabean sheets instead of *tofu*. Soak dried bean curd until soft (about 2 hours), then use like *tofu*.
6 In Southeast Asian countries where fresh garden peas are not available, use snow peas or 5 mm ($^1/_4$ in) lengths of diagonally sliced long beans or French beans.

Steamed Silken *Tofu* (cooling)

1 carton silken tofu
2 spring onions
1 thin slice ginger
cold-pressed sesame oil
pinch sea-salt
gomasio

1 Steam the silken *tofu* in a heat-proof dish.
2 Meanwhile, finely shred the spring onions and ginger.
3 Heat a wok. When hot, add enough oil to just coat the bottom. When the oil is hot, add the spring onions and a pinch of sea-salt and stir for 1 minute. Then add the ginger and stir for 1 minute.
4 Place this stir-fried mixture over the steaming *tofu* and steam for another minute.
5 Garnish with *gomasio*.

Variations:
1 Thin out 1 tsp of *mugi* or *genmai miso*. Pour sauce over the *tofu* and steam. Then garnish with the stir-fried mixture.

2 Add some finely shredded carrots to the stir-fried mixture.

3 Use *tempeh* diced into 1 cm ($^1/_2$ in) cubes instead of *tofu*.

Stir-fried *Tofu* with Watercress (*cooling*)

150 g (5 oz) tofu
pinch sea-salt
1 bunch watercress
1 clove garlic
cold-pressed sesame oil
shoyu, tamari or gomasio

1 Dice the *tofu* into 5 mm ($^1/_4$ in) cubes and marinate in a pinch of sea-salt.

2 Finely chop the watercress.

3 Finely mince the garlic.

4 Heat a wok. When hot, add enough oil to just coat the bottom. When the oil is hot, add the garlic and stir for 1 minute. Add the *tofu* and stir for 2 to 3 minutes. Then add the watercress and stir for 2 minutes or until cooked to your liking. (To make a sauce, add just enough water to cover the bottom of the wok and cover for 1 to 2 minutes. The watercress also cooks faster this way.)

5 Garnish with a dash of *shoyu* or *tamari*, or a sprinkling of *gomasio*.

Variations:

1 Use spinach instead of watercress.

2 Use baby carrots and baby carrot tops instead of watercress.

3 Substitute *tempeh* for *tofu*.

4 To make this dish less cooling add:
   • ginger, onions and carrots
   • ginger, leeks and carrots
   • ginger, leeks and pumpkin or

   • ginger, onion and pumpkin.

5 Use neutral vegetables like broccoli.

Tofu with Spinach and Black Mustard Seeds (*warming*)

The *tofu* and spinach in this dish have cooling energies. They are balanced by the warming energies of carrot, onions, black mustard seeds, garlic, ginger and by stir-frying.

150 g (5 oz) tofu
sea-salt
1 small onion
1 small carrot
50 g (2 oz) spinach
1 clove garlic
1 thin slice ginger
cold-pressed sesame oil
$^1/_4$ tsp whole black mustard seeds

1 Dice *tofu* into 5 mm ($^1/_4$ in) cubes and marinate with a pinch of sea-salt.

2 Dice onion and carrot into 5 mm ($^1/_4$ in) cubes.

3 Finely chop the spinach.

4 Finely mince the garlic and ginger.

5 Heat a wok. When hot, add enough oil to just coat the bottom. When the oil is hot, add the mustard seeds and stir until they start to pop.

6 Add the minced garlic and ginger and stir for 1 minute. Add the onions with a pinch of sea-salt and stir until limp.

7 Add the *tofu* and stir for 2 to 3 minutes, then add the spinach and stir for 3 minutes. Add the carrot and stir for 1 minute.

8 Finally, add just enough water to cover the bottom of the wok and cover for 2 minutes to let the aromas mix and to steam the spinach further. Serve.

Legumes and Pulses 55

Variation: Use *tempeh* instead of *tofu.*

Stir-fried *Tofu* with Spring Onions (*warming*)

150 g (5 oz) tofu
1 bunch spring onions
2 thin slices ginger
cold-pressed sesame oil
pinch sea-salt
freshly ground black pepper

1 Dice the *tofu* into 5 mm ($^1/_4$ in) cubes.
2 Slice spring onions into 5 mm ($^1/_4$ in) diagonal lengths.
3 Finely shred the ginger.
4 Heat a wok. When hot, add enough oil to just coat the bottom. When the oil is hot, add the spring onions and a pinch of sea-salt and stir for 1 minute. Add the ginger and stir for 1 minute. Then add the *tofu* and black pepper and stir for 2 to 3 minutes. Add a little water and simmer for 2 minutes. Serve.

Note: If you take this dish to sweat out a cold or chill, go to bed as soon as you finish the food and sweat it out under warm bedclothes.

For use as a winter dish to help you warm yourself up, try the following variations.

Variations:
1 Use leeks instead of spring onions.
2 Thin out 1 tsp *miso* into a sauce and add to the gently simmering dish; simmer for 15 minutes to reactivate the enzymes.
3 Use *tempeh* instead of *tofu.*

Baked Silken *Tofu* (*warming*)
Use this dish as a filling for wholewheat quiches.

1 carton silken tofu
1 medium leek
1 medium carrot
1 thin slice ginger
cold-pressed sesame oil
pinch sea-salt
parsley

1 Drain the silken *tofu.*
2 Finely shred the leek.
3 Dice the carrot into 5 mm ($^1/_4$ in) diamonds.
4 Mince the ginger.
5 Heat a wok. When hot, add enough oil to just coat the bottom. When the oil is hot, add the ginger and stir for 1 minute. Add the leek and a pinch of sea-salt and stir until limp. Add the carrot and stir for 1 minute. Then add the *tofu*, mash it into a cream and mix it thoroughly with the other vegetables.
6 Pour this mixture into a heatproof dish and bake in a moderate oven for 20 minutes.
7 Garnish with some finely chopped parsley.

Warming variations:
1 Use garlic, ginger, onions, *tofu* and thyme.
2 Use black mustard seeds, garlic, ginger, onions, carrots and *tofu.*
3 Use garlic, ginger, onions, nutmeg, spinach and *tofu.*

Less warming combinations:
1 Use garlic, ginger, watercress, carrots and *tofu.*

2 Use garlic, ginger, celery, carrots and *tofu*.

3 Use leeks, ginger, mushrooms and *tofu*.

Tofu Burger with Coriander Leaves (*warming*)

Baking the burgers makes them less oily, crisp on the outside and nice and soft in the centre. You can grill or fry them in a little oil if you like.

150 g (5 oz) tofu
$^1/_4$ cup brown rice flakes
1 small onion
small piece ginger
coriander leaves
pinch sea-salt
shoyu or tamari

1 Finely chop the *tofu*.

2 Mix brown rice flakes with just enough water to form a soft doughy consistency. Then add to the *tofu*.

3 Coarsely grate the onion. Finely grate the ginger and finely chop the coriander leaves. Add all three to the *tofu*.

4 Add a pinch of sea-salt and a dash of *shoyu* or *tamari* to the *tofu*.

5 Mix everything together thoroughly and form into burgers.

6 Grease a baking tray and bake the burgers in a hot oven for 15 minutes or until brown.

Variations:

1 Use spring onions or chives instead of coriander leaves.

2 Add carrots.

3 Use millet flakes instead of brown rice flakes for a less warming combination.

Soyabean Milk

Soyabean milk is very cooling and therefore ideal on hot summer days in temperate countries and during the hot season in the tropics. It is best freshly prepared and sweetened with barley malt extract. (Prepare it as you would black soyabean milk, see page 63, but it is not necessary to remove the seed coats.)

Soyabean milk is not advisable for individuals suffering from wind in the digestive system and those with weak constitutions or cooled blood systems.

Many people I know have given up cow's milk for soyabean milk. Personally I do not think this is a wise move. Firstly, prepacked soyabean milk is not fresh. Secondly, if you have a cooled blood system and drink tea (a cooling drink) with soyabean milk, you can cool yourself down even more if your diet is mainly raw salads. Even individuals with overheated blood systems can cool themselves down too much if they drink soyabean milk too often. Thirdly, soyabean milk can easily create wind in the digestive system.

I advise taking soyabean milk occasionally and only in accordance with the weather and your body condition.

Tempeh

Tempeh is a fermented soyabean product that originated in Indonesia as a nutritious, inexpensive meat substitute. It is also very popular among the Chinese and Malays in Singapore and Malaysia.

Tempeh recently found its way to the West and is being sold in macrobiotic shops. I had great fun helping my teacher prepare *tempeh*

for sale in London when he first discovered it.

Tempeh is versatile, nutritious and easily digested. Like *tofu*, it can be steamed, stir-fried, fried, stewed, grilled or baked.

Steamed Marinated *Tempeh*

150 g (5 oz) tempeh
pinch sea-salt
grated ginger
tamari
roasted sesame oil
spring onions

1 Dice the *tempeh* into 5 mm ($^1/_4$ in) cubes.
2 Marinate *tempeh* cubes for 30 minutes in a pinch of sea-salt, some grated ginger, some *tamari*, a drop or two of roasted sesame oil and some chopped spring onions.
3 Steam on top of a pot of steaming brown rice for 15 minutes.

Variations: Use parsley, chives or coriander leaves for the spring onions.

ADUKI BEANS
(Phaseolus angularis)
property: neutral

Aduki beans are very popular in China, Japan and among Chinese communities in Southeast Asia. For centuries, the Chinese have made sweet glutinous rice dumplings filled with aduki bean paste to celebrate the Dragonboat Festival on the fifth day of the fifth lunar month. They also used aduki bean paste to fill wheat steam buns for *dian xin* and mooncakes for the Moon Festival which falls on the fifteenth day of the eighth lunar month.

The Japanese also eat a great deal of aduki bean paste and Japanese shops sell it ready-made for busy housewives. In Southeast Asia, aduki beans are generally served with black glutinous rice.

According to the *Shen Nong Ben Cao* written by Shen Nong, God of Husbandry, aduki beans have diuretic properties and should be used medicinally to remove dampness from the body, for example in cases of oedema (water retention).

According to the *Nei Jing*, aduki beans harmonise the blood, are good for oedematous beri-beri, and cases of obesity due to water retention. But, the *Nei Jing* warns, aduki beans must not be eaten if you are very thin or have very dry skin.

Macrobiotic teachers recommend aduki beans for the spleen and pancreas.

Recently, researchers have discovered that aduki beans are rich in B vitamins (hence their use in the treatment of oedematous beri-beri), especially in vitamin B_1 (thiamine) which is required to metabolise carbohydrates. Vegans, vegetarians and macrobiotics should have aduki beans often to help metabolise the whole cereal grains, legumes and pulses in their diet.

The following are a few medicinal recipes using aduki beans.

Aduki Beans and Carrot
This macrobiotic dish is said to be good for the spleen and pancreas.

25 g (1 oz) aduki beans
1 cm ($^1/_2$ in) piece dried kombu (optional)
1 thin slice ginger (optional)
1 medium onion
1 medium carrot

pinch sea-salt

fresh parsley or spring onions

gomasio

1 Wash the beans overnight and soak them with the *kombu*, if desired.
2 The next day, bring the beans and *kombu* to a vigorous boil in an uncovered pot in their own soaking water. Finely shred the ginger and add it at the start of the cooking (if desired).
3 Dice the onion into 1 cm (¹/₂ in) cubes and add to the beans when they are boiling vigorously. Add a little more water if necessary to prevent burning.
4 Cut the carrot into 1 cm (¹/₂ in) wedges. When the onion looks cooked, add the carrot, replace the lid and continue boiling for another 10 minutes.
5 Simmer until the beans are soft, add sea-salt and continue to simmer for another 15 minutes.
6 Garnish with finely chopped parsley or spring onions and *gomasio*.

Note:
1 The finished dish should be fairly dry. I find that the longer this dish is allowed to simmer, the better it is. If you have time, leave the beans in a cool oven to simmer for 2 to 3 hours before adding the sea-salt and continue to simmer for another 15 minutes.
2 Use *kombu* only if your blood system is overheated. Use ginger only if your blood system is on the cool side. Those with neutral blood systems can use *kombu* and ginger.

Variations:
1 Use pumpkin instead of carrots in the autumn.

2 In Southeast Asia where pumpkins are always available, alternate between pumpkin and carrots to break the monotony.

Aduki Beans with Tangerine Peel

This dish is excellent for removing dampness from the body, but you should not eat it at night. It is best eaten on hot, humid summer days.

25 g (1 oz) aduki beans

2¹/₂ cm (1 in) piece dried tangerine peel

pinch sea-salt

1 Soak the beans overnight in plenty of water.
2 The next day, cook them with the tangerine peel until soft. (Follow steps 1 to 4 on page 48.)
3 Add a pinch of sea-salt and simmer for another 15 minutes before serving.

Aduki Beans with Peanuts

Although this dish is specifically for healing beri-beri, there is no harm in eating it regularly as an excellent source of B vitamins.

25 g (1 oz) aduki beans

1 cm (¹/₂ in) piece of dried kombu (optional)

50 g (2 oz) peanuts

1 thin slice ginger (optional)

1 medium onion

pinch sea-salt

1 Soak the beans overnight with *kombu*, if desired.
2 The next day, boil the peanuts with the beans and *kombu* in their own soaking water. Add the ginger at the start of the cooking, if desired.
3 Follow steps 3-4 on page 48.

Variation: Use 1 medium leek cut diagonally into 1 cm (¹/₂ in) sections instead of onion.

Note: In China, Hong Kong and Southeast Asia, you can get another variety of aduki beans (*chi xiao dou*) from the Chinese herbalist. This variety is said to strengthen the spinal column and is good for people who suffer from backaches. It is about the same size as the other type, but it is flatter, more rectangular and brownish red in colour. Cook it with onions and carrots, onions and peanuts, or simply with a thin slice of ginger.

BLACK-EYED BEANS
(Vigna unguiculata)
property: neutral

Black-eyed beans have been used for many years in China, especially among poor rural people, as a supplement to rice. They use them to make black-eyed bean *tofu*, flour and milk.

Black-eyed beans are easy to digest and therefore suitable for those with weak digestive systems, the very young and the elderly. According to the *Ben Cao Gang Mu* by Li Shi Zhen, black-eyed beans strengthen the stomach and supplement the kidneys.

They take only about 20 to 30 minutes to cook and are appropriate for quick meals.

Black-eyed Beans and Brown Rice

This is a typical recipe used by Chinese farmers. I usually prepare this one-pot meal in the morning and keep it hot in a food thermos for lunch at work.

25 g (1 oz) black-eyed beans
1¹/₂ cups water
¹/₂ cup brown rice
pinch sea-salt

1 Wash the beans and soak them in the water overnight.
2 The next day, drain the beans, but save the soaking water.
3 Wash and drain the brown rice and place it in a deep-sided pot.
4 Add the black-eyed beans. Measure the bean-soaking water. If it is less than 1¹/₂ cups, add tap water to make up the difference. Then add to the beans and rice.
5 Bring the contents of the pot to a boil.
6 When it is boiling vigorously remove the lid for 10 minutes.
7 After 10 minutes, replace the lid and simmer gently.
8 When most of the liquid has been absorbed, the beans should be cooked. Then add a pinch of sea-salt and stir. Continue to simmer until the brown rice is cooked.
9 Serve with stir-fried vegetables.

Variations:
1 Add diced onion and carrot and caraway seeds or thyme.
2 Add diced leek and carrot.

Black-eyed Beans and Peanuts
This is another favourite of the Chinese farmer.

25 g (1 oz) black-eyed beans
1¹/₂ cups water
50 g (2 oz) peanuts
pinch sea-salt

1 Wash the beans and soak them overnight in the water.
2 The next day, add the peanuts to the beans and soaking water and cook them as you would cook beans (see the basic recipe on page 48).

(see the basic recipe on page 48)

Variations:
1 Add a diced onion or a medium-sized leek, sliced.
2 Add diced onion or leek with diced carrot or pumpkin.
3 Season the cooked beans with *shoyu* or *tamari*.
4 Add *miso* 15 minutes before serving and simmer very gently until ready.

BLACK SOYABEANS
(Glycine max)
property: neutral

Black soyabeans are not often seen in the West except in Chinese supermarkets or macro-biotic shops. This is unfortunate because this bean has a great deal of medicinal value.

According to the *Nei Jing*, black soyabeans are good for the spleen, pancreas and kidneys. They stimulate blood circulation, promote diuresis (and, hence, are useful for oedema), and they have the ability to expel wind in sudden cases of rheumatism, arthritis, dizziness, and muscle or tendon spasms. They are also good for the eyes and are used to calm down overactive foetal activities in pregnant women. After childbirth, new mothers are given black soyabeans to relieve stiffness and to tonify the blood.

Note: It is not necessary to soak black soyabeans overnight. Just wash and drain them, and dry-roast in an oil-free wok or stainless steel pot until the skins begin to crack, revealing the green seed leaves. Cool before using.

Black Soyabeans and Chicken Feet Soup
This dish is good for strengthening the kidneys.

25 g (1 oz) black soyabeans
2 chicken feet
3 cups water
1 thin slice ginger
pinch sea-salt
spring onions
shoyu or tamari

1 Wash the black soyabeans, drain, dry-roast and leave to cool.
2 Meanwhile, wash and clean the chicken feet and place in a pot with 3 cups of water.
3 Add the ginger and bring to a fast rolling boil.
4 Then add the cooled dry-roasted beans and boil uncovered for 10 minutes.
5 Cover and simmer until the beans are cooked. Add a pinch of sea-salt and simmer for another 15 minutes.
6 Garnish with some chopped spring onions and a dash of *shoyu* or *tamari*.

Variations: Add a medium onion or a clove of garlic.

Black Soyabeans and Black-boned Chicken Soup
This dish is for new mothers to tonify their blood. It will increase the flow of *qi* and, eventually, help relieve stiffness.

If black-boned chicken is not available, fresh and free-range chickens are acceptable substitutes.

75 g (3 oz) black soyabeans
$^1/_2$ black-boned chicken
thumb-sized piece of fresh ginger
1 clove garlic
cold-pressed sesame oil
pinch sea-salt

1 Wash the black soyabeans, drain, dry-roast and leave to cool.
2 Clean the chicken and cut into bite-sized pieces.
3 Slice the ginger thinly and mince the garlic.
4 Heat a large pot. When hot, add enough oil to just coat the bottom. When the oil is hot, add the garlic and ginger and stir for 1 minute. Add the chicken pieces and stir for 2 to 3 minutes. Then add the cooled beans and enough water to cover. (Use more water if you prefer a thinner consistency.)
5 Bring to a fast rolling boil, then remove the lid for 10 minutes. Replace the lid and slowly simmer for 2 to 3 hours until the beans are cooked. Add a pinch or two of sea-salt to taste, then simmer for another 15 minutes.

Note: The long simmering adds warmth and strength and the ginger improves *qi* circulation, as well as warms up the body. If you are not used to so much ginger, smash it instead of slicing.

Take this soup twice a day, reheating before the second serving. NEVER drink soup cold or after it has been left overnight.

Black Soyabeans and Leek Stew

This stew is good for oedema, removing external wind which manifests itself as sudden onset of dizziness, arthritis, rheumatism, muscle and tendon spasms. The leeks improve circulation while the ginger drives out the wind, improves circulation and warms the body.

25 g (1 oz) black soyabeans
3 thin slices ginger
1 medium leek
2 cups water
pinch sea-salt

1 Wash the beans, drain, dry-roast and leave to cool.
2 Meanwhile, finely shred the ginger and leek and add to a pot of 2 cups of boiling water. Add the cooled beans and boil uncovered for 10 minutes or until the leek is cooked.
3 Replace the lid and simmer until the beans are cooked. Add a pinch of sea-salt and simmer another 15 minutes.
4 Serve with brown rice and other vegetables.

Black Soyabeans and Black Sesame Seed Stew

This stew helps improve eyesight and problems like blurred vision and spots before the eyes.

25 g (1 oz) black soyabeans
25 g (1 oz) black sesame seeds
1 cup water
1 thin slice ginger
pinch sea-salt

1. Wash the beans, drain, dry-roast and leave to cool.
2. Wash the sesame seeds and place in a pot with 1 cup water and the ginger.
3. Bring to a rolling boil, add the cooled beans and cook uncovered for 10 minutes. Cover and simmer until the beans are cooked.
4. Add a pinch of sea-salt and simmer for another 15 minutes.
5. Serve with brown rice and vegetables.

Black Soyabean Milk

This is even more nutritious but somewhat less cooling than regular soyabean milk. Black soyabeans are neutral, but the water in the milk makes them cooling.

25 g (1 oz) black soyabeans
1 cup water
barley or rice malt extract to taste

1. Wash and soak black soyabeans overnight in plenty of water.
2. The next day, remove all the black seed coats to reveal the green seed leaves. Rinse once.
3. Liquidise well in 1 cup fresh water.
4. Pour the contents into a finely woven muslin bag and squeeze the milk into a pot. Save the residue for cooking with vegetables.
5. Bring the milk to a boil while stirring constantly to prevent burning. Then simmer for 5 to 7 minutes.
6. Sweeten with barley or rice malt extract and drink hot or cold.

Note: Do not serve leftover soyabean milk. The Chinese believe that leftovers, especially of cooling foods, gather external wind overnight.

CHICK-PEAS
(Cicer arietinum)
property: neutral

Chick-peas are eaten frequently in India, the Middle East and the Mediterranean countries. They are very nutritious and have their own unique taste.

Chick-peas with Fresh Coriander Leaves

25 g (1 oz) chick-peas
sea-salt
1 clove garlic
1 medium onion
some fresh coriander leaves
cold-pressed sesame oil

1. Wash the chick-peas and soak them overnight in plenty of water.
2. The next day, drain and rinse them well.
3. Cook them in plenty of fresh water until soft. Then add a pinch of sea-salt and simmer for another 15 minutes. Reserve the chick-pea cooking water.
4. Meanwhile, finely mince the garlic.
5. Dice the onion into 5 mm ($^1/_4$ in) cubes.
6. Roughly chop the fresh coriander leaves.
7. When the chick-peas are done, heat a wok. When hot, add enough oil to coat the bottom. When the oil is hot, add the garlic and stir for 1 minute. Add the onion and a pinch of sea-salt and stir until soft. Add the chick-peas and stir for 1 minute. Add the coriander leaves and stir for 1 minute.
8. Add just enough of the reserved chick-pea cooking water to cover the bottom of the wok and cover for 1 to 2 minutes so the aromas can mix. Serve.

DRIED SOYABEAN

Dried soyabean sticks and fresh and dried soyabean sheets (*fu zhou*) are less cooling than *tofu* because they contain less water. The Chinese use them frequently in the preparation of Buddhist vegetarian dishes. They are found in Chinese supermarkets.

Dried Soyabean Stick Stew

50 g (2 oz) dried soyabean sticks
1 clove garlic
1 thin slice ginger
1 medium onion
1 medium carrot
cold-pressed sesame oil
pinch sea-salt
1 tsp miso
spring onions

1 Wash the soyabean sticks, break them into $2^1/_2$ cm (1 in) lengths, and soak for 3 hours in hot water until soft.
2 Finely mince the garlic and ginger.
3 Dice the onion into 1 cm ($^1/_2$ in) cubes.

4 Cut the carrot into 1 cm ($^1/_2$ in) wedges.
5 Heat a pot. When hot, add enough oil to just coat the bottom. When the oil is hot, add the garlic and ginger and stir for 1 minute. Add the onion and a pinch of sea-salt and stir until the onion is soft. Add the carrot and stir for 1 minute. Then add the soft soyabean sticks and the soaking water and bring to a fast rolling boil.
6 Simmer gently until most of the liquid has been absorbed.
7 Thin out the *miso*, add it to the pot and simmer very gently for another 15 minutes.
8 Garnish with some spring onions.

HARICOT BEANS
(Phaseolus vulgaris)
property: neutral

Haricot beans (baked beans) are popular throughout the world. The French use them often in their casseroles.

Like red kidney-beans, haricot beans help diabetics maintain their blood sugar levels. Do not eat the tinned variety as they are laden with sugar.

Haricot Beans with Pumpkin and Caraway Seeds
This dish is especially good for diabetics. The pumpkin is supposed to be good for the spleen and pancreas and the caraway seeds

aid digestion, give the dish a slightly sweet flavour and a wonderful aroma to stimulate the appetite.

25 g (1 oz) haricot beans
1 clove garlic
1 thin slice ginger
110 g (4 oz) pumpkin
1 medium onion
cold-pressed sesame oil
$^1/_8$ tsp caraway seeds
pinch sea-salt
parsley
gomasio

1 Wash the beans and soak them overnight in plenty of water.
2 The next day, finely mince the garlic and ginger.
3 Dice the pumpkin and the onion into 5 mm ($^1/_4$ in) cubes.
4 Heat a pot. When hot, add enough oil to coat the bottom. When the oil is hot, add the garlic and ginger and stir for 1 minute. Add the onion and caraway seeds and stir until the onion begins to soften. Add the pumpkin and stir for 2 minutes. Then add the haricot beans and enough soaking water to cover by $2^1/_2$ cm (1 in).
5 Bring to a rolling boil without the lid for 10 minutes. Cover the pot and simmer for 2 to 3 hours until the beans are soft. Then add a pinch of sea-salt and simmer for another 15 minutes. Add more water if necessary.
6 Serve either as it is, on the watery side, or remove the lid and bake in a very hot oven until you get a thick pumpkin sauce. (Mash the pumpkin before baking to give a smoother sauce.)
7 Garnish with parsley and *gomasio*.

Variations:
1 Use carrot instead of pumpkin.
2 Use a combination of leeks and swede.
3 Try other herbs like fennel leaves and seeds, dill leaves and seeds, bay leaf, parsley, thyme, etc., instead of caraway seeds.

HYACINTH BEANS
(Dolichos lablab)
property: neutral

Hyacinth beans are flattish white beans with a distinctive flavour. They are found only in China, Hong Kong and Southeast Asia.

According to the *Nei Jing*, hyacinth beans are good for the stomach, spleen and pancreas and they eliminate damp heat from the body.

The Chinese use hyacinth beans cooked in plenty of water for children with diarrhoea caused by damp heat. Elderly people who habitually pass loose stools – a sign that the spleen is weak – are often given hyacinth bean soup or hyacinth beans cooked with porridge oats.

In summer or in tropical countries, people tend to suffer from damp heat, the symptoms of which include lethargy, a heavy feeling in the body, loss of appetite, and possibly cystitis and gall bladder problems. To remedy this, cook the hyacinth beans with a fresh lotus leaf to make a sweet soup. (The method is the same as the one for cooking mung beans with fresh lotus leaf, page 53.)

Leucorrhoea due to damp heat (where the discharges are yellow) can be remedied by eating hyacinth beans. Just boil the beans on their own, add a pinch of sea-salt when they are soft, simmer another 15 minutes and serve. (Sweet soup with hyacinth beans and fresh lotus leaf can also be used.)

Peas
(Pisum sativum)
property: neutral

We are all familiar with several varieties of peas: fresh garden peas, mangetout (snow peas), dried whole green peas, marrowfat peas, and split green and yellow peas.

Pease pudding made from puréed peas and served with pork used to be a popular British dish. Now, they eat fish, chips and peas. The Dutch are still famous for thick green pea soup cooked with ham.

According to the *Nei Jing*, peas are good for the spleen, pancreas and stomach and they promote urination. They are said to counteract the toxic effects of ulcers and are advised for the treatment of beri-beri. Although beri-beri is almost unheard of now, there are still many people who suffer from a lack of B vitamins. Fresh and dried peas are an excellent source of B vitamins.

Try to use whole dried peas as much as possible. The skin gives added roughage and the pea embryo is still intact.

Thick Winter Pea Soup
This soup is a meal in itself. It is ideal for people who live on their own in bedsitters with only one gas or electric burner. The long simmering adds warmth to a cold room in winter.

25 g (1 oz) marrowfat peas
$^1/_4$ cup oat groats
1 clove garlic
1 thin slice ginger
1 medium leek
cold-pressed sesame oil
pinch sea-salt
parsley
gomasio

1 Wash the peas and soak them overnight in plenty of water.
2 The next day, rinse the peas thoroughly and drain.
3 Wash the oat groats and drain.
4 Finely mince the garlic and ginger.
5 Finely slice the washed leek.
6 Heat a pot. When hot, add enough oil to coat the bottom. When the oil is hot, add the garlic and ginger and stir for 1 minute. Add the leek and stir until limp. Then add the peas and oat groats and stir for 1 minute. Add plenty of water and bring to boil.
7 Remove the lid for 10 minutes. When the mixture is boiling vigorously, turn down the heat and simmer for 2 to 3 hours. Add more water if required.
8 Add a pinch of sea-salt 15 minutes before serving.
9 Serve with finely chopped parsley and a sprinkling of *gomasio*.

Note: With a solid fuel cooker, simmer peas in the cool oven.

Variations: Add $^1/_2$ cup diced swede, carrots, pumpkin, or mushrooms to give different flavours. (Do not use them all at once or flatulence may result.)

Steamed Fresh Garden Peas
In summer, try steaming fresh garden peas on top of some steaming brown rice. Simply de-pod the peas and steam them for 15 minutes. They are sweet and delicious done this way. Add 1 small diced baby carrot for extra colour.

Mangetout (Snow Peas) with *Tofu*

50 g (2 oz) button mushrooms
150 g (5 oz) tofu
sea-salt
6 fresh tender mangetout
1 clove garlic
1 thin slice ginger
cold-pressed sesame oil
shoyu or tamari

1 Wash the mushrooms and slice them about 3 mm ($^1/_8$ in) thick.
2 Drain the *tofu* and slice into 4 x 1 x $^1/_2$ cm ($1^1/_2$ x $^1/_2$ x $^1/_4$ in) rectangles. Marinate the slices in a pinch of sea-salt for 30 minutes.
3 Wash, top and tail the mangetout.
4 Finely mince the garlic and ginger.
5 Heat a wok. When hot, add enough oil to coat the bottom. When the oil is hot, add the garlic and ginger and stir for 1 minute. Add the *tofu* and stir gently for 2 minutes. Add the mushrooms with a pinch of sea-salt and stir until just cooked. Then add the mangetout and stir for 1 minute.
6 Add just enough water to cover the bottom of the wok and cover for 1 minute, or until the mangetout is just done (but still crisp and bright green). Add a dash of *shoyu* or *tamari* and serve.

Variations:
1 Use 3 dried Shiitake mushrooms instead of button mushrooms.
2 Use fresh garden peas instead of mangetout and dice the *tofu* and mushrooms into 5 mm ($^1/_4$ in) cubes.
3 Stir-fry the following combinations as above: fresh garden peas with diced *tofu*, baby carrots and onions; or fresh garden peas with diced baby radishes and onions.

RED KIDNEY-BEANS
(Phaseolus vulgaris)
property: neutral

Red kidney-beans have been popular in Mexico, South America and the Caribbean for many years. Scientists have recently learned that red kidney-beans lower blood cholesterol and help diabetics maintain their blood sugar levels.

Red Kidney-beans and Celery
The kidney-beans in this dish lower blood cholesterol and the celery lowers the blood pressure and contributes cooling energies.

25 g (1 oz) red kidney-beans
$1^1/_2$ cups water
sea-salt
3 stalks celery
1 clove garlic
cold-pressed sesame oil

1 Wash the red kidney-beans and soak them in the water overnight.
2 The next day, boil the beans in their own soaking water for 15 minutes with the lid off, then cover and simmer until cooked. Add a pinch of sea-salt and simmer gently for another 15 minutes or until nearly all the water has been absorbed. If the cooked beans are watery, drain them but save the cooking liquid for further use.
3 While the beans are cooking, wash and clean the celery stalks and slice them diagonally into 5 mm ($^1/_4$ in) pieces.
4 Finely mince the garlic.
5 When the beans are ready, heat a wok with enough oil to coat the bottom. When the oil is hot, add the garlic and stir for 1 minute. Add the celery and stir for 2

minutes with a pinch of sea-salt. Then add the cooked, drained beans and stir for 1 minute. Add just enough bean cooking liquid to cover the bottom of the wok and cover for 1 to 2 minutes to steam the celery and allow all the aromas to mix.

6   The celery should still be crispy when the dish is done. (Older people or those who have dentures should cook the dish in more water until the celery is soft.)

> **Variations:**
> 1   Substitute Chinese Peking cabbage for celery. This cabbage has cooling energies too.
> 2   Substitute yam bean, diced into 5 mm ($^1/_4$ in) pieces, for celery. Yam bean also has cooling energies.
> 3   Substitute Chinese flowering cabbage or broccoli for celery. These two vegetables have neutral energies and are suitable for diabetics with cooled blood systems.

LENTILS
(Lens esculenta)
property: warming

Lentils have been around since ancient times. Like chick-peas, they are a daily food in India, the Middle East and the Mediterranean countries.

Lentils are very nutritious and rich in iron. Like black-eyed beans, they cook in 20 to 30 minutes and are handy for quick meals. (Remember, of course, to presoak them overnight.)

When recipes call for minced meat, brown lentils are the best substitute. They are delicious as a filling for Shepherd's Pie or in Spaghetti Bolognese.

Green lentils can also be used instead of brown lentils (of course the taste and texture will be slightly different) but try not to use red lentils. They are actually brown lentils with the skins removed and therefore lack roughage and possibly the vital seed embryos. Remember – vital foods are healthier than processed foods.

Lentils and Thyme
This is the vegetarian equivalent to Shepherd's Pie filling. I prefer to serve it with brown rice, millet or even wholewheat pasta.

25 g (1 oz) brown lentils
1 clove garlic
1 medium onion
1 medium carrot
cold-pressed sesame oil
$^1/_4$ tsp dried thyme or some fresh thyme
pinch sea-salt
shoyu
parsley

1   Wash the lentils and soak them overnight.
2   The next day, finely mince the garlic and dice the onion and carrot into 5 mm ($^1/_4$ in) cubes.
3   Heat a pot. When hot, add enough oil to coat the bottom. When the oil is hot, add the garlic and stir for 1 minute. Add the onion and thyme and stir until just soft. Add the carrot and stir for 1 minute.
4   Now add the lentils and the soaking water and bring to a fast rolling boil for 10 minutes without the lid. Turn the heat down, cover and simmer gently until the lentils are soft. Add a pinch of sea-salt and simmer for another 15 minutes. Add a dash of *shoyu* before serving.
5   Garnish with some parsley.

Variations:
1   Add diced mushrooms and use mixed herbs such as parsley, sage, thyme and oregano for a vegetarian version of Spaghetti Bolognese sauce. One teaspoon of *miso* will make it even better.
2   Use a combination of lentils, onions and celeriac for an unusual flavour.

Lentils and Brown Rice

This is another one-pot meal which I prepare for cold winter days. The carrot, ginger, cumin seeds and lentils all give warming energies.

25 g (1 oz) brown lentils
1 cup water
$^1/_3$ cup brown rice
1 small carrot
2-3 white cabbage leaves
1 thin slice ginger
$^1/_8$ tsp cumin seeds
pinch sea-salt
spring onions

1   Wash the lentils and soak them overnight in 1 cup of water.
2   The next day, drain the lentils but save the water. (If it is less than 1 cup, top it up.)
3   Wash and drain the rice. Dice the carrot into 5 mm ($^1/_4$ in) cubes. Finely chop the cabbage and finely grate the ginger.
4   Place the brown rice, lentils, carrot, cabbage, ginger, cumin seeds and the reserved cup of water in a deep pot. Bring to a boil and remove the lid for 10 minutes. Then simmer slowly until almost all the water has been absorbed and the lentils are cooked. Stir a pinch of sea-salt into the brown rice and lentils. Continue to simmer until the rice is done.
5   Garnish with some chopped spring onions.

Variations:
1   In summer, add fresh garden peas during the last 15 minutes of the brown rice cooking time and leave out the cumin seeds.
2   In autumn, use pumpkin instead of carrot and caraway seeds instead of cumin seeds.
3   Use a combination of brown rice, brown lentils, ginger, onion and *miso*.

Lentil Burgers

25 g (1 oz) lentils
1 cup water
1 clove garlic
pinch sea-salt
cold-pressed sesame oil
shoyu or tamari

1   Wash the lentils and soak them overnight in the water.
2   The next day, finely mince the garlic and add it to the lentils and soaking water. Bring to a boil, remove the lid for 10 minutes, then simmer until the lentils are soft. Add a pinch of sea-salt. Simmer for another 15 minutes until the lentils are soft and dry. If they are watery, reduce the liquid by simmering with the lid off.
3   When the lentils are done, mash, form into flat, round patties, and place them on a greased baking tray.
4   Mix equal portions of oil and *shoyu* or *tamari* and brush the tops of the patties with the mixture. Bake them in a hot oven for 15 minutes.

5 Serve with brown rice and plenty of vegetables.

LEGUMES AND PULSES FOR BABIES AND INFANTS

Legumes and pulses should not be given to very young babies because their digestive systems are not developed enough to handle them. Consumption can lead to flatulence and/or too much phlegm or mucus, a runny nose and respiratory problems.

Babies and infants can, however, have the top liquid of a pot of boiling legumes or pulses (before any sea-salt is added) once or twice a week to allow their digestive systems to get used to them. You can increase the frequency as they grow older.

Once the child is old enough to chew properly, he can be given well cooked, well mashed legumes or pulses with cooked grains and vegetables once a week. Increase frequency to twice a week, and so on, until he can have it daily.

Any time the child shows signs of too much flatulence and/or respiratory problems, cut out the legumes or pulses for one to three months until the problems clear. Then slowly reintroduce the legumes or pulses and again build up the frequency. If the child cannot tolerate them more than two to three times a week, just stay at this frequency.

Tofu is usually easier for children to tolerate, but they should not eat it too often because of its cooling properties. It is difficult to advise just how often to feed it to children because they vary so much in constitution and in blood system. Use your own judgement to determine how much *tofu* to give your child.

Miso is also easily digested, but because of its salt content, it should not be given to children until about age three. Children should have *miso* soup with a hint of saltiness (i.e., half a level teaspoon of *miso* to a rice bowl of soup) about once or twice a week. Increase the frequency as the child grows older.

4 Seeds and Nuts

Seeds and nuts are concentrated packets of energy. They contain a very high proportion of poly-unsaturated oils, vitamins E and B, and lots of essential minerals and trace elements.

Seeds and nuts should not exceed 5 per cent of your daily food intake because they contain too much oil and are therefore hard to digest. If you lightly dry-roast or boil them rather than eat them raw, the polyunsaturated oils will be easier to digest.

They must be stored in a cool, dry place to prevent them from going rancid. Buy them in small amounts to ensure freshness.

BITTER APRICOT KERNELS
(Prunus armeniaca)
property: cooling (see page 72)

GINKGO NUTS
(Ginkgo biloba)
property: cooling

The Chinese use ginkgo nuts for dry coughs, some forms of asthma and leucorrhoea caused by damp heat.

Li Shi Zhen cautions that excessive consumption of ginkgo nuts can harm the body. People with cooled blood systems, pregnant women or those who wish to conceive should avoid ginkgo nuts.

Sweet Tea with Ginkgo Nuts, *Fu Zhou* and Apricot Kernels
This tea helps clear the lungs of dry heat. It is also good for dry coughs. Boil 5 ginkgo nuts with 1 dried sheet of pre-soaked *fu zhou* and 10 sweet apricot kernel halves in 2 cups of water. The tea will be done when the nuts and kernels are soft, after about 1 to 1 $^1/_2$ hours. Sweeten the tea with barley malt extract.

Ginkgo Nut and *Euryale ferox* Sweet Tea
This tea helps clear leucorrhoea with a yellow, strong smelling discharge caused by damp heat. Consult a Chinese herbalist regarding the proportions of ginkgo nut, water and *Euryale ferox* (芡 实) for the tea. Boil the ingredients and sweeten with barley malt extract. Ask the herbalist how often you should take the tea.

ALMONDS
(Prunus amygdalus)
property: neutral

Almonds are rich in calcium and protein. Almond milk is an excellent alternative to cow's or goat's milk. (See page 182 for the recipe and more information.)

To make almond cream: liquidise some blanched almonds in less water than you would use for almond milk. Almonds can also be served lightly dry-roasted with *tamari*. Dry-roast them in an oil-free wok until just lightly browned. Cool for 2 to 3 minutes then add a dash of *tamari* and mix thoroughly. Cook them with brown rice for an unusual texture and taste, or chop them and add to a *tofu* and coriander burger (see recipe on page 57).

APRICOT KERNELS
(Prunus armeniaca)
property: neutral (sweet variety),
cooling (bitter variety)

There are two types of apricot kernels – bitter and sweet. Both are heart-shaped, but the bitter variety is yellowish-brown because it has more oil. It is also cooling, while the sweet variety is neutral.

Bitter apricot kernels are slightly toxic but are not dangerous, so long as they are taken in small quantities, as suggested in the recipes. Sweet apricot kernels are non-toxic but overconsumption can cause indigestion.

Bitter and sweet apricot kernels are used together to dispel heat or damp heat from the lungs, to stop or relieve dry coughs, to strengthen the lungs and to help resolve phlegm.

Apricot Kernel, Dried White Cabbage and Date Tea
This tea helps dispel coughs and wind heat from the lungs.

Boil 30 g (1 oz) sweet apricot kernels, only 3 g bitter apricot kernels, some dried white cabbage (白菜干) and some unsweetened brown dates in some water. Boil until the

kernels are soft, and drink the tea.

Apricot Kernel Milk
This milky tea helps stop or quiet dry coughs and strengthens the lungs.

Soak 60 g (2 oz) sweet apricot kernels with only 6 g bitter apricot kernels overnight. Next day, boil with some cooked brown rice and water until the kernels are soft. Liquidise into a creamy milk. Reheat and sweeten with barley malt extract.

LOTUS SEED
(Nelumbo nucifera)
property: neutral

According to the *Nei Jing,* lotus seeds are good for the heart, spleen and kidneys. They nourish the heart (to prevent insomnia), tone up the spleen (to correct diarrhoea caused by spleen deficiency), and tone up the kidneys (to help urinary disorders, spermatorrhoea, leucorrhoea and vaginal bleeding).

The *Nei Jing* advises against using lotus seeds in cases of congestion in the middle *jiao* with swelling in the epigastrium (the area below the sternum or breast bone) or hypochondrium (the area below the lower rib cage on either side of the sternum) or constipation with dry stools.

Lotus Seed and Egg Drop Soup
This soup helps nourish the heart to prevent dream-disturbed sleep or insomnia.

20 lotus seed halves (dried)
2 cups water
1 thin slice ginger
pinch sea-salt

1 free-range egg

1 spring onion

1 Wash the dried lotus seeds. Boil in 2 cups of water with the ginger until the liquid is reduced to 1 cup.
2 Add a pinch of sea-salt, quickly break the egg into the boiling liquid and stir for 1 to 2 minutes until the egg is cooked.
3 Garnish with finely chopped spring onion.

Lotus Seed and Brown Rice Congee

This congee tones up the spleen to correct spleen deficient diarrhoea.

20 lotus seed halves (dried)

$\frac{1}{4}$ cup brown rice

10 Chinese red dates (stones removed)

1 thin slice ginger

pinch sea-salt

2-3 cups water

Bring all the ingredients to a boil and simmer gently until the brown rice becomes a soft congee.

Lotus Seed and Lotus Root Tea

This tea is good for vaginal bleeding that occurs between menstrual cycles. (See a doctor or a qualified acupuncturist as soon as possible. This is only a home remedy to supplement other treatment.)

20 lotus seed halves (dried)

2-3 slices lotus root (dried)

2 cups water

pinch sea-salt

1 Wash the lotus seeds and root and soak in 2 cups of cold water.
2 When the lotus root has swelled, boil everything with a tiny pinch of sea-salt until 1 cup of liquid is left.
3 Drink the tea and eat the seeds and root.

PEANUTS
(Arachis hypogaea)
property: neutral

Peanuts are really legumes. They are good sources of vitamin B and protein but can form mucus, phlegm or catarrh if taken in excess.

Dry-roast peanuts in an oil-free wok. Boil them until they are soft and liquidise into a milk or cream, or boil them with beans. Buy smooth or crunchy peanut butter – free from additives – at health food shops to use as a spread or a sauce.

Note: Peanuts have neutral properties, but once roasted they become warming. When boiled, they become slightly more cooling.

CHESTNUTS
(Castanea sativa)
property: warming

Chestnuts are one of the most warming foods. In Chinese medicine they are used to warm up the kidneys, to strengthen the lower back and knees, and to warm up the whole body. They can also help in mild cases of diarrhoea.

Caution: People with weak digestive systems should not eat too many chestnuts. They are very difficult to digest and must be chewed thoroughly before swallowing.

Roasted Chestnuts

This is a remedy for someone who suffers

from what the Chinese call 'internal cold', or the inability to warm up, even in warm weather. For internal cold, eat 20 to 30 roasted chestnuts daily until your condition improves.

Chestnut and Brown Rice Congee

This congee helps strengthen the lower back and knees. It must be taken daily for a long time before there is any improvement.

10 dried chestnuts
2 cups water
$^1/_4$ cup brown rice
tiny pinch sea-salt

1 Wash the chestnuts and soak them for 8 hours in 2 cups of water. Drain the soaking liquid into the pot in which you will cook the congee.
2 Remove any reddish brown skins still attached to the chestnuts. Cut them up into small pieces and add them to the pot.
3 Add the washed brown rice and a tiny pinch of sea-salt. Bring to a fast rolling boil, then simmer on a medium flame.
4 Cook until the brown rice and chestnuts are soft.

Chestnuts and Brussels Sprouts

This winter dish is very simple to make. Wash and soak the chestnuts overnight in plenty of water. Next day, remove the reddish brown skins and cook the chestnuts until soft in their own soaking liquid. Add Brussels sprouts and a tiny pinch of sea-salt and cook until the Brussels sprouts are just done. For a very nourishing, high-protein dish, add *tofu*.

PUMPKIN SEEDS
(Cucurbita maxima)
property: warming

The Chinese have been giving children these large green seeds for years to expel intestinal worms. The Hungarian gypsies, Bulgarians, Anatolian Turks, Ukranians and Transylvanian Germans have known for centuries that pumpkin seeds can prevent prostate gland troubles in older men.

Someone I know had prostate gland trouble. After I recommended that he take 10 pumpkin seeds a day, his problem cleared. I must stress, however, that the problem took from six months to a year to clear completely.

Pumpkin seeds can be eaten raw, very lightly dry-roasted or cooked.

A health food shop in West Berlin sells delicious wholewheat pumpkin seed bread. If you bake your own bread, just add some pumpkin seeds to the dough. A patient of mine from Ghana eats cooked pumpkin seeds and onions as a side dish with his rice. You can also sauté or boil onions with pumpkin seeds and simmer them in a little water for 30 to 45 minutes to make a sauce. Add some nice fresh herbs to make it more aromatic and appealing. Or add pumpkin seeds to your muesli or jumbo oats for breakfast.

BEIGE SESAME SEEDS
(Sesamum indicum)
property: warming

Beige sesame seeds are used more as a food garnish than for medicinal purposes. In their natural state they have warming energies. When dry-roasted they become more heating. Similarly, if baked with biscuits or cakes they

also tend to have more heating energies. If boiled, they become more cooling. In any state, they are rich sources of calcium.

The best quality sesame seeds have the beige skins intact. (They are available in health food shops.) The white sesame seeds you get in Chinese supermarkets are without skins so they lack roughage and extra vitamins, especially B vitamins.

Dry-roasted Sesame Seeds

Dry-roasted sesame seeds go very well with raw, blanched or hot-tossed salads. The heating properties of the seeds balance the cooling properties of raw or lightly cooked vegetables.

The Japanese like to garnish food with *gomasio* (i.e., roasted sea-salt ground with roasted sesame seeds in a ratio of about 1 to 15). The Japanese grind *gomasio* in a *suribachi* with a wooden pestle until the mixture is only about 75 per cent ground sesame seeds. *Gomasio* is highly aromatic and excellent in promoting salivary secretion to aid digestion. Some people say that it can stop morning sickness.

To make salt-free *gomasio* simply grind roasted sesame seeds in a *suribachi* until only 25 per cent of the whole seeds are left. Sprinkle on your food and your children's to build strong teeth and bones.

Roasted Sesame Seeds

Wash the seeds well as they tend to have lots of sand and grit. Drain thoroughly, then dry-roast on a medium flame in a heavy-based stainless steel pan, wok or cast-iron pan. Stir the wet seeds constantly to ensure even roasting. When the seeds start to pop, lower the heat and roast until they are easily crushed between the thumb and little finger. By this time the seeds should be a lovely pale gold and the aroma should be very fragrant. Use the roasted seeds as they are or crush them in a *suribachi* to make *gomasio*.

Sesame seed milk or cream is better for young babies as their digestive systems are not strong enough to digest whole seeds properly. Sesame seed milk or cream is better than soyabean milk as it is far less cooling. Once a baby's system is cooled down too much he may become permanently weak.

Sesame seed milk or cream is also suitable for adults who suffer from constipation due to too much heat, but unsuitable for babies or adults with loose stools or diarrhoea.

To make milk or cream, liquidise the seeds after they have been boiled with brown rice and water. The thickness of the milk or cream will depend on the amount of water used.

Tahini

Tahini, or sesame paste, is made by grinding raw sesame seeds. Some companies make *tahini* from roasted sesame seeds. This version, of course, tends to be more heating but also more aromatic.

Tahini is very thick and oily so I thin it out with some hot water and a variety of ingredients to make sauces for pastas or spreads for wholemeal bread.

Note: Tahini is difficult to digest and should be avoided by people who tend to suffer from or are prone to catarrh, mucus or phlegm.

BLACK SESAME SEEDS
(Sesamum indicum)
property: warming

The Chinese use black sesame seeds as a

medicine for the liver and kidneys, to lubricate the large intestines and the skin, to darken prematurely grey hair, and to improve eyesight.

In the old days in China, adults who suffered from constipation with hard, dry stools were advised to take a soup of pig's intestines stuffed with black sesame seeds. This soup was supposed to moisten and lubricate the stools. Children who suffer from constipation with hard, dry stools and heat in the gastrointestinal tract are given ground black sesame seed meal mixed with honey and formed into little balls to free the large intestines and soften the stools.

To restore grey hair, mix 600 g (20 oz) of black sesame seed meal with 300 g (10 oz) of a herb called *Polygonum multiflorum* (何首乌) and a little brown sugar. Boil with some hot water to form a cream. Take 1 cup of this mixture in the morning and at night.

To improve the eyesight, take black sesame seeds daily.

> *Note:* People who tend to have loose stools or diarrhoea should avoid black sesame seeds. Those with overheated blood systems or tendencies towards them should eat boiled black sesame seeds.

SUNFLOWER SEEDS
(Helianthus annuus)
property: warming

Sunflower seeds are rich in vitamin B_6. Their warming properties make them excellent for women who suffer from pre-menstrual tension (PMT) with pain before or during menstruation, especially in the lower abdomen.

Those who suffer from stress and tension can also benefit from the vitamin B_6 in sunflower seeds. Like pumpkin seeds, sunflower seeds can be used to expel intestinal worms.

They can be eaten raw, lightly dry-roasted, baked in wholewheat breads or cooked with muesli or jumbo oats.

Dry-roasted Sunflower Seeds with *Tamari*
For tidbits on special occasions I dry-roast sunflower seeds in an oil-free, cast-iron pan until they are golden and very aromatic. Then I cool them for about 3 minutes, sprinkle them with *tamari* and mix thoroughly. Sprinkle over brown rice, other wholegrains, pastas or salads.

Sunflower Seed Milk or Cream
Boil some sunflower seeds until they are soft, then liquidise into milk or cream to pour over baked fruits or compotes. They are deliciously nutty this way.

On occasion, give babies and infants sunflower seed milk as a supplement to mother's milk. Carefully sort the seeds from the grit and stones before washing them.

WALNUTS
(Juglans regia; Juglans nigra)
property: warming

According to Li Shi Zhen, walnuts are good for the kidneys and the brain. In the old days, children were given walnuts as presents on Chinese New Year to nourish the brain. The Chinese also take walnuts for insomnia and to keep their complexions youthful.

Creamy Walnut Milk

Wealthy Chinese ladies used to drink this tea daily to preserve their complexions.

Boil 10 whole walnuts in some water with a few grains of cooked brown rice, then liquidise. The amount of water and brown rice you use will determine the consistency of the milk.

Walnuts and Brown Rice

Take this daily for a minimum of three months to prevent frequent urination during the night. The longer you have had the problem, the longer it will take to cure.

6-10 walnut halves
$^1/_3$ *cup brown rice*
$^2/_3$ *cup water*
tiny pinch sea-salt

Cook as you would brown rice (see page 37).

Walnut and Chinese Red Date Tea

This tea is good for insomnia and the complexion.

10 whole walnuts
10 Chinese red dates (stones removed)
2 cups water

Boil all the ingredients until only 1 cup is left. Drink the tea and eat the other ingredients. If you find it bitter, blanch the walnuts to remove the skins before boiling.

> *Note:* Walnuts contain a lot of oil and can turn rancid easily. Buy in small amounts each time to ensure freshness. (Walnuts in the shell are freshest around Christmas time.)

> *Variations:* Walnuts can also be stir-fried with *tofu* or vegetables.

LINSEED
(Linum usitatissimum)

Linseed, or flaxseed, is often used in Germany as an ingredient in muesli. Linseed comes in golden yellow or reddish brown. They are slightly longer than sesame seeds.

Modern research has shown that linseed benefits the lungs, heart, stomach, intestines, kidneys and liver. In fact, linseed is better than bran in helping constipation. It has a mucilaginous property which helps lubricate and soothe the intestines, and causes less flatulence. As a whole seed, it contains vitamin E, which is essential in the growth of new cells lining the digestive tract. (Unfortunately, the property of linseed is unknown.)

Linseed also contains: enzymes, which help in the digestion of food; lipase, which separates fats into glycerol and fatty acids; protease, which breaks down protein; and diastase, which reduces starch to dextrose.

Like the Germans, I occasionally add linseed to muesli made from jumbo oats, raisins and walnuts. You can also cook linseed with brown rice or other foods.

> *Note:* Do not have linseed daily unless you suffer from chronic constipation.

Seeds and Nuts for Babies and Infants

Milk made from seeds or nuts is much better for babies and infants than soyabean milk because it is not as cooling.

The younger the baby, the thinner and more dilute the seed or nut milk should be because the baby's digestive system cannot easily digest the seed and nut oils. Give babies and infants a combination of grains and seed or nut milks to ensure intake of complementary proteins. This is especially so for vegan and vegetarian babies and infants. Of course, mother's milk is still required as the main source of protein and nourishment.

As the baby grows older, thicken the milk and add well-cooked vegetables to the grains, seeds and nuts.

> *Note:* Seeds and nuts must be blanched before being liquidised into milk. Young babies and infants cannot handle the indigestible skins.

5 Seaweeds

Seaweeds are excellent sources of minerals. In fact, they contain even more minerals than land plants. Every time it rains, minerals from the soil are washed into streams and rivers which flow into seas and oceans. If you eat seaweeds, you are getting back what is missing from land plants. Besides, land plants are now sprayed with harmful insecticides and chemical fertilisers, while seaweeds grow naturally in the seas and oceans.

Some of you may ask, 'What about the increasing pollution in the seas and oceans, especially in those off the coast of Japan and China where most seaweeds are harvested?' According to studies by a research team at McGill University, Montreal, all seaweeds have the ability to remove heavy metals like strontium 90, barium, etc., from the body. This is because they contain a substance called alginic acid which binds to certain metallic ions and passes with them out of the body without being absorbed. Therefore, even though seaweeds grow in highly polluted waters, the pollutants they contain pass out of the digestive system unchanged.

Compared to land plants, seaweeds are richer in magnesium, iron, iodine, sodium, calcium, phosphorus and vitamins A, B$_1$, B$_{12}$, C and E. They also contain protein and an easily digested carbohydrate called futose. All these nutrients give seaweeds an alkalising effect on the blood, i.e. they purify the blood by eliminating the acidic effects of too much sugar, fruits, dairy products, animal fats and meats.

Seaweeds have been used for centuries in China and Japan to help eliminate high blood pressure, high blood cholesterol, goitre, certain types of arthritis and rheumatism, constipation and lung problems caused by heat, some types of oedema, leucorrhoea caused by damp heat, enlarged lymph nodes and certain types of tumours.

ADVERSE EFFECTS OF EXCESS INTAKE

Although seaweeds are rich in minerals and capable of healing various ailments, they are also *yin* and very cooling, and should not be eaten every day. When I first began eating them I was unaware that they could cause very low blood pressure, fatigue, lassitude, loose stools, sore back and weak knees, if eaten in large quantities. Suddenly, I began to feel cold all the time and no amount of clothing or warm gas fires could warm me up. I wanted to lie down and sleep all the time (a condition the acupuncturist calls 'Kidney *Yang* Deficient Syndrome'). Luckily, at that time I was studying acupuncture and became interested in the medicinal properties of food

according to Taoist principles; I soon realised the cause of my problems.

I immediately stopped eating seaweeds and started to warm myself up with lots of ginger, cinnamon, black pepper, walnuts, chestnuts, garlic, leeks and eggs. Once a month in winter I drink ginseng double-boiled with longan to warm me up. I also combined the dietary change with reflexology, meditation and chanting to speed up the healing process.

It has taken me one and a half years to build myself up again and I am still not 100 per cent healed. I still get easily tired and cold if I do not have three properly cooked meals a day.

A macrobiotic friend who had been eating seaweeds daily for about a year also started to feel tired for no apparent reason. After I shared my experiences with her and advised her to cut down on seaweeds her energy level returned to normal again. Another macro-biotic friend noticed that her blood pressure had dropped considerably after taking seaweed for a few months. She, too, decreased the quantity and frequency of her seaweed intake, and eventually her blood pressure returned to normal.

I would advise people to eat seaweeds with care – two or three times a week at most. If you start to tire for no apparent reason, stop taking the seaweeds and visit the doctor to have your blood pressure checked.

People who have weak constitutions or cooled blood systems must not take seaweeds at all. Even those who tend to have heated blood systems should cook seaweeds with a little ginger to reduce their cooling properties.

Seaweeds can be purchased in health food shops, Chinese supermarkets and shops that stock Japanese foodstuffs. In Wales, laverbread can be bought fresh from the fishmongers.

Dried seaweed will keep for years in an airtight container in a cool, dry place but fresh laverbread or dulse must be used within a day or two of purchase.

KOMBU, HOI TAI AND KELP
property: cooling

These seaweeds are very similar. *Kombu* comes from Japan, *hoi tai* from China, and kelp from the western coasts of the British Isles. In the old days, the Japanese used *kombu* extract (instead of MSG) to flavour their foods. Today, *kombu* is used when cooking beans to reduce the cooking time and to improve their flavour and digestibility. It is also used to make vegetarian stocks. *Hoi tai* and kelp can be used the same way as *kombu*.

Black Soyabeans and *Kombu*

25 g (1 oz) black soyabeans
2¹/₂ cm (1 in) piece dried kombu
1 cup water
2 thin slices ginger
pinch sea-salt
spring onion

1 Wash and drain the beans.
2 Break the *kombu* into tiny pieces and soak in the water.
3 Dry-roast the beans in a dry wok without any oil until skins split open revealing the green seed coats. Set aside to cool.
4 Boil the water with the soft *kombu* pieces and add the ginger.
5 Add the cooled dry-roasted black soyabeans to the water and boil vigorously

for 10 to 15 minutes. Then simmer until the beans are soft. Add more water if necessary.

6 When the beans are cooked, add sea-salt and simmer for another 15 minutes.

7 Garnish with some chopped spring onion.

Note: The black soyabeans will be somewhat nutty because they have been dry-roasted.

Variations: Add garlic, onion or leek to give more flavour.

Fish, *Kombu* and *Miso* Soup

If you have vegetables and brown rice with this dish you will have a complete meal.

2¹/₂ (1 in) piece of dried kombu
2 cups water
3 thin slices ginger
pinch sea-salt
1 tsp genmai miso
110 g (4 oz) white fish
spring onion

1 Place the *kombu*, water and ginger in a pot to soak.

2 When the *kombu* has softened, add the sea-salt and boil until it becomes very soft. Reduce heat to a gentle simmer.

3 Thin the *miso* with a little of the *kombu* stock. Cube the fish into bite-sized pieces.

4 Add the fish cubes and the *miso* to the *kombu* stock. Simmer for 10 minutes or until the fish is just cooked.

5 Garnish with spring onion.

Variations: Change the flavour by adding either garlic, onion, leek, carrot or white cabbage.

WAKAME
property: cooling

Wakame is often used for making soups, especially *miso.*

Wakame, Onion and *Miso* Soup

7¹/₂ cm (3 in) strip dried wakame
2 cups water
1 large onion
cold-pressed sesame oil
1 thin slice ginger
pinch sea-salt
1 tsp genmai miso
spring onion

1 Soak the *wakame* in the water.

2 Cut the onion in half from top to bottom and slice finely into half moon slices.

3 Drain and finely slice the *wakame* into strips. Save the soaking water.

4 Heat a pot. When hot, add enough oil to coat the bottom. When the oil is hot, stir-fry the ginger for 1 minute. Add the onion slices and sea-salt and stir until the onion is limp. Add the *wakame* and the soaking water, taking care not to add the little bits of grit or sand at the bottom of the bowl.

5 Boil for 15 minutes. Meanwhile, thin out the *miso* with some of the stock.

6 Reduce the heat to a very gentle simmer, add the *miso* and simmer another 15 minutes.

7 Garnish with some chopped spring onion.

Note: The longer you simmer the stock after it has come to a boil, the sweeter the soup will be.

HIZIKI
property: cooling

According to Japanese folk legends, this seaweed is an excellent food for maintaining healthy hair. When dried, it does resemble black hair, but when soaked, it looks like thick black strings. *Hiziki* should not be cooked with oil; the combination can make you ill.

Slow-cooked *Hiziki* with Cabbage, Carrot and Long Bean
Slow-cooked dishes like this one are deliciously and naturally sweet.

pinch dried hiziki
pinch grated ginger
1 long bean
1 small carrot
1 large white cabbage leaf
pinch sea-salt
tamari or shoyu
roasted sesame seeds

1 Place *hiziki* and ginger at the bottom of a pot with some water.
2 Break the long bean into 2¹/₂ cm (1 in) lengths, cut the carrot into the same shape and size as the bean, and shred the cabbage.
3 Layer the cabbage over the softened *hiziki* and top with the carrot and long bean.

4 Add enough water to cover the cabbage and sprinkle sea-salt over everything.
5 Slowly bring the water to a boil, then simmer vegetables for 45 minutes. Add more water if necessary, but only enough to moisten the dish.
6 Add *tamari* or *shoyu* and mix thoroughly.
7 Garnish with roasted sesame seeds.

ARAME
property: cooling

This seaweed also looks like hair. It is delicious stir-fried with onions, carrots and cabbage.

Stir-Fried *Arame*, Onion and Carrot

pinch dried arame
1 small onion
1 small carrot
cold-pressed sesame oil
pinch finely shredded ginger
pinch sea-salt
tamari or shoyu
coriander leaves or parsley

1 Soak *arame* in as little water as possible.
2 Finely shred the onion and carrot.
3 Heat a wok. When hot, add just enough oil to coat the bottom. When the oil is hot, add the ginger and stir for 1 minute. Add the onion and sea-salt and stir until limp.

Add the carrot and stir for 2 minutes, then add the *arame* and the soaking water. Cover and simmer until the carrots are soft.

4 Add a dash of *tamari* or *shoyu*.
5 Garnish with finely chopped coriander or parsley.

Variations:

1 Use leek instead of onion.
2 Add white or Chinese Peking cabbage.
3 Use *genmai miso* instead of *tamari* or *shoyu*.
4 Add long beans, French beans or string beans to make the dish more colourful.

NORI
property: cooling

There are actually three names for this seaweed: the Japanese call it *nori*; the Chinese call it purple seaweed (紫菜); and the Welsh call it laverbread.

In Japan, *nori* sheets are used to wrap rolls of rice called *sushi*. Sometimes, bits of *nori* are just sprinkled on top of rice. The Chinese like to cook soup with purple seaweed or sprinkle fine toasted strips of it over soups. The Welsh mix fresh laverbread with fine oatmeal or cook it in bacon fat and serve it with bacon for breakfast.

Laverbread Burgers

50 g (2 oz) fresh laverbread
oatgerm and oat bran (or fine oatmeal)
1 clove garlic
3 thin slices ginger
1 medium leek
cold-pressed sesame oil
pinch sea-salt
2 small turnips

1 Mix the laverbread with the oatgerm and oat bran to form mini-burgers. (Use just enough to hold the burgers together.)
2 Finely mince the garlic and ginger.
3 Finely cut the leek into diagonal slices.
4 Heat a pan. When hot, add just enough oil to coat the bottom. When the oil is hot, add the garlic and ginger and stir for 1 minute. Add the leek and sea-salt and stir for 1 minute. Reduce the heat and add the mini-burgers. Continue to stir the leek. Turn the burgers when one side is cooked. When the burgers are cooked, the leek should be limp.
5 Serve with the leek and some mashed, boiled turnips.

Note: The smaller the burgers, the tastier they will be and the quicker they will cook. The turnips help in the digestion of the burgers, which tend to be quite filling.

FAT CHOY (BLACK MOSS)
property: cooling

It is misleading to call *fat choy* black moss, because it is really a seaweed. It looks like very fine, dry black hair. The Chinese eat it often because they believe it contains lots of iron and gives a healthy head of jet black hair. It is a very important ingredient in a special Cantonese Chinese New Year dish called *ho see fat choy*, which consists of dried oysters and seaweed.

Fat Choy and Dried Oysters
The original Chinese New Year dish, *ho see*

fat choy, calls for roast belly pork and oyster sauce. I have substituted onions here for the pork and *miso* for the oyster sauce. These substitutes are free of hormones, antibiotics, additives, sugar and preservatives.

6 dried oysters
1 tsp dried fat choy
3 small dried Shiitake mushrooms
1 clove garlic
3 thin slices ginger
1 medium onion
cold-pressed sesame oil
pinch sea-salt
1 tsp genmai miso
spring onion

1 Wash the oysters and soak them overnight.
2 The next day, soak the *fat choy* for 2 to 3 hours, wash off any impurities and drain.
3 Soak the Shiitake mushrooms in hot water for 20 to 30 minutes.
4 Finely mince the garlic and ginger.
5 Finely dice the onion.
6 Drain the oysters and Shiitake mushrooms but save the soaking water.
7 Heat a pot. When hot, add enough oil to just coat the bottom. When the oil is hot, add the garlic and ginger and stir for 1 minute. Add the onion and sea-salt and stir for 3 to 4 minutes or until brown. Add the drained *fat choy*, mushrooms and oysters and stir for 2 minutes. Add the soaking liquid. Bring to a boil, then simmer until most of the liquid has evaporated.
8 Thin out the *miso* with some of the liquid and add it to the pot. Reduce the heat to a very gentle simmer and cook another 15 minutes.

9 Garnish with chopped spring onion.

Variations:
1 Use leek instead of onion.
2 Use *mugi miso* instead of *genmai miso*.

DULSE
property: cooling

This purple seaweed is also found along the western coasts of Britain. The Irish cook fresh dulse with onions and black pepper.

CARRAGEEN
property: cooling

This seaweed from the western coasts of Britain is normally bleached white by the sun before being sold. It soothes lung pains and irritating diseases of the bladder and kidneys caused by too much heat or damp heat.

AGAR-AGAR
property: cooling

The Chinese, Malays and Indonesians use this for making jelly. It is also a mild laxative that relieves constipation caused by heat.

Barley Malt Jelly

1 cup water
2 tbsp barley malt
2 tsp agar flakes
roasted sesame seeds

1 Bring the water to a boil.
2 Add barley malt and mix thoroughly.

3 Sprinkle in the agar flakes and stir until all the flakes dissolve. Continue cooking and stirring for another 5 minutes.

4 Pour into a rinsed mould and leave to set in a cool place for 5 to 6 hours.

5 Sprinkle with roasted sesame seeds.

Note: This is a soft jelly. If you prefer a harder jelly, use 3-4 teaspoons of agar flakes.

Apple and Raisin Jelly

1 red dessert apple
water
pinch sea-salt
50 g (2 oz) raisins
2 tsp agar flakes
chopped roasted hazelnuts

1 Cut the apple into bite-sized pieces.

2 Steam the apple pieces in a small quantity of water with sea-salt for 1 to 2 minutes.

3 Place the steamed apple in a rinsed mould.

4 Combine 1 cup of water with the raisins and another pinch of sea-salt. Boil for 5 minutes.

5 Sprinkle agar flakes into the pot and stir until all the flakes have dissolved. Cook for another 5 minutes while stirring constantly.

6 Pour mixture over the steamed apple and leave to set in a cool place for 5 to 6 hours.

7 Garnish with chopped roasted hazelnuts.

Note: This is a soft jelly. If you prefer a harder jelly, use 3 to 4 teaspoons of agar flakes.

Variations: Use pear and sultanas instead of apple and raisins, and add a pinch of ground cinnamon.

SEAWEEDS FOR BABIES AND TEENAGERS

I would not advise mothers to give seaweeds to babies under three years of age. If the babies become weak they will have difficulty regaining their strength. Under certain circumstances, however, seaweeds can be used as a medicine, for example when the baby is suffering from heat rash.

A child over three can have seaweeds approximately once or twice a week to improve bone growth and development. They can take *wakame* or *kombu* powder sprinkled on brown rice, soups or vegetables and *wakame,* onion and *miso* soup occasionally. Brown rice *sushis* are also acceptable.

Teenagers, especially those who suffer from acne and spots, can have seaweeds more frequently. According to Chinese physicians, acne comes from too much heat in the blood. As you know, the cooling properties of seaweeds can counteract the heat. The Chinese also believe that if young girls eat *fat choy* regularly, they will have black silky hair when they mature.

Adults and children of any age who become tired for no apparent reason after eating seaweeds on a regular basis should stop eating them immediately.

Kombu or Wakame Powder

Wipe dried seaweed with a damp cloth to remove any sand or grit. Dry-roast the seaweed in a hot oven until crisp, then grind the sheets into a fine powder using a *suribachi* (available from Japanese shops). Store the powder in an airtight bottle in a cool, dry place.

6 Vegetables

Open air markets with stall upon stall of different fresh vegetables are a real feast for the eyes. And the smell of fresh vegetables is heaven! I have been to such wonderful markets in England, Spain, Germany, Switzerland, Austria, Italy, Calcutta, Thailand, Malaysia, Singapore and Hong Kong. Each country has its own selection of local and imported vegetables.

Singapore and Hong Kong are unique because neither place has enough land to grow vegetables. Singapore imports vegetables from Malaysia, Australia and other parts of the world, while Hong Kong imports vegetables mostly from mainland China. In Hong Kong, vegetable markets are open from early morning to evening because Hong Kong housewives demand freshness: they shop in the morning for lunch and again in the afternoon for dinner.

Fresh vegetables should comprise one quarter of the Taoist diet because they contain lots of vitamins, minerals and roughage. Ideally, vegetables should be organically grown at home to achieve maximum freshness and to ensure an abundance of vitamins and minerals. Once a vegetable is cut, it begins to lose vitamins. If you cannot have your own garden, buy organically grown vegetables from health food shops or supermarkets. Choose mainly local and seasonal varieties. If organically grown produce is unavailable, buy fresh vegetables from greengrocers or supermarkets. There is no need to peel organically grown root vegetables. Just scrub them clean with a nail brush; the skin gives added vitamins, minerals and roughage.

Eat a wide variety of local and seasonal greens and roots throughout the year to get a good range of vitamins and minerals. Eat local rather than imported vegetables to be in tune with your own environment. In temperate countries during winter, local vegetables such as winter greens, Savoy cabbages, Brussels sprouts, turnips, swedes, carrots, parsnips and onions are naturally more warming and neutral than imported cooling summer vegetables such as cucumbers, courgettes, asparagus and lettuce. If you have had a harsh winter, buy imported winter vegetables grown in milder temperate countries. In summer, eat fresh garden peas, French beans, cucumbers, courgettes, asparagus and lettuces instead of imported swedes, turnips and parsnips. Similarly, people in the tropics should avoid imported vegetables and opt for their local varieties. Fortunately, local and seasonal vegetables are much less expensive than imported ones.

On the whole, vegetables are more cooling than whole cereal grains, legumes, pulses, seeds and nuts, because they contain more

water, but less cooling than seaweeds, because they are land plants. The Chinese classify vegetables according to cooling, neutral and warming energies, as they do other foods. The following sections on different types of vegetables from both temperate and tropical countries will be grouped accordingly.

> *Note:* The recipes that follow do not include sea-salt. Cooks can add a pinch at their discretion.

COOLING VEGETABLES

Cooling vegetables are best for the young, active and robust, and those with overheated blood systems or tendencies towards them. Such people can have cooling vegetables raw or lightly cooked.

The weak, elderly or those with cooled blood systems or tendencies towards them should have cooling vegetables only once or twice a week. They should be stir-fried with warming energy vegetables, herbs or spices, eggs, fish or chicken to make them less cooling, and eaten only at lunchtime, when the day is at its hottest.

ALFALFA SPROUTS
(Medicago sativa)
property: cooling

Alfalfa sprouts are easy to grow on your kitchen window sill. They are full of vitamins, especially vitamin C. In fact, alfalfa sprouts are richer in vitamin C than oranges because they are harvested just before eating. Use them as a side-dish to supplement your daily vitamin C intake.

> *To use alfalfa sprouts as a cooling vegetable:*
> Eat them raw on their own.
>
> *To make alfalfa sprouts less cooling:*
> 1 Marinate in fresh ginger juice.
> 2 Mix with grated fresh ginger.
> 3 Mix with grated fresh ginger and roasted sesame seeds.
> 4 Toss with some ground black pepper and chopped spring onions.
> 5 Toss with some black mustard seeds roasted in a little oil.
> 6 Toss with some minced garlic that has been stir-fried in a little cold-pressed oil until golden and fragrant.
> 7 Stir-fry with warming energy vegetables, herbs or spices.

ANGLED LUFFA
(Luffa acutangula)
property: cooling

This Eastern vegetable is usually stir-fried with other vegetables, and occasionally used in soups.

Angled Luffa Soup

cold-pressed oil
garlic, minced
ginger, minced
Shiitake mushrooms, soaked and diced
carrot, diced
angled luffa, diced
mung bean threads, soaked
fried tofu, cubed
spring onion, chopped

1 Heat a pot. When hot, add just enough cold-pressed oil to coat the bottom.

2 When the oil is hot, add the garlic and ginger and stir for 1 minute. Add the mushrooms and stir for 2 minutes. Add the carrot and luffa and stir for 2 minutes.

3 Add water, the mung bean threads and fried *tofu* cubes. Simmer for 15 minutes.

4 Garnish with some chopped spring onions.

To make angled luffa less cooling:
Stir-fry with garlic, ginger, Shiitake mushrooms, black wood ears, water chestnuts, carrots and *tofu*. Then simmer for 15 minutes.

To make angled luffa even less cooling:
1 Stir-fry with garlic, ginger, leeks, *tofu*, walnuts and some freshly ground black pepper. Then simmer for 15 minutes.
2 Stir-fry with onions and eggs.
3 Stir-fry with garlic, ginger, fish and fennel seeds.
4 Stir-fry with garlic, ginger, chicken and black pepper.

ARROWHEAD TUBERS
(Sagittaria sinensis)
property: cooling

The Chinese usually braise this vegetable.

To make arrowhead tubers less cooling:
1 Stir-fry with garlic and ginger. Then simmer very gently with *miso*.
2 Stir-fry with spring onions, ginger and fermented black soyabeans. Then simmer very gently.

ASPARAGUS
(Asparagus officinalis)
property: cooling

This delicate shoot can be prepared to retain its cooling properties and made less cooling. May and June are the months for home-grown asparagus in Britain.

To make asparagus a cooling vegetable:
Steam and serve with some herb seed or nut cream. To prepare seed cream: boil some seeds for 10-15 minutes (or until soft) in enough water to cover. Liquidise into a cream with herbs such as parsley, thyme, chives or fennel leaves. Vary the consistency of the cream by changing the amount of water. To prepare nut cream: boil some nuts (for example, almonds, which must be blanched first) in water to cover for about 15-20 minutes or until soft. Liquidise into a cream with garlic, spring onions, chives or parsley.

To make asparagus less cooling:
1 Stir-fry with garlic and ginger.
2 Stir-fry with garlic and ginger, then add a dash of *tamari* and some chopped herbs.
3 Stir-fry with garlic, ginger, onions, carrots or beetroot.

BEETROOT GREENS
(Beta vulgaris)
property: cooling

Available from June to November, this lovely vegetable with its green leaves, red stems and red veins is rich in iron. (See section on beetroot for more information.)

To use beetroot greens as a cooling vegetable:
Lightly steam with a dash of *tamari* or *shoyu*.

BITTER GOURD
(Momordica charantia)
property: cooling

This vegetable is recommended for people who suffer from pimples, spots, acne, boils, skin diseases such as eczema and psoriasis, high blood pressure, high blood cholesterol, and some forms of diabetes where there is a history of high blood pressure and high blood cholesterol. This type of diabetic is often strong and robust, and feels uncomfortable in the heat.

The Chinese usually cut up and blanch bitter gourd in boiling water with a pinch of sea-salt for 2 to 3 minutes to remove the bitterness. Then they stir-fry it.

CELERY
(Apium graveolens)
property: cooling

English celery is less aromatic, has wider stems and is juicier than Chinese celery. The Chinese variety is greener, stringy and very aromatic. Both types of celery are cooling and help lower high blood pressure and relieve certain forms of arthritis and rheumatism where the joints are inflamed and feel hot. Celery is also good for constipation caused by too much heat in the blood system.

CHICORY
(Cichorium intybus)
property: cooling

This slightly bitter shoot aids digestion. It can be eaten raw or cooked.

To make chicory less cooling:

Blanch in boiling water with a pinch of sea-salt for 2 to 3 minutes to remove the bitterness, then:

1   Stir-fry with garlic, ginger and parsley.
2   Stir-fry with onions and chicken.

CHINESE BOX THORN LEAVES
(Lycium chinense)
property: cooling

The Chinese use this vegetable to make a cooling medicinal soup that cools down heat in the liver when the symptoms include sore, red eyes, irritability and headaches.

To use Chinese box thorn leaves as a cooling vegetable:

Stir-fry with a thin slice of ginger until limp. Add water for soup and simmer for 10 minutes. Season with sea-salt before serving.

Variations:

1   Add thin slices of white fish during the last 2 to 3 minutes.
2   Use fish or chicken bones for stock.

CHINESE PEKING CABBAGE
(Brassica pekinensis)
property: cooling

This vegetable is so cooling that it is said to bring on an asthmatic attack. Chinese mothers will not allow their asthmatic children to eat Chinese Peking cabbage or to drink the cabbage juices.

To use Peking cabbage as a cooling vegetable:

1   Eat it raw.

2   Toss in a hot oil-free pan with some freshly grated ginger.
3   Simmer slowly in its own juices with some grated ginger. (This variation is delicious.)

To make Chinese Peking cabbage less cooling:

1   Stir-fry with garlic, ginger and other warming energy vegetables.
2   Stir-fry with garlic, ginger and dried shrimps.
3   Stir-fry and braise with garlic, ginger, fried *tofu*, Shiitake mushrooms, carrots and *miso*.
4   Stir-fry and braise with garlic, ginger, carrots, Shiitake mushrooms and chicken.

CHINESE RADISH
(Raphanus sativus L. var. longipinnatus)
property: cooling

Southern Chinese use this long white vegetable in hot, dry weather to keep the lungs moist. Northern Chinese use it in winter to counteract the drying effects of coal dust and smoke on the lungs. It can also be used to counteract the drying effects of modern gas fires and central heating. (Try the soup and leek variations below for this particular problem.)

To use Chinese radish as a cooling vegetable:

1   Eat it raw.
2   Boil with an equal quantity of carrots and some white fish for a soup. If you are a vegetarian, substitute *tofu* or *fu zhou* for the fish. If you are weak or have a cooled blood system simmer the soup for at least 6 hours. Take only at lunch, in hot, dry weather, to help keep your lungs moist.

Stir-fry, then simmer for 30 minutes with some leeks. (The proportion of Chinese radish to leek should be 3 to 1.)

Note: Raw Chinese radish is an antidote for ginseng poisoning. (See page 131.)

CHINESE SPINACH
(Amaranthus gangeticus)
property: cooling

This delicate, pretty vegetable with the reddish-purple stems is used in Chinese homes to remedy constipation caused by too much heat in the blood system. I was recently told that Chinese spinach and duck egg soup is good for smoker's lungs.

To use Chinese spinach as a cooling vegetable:
Stir-fry a clove of garlic. Add enough water for soup and bring to a boil. Add the washed Chinese spinach and simmer until tender. Season with sea-salt and a dash of *tamari*. For smoker's lungs, break a duck egg into the boiling stock just before serving.

To make Chinese spinach less cooling:
1   Stir-fry with garlic and ginger.
2   Stir-fry with ginger and onions and use as an omelette filling.
3   Stir-fry with garlic and chicken.

CHINESE WHITE CABBAGE
(Brassica chinensis Jus. var. chinensis)
property: cooling

The Chinese usually use this vegetable in soups or stir-fried with meats. There are two varieties: large and small.

To use Chinese white cabbage as a cooling vegetable:
1   Boil in a soup with chicken bones.
2   Boil in a soup with 1 portion bitter apricot kernels and 10 portions sweet apricot kernels to clear heat from the lungs during hot, dry weather.
3   Boil in a soup with onions, carrots and *tofu*.
4   Blanch and serve with an onion or garlic *miso* sauce.

To make Chinese white cabbage less cooling:
1   Stir-fry with garlic and ginger.
2   Stir-fry with garlic, ginger and onions and simmer in *miso* sauce.
3   Stir-fry with onions and chicken.

COURGETTE
(Cucurbita pepo ovifera)
property: cooling

I love to stir-fry and simmer this lovely summer and autumn vegetable to allow it to soak up the juices of the other vegetables or a *miso* sauce.

Like cucumber, courgette has a milky sap in the skin that can be difficult to digest. To draw out the sap: cut a 5 mm ($^1/_4$ in) piece off the stalk end. Sprinkle the piece with sea-salt and rub it on the end of the courgette until no more sap or foam appears. Repeat with the other end.

To use courgette as a cooling vegetable:
1   Slice tender courgette diagonally into 3 mm ($^1/_8$ in) slices, place on top of some steaming brown rice and sprinkle with chopped parsley or spring onions. They will be done when the brown rice is cooked.

2   Steam with other vegetables, *tofu*, fish or chicken.

To make courgette less cooling:

1   Stir-fry with garlic, ginger, onions and carrots. Simmer in *miso* sauce and garnish with parsley. Use pumpkin instead of carrots.
2   Stir-fry with spring onions, ginger and fermented black soyabeans.
3   Stir-fry with garlic, ginger and dried shrimps.
4   Stir-fry with garlic, ginger, fresh mushrooms and chicken. Then simmer.
5   Stew with lentils, herbs and spices.
6   Stuff with lentils, herbs and spices, and bake.

CRESS
(Lepidum sativum)
property: cooling

Cress is primarily used in salads or as a sandwich filling.

To use cress as a cooling sandwich filling:

1   Use with cucumber.
2   Use with celery.
3   Use with seed or nut cream. (See page 88.)

To use cress as a less cooling sandwich filling:

1   Use with *tahini*.
2   Use with peanut butter.
3   Use with eggs.
4   Use with fish and ginger.
5   Use with chicken.

CUCUMBER
(Cucumis sativus)
property: cooling

Green cucumber is excellent in summer or all year round in tropical countries to cool the blood system.

If you have difficulty digesting the cucumber skin because of the white sap, either peel the vegetable or follow the Chinese way of drawing out the sap. (See Courgette, page 91.)

To use cucumber as a cooling vegetable:

1   Eat it raw.
2   Shred finely and toss in a hot oil-free pan with a tiny pinch of sea-salt.
3   Make a clear cucumber and peppermint soup.

To make cucumber less cooling:

1   Stir-fry with warming energy vegetables, herbs or spices.
2   Stuff with a lentil herb stew and bake.

DANDELION LEAVES
(Taraxacum officinale)
property: cooling

This garden weed has many medicinal properties. It is a good, safe diuretic because it contains potassium. It also helps tonify the liver in the spring.

To use dandelion leaves as a cooling vegetable:
Eat raw in a salad.

To make dandelion leaves less cooling:

1   Stir-fry with garlic and ginger.

2 Stir-fry with onion and freshly ground black pepper.

3 Stir-fry with ginger and chicken.

ENDIVE
(Cichorium endivia)
property: cooling

Serve this summer vegetable raw in a salad. It is nice and cooling on hot summer days.

To make endive less cooling:

1 Serve with a dressing of minced garlic, ginger, apple cider vinegar and a few drops of roasted sesame oil.

2 Toss with lots of black mustard seeds that have been roasted in a little oil until they start to pop.

3 Serve with piping hot popcorn.

FUZZY MELON
(Benincasa hispida)
property: cooling

Fuzzy melon is the Eastern version of the Western courgette. The Chinese boil, steam, stir-fry or braise it.

To use fuzzy melon as a cooling vegetable:

1 Boil with onions, Shiitake mushrooms, mung bean threads and salted duck eggs.

2 Boil with onions and carrots in a stock made from fish or chicken bones.

3 Shred finely and simmer slowly in its own juices with a pinch of sea-salt. Use just enough water to cover the bottom of the pot to prevent burning. Add other finely shredded vegetables.

To make fuzzy melon less cooling:

1 Stir-fry with garlic and ginger and simmer in *miso* sauce. Add other vegetables such as onions, leeks, carrots, pumpkin or white cabbage. Add dried ingredients such as Shiitake mushrooms or black wood ears.

2 Stir-fry with spring onions, ginger and fermented black soyabeans.

3 Stir-fry with garlic, ginger and walnuts.

4 Stir-fry with ginger, onions and eggs.

5 Stir-fry with garlic, ginger, fish, fresh or dried shrimps or chicken.

KOHLRABI
(Brassica oleracea L. var. gongylodes L.)
property: cooling

This unusual stem vegetable can be eaten raw or cooked. The Chinese prefer to cook it.

To use kohlrabi as a cooling vegetable:

1 Serve raw with a *tahini* dip or a peanut butter sauce.

2 Steam with other vegetables.

3 Steam with chicken.

To make kohlrabi less cooling:

1 Parboil it, then bake.

2 Stir-fry with garlic, ginger and other warming energy vegetables, herbs or spices.

3 Stir-fry with garlic, ginger, dried shrimps or chicken.

LETTUCE
(Lactuca sativa)
property: cooling

Everyone knows how cooling crispy lettuce leaves are on a hot summer's day or in hot

countries. They are best eaten raw in a salad. The Chinese serve raw lettuce and hot rice congee to the young, active and robust to help cool their blood systems.

To make lettuce less cooling:

1   Shred finely and toss in a hot oil-free pan for 1 to 2 minutes with some ginger juice and a pinch of sea-salt.
2   Stir-fry with garlic and ginger and serve with a dash of *tamari* or *shoyu*.
3   Stir-fry with garlic, ginger and chicken.

LOTUS ROOT
(Nelumbo nucifera)
property: cooling

The Chinese use lotus root for medicinal purposes. It is available raw in Asian countries or in large Chinese communities in the West. Dried lotus root can be found in Chinese supermarkets, but it must be soaked for 4 to 6 hours before cooking.

Raw lotus root and raw lotus root juice are used to cool the body. Years ago, before surgery was widely performed in China, if someone suffered from acute bleeding of the stomach or lungs, he would be given raw lotus root juice mixed with a little sea-salt for several days to prevent clot formation. Today, this remedy should be used only in conjunction with advice by a Chinese or Western-trained physician.

Teenagers or adults who suffer from spots, pimples, acne, skin rashes, eczema or psoriasis can also drink raw lotus root juice or fresh or dried lotus root and mung beans boiled into a soup to help cool the blood system.

Fresh or dried lotus root boiled with black soyabeans to make a bean stew is said to be good for the anaemic, the weak and those with cooled blood systems. To make the stew less cooling, add a thick slice of ginger and stew the beans for 2 hours.

Lotus root soup boiled with dried octopus is a good tonic for the blood. Simmer at least 4 to 6 hours with a slice of ginger if you are weak, have a cooled blood system or a tendency towards one. (See the recipe on page 129 for Lotus Root and Dried Squid Soup.)

To make a blood tonic for vegetarians, slowly simmer a soup of lotus root, Chinese red dates (stoned), a handful of peanuts and a slice of ginger for at least 4 to 6 hours.

MARROW
(Cucurbita pepo ovifera)
property: cooling

Use marrow as you would courgette (see page 91).

MUNG BEAN SPROUTS
(Phaseolus aureus)
property: cooling

Unlike alfalfa sprouts, mung bean sprouts are not eaten raw by the Chinese. They should be clean, clear and white from head to tail. Do not buy mung bean sprouts if you can see most of the embryo emerging between the pale yellow seed leaves. At this stage, most of the valuable vitamins, protein, enzymes and minerals will be gone. Do not buy sprouts tinged with brown, purple or green.

Like alfalfa sprouts, mung bean sprouts are rich sources of vitamins, protein, enzymes and minerals. People with overheated blood

systems or tendencies towards them will find mung bean sprouts very cooling. They are available all year round.

To use mung bean sprouts as a cooling vegetable:
1 Steam or blanch and toss in a *tamari* and spring onion sauce.
2 Steam or blanch and toss in a *miso* and coriander leaf sauce.
3 Toss in a hot oil-free wok with other finely shredded vegetables like carrots and spring onions. Garnish with roasted sunflower seeds.

To make mung bean sprouts less cooling:
1 Stir-fry with warming energy vegetables, herbs or spices.
2 Stir-fry with an egg.
3 Stir-fry with fish, fresh or dried shrimps, or chicken.

MUSHROOMS
(Agaricus campestris)
property: cooling

Fresh mushrooms are cooling. Although button mushrooms can be eaten raw in salads, the Chinese always cook them. I like them stir-fried with spring onions or coriander leaves and then slowly simmered in *miso* sauce.

To make mushrooms less cooling:
1 Stir-fry with garlic, ginger and coriander leaves, and slowly simmer with *miso*.
2 Stir-fry with ginger, leeks and eggs.
3 Stir-fry with spring onions, ginger and chicken.

NETTLES
(Urtica dioica)
property: cooling

This wild vegetable helps purify and tonify the blood in spring. It is also a rich source of iron.

To use nettles as a cooling vegetable:
1 Make a soup.
2 Steam the nettles.

To make nettles less cooling:
1 Make a soup with garlic, ginger and onion.
2 Stir-fry with garlic, ginger, onions and carrots.
3 Stir-fry with garlic, ginger, leeks and silken *tofu*. Then bake as a quiche filling.
4 Stir-fry with garlic, ginger and chicken.

RADICCHIO ROSSO
(Cichorium endivia)
property: cooling

This vegetable adds a bit of deep red to the green lettuce leaves in a salad. It is nice and cooling on hot summer days.

RADISH
(Raphanus sativus)
property: cooling

These small red vegetables always cheer up a green salad, and are usually eaten raw. Although they taste hot, they have cooling energies. I have tried unsuccessfully to cook them so they both look nice and taste nice. I do not recommend them for the weak, the

elderly, or those with cooled blood systems or tendencies towards them.

RED CABBAGE
(Brassica oleracea)
property: cooling

This attractive reddish purple vegetable is usually served raw or as a pickle; sometimes it is cooked with apples.

To use red cabbage as a cooling vegetable:
1 Serve raw.
2 Pickle with sea-salt and bottle until ready to eat.

To make less cooling:
1 Stir-fry with garlic, ginger, onions and caraway seeds, and then simmer until tender. The longer you simmer this vegetable, the sweeter it becomes.
2 Stir-fry with garlic, ginger, onions and thyme, and then simmer until tender.

SLIPPERY VEGETABLE
(Basella alba)
property: cooling

This unusual vegetable is also called Ceylon spinach. As the name suggests, it is a slippery mucilaginous vegetable. The Chinese use it only in soups to help lubricate the digestive tract for people suffering from constipation with hard, dry stools.

To use slippery vegetable as a cooling vegetable:
Stir-fry a slice of ginger in a little oil for 1 to 2 minutes. Add enough water for soup and bring

to a boil. Then add the vegetable and simmer for 5 to 10 minutes.

Variations:
1 Use a stock made from fish or chicken bones.
2 Add *tofu*.
3 Beat in an egg just before serving.

SOYABEAN SPROUTS
(Glycine max)
property: cooling

Soyabean sprouts are nutritious, rich in protein and very cooling. The Chinese always cook them to destroy a protein inhibitor in the bean. When cooked, the sprouts will still be nutty in texture but the raw taste will disappear.

To use soyabean sprouts as a cooling vegetable:
Boil with onions and carrots to make a vegetable soup to cool you down in hot weather, especially if you have an overheated blood system or a tendency towards one.

To make soyabean sprouts less cooling:
1 Stir-fry with garlic and ginger, or any other warming energy vegetables, herbs or spices.
2 Stir-fry with garlic, ginger, vegetables and chicken.

SPINACH
(Spinacia oleracea)
property: cooling

This delicate green vegetable is a rich source of iron. Although very tender young leaves can be eaten raw in salads, to me, they taste better cooked.

To use spinach as a cooling vegetable:
1   Eat raw, very tender young green leaves.
2   Make a soup.
3   Steam or blanch.

To make spinach less cooling:
1   Stir-fry with black mustard seeds, garlic and ginger.
2   Stir-fry with garlic, ginger, onions and freshly grated nutmeg.
3   Stir-fry with onions and ginger and use as a filling for omelettes.
4   Stir-fry with garlic, ginger and chicken.

SWATOW MUSTARD CABBAGE
(Brassica juncea var. rugosa)
property: cooling

The early Chinese who settled in Malaysia found this very cooling vegetable excellent in helping them cope with the hot weather. It is not appropriate for the weak, the elderly, or people with cooled blood systems or tendencies towards them. It is usually used in soups, but the salted variety is often stir-fried with squid or pork.

To use Swatow mustard cabbage as a cooling vegetable:
1   Boil with sweet potato to make a cooling soup.
2   Boil with *tofu*, fish or chicken bone stock and a thin slice of ginger.

SWISS CHARD
(Beta vulgaris)
property: cooling

Swiss chard is from the beetroot family.

To use Swiss chard as a cooling vegetable:
1   Blanch and serve with an onion *miso* sauce.
2   Shred finely and toss in a hot oil-free pan to make a hot salad.

To make Swiss chard less cooling:
1   Stir-fry with garlic, ginger and black pepper.
2   Stir-fry with onions and carrots.
3   Stir-fry with garlic, ginger and dried shrimps.
4   Stir-fry with onions, carrots and chicken.

WATER CHESTNUTS
(Eleocharis dulcis)
property: cooling

The Chinese eat water chestnuts as a cooling snack. They simply peel, wash, and eat them. People with spots, pimples, acne, boils, skin rashes, eczema or psoriasis will find them very helpful.

Water chestnuts can be stir-fried with other warming energy vegetables to make them less cooling, and to give a mixture of textures and tastes.

WATERCRESS
(Nasturtium officinale)
property: cooling

In the West, watercress is usually eaten raw, as a salad ingredient or as a herb. It is also used to purify and cleanse the blood. The Chinese usually boil watercress in soups or as a medicine to clear heat and phlegm from the lungs and to stop bleeding in the stomach.

To make traditional Chinese watercress soup, combine chicken bones for the stock,

watercress, dried duck's kidneys, dried tangerine peel and Chinese bitter and sweet almonds (1 part bitter almonds to 10 sweet).

To make a soup that helps clear heat and phlegm from the lungs, use the same ingredients but leave out the chicken bone stock and dried duck's kidneys, and simmer for 2 hours after bringing to a boil. If you have a weak constitution or a tendency towards a cooled blood system and you are suffering temporarily from too much heat in the lungs, simmer the soup for at least 4 to 6 hours. Drink the soup at midday, when the day is at its hottest.

In the old days, raw watercress juice with a pinch of sea-salt was given to people who vomited blood as a result of too much heat in the body. The patient would be advised to drink the juice with sea-salt for a couple of days to prevent the formation of clots in the stomach. (Never use this remedy today without consulting your physician. If you have a weak constitution or a tendency toward one, warm – do not boil – the juice before drinking.)

Never pick wild watercress – it could be contaminated with liver flukes.

To use watercress as a cooling vegetable:
1. Eat it raw.
2. Boil in soup.

To make watercress less cooling:
1. Stir-fry with warming energy vegetables, herbs or spices.
2. Stir-fry with onions, ginger and eggs.
3. Stir-fry with garlic, ginger, fish or chicken.

WATER SPINACH/WATER CONVOLVULUS
(Ipomoea aquatica)
property: cooling

This vegetable is also known as *kangkung* in Southeast Asia. The Chinese eat *kangkung* with caution because they believe it can cause cramps if taken too often.

To use water spinach as a cooling vegetable:
1. Blanch and serve as a salad ingredient.
2. Blanch and serve with *tahini miso* sauce.
3. Blanch and serve with onion *miso* sauce.

To make water spinach less cooling:
1. Stir-fry with garlic and ginger.
2. Stir-fry with garlic, ginger and fermented soyabean cheese.
3. Stir-fry with garlic, ginger, dried shrimps or dried shredded squid.

WINTER MELON
(Benincasa hispida)
property: cooling

Winter melon is mainly used in soups to cool the blood system. Those who cannot tolerate cooling energy foods can stir-fry it.

To use winter melon as a cooling vegetable:
1. Boil with Job's tears and hyacinth beans to make a cooling soup for hot, dry weather.
2. Boil with onions and Shiitake mushrooms.
3. Boil with salted duck eggs.
4. Boil with dried shrimps, ginger and mung bean threads.
5. Boil in a stock made from fish or chicken bones.

YAM BEAN
(Pacchyrhizus erosus)
property: cooling

In Malaysia, yam bean is called *sengkuang* or *bangkuang*. The street hawkers sell it in peeled raw chunks or slices to passers-by who need cooling off. Yam bean is an important ingredient in Nonya dishes like *bosomboh*, Penang *rojak, gado-gado, po-piah* and *jiu hu char* (or shredded cuttlefish with yam bean). In all these dishes the cooling yam bean balances the warming energy vegetables, sauces or spices.

YELLOW CUCUMBER
(Cucumis sativum)
property: cooling

Yellow cucumbers are larger than green ones, and have a tough brown skin and yellow flesh. They are available in China, Hong Kong, Malaysia, Singapore and other places where there is a large Chinese community.

NEUTRAL VEGETABLES

People with cooled and overheated blood systems should eat lots of neutral vegetables every day. When you boil neutral vegetables they become more cooling; if you stir-fry them, they become more warming.

BEETROOT
(Beta vulgaris)
property: neutral

This lovely red root is deliciously sweet, especially when cooked. Beetroot is said to be blood-building – perhaps it is all that red! It can be eaten raw or cooked.

To use beetroot as a neutral vegetable:
1 Serve raw in salads.
2 Boil and serve as a hot vegetable.
3 Boil into a thick, creamy soup with oat groats and onions.
4 Boil in chicken stock to make a clear red soup.

To make beetroot more warming:
1 Stir-fry with garlic, ginger, onions and oat groats, then boil with a dash of freshly ground black pepper to make a very warming, thick, creamy winter soup. Add some black-eyed beans to make a complete winter meal.
2 Stir-fry with garlic, ginger and beetroot tops.
3 Stir-fry with ginger and onions.

BROAD BEANS
(Vicia faba)
property: neutral

Fresh summer broad beans are a welcome change from the old leathery brown ones we get in winter. Young, tender broad beans do not contain enough protein, however, so they should only be eaten in summer with other proteins.

To use broad beans as a neutral vegetable:
1 Steam on top of steaming brown rice with chopped herbs.
2 Boil with brown rice and onions.

To make broad beans more warming:
1 Stir-fry with onions, fresh mushrooms and parsley.
2 Stir-fry with garlic, *tofu* and *miso* or *tamari*.
3 Stir-fry with garlic, ginger, onions and Shiitake mushrooms.
4 Stir-fry with garlic, ginger, fish, fresh or dried shrimps, or chicken.

BROCCOLI
(Brassica oleracea L. var. botrytis)
property: neutral

Broccoli is my favourite autumn vegetable. It is delicious when freshly picked, steamed on its own, or with other vegetables for colour contrast.

To use broccoli as a neutral vegetable:
1 Steam with a slice of ginger.
2 Steam with pumpkin or squash.
3 Blanch, toss with other salad ingredients and serve with a dressing made from garlic, ginger and roasted sesame oil.

To make broccoli more warming:
1 Stir-fry with garlic and ginger, and add *miso* at the last minute according to taste.
2 Stir-fry with onions and carrots, onions and squash, or onions and pumpkin.
3 Stir-fry with garlic, ginger and fresh mushrooms.

BRUSSELS SPROUTS
(Brassica oleracea)
property: neutral

These miniature green cabbages are my winter favourites. They are best after the first frost of winter. When I first tried them at boarding school, I disliked them wholeheartedly – the smell and bitter taste put me off for years. I later discovered that they can be very nice simply steamed with just a slice of ginger.

To speed up the cooking time, cut a deep cross almost three-quarters of the way down from the stalk end to the top of each sprout. Do this whether you steam, blanch or stir-fry them.

To use Brussels sprouts as a neutral vegetable:
1. Steam with a slice of ginger.
2. Steam with squash, pumpkin or any other vegetable.
3. Steam with some fresh or dried chestnuts. If you use wind-dried chestnuts, soak them overnight, boil them until they are soft and most of the cooking liquid has evaporated. Then add the prepared Brussels sprouts and steam in the remaining chestnut cooking water.

To make Brussels sprouts more warming:
1. Stir-fry with garlic, ginger and oregano.
2. Stir-fry with garlic and ginger and add *miso* in the last 5 minutes.
3. Stir-fry with garlic, ginger, onions and fermented black soyabeans.
4. Stir-fry with garlic, ginger, onion, carrots, fresh mushrooms, leftover brown rice and some fresh parsley or thyme.

Note: After stir-frying Brussels sprouts, add just enough water to cover the bottom of the pan, and steam until just cooked.

CABBAGE
(Brassica family)
property: neutral

Cabbage, especially the green varieties, should be taken daily because it contains a lot of fibre, and various vitamins and minerals that are good for the complexion.

I have some form of cabbage at least once a day. In winter I have a choice of: Brussels sprouts, Savoy cabbage, white cabbage, green cabbage, winter greens or kale. In spring I have either spring greens, white or green cabbage or purple sprouting broccoli. In summer there is cauliflower or white cabbage. And in autumn there is broccoli, cauliflower or white or green cabbage.

Many people, especially children, do not like cabbage because of the odour. I still have memories of the unpleasant smell of boiling vegetables from my boarding school days. To get rid of the odour, just lightly steam or stir-fry the cabbage with onions, ginger and garlic.

To use white cabbage（椰菜）as a neutral vegetable:
1. Serve raw in salads.
2. Shred and simmer gently with caraway seeds in a little water until tender and deliciously sweet.

To make white cabbage more warming:
1. Stir-fry with garlic and ginger, and simmer. Add a dash of *tamari* before serving.
2. Stir-fry with garlic and ginger and simmer

very gently in *miso*.
3 Stir-fry with other kinds of vegetables, and simmer.
4 Stir-fry with garlic, ginger, *tofu* or *fu zhou*, Shiitake mushrooms and carrots, and simmer with *miso*.

GREEN AND SAVOY CABBAGE
property: neutral

Stir-fry as you would white cabbage (see above).

WINTER GREENS, SPRING GREENS AND KALE
property: neutral

Stir-fry with garlic and ginger, and gently simmer for 1 to 2 minutes until just tender. They are a lovely green when cooked. Add a dash of *tamari* or *shoyu* and a sprinkle of roasted sesame seeds.

CAULIFLOWER
(Brassica oleracea L. var. botrytis)
property: neutral

This white member of the *Brassica* family makes a nice visual contrast to other cabbages. They taste completely different when raw.

To use cauliflower as a neutral vegetable:
1 Serve raw with carrots.
2 Blanch and toss with broccoli and carrots for a colourful salad. Serve with herbs, roasted seeds or nuts.
3 Steam with sections of corn on the cob,

broccoli and carrots for a colourful autumn vegetable dish. Serve with a *tofu* dip.

To make cauliflower more warming:
1 Stir-fry with garlic, ginger and coriander leaves, and simmer for 2 to 3 minutes.
2 Stir-fry with onions, broccoli, fresh mushrooms and carrots, and simmer until just cooked.
3 Stir-fry with garlic, ginger, thyme and courgettes.

CELERIAC
(Apium graveolens var. rapaceum)
property: neutral

This root vegetable comes from the same family as celery. It can be eaten raw, but I like it cooked with lentils. (I am afraid that this is the only way I know to make this vegetable tasty.)

Stir-fry onions and celeriac until the onions are limp. Add some soaked brown lentils and water and bring to a boil. Stew until the lentils are soft, then add a pinch of sea-salt, and simmer for another 15 minutes. Serve with a dash of *tamari* and some finely chopped parsley.

CHINESE FLOWERING CABBAGE
(Brassica chinensis Jus. var. parachinensis)
property: neutral

The Chinese eat flowering cabbage almost every day. It is available all year round in Southeast Asia. Do not buy the older, tougher ones with the yellow flowers. Choose the tender young cabbages.

To use Chinese flowering cabbage as a neutral vegetable:

Blanch and serve with:

1 a garlic oil dressing
2 a garlic, *tamari* and roasted sesame oil dressing
3 a *tamari* and spring onion dressing
4 a garlic, shallot or onion *miso* dressing.

To make Chinese flowering cabbage more warming:

1 Stir-fry with garlic and ginger.
2 Stir-fry with other warming energy vegetables.
3 Stir-fry with garlic, ginger, fish, fresh or dried shrimps, squid or chicken.

CHINESE KALE
(Brassica alboglabra)
property: neutral

The Chinese eat only the tender crispy stems of this delicate vegetable and discard the tough, waxy leaves. Stir-fry as you would Chinese flowering cabbage (see above).

FENNEL
(Foeniculum vulgare)
property: neutral

This unusual looking bulb has a lovely aniseed aroma. It can be eaten raw or cooked.

To use fennel as a neutral vegetable:

1 Chop and mix with other salad ingredients.
2 Boil and liquidise to make a sauce for other vegetables, pasta, fish or chicken.
3 Boil with carrots and onions to make a stock for poaching fish or chicken.
4 Chop and steam with fish or chicken.

To make fennel more warming:

1 Stir-fry with garlic, ginger and fennel seeds, simmer in a small amount of water, and poach with mackerel. (This is my favourite new discovery.) Try fennel with other oily fish such as trout, sardines or herring.
2 Braise or bake in the oven.

FOUR-ANGLED BEANS
property: neutral

These unusual beans are tasty and full of roughage. My mother used to grow them in the garden in Penang and we often enjoyed them freshly picked. I have not seen them outside Southeast Asia and can only remember eating them stir-fried with garlic, ginger and dried shrimps. I am sure they can be stir-fried with all kinds of vegetables too. Be adventurous and cook them as you would long beans (see page 104).

FRENCH BEANS
(Phaseolus vulgaris)
property: neutral

French beans are my favourite summer vegetable. They are a rich source of fibre.

To use French beans as a neutral vegetable:

1 Steam on top of some brown rice.
2 Boil with brown rice and other vegetables.
3 Blanch and serve with dry roasted seeds or nuts.

4 Blanch and serve with onion *miso* sauce or other sauces.

5 Blanch, shred finely and mix with other salad ingredients.

6 Stir-fry with garlic, ginger, onions and *arame*, and simmer in *miso*.

To make French beans more warming:

1 Stir-fry with garlic and ginger, and add other vegetables according to taste.

2 Stir-fry with garlic, ginger and fermented black soyabeans.

3 Stir-fry with garlic and fermented soyabean cheese.

4 Stir-fry with *tofu*, and add other vegetables according to taste.

5 Stir-fry with onions and simmer in *miso*.

6 Stir-fry with garlic, ginger, fish, fresh or dried shrimps, squid or chicken.

GARLAND CHRYSANTHEMUM
(Chrysanthemum coronarium L. var. spatiosum)
property: neutral

This delicate member of the *Chrysanthemum* family has a unique flavour. Garland chrysanthemum is one of the more important green vegetables in a Chinese steamboat dinner because it cooks in seconds and is so delicious and tender. Blanch them in boiling water for a minute or two, and serve with one of the dressings for Chinese flowering cabbage (see page 103).

LAMB'S LETTUCE
(Valerianella olitoria)
property: neutral

This delicate green is usually eaten raw as a winter salad. I prefer to blanch and serve them with a thin *tamari,* garlic and roasted sesame oil dressing. They are also good stir-fried with garlic and ginger.

LANDCRESS
(Barbarea verna)
property: neutral

Landcress is like watercress but it grows on land. Hence, it is less cooling. Although it can be eaten raw or cooked, I stir-fry it as I would watercress (see page 98).

LONG BEANS
(Vigna sesquipedalis)
property: neutral

Long beans are my favourite Southeast Asian vegetable. Whenever I am home in Penang my mother cooks them for my first meal. Like French beans, they are rich in roughage.

To use long beans as a neutral vegetable:

1 Blanch and mix with some raw yam bean and carrots. Serve with dry roasted seeds or nuts or with a sauce.

2 Boil with brown rice and other vegetables.

3 Steam on top of some brown rice.

To make long beans more warming:

1 Stir-fry with shallots and *fu zhou,* and simmer in *miso*.

2 Stir-fry with shallots, *tofu,* Shiitake mushrooms, carrots and *tamari* or *miso*.

3 Stir-fry with shallots, ginger and fermented black soyabeans.

4 Stir-fry with garlic and fermented soyabean cheese.

5   Stir-fry with ginger and eggs.

6   Stir-fry with garlic and either fish, fresh or dried shrimps, or chicken.

PARSNIP
(Pastinaca sativa)
property: neutral

This winter white root vegetable takes some getting used to. It has its own unique flavour. Steaming parsnips with a pinch of sea-salt brings out their flavour, but for a more warming root, try baking. You can also stir-fry and simmer with leek or spring onion.

PEA SHOOTS
(Pisum sativum)
property: neutral

These tender little shoots are best just stir-fried with garlic and ginger and served with a dash of *tamari*. You can also stir-fry them as you would Chinese flowering cabbage (see page 103).

PUMPKIN
(Cucurbita maxima)
property: neutral

Before the introduction of tomatoes from the New World, pumpkin was a popular vegetable in the Middle East, Europe and Asia. Unlike greenhouse-grown tomatoes, they grow easily in temperate climates, without insecticides or pesticides, and store well from autumn to spring, provided their stalks are intact and they are kept in a cool, dry place.

When rice was scarce in China during a famine, pumpkin was used to stretch the rice or eaten instead of rice. Today pumpkin is grown in many country homes where there is a small plot of earth.

To use pumpkin as a neutral vegetable:

1   Steam on its own, or with cauliflower and broccoli for colour and texture contrast.

2   Boil with caraway seeds until soft, then mash to make a sauce for other vegetables. Use other herbs or spices for various sauces.

3   Boil with onions for a colourful autumn soup.

To make pumpkin more warming:

1   Slice, brush with *tamari* and cold-pressed sesame oil, and bake until soft.

2   Stew with chick-peas or other beans.

3   Stir-fry with onions, broccoli and cauliflower.

4   Stir-fry with garlic, ginger, onions, fresh mushrooms and courgettes. Add some fresh basil for more flavour.

RUNNER BEANS
(Phaseolus multiflorus)
property: neutral

This inexpensive summer vegetable is full of fibre. Runner beans are best young and tender; shop-bought ones tend to be a bit stringy. (Perhaps that is why they are sometimes called 'string' beans.)

Cook them as you would French beans (pages 103-104). For stringy old runner beans: slice finely at a slant, stir-fry with garlic, ginger, onions, fresh mushrooms and carrots, and simmer until tender. Then add *miso* or *tamari* and simmer very gently for another 5

minutes. Slice all the vegetables finely for uniformity and visual appeal.

SNOW PEAS
(Phaseolus sativum L. var. macrocarpon)
property: neutral

This is another delightful summer vegetable that is full of roughage and so tender and sweet that it needs very little cooking.

To use snow peas as a neutral vegetable:
1   Steam on top of brown rice.
2   Steam with *tofu* and serve with a sauce made from spring onion and *miso*, or *tamari*, ginger, spring onion and roasted sesame oil.
3   Steam with other vegetables such as white cabbage and carrots, white cabbage and baby sweet corn, pumpkin or squash, and serve with dry-roasted seeds or sauce.

To make snow peas more warming:
1   Stir-fry with garlic, ginger and water chestnuts.
2   Stir-fry with garlic, ginger, white cabbage and baby sweet corn or sweet corn kernels.
3   Stir-fry with garlic, ginger, *tofu*, Shiitake mushrooms and carrots.
4   Stir-fry with garlic, ginger, fish, fresh or dried shrimps, squid or chicken.

SQUASH
(Cucurbita moschata)
property: neutral

Use the same way as pumpkin (see page 105).

SWEDE
(Brassica rutabaga)
property: neutral

This large golden-purple winter root has its own subtle flavour, but is much easier to acquire a taste for than parsnips. According to the Welsh, you can help gall bladder problems by drinking swede water and eating plenty of swedes.

To use swedes as a neutral vegetable:
1   Boil with leeks, marrowfat peas and oat groats for a winter soup meal.
2   Boil on their own to help gall bladder problems.
3   Steam with broccoli and a slice of ginger.

To make swedes more warming:
1   Stir-fry with onions or leeks.
2   Blanch, and then stir-fry with garlic, ginger, broccoli and cauliflower.
3   Bake.
4   Roast.

Note: Large swedes contain a woody core, and will need to cook for about 45 minutes. Use small swedes whenever possible for the above dishes.

SWEET CORN
(Zea mays)
property: neutral

This delicious whole cereal grain can be used as a vegetable. Baby sweet corn, the miniature hybrid very popular in the East, is too tender and young to have much protein value as a whole cereal grain.

SWEET POTATO
(Ipomoea batatas)
property: neutral

Sweet potatoes are often boiled with Swatow mustard cabbage in Southeast Asia to make a cooling soup during the hot, dry season.

As children, we used to have them boiled and mashed with finely chopped spring onions for breakfast. They can also be baked on a charcoal fire. The skin will burn until it has a papery quality and will peel easily. The potato can then be served with all kinds of sauces.

SWEET POTATO LEAVES
(Ipomoea batatas)
property: neutral

Sweet potato leaves are delicious and a welcome change from cabbage. They are very tough and grow like weeds – usually without pesticides or insecticides. Blanch them before stir-frying to remove the unpleasant taste of the sap.

TARO
(Colocasia esculenta)
property: neutral

This starchy root tuber is usually served in Chinese homes on the night of the full moon during the Mid-Autumn Festival. It is simply boiled, skinned and eaten as a snack. Sometimes it is dipped in a *tamari* and roasted sesame oil dressing.

TURNIP
(Brassica rapa)
property: neutral

This flattish round root has a green top in winter and a purple top in early spring. It is

very easy to grow and the leaves can be used as an alternative to cabbage. Some people believe that regular consumption of turnips can prevent the formation of gallstones.

> **To use turnips as a neutral vegetable:**
> 1 Boil with onions, carrots and marrowfat peas for a hearty, warming winter vegetable soup.
> 2 Boil, mash and serve with some laverbread.
>
> **To make turnips more warming:**
> 1 Stir-fry with leeks.
> 2 Stir-fry with garlic and oregano.

YAM
(Dioscerea alata)
property: neutral

Cook this large root vegetable as you would taro (see page 107).

> *Note:* People with skin diseases or healing wounds should avoid yam. It may aggravate the condition.

WARMING VEGETABLES

Warming vegetables are often used with cooling vegetables to make them less cooling. They should not be eaten in excess by people with overheated blood systems or tendencies towards them. Boil warming vegetables to make them more neutral or stir-fry them with cooling vegetables.

CARROT
(Daucus carota)
property: warming

Carrots are eaten in winter in temperate countries to strengthen the mucus membrane against colds and 'flus. They are a rich source of pro-vitamin A or carotene, and are sweet enough to be eaten raw or cooked.

In summer, baby carrots can be eaten with their fern-like tops, which have a distinctive flavour. In winter the tops are stringy and fibrous, so they need to be cooked longer.

> **To use carrots as a warming vegetable:**
> 1 Serve raw in salads.
> 2 Slice thinly and steam on top of some brown rice.
> 3 Steam with other vegetables.
> 4 Boil to make carrot soup.
> 5 Cut into chunks and simmer gently, on their own or with other vegetables, for 30 minutes, in as little water as possible. (They are very sweet this way.)
> 6 Stir-fry with their tops or other vegetables.
> 7 Stir-fry with other vegetables and simmer gently for a few minutes.
>
> **To make carrots more warming:**
> 1 Bake or roast them.

CHINESE CHIVES
(Allium tuberosum)
property: warming

The Chinese stir-fry Chinese chives with ribbon rice noodles (*kway teow*), *tofu* and fish or other seafoods.

Note: Some Chinese believe this vegetable has some toxic properties. Anyone with a skin disease or a healing wound should avoid it; it may make the skin disease worse or the wound septic.

LEEK
(Allium porrum)
property: warming

Leeks are an excellent vegetable in winter because they keep us warm and help us resist colds and 'flus. The Northern Chinese, who are known for their strength and health, eat them often. They are delicious stir-fried or braised.

To use leeks as a warming vegetable:
1 Very gently simmer in as little water as possible.
2 Boil in a soup.
3 Stir-fry with ginger, *tofu* and freshly ground black pepper or black mustard seeds for a really warming winter dish. Add *miso* or *tamari*.
4 Stir-fry with ginger, *arame* and carrots.
5 Stir-fry with ginger and Chinese Peking cabbage.
6 Stir-fry with ginger, mung bean sprouts and carrots.
7 Stir-fry with ginger, eggs and fresh mushrooms.
8 Stir-fry with ginger, fish, fresh or dried shrimps, squid or chicken.

ONION
(Allium cepa)
property: warming

Vegetarian meals without onions are tasteless, so I use them often when I cook. Like leeks, they warm the body and help resist colds and 'flus. Scientific research has shown that an onion a day can help lower blood pressure and blood cholesterol levels. Because onions contain a lot of roughage, they are also very good for some forms of constipation.

Onion *Miso* Sauce

1 medium onion
cold-pressed sesame oil
pinch sea-salt
1 tsp miso

1 Finely dice the onion.
2 Sauté in just enough cold-pressed oil to coat the bottom of the pot. Add sea-salt and sauté until soft.
3 Add just enough water to cover and simmer gently for 15 minutes.
4 Add *miso* which has been thinned out with a little onion stock. Simmer gently for another 15 minutes.
5 Pour over whole wheat pasta, vegetable or fish.

Variations:
1 Use garlic, leeks, carrots or fennel instead of onion.
2 Use a combination of: garlic, ginger and onion; garlic, leek and parsley; or onion, carrot and thyme.

SHALLOT
(Allium cepa L. var. aggregatum)
property: warming

These little purple bulbs are used often in Southeast Asia. Their pungency lies somewhere between that of garlic and onion. When I am in the East, I use shallots instead of onions for a more aromatic dish, for example in fried brown rice.

Although shallots are used often in Southeast Asia as a deep-fried garnish for salads, bowls of noodles or soups, I find them too greasy for the digestive tract.

SPRING ONION
(Allium cepa L. var. aggregatum)
property: warming

Spring onions are used internationally as a salad ingredient or a food garnish. To the Chinese they are more than that: they mask the strong aromas of raw vegetables, fish, seafoods, poultry and meats, and warm up cooling energy foods.

Spring onion whites are used medicinally to induce sweating at the start of a cold or 'flu, to clear phlegm, and as a diuretic.

In winter, stir-fry spring onions with *tofu* to warm the stomach and keep colds away. I often have this in winter with home-grown Welsh onion *(Allium fistulosum).*

Spring Onions for Cold and 'Flus

10 spring onion whites
12 $^1/_2$ g ($^1/_2$ oz) fermented black soyabeans
5 slices ginger
3 cups water

1   Boil all the ingredients together until only 1 cup of liquid remains.
2   Drink the liquid and get into bed immediately under plenty of bedclothes, to sweat out the cold or 'flu.

Note: This remedy is applicable for fever, headache, blocked nose and aching bones.

Caution: Only the young and strong may use this remedy. Sweating can deplete the old and weak even further.

To use spring onions as a warming vegetable:
1   Serve raw in salads.
2   Stir-fry with cooling vegetables to make them less cooling.
3   Stir-fry with eggs, pasta, fish, other seafoods or chicken.

Vegetables for Babies and Infants

Babies and infants can be given mashed or puréed vegetables in small quantities as soon as they start teething. Give them mostly neutral vegetables with more warming vegetables in winter and cooling ones in summer.

You can determine the nature of the baby's blood system by his appearance. If he has heat rashes; give him cooling and neutral vegetables. Dark, scanty urine or hard, dark stools also indicate heat. If the child looks or feels cold, and often has a runny nose with clear watery mucus, then he needs more warming vegetables. Frequent urination and pale, loose stools are further indications of cold.

If young children refuse to eat steamed or boiled cabbage, stir-fry them with some sweet root vegetables such as onions or carrots. Alternatively, chop the cabbage, boil it in a soup, and liquidise it so that it is not noticeable.

7 Herbs and Spices

Like whole cereal grains, legumes, pulses, seeds, nuts, seaweeds and vegetables, herbs and spices have been used since early civilisation. Through trial and error, we have discovered that herbs and spices have medicinal properties and that they stimulate the salivary glands and aid digestion.

In my travels I have noticed that each country has its own particular blend of herbs and spices. Every time I walk through the wholefood shop near the clinic where I work, I get a wonderful whiff of Western herbs and spices blended with whole cereal grains, legumes, pulses, seeds, nuts and organic vegetables. The smell is different when I walk through Culpeper's in Covent Garden where they have drawers of dried herbs and different types of potpourri. In Italy, the air has a blend of garlic, basil, oregano and tomatoes.

In Calcutta, as the airport bus nears the city at dusk, the smell of spicy cooking fills the air. In Bangkok the smell is in the airport itself! In Penang, where there are many Indian shops, there is a wonderful, rich, spicy aroma. In Chinese medicinal shops the smell is completely different and I am attracted to the calming effect of the Chinese herbs. The *pasar malam* (night market) is the best place to sample the whiffs of the four different types of cooking: Chinese, Nonya, Malay and Indian. As you walk from stall to stall the different smells of the spices make your mouth water.

Fresh herbs are easy to grow in pots on the kitchen window sill. Their freshness adds extra vitamins to your diet and ensures that the essential oils are at their most potent. You can be shivering in England during a cold winter and still grow fresh outdoor herbs like Welsh onion, rosemary, thyme, winter savory and sweet bay leaves. In summer, you can grow chives, mint, lemon balm, sage, comfrey, parsley, coriander, basil and fennel, to name a few.

Herbs and spices are good for the health but they must be taken in moderation and with discretion. Consult the following list of herbs to discover their cooling, neutral and warming energies and to determine which are appropriate for you.

Many of the recipes that follow are for herbal tea infusions. Just mix one teaspoon of the dried herb with one cup boiling water, infuse for 10-15 minutes, strain and drink. Use a small thermos flask for infusions rather than a teapot. A flask will extract the volatile oils better.

Like many other beverages, all herbal teas must be freshly prepared. The medicinal properties are lost if the tea is kept overnight.

COOLING HERBS AND SPICES

Cooling herbs and spices should not be eaten by people who are weak, old, have cooled blood systems or tendencies towards them.

ALOE VERA
property: cooling

This succulent plant is included here for its healing rather than eating purposes. Its cooling nature can soothe burns and certain types of skin diseases like eczema, psoriasis, pimples, spots, boils, acne and cold sores. It is also used to heal skin cancer.

To use, just cut a leaf and apply the oozing gel-like sap to the affected area. Wrap the rest of the leaf in a piece of paper and store in a cool, dry place for future use. NEVER wrap in plastic or cling-film or the leaf will rot.

BORAGE
(Borago officinalis)
property: cooling

Borage tea helps restore the adrenal cortex after treatment with cortisone or steroids. It is also used as an anti-inflammatory herb in cases of pleurisy.

2 tsp dried borage
1 cup boiling water

Infuse the dried herb in boiling water for 10 to 15 minutes. Drink three times a day.

Borage as food:
1 Serve the young, tender leaves raw in salads.
2 Steam and serve borage with chopped chives or spring onions.

BURDOCK
(Arctium lappa)
property: cooling

Burdock is one of the classic blood purifiers. Burdock tea is good for skin diseases like eczema and psoriasis caused by too much heat in the blood system.

25 g (1 oz) burdock root
1 ¹/₂ pints water

Boil the root in the water until liquid is reduced to a pint. Drink a wineglassful 4 times a day before meals.

Burdock as food: Burdock grows wild. The stalks must be harvested before the flowers open. Peel the tough rind, slice the stalks diagonally and boil in as little water as possible. Serve as a cooked vegetable with a dash of *tamari*. Burdock root is also edible. Cook as you would parsnips (see page 105).

CHAMOMILE, GERMAN
(Matricaria chamomilla)
property: cooling

Chamomile tea is fragrant and now very popular with people who are trying to give up coffee and Indian, Ceylonese or Chinese

tea. It can help you relax if you suffer from migraines, anxiety or insomnia. Slowly sip the tea and inhale the chamomile fragrance. Chamomile is also used to cool down overheated blood systems with symptoms like gingivitis (inflammation of the gums), sore throat, inflamed, sore eyes and gastritis.

Infuse and drink throughout the day. For sore, inflamed eyes, place cooled, moist chamomile tea bags over the closed eyes for 30 minutes.

If you suffer from migraines, anxiety or insomnia keep a chamomile plant near you so you can inhale its soothing fragrance when you rub the leaves between your fingers.

CHICKWEED
(Stellaria media)
property: cooling

This wild, delicate weed has soothing properties: it is used as an external remedy for cuts, wounds, itching and irritation. Poultices of chickweed can help ease eczema or psoriasis.

Chickweed as food:
1 Serve raw in salads and as a sandwich filling.
2 Steam in a minimum amount of water and serve as you would spinach (see page 97).

CHRYSANTHEMUM
(Chrysanthemum indicum)
property: cooling

Chrysanthemum tea is cooling and has antibiotic and anti-inflammatory properties. As a child I was given this tea once a week to

keep cool during the hot, dry season in Penang. It is appropriate for headaches caused by too much heat, red and sore eyes, bad breath, bitter taste in the mouth, spots, pimples, acne, boils, heat rashes, eczema and psoriasis.

3-6 whole dried flowers
1 cup boiling water

Infuse the dried flowers in a cup of boiling water for 10 to 15 minutes. Drink throughout the day until the condition improves. Use no more than 6 dried flowers per cup of boiling water.

COMFREY
(Symphytum officinale)
property: cooling

I used to use comfrey as a mulch for my plants, until one day, a patient told me that she used comfrey to heal the numerous cuts, bruises and wounds she received while working on a farm. She would cut up a few leaves and mash them to form a poultice which she would apply directly to the affected area.

Nowadays, health food shops stock comfrey ointment to heal bruises and sprains. They also sell tablets that help fractured bones.

Comfrey tea acts as an expectorant in cases of too much heat in the lungs, e.g. in heat-caused bronchitis and irritable coughs. It also soothes inflamed gastric and duodenal ulcers.

1-3 tsp dried comfrey
1 cup water

1 Put the dried herb in a cup of water. Bring to a boil and let simmer for 10 to 15 minutes.
2 Strain and drink three times a day until the condition eases.

Comfrey as food: Steam the tender young leaves as you would spinach (see page 97). Add some freshly grated nutmeg for extra flavour.

CORN SILK
(Zea mays)
property: cooling

Traditionally, corn silk tea was used in China to treat diabetes and infections such as nephritis, cystitis and prostatitis. It also helps lower high blood pressure.

1 tbsp dried corn silk
1 cup boiling water

Infuse dried corn silk in boiling water for 10-15 minutes in a thermos flask. Strain and drink 3 times a day.

DANDELION
(Taraxacum officinale)
property: cooling

This wild weed is also listed under cooling vegetables (see page 92).

Dandelion root has antibiotic, anti-inflammatory and anti-swelling properties. It is used to treat mastitis (inflammation of the breast), sores, chronic gastritis, urinary tract infections, gall bladder inflammation, hepatitis, bronchitis and tonsilitis.

For mastitis, drink the tea and apply a fresh poultice of dandelion leaves to the affected area.

25 g (1 oz) dandelion root
2 cups water

1 Boil the dandelion root in water until only 1 cup remains.
2 Strain and drink once daily until the condition clears. If you find the root too bitter, use the same quantity of dried leaves.

LEMON BALM
(Melissa officinalis)
property: cooling

Lemon balm tea is a cooling drink for hot summer days. It has a lovely lemony fragrance.

3-4 sprays fresh lemon leaves or
1 tsp dried leaves
1 cup boiling water

Infuse fresh or dried leaves in the boiling water. Leave for 10 to 15 minutes. Strain and drink.

Lemon balm with food:
1 Chop finely and toss with salads to give a lemony aroma.
2 Add to stews and casseroles.

SLIPPERY ELM
(Ulmus fulva)
property: cooling

When boiled with water, this fine beige powder helps soothe inflamed digestive tract diseases such as gastritis, gastric and duodenal ulcers, enteritis and colitis.

1 part powdered bark
8 parts water

1 Mix the powder in a little water first to make a thick paste then slowly add the rest of the water.
2 Bring to a boil and gently simmer for 10 to 15 minutes.
3 Drink half a cup three times a day. If you have an ulcer and cannot eat solid food, use more slippery elm for a thicker consistency. Eat a bowl at every meal until you are able to resume eating solids.

TAMARIND
(Tamarindus indica)
property: cooling

In Malaysia, tamarind (*assam*) trees grow to great heights and bear lots of fruit pods. The fruit is used in cooking to aid digestion, add a sour taste, and to act as a mild laxative. Try marinating mackerel in tamarind paste, and then lightly frying, grilling or baking the fish.

TARRAGON
(Artemisia dracunculus)
property: cooling

Tarragon tea is a diuretic and a mild laxative

MINT, CORNMINT, PEPPERMINT
(Mentha arvensis, Mentha piperita)
property: cooling

Tea made with these mints is used to treat colds, headaches, red and sore eyes, mouth and tongue ulcers, toothache, heat rashes, spots, pimples, acne, boils, eczema and psoriasis.

Infuse and drink throughout the day until the condition improves.

Mint with food:
1 Serve raw in salads.
2 Boil plain or with cucumbers to make a clear soup.

Note: Nursing mothers should avoid mint teas. They may decrease milk production.

PURPLE SAGE
(Salvia purpurascens)
property: cooling

Purple sage is a medicinal herb. Unlike garden sage, it has cooling properties and can help sore throats. (See sage and honey gargle on page 119.)

and helps alleviate painful menstrual periods.

Infuse and drink 2 to 3 times a day if the problem is acute, once a day otherwise.

> **Tarragon with food:**
> 1 Chop and add to salads.
> 2 Use as a *bouquet garni* when cooking fish or chicken.
> 3 Use as a stuffing for fish.
> 4 Use with chicken stews or casseroles.

TURMERIC
(Curcuma longa)
property: cooling

This cooling yellow spice is one of the ingredients in Indian curry. Mixed with hot spices to make them less heating, turmeric also has antibiotic properties. Meat cooked with turmeric can keep longer. In Asia, you can buy either the ground yellow powder or the fresh rhizome.

Turmeric also has the ability to resolve blood stagnation caused by trauma, for example a bruise from a harsh blow or fall.

1 medium onion, sliced
$^1/_8$ tsp turmeric powder
$^1/_8$ tsp cayenne
25 g (1 oz) beans or
110-175 g (4-6 oz) fish/chicken

Stir-fry the ingredients and simmer with a little water. Season lightly with sea-salt. Take this stew several times a week until the condition improves.

> *Note:* Cayenne helps improve blood circulation, but use it sparingly if you suffer from high blood pressure, high blood cholesterol or an overheated blood system.
>
> Do not use turmeric in your cooking if you wish to get pregnant. In a recent study in China it was discovered that water and petroleum-ether extracts of turmeric were 100 per cent effective in preventing pregnancy in female rats.
>
> **Turmeric with food:**
> 1 Cook brown rice with turmeric instead of expensive saffron to give a yellow colour.
> 2 Marinate oily fish with turmeric before shallow-frying, grilling or baking.

VERVAIN
(Verbena officinalis)
property: cooling

Vervain tea helps relieve stress and tension. It is also useful in cases of inflammation of the gall bladder and jaundice.

Infuse and drink 3 times a day until the condition improves.

NEUTRAL HERBS AND SPICES

Neutral herbs and spices can be used daily, in moderation, by people with all types of blood systems.

ELDERBERRY
(Sambucus nigra)
property: neutral

The British countryside is full of wild elderberry trees. In early summer, the trees

are covered with clusters of tiny flowers. In autumn, they are dotted with black elderberries.

Elderberry flowers are often used with peppermint to sweat out colds and 'flus and, in Britain, elderberry cordial is used to prevent these diseases.

> **Elderberries as food:**
> 1 Stew with apples, cinnamon and cloves for a warming autumn dessert. Add blackberries, which are in season at the same time.
> 2 Boil in soups with ginger and onions.

LIQUORICE
(Glycyrrhiza glabra)
property: neutral

Liquorice is said to help revitalise the adrenals of people who have had a course of steroids. It is also used for sore throats and coughs.

---
1 tsp dried liquorice root
1 cup water

Boil the dried root in water for 10 to 15 minutes. Strain and drink 3 times a day.

> **Liquorice with food:**
> 1 Stew with apples for a dessert.
> 2 Stew with chicken.
>
> **Note:** Liquorice can leach potassium from the body. Eat in moderation.

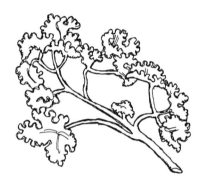

PARSLEY
(Carum petroselinum or Petroselinum crispum)
property: neutral

This is the most popular herb in the West. It is rich in iron, vitamins A and C, good for the bladder, kidneys, gall bladder and liver, and helpful in cases of painful menstrual periods, delayed periods and pre-menstrual water retention. Use dried parsley in winter when fresh parsley is unavailable.

Infuse and drink 1 to 3 times a day depending on the severity of the condition. Stop as soon as the problem eases.

> **Parsley with food:**
> 1 Chop and mix with salads.
> 2 Sprinkle on all kinds of food.

RASPBERRY
(Rubus idaeus)
property: neutral

Raspberry leaf tea may help expectant mothers have a smooth, quick delivery, if taken during the last three months of pregnancy.

Infuse and drink 3 times a day.

ROSEMARY
(Rosmarinus officinalis)
property: neutral

This wonderful herbaceous plant grows year round, even when it snows. It is a strong antiseptic and a diuretic, and it benefits the liver.

Infuse and drink 1 to 3 times a day, depending on the severity of your condition.

> **Rosemary with food:**
> 1 Cook with fish, especially mackerel and herring, to help digest the oil.
> 2 Cook a sprig with brown rice for extra aroma.
> 3 Use with legumes, pulses and *tofu*.
> 4 Cook with chicken to help digestion.
>
> *Note:* Rosemary can increase blood pressure.

SAGE
(Salvia officinalis)
property: neutral

Sage is another popular herb. It helps promote and regulate menstruation.

Infuse and drink 1 to 3 times a day depending on the severity of your condition.

> **Sage and honey gargle:** For sore throat, simmer 25 g (1 oz) dried sage in 570 ml (1 pint) water for 10 minutes. Leave to cool, strain, and add 1 teaspoon honey. Use often until condition clears, but remember to warm up mixture each time before gargling.

> **Sage with food:**
> 1 Sauté with onions and buckwheat.
> 2 Add to chicken and other foods.

SCREWPINE LEAVES
(Pandanus odorus)
property: neutral

These very aromatic dark green leaves are often used in Nonya sweet dishes. They stimulate the salivary glands and colour foods. For aromatic brown rice, boil with a screwpine leaf and remove before serving.

THYME
(Thymus vulgaris)
property: neutral

Like rosemary, thyme is an evergreen. It is good for people who suffer from catarrh and it aids digestion. Thyme is also a good antiseptic for the digestive tract, for example in cases of gastritis. (For this, just infuse and drink 3 times a day.) According to some, if you cook lentils with thyme and caraway seeds they will not lose iron during cooking.

> **Thyme with food:**
> 1 Cook with lentils, garlic, onions, ginger and caraway seeds.

2 Cook with courgettes, carrots, onions and mushrooms.

3 Cook with *miso*.

WARMING HERBS AND SPICES

Warming herbs and spices are beneficial to the weak, the elderly, those with cooled blood systems or tendencies towards them.

BASIL
(Ocymum basilicum)
property: warming

This very aromatic herb always reminds me of my Italian aunt who uses it with garlic, ground almonds and olive oil to make a special *pesto* for all kinds of pasta.

Basil is good for the nerves and stomach, it aids digestion, and helps promote and regulate menstruation. Women who suffer from irregular or painful periods should use basil frequently in their cooking.

I sauté basil with fresh mushrooms and *miso* or, in summer, I chop up the fresh leaves and add them to salads.

BAY LEAVES
(Laurus nobilis)
property: warming

Bay leaves are often used to flavour stocks, legumes or pulses.

Add some dried bay leaves to dried grains, legumes, pulses, seeds or nuts to keep insects away.

CARAWAY
(Carum carvi)
property: warming

The Germans use sweet caraway seed in breads and cakes to make them more digestible. They are also said to relieve menstrual pains.

Caraway seeds with food: Cook with millet, onions, pumpkin or squash.

CARDAMOM
(Elettaria cardamomum)
property: warming

Cardamom is used often in Indian cooking (even in tea), to make food more spicy.

Sometimes I add one or two cardamom pods to my boiling brown rice to give an interesting taste and aroma. They also aid digestion.

CHIVES
(Allium schoenoprasum)
property: warming

My German aunt used to serve chopped chives with chopped hardboiled eggs. Chives are a good source of vitamin C, they aid the digestion of eggs and ensure that the cholesterol level is not raised. I use chives as I would spring onions (see page 110).

CINNAMON
(Cinnamomum zeylanicum)
property: warming

This type of cinnamon is quill-shaped and popular in the west. The Chinese use a bark-like type of cinnamon (*Cinnamomum cassia*) to warm up the kidneys, and to treat cold hands and feet, backache, weak knees, early morning coughs and menstrual pains. Cinnamon is also useful in treating arthritis, rheumatism, or 'flus caused by sudden exposure to wind and cold. Use the variety available in your area.

Cinnamon with food:

1   Add to breakfast oat groats or frumenty. (See pages 33-34 and 44.)
2   Add to *fu zhou* stewed with garlic, ginger, onions, carrots and *miso*.
3   Use in a casserole with chicken, Chinese red dates, chestnuts and Shiitake mushrooms.
4   Use in fruit stews with pineapple, apples, pears, plums and peaches.

Note: Do not eat too much cinnamon; it may cause nosebleeds. Antidotes include chrysanthemum tea or mung bean stew.

CLOVES
(Eugenia caryophyllata)
property: warming

In the old days, dentists used to deaden the nerves in the gums with oil of clove. Unfortunately, it is no longer in use.

Cloves are used in winter in Christmas cakes, puddings, mince pies and hot punches because of their aroma, warming properties and antiseptic effects. Oil of clove can be used externally for neuralgia and rheumatic pain.

To sweat out a cold or 'flu, boil elderberry with cloves, ginger, cinnamon and brown sugar.

CORIANDER
(Coriandrum sativum)
property: warming

The Chinese use coriander leaves with fish and other seafood because it masks fishy odours. It also aids digestion. Coriander seed is one of the ingredients in Indian *garam masala* (curry paste).

Coriander with food:

1   Steam with fish.
2   Stir-fry with fresh mushrooms, *tofu* or prawns.
3   Use as a garnish.
4   Add a few seeds to any legume or pulse stew, or casserole.

CUMIN
(Cuminum cyminum)
property: warming

This is another popular Indian spice that is good for digestion.

Cumin with food:

1   Stir-fry in a little cold-pressed oil with garlic and pour over stewed legumes or pulses, especially brown lentils.
2   Cook with fish.

DILL
(Anethum graveolens)
property: warming

In Europe, dill leaves and seeds are used with fish, cabbage and gherkins. Dill also aids digestion.

FENNEL
(Foeniculum vulgare)
property: warming

Fennel leaves and seeds help the digestion of oily fish such as trout, sardines, herring and mackerel.

Fennel seed tea is said to promote milk flow in nursing mothers.

1 tsp bruised fennel seeds
1 cup boiling water

Infuse the bruised seeds in boiling water for 10 to 15 minutes. Strain and drink 3 times a day until the condition improves.

FENUGREEK
(Trigonella foenum-graecum)
property: warming

These flattish, rectangular looking brown seeds are said to warm the kidneys. They are used to treat cold hands and feet, backaches, weak knees and painful periods.

1 tsp bruised fenugreek
1 cup boiling water

Infuse the bruised seed in boiling water for 10 to 15 minutes. Strain and drink 3 times a day.

Fenugreek with food: Cook with all kinds of legumes and pulses to warm up the kidneys.

Note: Overconsumption can overheat the blood system. Take in moderation, even after the condition improves.

GARLIC
(Allium sativum)
property: warming

Garlic has antibiotic and anti-inflammatory properties, and helps lower blood pressure and blood cholesterol.

The Northern Chinese, who use a lot of garlic, are known for their strength and good health. The Indians say garlic aids the digestion of all kinds of food.

I use garlic nearly every day because it improves the flavour of all kinds of foods, especially whole cereal grains, legumes, pulses and fresh vegetables. What is more, the aroma encourages the secretion of the salivary

glands to further aid digestion.

The frequent use of garlic is most appropriate in autumn, winter and spring to prevent colds, 'flus and all kinds of respiratory problems.

> *Note:* Do not cook garlic with eggs.

GINGER
(Zingiber officinale)
property: warming

The Chinese and Indians use ginger a lot in their cooking to aid digestion. The Chinese always use ginger with fish and all kinds of seafood to remove fishy odours. It is also stir-fried with leafy and other cooling vegetables to make them less cooling.

Medicinally, ginger is used: to prevent motion sickness; to sweat out colds or 'flus; as a remedy for coughs with lots of clear watery mucus, sputum or phlegm; to remove cold and damp; to improve the circulation of arthritic and rheumatic joints; and to decongest sinuses by improving circulation.

> *To improve circulation:* Grate a handful of fresh ginger and place in a muslin bag. Bring a pot of water just to the boil and turn off the heat. Squeeze out the ginger juice into the pot until the water turns yellow. Soak an old piece of towel in the water, wring out and place on the stiff joint or congested sinus area. Then put a thick dry towel over the wet one to keep in the heat. Change the towel as soon as it begins to cool. Discontinue treatment when the ginger water cools. Repeat the treatment every evening until the problem clears.

Ginger is available fresh from Chinese, Indian, and some Western supermarkets and greengrocers. Store ginger in moist peat in a cool, dry place to keep it fresh for months. It may even start to sprout. (Discard if the ginger begins to grow green leaves.)

LEMONGRASS
(Cymbopogon species)
property: warming

Lemongrass grows wild in Malaysia and is used a lot in Nonya curries to aid the digestion of the rich sauce and fatty meat.

NUTMEG
(Myristica fragrans)
property: warming

Penang is famous in Malaysia for its fresh nutmeg and nutmeg products, for example mace, preserved nutmeg, nutmeg oil and nutmeg balm.

Nutmeg aids digestion and is used in cases of vomiting, indigestion, stomach-ache, and diarrhoea due to excessive eating.

> *Nutmeg with food:*
> 1 Grate over spinach and green cabbage to aid digestion.
> 2 Grate or use a small piece of mace in brown rice puddings made with fresh soyabean milk.
> 3 Grate or use a small piece of mace in stewed fruits such as apples, pears, plums or pineapple.
> 4 Use in rich Christmas cakes, puddings and mince pies to aid digestion and to enrich the aroma.

MUGWORT
(Artemisia vulgaris)
property: warming

Chinese acupuncturists use mugwort often to treat their patients.

Mugwort tea helps promote and regulate menstruation. Normally, it is taken between ovulation and menstruation.

Infuse and drink 1 to 3 times a day, depending on the severity of your condition, until the problem clears. Stop as soon as the problem has eased.

Mugwort as food: Stir-fry with eggs to build up the blood and remove wind from the body. (A friend from China also says it can be cooked as a vegetable with pork.)

MUSTARD
(Brassica alba, Brassica nigra)
property: warming

Mustard aids the digestion of fatty foods such as oily fish and meats. The Indians fry black mustard seeds with vegetables, while the British use them in pickles and sauces.

Soak the feet in a hot mustard bath to drive away a cold. Place mustard plasters over the forehead to decongest the sinuses, or on the knees to ease arthritis or rheumatism.

Mustard with food:
1 Stir-fry black mustard seeds with vegetables.
2 Use the freshly prepared yellow type with oily fish such as sardines, herring and mackerel.

OREGANO
(Origanum vulgare)
property: warming

Oregano is often used to aid the digestion of cabbages, Brussels sprouts and turnips. My Italian aunt uses it often with garlic and basil.

Note: Only use a pinch or two of oregano at a time. Too much can make the food bitter.

PEPPER
(Piper nigrum)
property: warming

Pepper is appropriate for winter because it warms the body. It can benefit those who suffer from cold hands and feet, and arthritic and rheumatic joints that are more painful on cold days.

SAVORY, SUMMER AND WINTER
(Satureja hortensis, Satureja montana)
property: warming

Summer and winter savory should be cooked with legumes and pulses to aid digestion.

SICHUAN PEPPER
(Zanthoxylum bungeanum)
property: warming

The Chinese marinate fresh prawns in ground Sichuan pepper before stir-frying or deep-frying to make them less cooling. It is also an ingredient in Chinese five-spice powder.

SPEARMINT
(Mentha spicata)
property: warming

Unlike cornmint and peppermint, spearmint has warming properties. It also has the ability to get rid of colds and 'flus and to aid digestion.

> ***Spearmint with food:***
> 1   Chop and add to salads.
> 2   Add to food, strawberries for instance, to give a minty flavour.

STAR ANISE
(Illicium verum)
property: warming

The Chinese use this in stews and casseroles to warm the body. I add it to *tofu* or *fu zhou* stew, with *miso*. It is one of the spices in Chinese five-spice powder.

8 Dried Ingredients

The following ingredients and their uses are peculiar to Chinese cooking. In the days before refrigeration, many foods were sun or wind dried. Dried ingredients are used as flavourers or medicines, as opposed to main ingredients, and constitute only a small part of a dish.

In this section I have included some popular Chinese herbs used as tonics. (A warning for the uninitiated: Chinese herbs often taste bitter!)

COOLING DRIED INGREDIENTS

BUDDHA'S FRUIT
(Momordica grosvenori, luo han guo)
property: cooling

This lightweight dark brown fruit is excellent for resolving phlegm in the chest.

> *To resolve thick, yellow-green sputum, mucus or phlegm:* Place ¹/₂ to 1 Buddha's fruit (broken into small pieces), a little snow ear fungus and 2 cups of water in a pot. Boil down to 1 cup. (Soak snow ear fungus overnight before cooking.)
>
> Drink this brew once a day until condition improves. Do not be surprised if you begin coughing up lots of lumpy yellow mucus; it

means the medicine is working and your chest will feel better. You may also find the bowel movements a bit loose or the stools coated with mucus or slime. This means you are passing out the sputum, mucus or phlegm.

> *To resolve thick white sputum, mucus or phlegm:* Place ¹/₄ to ¹/₂ Buddha's fruit, 25 g (1 oz) to 50 g (2 oz) dried longan and 2 cups of water in a pot. Boil down to 1 cup. (Substitute a 2¹/₂ cm (1 in) stick of cinnamon for dried longan if preferred. The longan and cinnamon have warming energies to balance the cooling energies of the Buddha's fruit.)
>
> Drink this once a day until the condition clears. You may begin coughing up a lot of mucus or urinating more frequently or pass loose stools coated with mucus or slime to expel the mucus.

CHINESE BOX THORN BERRIES
(Lycium chinese)
property: cooling

Box thorn berries are a member of the *Solanaceae* family. Unlike potatoes, tomatoes, aubergines, sweet bell peppers and chillies, they have medicinal values. They are used for heat in the liver that gives rise to sore, red eyes, headaches, a red face, bad breath and a bitter taste in the mouth.

Box thorn berries are usually added to soups (such as box thorn leaf soup, see page 90) or a chicken stew to help the old and weak build up their eyesight.

FIGS
(Ficus carica)
property: cooling

Dried figs boiled with brown rice in a congee or gruel are excellent for heat-caused constipation and dry, hard stools. You can also boil them with pot barley to make a more cooling congee or gruel.

GOLDEN NEEDLES
(Hemerocallis fulva)
property: cooling

Golden needles are supposed to be rich in iron. The Chinese usually cook them with black hair moss and black wood ears in a vegetarian dish. Try stir-frying soaked needles with other vegetables to boost your iron intake.

JOB'S TEARS
(Coix lachryma-jobi)
property: cooling

This strange looking grain of the grass family is excellent in expelling damp heat from the body and in treating cases of: gall bladder inflammation, cystitis, prostatitis, leucorrhoea with yellow discharge, pelvic inflammation, etc. Just boil 1 part Job's tears with 7-8 parts water until the grains are soft. Drink the liquid all day until the condition im-

proves. (Eat the Job's tears as well.)

Use this tea as a diuretic if you suffer from water retention.

> **Note:** Always prepare fresh Job's tears tea daily. Throw away all leftovers.

PERSIMMON
(Diospyros kaki)
property: cooling

Dried persimmons are not as cooling as fresh, but they can still be used to cool the body.

Use persimmon tea to treat diarrhoea and dysentery caused by deep-fried foods where the patient has a parched throat and mouth, especially during the hot, dry seasons. Boil 1 dried persimmon in 2 cups of water until the fruit is soft and mushy. Drink only the sweet tea and discard the residue.

Try persimmon congee for heat-caused constipation where the stools are hard, dry and knobbly.

SNOW EAR FUNGUS
(Tremella fuciformis)
property: cooling

Snow ear fungus is good for the lungs, especially for lung heat problems like thick yellow or greenish foul-smelling sputum sometimes speckled with blood.

You should see a doctor for the above symptoms because you need antibiotics. However, you can also use the remedy below in conjunction with antibiotics if the symptoms are taking a long time to clear (that is, more than one week on antibiotics and still no improvement).

Snow ear fungus can be boiled on its own, to make a tea or soup, and sweetened with barley malt extract. The weak or elderly who need strength and nourishment to overcome illness should gently simmer snow ear fungus or stew it with chicken.

NEUTRAL DRIED INGREDIENTS

BLACK WOOD EARS
(Auricularia auricula-judae)
property: neutral

This odd-looking fungus has been scientifically proven to help blood cholesterol. The Chinese normally cook it with vegetables, chicken or pork.

Those who already suffer from high blood cholesterol or whose arteries are furred up with cholesterol deposits should soak the fungus and cook it with vegetables. Those who have a tendency towards high cholesterol but still love meat should stew presoaked black wood ears with meat or, better yet, with chicken. Add Shiitake mushrooms to make an even healthier dish.

DRIED ABALONE
property: neutral

The Chinese regard dried abalone as a nourishing food. Those who can afford it usually make a chicken and abalone tonic soup that is slowly simmered for hours to extract the goodness out of the ingredients. Abalone is said to nourish the body's *yin* or, in acupuncture terms, to maintain the blood and body fluids so the body does not dry out. Abalone, then, is appropriate for old, creaky

joints that lack lubrication (synovial fluids).

DRIED OYSTERS
property: neutral

The Chinese prefer to eat dried oysters because they know fresh oysters are very difficult to digest. Dried oysters help increase breast milk in nursing mothers and help build up the blood in anaemics.

> ***Soup for increasing breast milk:*** Boil some presoaked dried oysters with white fish and a thin slice of ginger (or a few fennel seeds) to make a nourishing soup. The longer the soup simmers the more nourishing it becomes.
>
> ***Soup for blood building:*** Stew dried oysters with some black hair moss (*facai* or *fat choy*). See pages 83-84.
>
> ***Note:*** People with the following ailments must not eat fresh or dried oysters.
>> Indigestion problems
>> Gastric problems
>> Damp heat in the blood system
>> Typhoid (especially if the person is not completely cured).

DRIED SCALLOPS
property neutral

This expensive nourishing food helps strengthen the *yin of* the body. It is most appropriate for those who suffer from high blood pressure as a result of eating too many rich, greasy foods. Such people tend to have overheated blood systems.

Dried Scallops and *Kombu* Stew

Take this dish twice a week, making sure to check on blood pressure weekly. As soon as it normalises, stop eating this dish.

1 dried scallop
5 cm (2 in) piece of dried kombu
3 dried Shiitake mushrooms
1 medium onion
1 small carrot
1 thin slice ginger
pinch sea-salt
tamari
spring onions

1 Wash the dried scallop, *kombu* and Shiitake mushrooms and soak them overnight. The next day, tease the scallop into fine shreds and finely slice the *kombu* and Shiitake mushrooms. Place them all in a pot with the soaking water.

2 Finely slice the onion and carrot and put them in the pot. Add the ginger and a tiny pinch of sea-salt. Add plenty of water, bring to a boil, then simmer for 2 to 3 hours until the scallop shreds are tender. Add more or less water depending on your preference.

3 Add a dash of *tamari* just before serving and garnish with fresh spring onions.

Variation: Add finely shredded Chinese Peking cabbage.

Note: Asthmatics should not take this dish with Chinese Peking cabbage. People with cooled blood systems should avoid this dish altogether.

DRIED SHRIMPS
property: neutral

The Chinese often use presoaked dried shrimps to flavour rice and vegetables. Dried shrimps are good for those who are weak and lack energy because, when alive, shrimps are full of vital energy. Those with high blood pressure or high blood cholesterol should not eat shrimps and others should eat them in moderation, about once or twice a week.

DRIED SQUID
property: neutral

Dried squid is sold in many forms – small, large or finely shredded. Like dried shrimps, dried squid is used to flavour foods and to give vitality. It is also supposed to be good for blood building.

Dried Squid, Lotus Root and Chinese Red Date Soup

Boil 2 small dried squids with fresh or dried lotus root (3 large dried slices) and 10 Chinese red dates (stones removed) in 3 cups of water. Boil down to 1 cup.

RAISINS
(Vitis vinifera)
property: neutral

Raisins are excellent for constipation sufferers. They are also a rich source of iron. Raw raisins can cause flatulence (due to the sugar, they start to ferment in the bowels) and are best cooked.

For heat-caused constipation, see recipe for Apple and Raisin Jelly (page 85). Cook raisins for breakfast with brown rice, jumbo oats or oat groats to help relieve other kinds of constipation.

SHIITAKE MUSHROOMS
(Lentinus edodes)
property: neutral

Like black wood ears, Shiitake mushrooms have been scientifically proven to lower blood pressure and blood cholesterol. They are also said to help diabetes, anaemia, rickets, colds, 'flus, gall stones, hyperacidity, stomach ulcers and cancer.

Shiitake can be cooked with all kinds of food; the best way is to stew, braise or cook them in a casserole.

Note: Excessive consumption may lead to a condition called 'internal wind', or travelling aches and pains in the joints.

WARMING DRIED INGREDIENTS

CHINESE BLACK DATES
property: warming

Black dates are often used in Chinese medicine to neutralise medications so that they are neither too *yin* nor too *yang*. They are said to improve *qi* flow, strengthen the body, and build blood. Sometimes, I add Chinese black dates to my brown rice or oat groats for breakfast.

CHINESE RED DATES
(Zizyphus jujuba)
property: warming

Like Chinese black dates, red dates are good for building the blood. They are also used to strengthen the legs. Some Chinese families like to steam fish with Chinese red dates to remove the fishy odour.

Leg Strengthening Tea
This tea is good for strengthening the leg muscles. Boil some Chinese red dates (without the stones) with peanuts until the peanuts are soft. Liquidise this to make a creamy soup or tea. Drink the liquid.

Blood Building Soup
Boil Chinese red dates with fresh or dried lotus root. Those who are old, weak, have a cooled blood system or a tendency towards one must simmer this soup for at least 4 to 6 hours to make it less cooling. You can add fish or chicken to make it more delicious and nourishing.

Note: Always remove the stones in red dates before cooking because the stones create damp heat.

DANG GUI
(Angelica polymorpha Maxim. var. sinensis)
property: warming

Dang gui is the herb for women, while ginseng is the herb for men. Traditional Chinese women always drink *dang gui* tea at the end of their menstruation to build the blood up again and to give more energy. New mothers

also build themselves up with *dang gui* after childbirth.

Please note that *dang gui* is a warming herb. It is therefore not for anyone with an overheated blood system or tendencies towards one.

Dang gui is available only from Chinese herbalists. It comes in different shapes and sizes: roots the size of a little finger or thumb, or thin, rolled out sheets from 10 to 20 cm (4 to 8 in) long.

> *Warning: Dang gui* is very bitter and may take some getting used to. Please do not sweeten any *dang gui* tonic brews with honey or sugar to make it more palatable. This will negate the medicinal properties. Taking honey or honey water to sweeten the taste buds after a tonic brew also has the same negating effects. However, you can get rid of the bitter tonic taste by sucking one or two pieces of dried longan.

DANG SHEN
(Campanumaea pilosula)
property: warming

The Chinese use this as a poor man's substitute for ginseng. It improves the body's *qi* flow and strengthens the spleen and stomach. *Dang shen* is available from Chinese herbalists in the form of narrow, wrinkled brown roots, $3\,^3/_4$ to 20 cm ($1\,^1/_2$ to 8 in) long.

PANAX GINSENG
property: warming

Panax ginseng is the herb for men (and by that I do not mean it increases their sexual

powers). According to Chinese medicine, men have more *qi* than women, while women have more blood. In addition, men usually suffer from *qi* diseases while women usually suffer from blood diseases. Hence, *Panax ginseng* is the herb for men, because it strengthens *qi* and *dang gui* is the herb for women, because it builds the blood.

There are circumstances, however, when women suffer from lack of *qi*, especially after childbirth, in old age, or from exhaustion due to overwork. *Panax ginseng* is applicable for women in these instances.

Panax ginseng was not traditionally taken in tablet form. It was usually steeped in wine and sipped from a small glass in the evening, or double-boiled for $1^1/_2$ to 2 hours. Do not eat fish, vegetables, seaweeds, fruit or drink tea and anything with cooling energies for 24 hours after taking *Panax ginseng* or you will negate the warming effects of the herb.

> *Note: Panax ginseng* must not be taken if you have a cold (it will push the cold deeper into the body), 'flu, high blood pressure, an overheated blood system or a tendency towards one.
>
> Too much *Panax ginseng* can be dangerous, especially if you have a history of high blood pressure or if you have low blood pressure and start with too strong a dose. *Panax ginseng* should be taken cautiously.
>
> The symptoms of *Panax ginseng* poisoning are similar to those of high blood pressure: dizziness, palpitations, fast heartbeat, tightness in the chest and discomfort in the head. The antidote to *Panax ginseng* poisoning is raw Chinese radish. Start with a small raw Chinese radish. If the symptoms persist have another. Continue to take it until the symptoms clear.

HUANG SHI
(Astragalus hoantchy)
property: warming

This root strengthens the body's defensive *qi* (or *wei qi,* as it is called in acupuncture), by building up the body's resistance to external wind, cold or damp.

Chinese herbalists sell *huang shi* in long yellowish slices. Some are narrow and about 10 to 15 cm (4 to 6 in) long; others are $1^1/_4$ cm ($^1/_2$ in) wide and 20 to 30 cm (8 to 12 in) long.

DRIED LONGAN
(Nephelium longana, long yan rou)
property: warming

Dried longan is used to build up and tonify the blood for anaemia, after childbirth, when the mother has lost a lot of blood, and at the end of menstruation, to rebuild the blood.

I often cook dried longan for breakfast with brown rice, jumbo oats or oat groats.

SILVER FISH
property: warming

According to the Chinese, the vitality these fish had when they were alive is passed to us when we eat them. Their tiny edible bones are good sources of calcium and iodine.

For vitality: Wash and drain the silver fish and marinate them in ginger juice and roasted sesame oil for 1 hour. Steam on top of a pot of steaming brown rice.

For strengthening during confinement: Wash and drain the silver fish and marinate them in ginger juice and rice wine for 1 hour. Steam on top of a pot of steaming brown rice.

Note: If silver fish are not available use *ikan bilis* (dried anchovies) or tiny dried Japanese sardines. They are all available from Chinese supermarkets all over the world.

TANGERINE PEEL
(Citrus reticulata)
property: warming

When a Chinese child starts to sneeze, his mother will often give him a piece of dried tangerine peel to suck. It is a rich source of vitamin C; it aids digestion when used to make brown rice congee; it helps expel phlegm from the lungs in productive coughs (i.e., mucus is easily coughed out) with white sputum; and is used as a diuretic when cooked with aduki beans.

TONICS

Tonics are taken by the Chinese to build up the body. They are usually slowly simmered or double-boiled for a couple of hours to extract the goodness out of herbs.

Although I am not a herbalist, I am very interested in Chinese and Western herbs and their medicinal properties. The following recipes are my own concoctions which I have found very helpful. They are not for those with high blood pressure, overheated blood systems (or those who tend towards them), the strong, active or robust.

Vitality Tea
This tea is good for insomnia due to anaemia

because all the ingredients help build and tonify the blood and strengthen the spleen.

10 Chinese red dates (remove the stones)
10 lotus seeds (20 lotus seed halves)
10 pieces dried longan
2 cups water

Boil all the ingredients in a Chinese earthenware herbal pot or stainless steel pot until it has boiled down to 1 cup. Drink the liquid and eat the residue once or twice a week or daily until you are better. Then, decrease the frequency.

> *Note:* Remove the stones from the red dates before cooking, or their damp heat properties will spoil the tea.

Tea for Building Up Defensive *Qi* in Autumn, Winter and Spring

a 20-30 cm (8-12 in) slice huang shi
a 20-30 cm (8-12 in) dang shen root
10 Chinese black dates
2 cups water

1 Cut the roots into $2^1/_2$ cm (1 in) pieces.
2 Wash the dates and make a deep slit in each one so the medicinal properties will leach out during boiling.
3 Boil all the ingredients in a Chinese earthenware herbal pot or stainless steel pot until it has boiled down to 1 cup.

> *Note:* Take this tea and the black dates once a week in autumn, winter and spring. Do not eat the roots.
>
> Do not take this tea if you have a cold or 'flu or you can trap the disease in the body.

Tonic for Building Up Defensive *Qi* in the Old, Weak or Exhausted

This tonic is ideal for very cold winters. Use black-boned chicken if available.

a 20-30 cm (8-12 in) slice huang shi
a 20-30 cm (8-12 in) dang shen root
10 Chinese black dates (slit each one)
1 small portion of fresh chicken leg
1 thin slice ginger
a tiny pinch sea-salt
2 cups water

1 Remove all the skin and fat from the chicken.
2 Wash and place the chicken, and all the other ingredients, in a stainless steel or earthenware pot and bring to boil. Then simmer until only 1 cup of liquid is left. By this time, the chicken should be cooked. If not, add more water and simmer until the chicken is done.

> *Note:* Drink the soup and eat the chicken and dates. Discard the roots and ginger.
>
> Double-boil this dish to make it even more strengthening. Use only 1 cup of water and double-boil as long as possible – even up to 4 to 6 hours.
>
> Do not take this tea if you have a cold or 'flu or you can trap the disease in the body.

Tonic to Build Blood at the End of a Menstrual Period

Take this tonic on the last day of the period, or the day after. If you suffer from anaemia, take it once a week until you improve.

1 dang gui root the size of a thumb
10 Chinese red dates (remove all the stones)
5 Chinese black dates (slit each one)
2 cups water

1 Bring all the ingredients to a boil in a Chinese earthenware herbal pot or stainless steel pot until only 1 cup of liquid is left.
2 After about 20 to 30 minutes, take out the *dang gui* root, slice it very thinly and return to the pot. Drink the liquid and eat the root and dates.

> *Variation:* Use a handful of dried longan instead of the dates if you suffer from anaemia.
>
> *Warning: Dang gui* is very bitter. You may need to acquire a taste for it before you eat it regularly.

Blood Building Tonic for the Old, Weak and Anaemic

1 dang gui root the size of a thumb
1 small portion fresh chicken leg
cold-pressed sesame oil
1 thin slice ginger
tiny pinch sea-salt
10 Chinese red dates (remove all stones)

1 Steam the *dang gui* on top of a pot of steaming brown rice to soften, then slice very thinly. (I normally prepare the *dang gui* in my brown rice at lunch and cook this dish for dinner.)
2 Remove the skin and fat from the chicken. Wash and drain.
3 Heat a stainless steel or earthenware pot. Add just enough oil to coat the bottom. When the oil is hot, add the ginger slice and stir for 1 minute. Add the chicken and brown on both sides. Add 2 bowls of water, a tiny pinch of sea-salt, the prepared dates and *dang gui*. Bring to a boil and simmer until one bowl of liquid is left. Drink the liquid and eat all the contents.

Double-boiled *Panax Ginseng* and Dried Longan

The amount of *Panax ginseng* you use depends on your level of exhaustion and fatigue. I use the smallest amount for myself to boost my energy when I eat too much seaweed. If possible, consult a Chinese herbalist to determine how much is best for you.

1 handful dried longan
2 cups water
2 ¹/₂ cm (1 in) sliver Panax ginseng

1 Boil the dried longan and the water in a Chinese earthenware herbal pot until 1 cup is left (to extract the sweetness and goodness from the longan).
2 Strain the tea, add the *Panax ginseng* and double-boil for 1¹/₂ hours. Drink the tea and eat the softened *Panax ginseng*.

> *Note:* The combination of *Panax ginseng* and dried longan both improves the *qi* and builds up the blood. Therefore, it is excellent for new mothers who need to regain their strength.
>
> Remember, *Panax ginseng* must not be taken for a cold or 'flu. Wait until you have completely recovered before drinking it again. Do not eat the following foods 24 hours after taking *Panax ginseng:* fish, vegetables, seaweeds, fruits, tea, anything with cooling energies or ice-cold, refrigerated or leftover foods.

9 Eggs

Eggs are compact little bundles of nutrients essential for the growth of the embryos they contain. Man can use them to give him vitality too. However, be careful not to take too many for the reasons given below.

CHICKEN EGGS
property: warming

The Chinese use chicken eggs to nourish the old, weak and exhausted. Eggs should not be eaten by people with high blood pressure, high blood cholesterol and those who are prone to catarrh, sputum, phlegm or mucus. They are mucus forming and, because of their rich protein content, difficult to digest.

Vegetarians who use chicken eggs as a protein source should cook them in the manner described below to aid digestion.

One large egg is enough for one person per meal, and two to three large eggs per week is sufficient. The body cannot cope with more than that, especially if you do not exercise daily, have a sluggish metabolism, are approaching middle age, or are more than 70 years old.

However, if you are a manual labourer or a vegetarian who lives on beans and eggs, then five to six large eggs a week is safe. If you eat cheese as well, then two to three large

eggs a week is more than enough.

Only free-range eggs are recommended. Battery eggs are not advisable because the hens are fed all kinds of chemicals, including hormones and antibiotics.

Note: The following foods aid the digestibility of eggs (and pasta and noodles): ginger, leeks, onions, chives, Chinese chives, shallots, spring onions, Shiitake mushrooms, black wood ears, parsley, marjoram and thyme. They appear quite often in the following recipes.

Egg Drop Soup
This recipe makes chicken eggs more cooling and easier on the digestion. Egg drop soup is suitable for people with high blood cholesterol and high blood pressure who just cannot give up chicken eggs. It is also appropriate for hot summer days or hot climates.

3 dried Shiitake mushrooms
tiny pinch sea-salt
1 medium leek
ginger
1 large egg
roasted sesame oil

1   Wash the Shiitake mushrooms and soak them in 1 cup of hot water. When soft, cut into thin slices. Save the soaking water.

2 Put the soaking water and another cup of fresh water into a pot. Add the Shiitake slices and bring to a fast rolling boil with a tiny pinch of sea-salt.
3 Wash and finely slice the leek. Add to the boiling stock with a thin slice of ginger. Boil the stock down to 1 cup.
4 Just before serving, crack an egg into the stock and stir vigorously so that you get fine strands of yellow 'egg webs'. Add a drop of roasted sesame oil for aroma.

Variations: Make a stock as above using the following ingredients.
1   Ginger, onion, carrot, angled luffa, black wood ears and Shiitake mushrooms.
2   Ginger, onion, carrot, Chinese Peking cabbage and tender green peas.
3   Ginger, onion, carrot and celery.
4   Ginger, onion and peppermint.
5   Ginger, onion and nettles.
*6 Ginger, cooked brown rice, onion, Shiitake mushroom and roasted sesame oil.
*7 Substitute cooked pot barley or oat groats for cooked brown rice in no. 6.
*8 Ginger, whole wheat pasta, onion, carrot, fresh mushrooms and thyme.
*9 Ginger, whole wheat pasta, onion, Brussels sprouts and marjoram.

* This is a complete meal because it contains grain, egg and vegetables.

Steamed Eggs

The best way to make chicken eggs more neutral is to steam them. Steamed eggs are very easy to digest and, therefore, excellent for young children, invalids and the elderly. They are ideal on hot summer days or in hot climates.

1 large egg
ginger
tiny pinch sea-salt
roasted sesame oil
tamari
fresh herbs

1 Break an egg into a heat-proof dish.
2 Add an equal portion of water. (I measure half an egg-shellful of water twice.)
3 Add a little grated ginger, a pinch of sea-salt and a drop of roasted sesame oil for aroma and taste. Beat thoroughly to mix. Place the heat-proof dish with the egg mixture in a steaming basket and steam on gentle heat for 5 to 7 minutes in a covered wok or pot until the egg sets.
4 Add a dash of *tamari* and garnish with some finely chopped fresh herbs like spring onion, parsley or chives.

Note: If you do not wish to eat the ginger, use a thin slice of ginger which can be removed. Leave out the ginger if serving to children.

Variations:
1   Steam the finely chopped herbs together with the egg.
2   Try other herbs and spices such as nutmeg, marjoram, thyme and bay leaves.
3   In summer, add fresh tender green peas. If the peas are old, blanch them until just cooked, then add to the egg mixture.
4   Mince and stir-fry the following ingredients, then add them to the egg mixture to be steamed
    • onion (garnish steamed egg with a bay leaf)
    • onion (or leek) and 3 presoaked Shiitake mushrooms

- leek (or spring onions) and Chinese Peking cabbage
- onion (or shallots), tender young spinach and nutmeg
- onion (or shallots), watercress and black pepper
- onion (or leek), celery and black pepper

Scrambled Eggs

Scrambling eggs in a little hot oil with ginger makes them even more warming. Such dishes are for the weak and those who feel the cold easily. They are appropriate for cold autumn, winter and spring days.

1 large egg
sea-salt
roasted sesame oil
ginger
chives or Chinese chives
cold-pressed sesame oil

1 Break the egg into a bowl. Add half an egg-shellful of water. Beat with a tiny pinch of sea-salt and 1 drop of roasted sesame oil.
2 Finely mince the ginger. Wash the chives and cut into $2^1/_2$ cm (1 in) lengths.
3 Heat a wok. When hot, add just enough oil to coat the bottom. When the oil is hot, add the ginger and stir for 1 minute. Add the chives and a tiny pinch of sea-salt and stir until limp. Then add the egg mixture and stir until cooked.

Variations: Stir-fry the following ingredients before adding the egg mixture.
1 Ginger, onion, fresh mushrooms and parsley (or thyme)
2 Ginger, leek and Shiitake mushrooms

3 Ginger, leek and celery
4 Ginger, onion and peppermint
5 Ginger, onion, angled luffa (or fuzzy melon) and black wood ears.

QUAIL EGGS
property: warming

Quail eggs are as warming and nourishing as chicken eggs and can be prepared the same way (see recipes above). Two or three quail eggs are equivalent to one large chicken egg. The Chinese often use quail eggs as garnishes.

Note: Use only free-range quail eggs.

PRESERVED QUAIL EGGS
property: cooling

Quail eggs become cooling once they have been fermented. They are not as cooling as preserved duck eggs, however, because duck eggs have cooling properties to begin with. If you like preserved eggs and have a cooled blood system (or a tendency towards one) then eat preserved quail eggs instead. Do not have more than three in a fortnight and serve them with ginger pickled only in sea-salt and rice vinegar.

DUCK EGGS
property: cooling

These large blue-green eggs are not considered as nourishing as chicken eggs because they have cooling energies. The Chinese do not use them often because of their strong odour and taste.

The cooling natures of duck eggs and Chinese spinach help cool down the overheated lungs of smokers. See recipe on page 91.

> *Note:* Duck eggs are said to be mildly irritating. If you have a skin infection or wound which is healing it may make it itch. People with skin diseases, infections or healing wounds should avoid them until they are completely well.

SALTED DUCK EGGS
property: cooling

Salted duck eggs are soaked in brine and charcoal dust for a period of time, and dried, scraped and washed before cooking.

They are used in egg drop soups and congees for a cooling meal, especially during the hot, dry seasons. They can be beaten with a chicken egg and steamed to make the chicken egg less warming.

Salted duck eggs should not be taken by anyone with high blood pressure or high blood cholesterol, or anyone suffering from water retention or kidney problems.

> *Note:* Salted duck eggs are mildly irritating, causing itches if you have a skin infection or healing wound. People with skin diseases, infections or healing wounds should avoid them.

PRESERVED DUCK EGGS
property: cooling

Duck eggs are preserved in wood chips and mud for about 100 days. During that time, certain types of bacteria transform them into hard-boiled eggs – the egg white turns into a black gelatin-like substance while the yolk becomes soft, pasty and green/grey/black in colour. Such eggs have a very strong odour and taste that is definitely acquired.

Preserved duck eggs are usually served with pickled stem ginger. The pickles stimulate the salivary glands while the ginger aids the digestion of the egg. Sometimes preserved eggs are minced and steamed with beaten chicken eggs or chopped and added to a fish and coriander soup.

Preserved duck eggs are not to be eaten frequently because they are very difficult to digest. The occasional egg is fine as long as it is prepared with plenty of ginger to aid digestion.

> *Note:* Like all types of duck eggs, preserved eggs are not for those with skin diseases, infections or healing wounds.

FISH EGGS
property: cooling

Because fish are cooling, their eggs are cooling too. Like chicken, quail and duck eggs, fish eggs are rich in cholesterol and must be avoided by people with high blood pressure and high blood cholesterol. Fish eggs are not as mucus-forming as the others but they are equally difficult to digest and should be cooked with ginger, onions, leeks, chives, shallots, spring onions, Shiitake mushrooms, black wood ears, parsley, marjoram or thyme. You can also add coriander, dill, or fennel leaves and seeds to aid digestion and remove the fishy odour.

Poached Cod Roe

110 g (4 oz) cod roe
ginger
1 medium onion
fresh coriander leaves
cold-pressed sesame oil
tiny pinch sea-salt
roasted sesame oil

1 Wash and drain the cod roe.
2 Finely mince a thin slice of ginger, finely dice the onion and finely chop the fresh coriander leaves.
3 Heat a wok. When hot, add just enough oil to coat the bottom. When the oil is hot, add the ginger and stir 1 minute. Add the onion and a tiny pinch of sea-salt and stir until glassy. Add the coriander leaves and stir for 1 minute. Then add just enough water to cover. Simmer for 30 minutes.
4 Add the cod roe to the simmering stock and poach for 5 to 7 minutes or until the roe is cooked.
5 Add a drop of roasted sesame oil just before serving.

Variations:
1 Use ginger, onion, coriander seeds and leaves.
2 Use ginger, onion, dill weed and seeds.
3 Use ginger, onion and fennel bulb, leaves and seeds.
4 Use ginger, leeks and black pepper.
5 Use ginger, onion, fresh mushrooms and thyme.

Note: Fish eggs are mild irritants. Anyone with a skin disease, infection or a healing wound should avoid them.

EGGS FOR BABIES AND INFANTS

Very young babies should not be given eggs because they are difficult to digest, and can make them susceptible to catarrh or lung infections.

Once the infants begin to chew their food, give them no more than one small egg a week. Increase their allowance to three small eggs per week maximum, then from small eggs to medium to large eggs. If the child shows symptoms of catarrh such as runny, stuffy or blocked nose, frequent colds, etc., stop the eggs altogether until the condition improves. Then build the child's intake up to only one to two eggs a week maximum.

Start giving children eggs in the form of egg drop soup or egg drop congee using a vegetable stock of onion, leek, celery, spinach or watercress.

To make egg drop congee, just break an egg into a bowl of piping hot brown rice congee and stir vigorously to break up the egg. Serve with a dash of *tamari* and chopped spring onions. For variety, make brown rice congee with vegetables like onion, leek, celery, spinach or watercress.

The warming onion or leek brown rice congees are more suitable for winter, or for a child who suffers from the cold easily. The cooling vegetable brown rice congees of celery, spinach or watercress are more for the

summer or hot countries and for children who tend to suffer from constipation with hard, dry stools.

As children grow older, give them plain steamed eggs. The variation with stir-fried vegetables (see pages 136-137) may be too difficult to chew so you can liquidise them before steaming. Once children can chew, give them poached cod roe, but use a vegetable stock without fennel, coriander and dill seeds.

I would not advise giving young children duck eggs in any form. Chicken and quail eggs are fine, provided they are free-range.

10 Fish and Other Seafoods

The Chinese regard fish as the second most important source of protein – after *tofu* and other soyabean products, and before chicken, duck, goose and quail eggs. Fish also contains minerals like iodine that are lacking in land plants.

The Chinese prefer fish to eggs and chicken because it is very easy to digest. To the Chinese, a food must be easily digested or it will tax the body's strength and metabolism. Undigested or poorly digested food easily accumulates in the body in the form of fatty deposits. People who wish to lose or maintain their weight should go on a grain, legume, pulse, vegetable and fish diet.

Scientists have recently discovered that oily fish contain a special polyunsaturated fatty acid, called docosahexaenoic acid (DHA), essential for brain functions. Now we know that there is truth in the saying 'fish is good for the brain'. Oily fish also contains another polyunsaturated fatty acid called eicosapentaenoic acid (EPA) which helps prevent blood clots and therefore heart attacks. White fish also contains DHA and EPA but to a lesser quantity.

Unfortunately, many people avoid fish because they are put off by fishy odours. If fish is fresh, however, the odour is hardly noticeable. Look around for a fishmonger in your area who stocks fresh fish daily and ask him what time his orders come in.

Some fishmongers in Germany only sell fish on days when they can get it fresh. The French are as particular as the Chinese about freshness and in Spain and Italy I saw people selling fresh fish daily. In Penang and Singapore, the fish is very fresh, but not as fresh as that sold in Hong Kong, where you can choose live fish from tanks of fresh or salt water. The fishmonger cleans and prepares the fish for you – all you have to do is add the ingredients and cook.

Throughout the world, people of different cultures have taken great pains to find out which herbs or spices can remove fishy odours. The Chinese use ginger, garlic, leeks, shallots, chives, Chinese chives, spring onions, coriander leaves, black pepper, Chinese red dates, rice wine or rice vinegar. The Indians use ginger, garlic, coriander seeds and leaves, cumin seeds, turmeric and lemon.

The Malays use garlic, spring onion, Chinese celery, coriander leaves and seeds, fennel seeds, cumin seeds, mustard seeds, turmeric, black pepper, tamarind and lemon or lime leaves, while Penang Peranakans (Straits Chinese) prefer ginger, garlic, shallots, spring onions, Chinese celery, coriander leaves, black pepper, tamarind, lemongrass, lime, turmeric and rice vinegar. The Northern Europeans use lemon, dill seeds, dill weed, bay leaf, mustard, black pepper, parsley,

vinegar or wine, and the Southern Europeans like garlic, lemon, fennel bulb, leaves and seeds, mustard, black pepper, parsley, tarragon, oregano, marjoram, rosemary, wine or vinegar.

All types of fish have cooling energies because they are aquatic creatures. However, within this cooling energy group, some kinds of fish have more neutral or warmer energies compared to others. If you wish to cool an overheated blood system, select the cooler energy fishes. If you wish to maintain a neutral blood system, eat the more neutral varieties. And, if you wish to warm yourself up for autumn and winter, choose more warming fish.

In this chapter, I have grouped the different kinds of fish into white and oily varieties. White fish are easier to digest than oily fish, and oily fish tend to have a stronger odour, especially when they are not fresh.

TEMPERATE WATER FISH

(The months in brackets indicate the period during which the fish is in season and hence at its best and freshest.)

White Fish
Bass *(May – Aug)*
Bream, sea *(Jun – Dec)*
Brill *(Jan – Apr)*
Cod *(Oct – Apr) Warming*
Coley *(all year round)*
Dab *(Apr – Jan)*
Dogfish, huss, rigg, flake *(Sep – May)*
Flounder *(Sep – Feb)*
Haddock *(Nov – Feb)*

Hake *(Jul – Mar)*
Halibut *(Aug – Apr)*
Plaice *(Jan – Apr)*
Rockfish, catfish *(Sep – Feb)*
Skate *(Oct – Apr)*
Sole, Dover *(May – Feb)*
Sole, lemon *(Dec – Mar)*
Turbot *(Apr – Jul)*
Whiting *(all year round)*
Witch, Aberdeen dole, megrim *(Aug – Apr)*

Oily Fish
*Carp *(mid Jun – Mar) Warming*
*Eel, common *(autumn – early winter) Warming*
Eel, conger *(Mar – Oct) Cooling*
Herring *(Jun – Mar) Neutral*
Mackerel *(winter and spring) Neutral*
*Mullet, grey *(Jul – Feb)*
Mullet, red *(May – Sep)*
*Perch *(Jun 16 – Mar 14)*
*Pike *(Jun 16 – Mar 14)*
Salmon *(May – Jul)*
Sardine *(Mar – Sep) Neutral*
Smelt or sparling *(Jan – Mar)*
Sprat *(Nov – Mar)*
*Trout, rainbow *(all year round) Warming*
Whitebait *(Feb – Jul)*

* These are freshwater fish. The grey mullet is an estuary fish.

TROPICAL WATER FISH

White Fish
Grouper
Plaice
Pomfret *(ikan bawal putih)*
Red lipped half-beak *(ikan jolong-jolong)*
Red snapper *(ikan merah)*
Sea perch *(ikan siakap or ikan kerapu)*
Sole *(ikan lidah)*
Threadfin *(ikan kurau)*
Whiting *(ikan bulos-bulos)*

Oily Fish
Herring *(ikan parang)*
Mackerel family *(ikan tongkol, ikan kembong, ikan selar, ikan kuning, ikan tenggiri)*
Sardine *(ikan tambon siseh)*
Torpedo *(ikan cencaru)*

COOLING COOKING METHODS

White Fish Soup
This dish is very easy to digest, and suitable for young children, the elderly, invalids, people with high blood pressure, high blood cholesterol and overheated blood systems. It is excellent for hot summer days or hot climates.

1 small whole white fish
sea-salt
1 thin slice ginger
3 spring onions
freshly ground black pepper
1 drop roasted sesame oil

1 Scale and gut the fish and discard the entrails. Cut off the head and tail and fillet the fish.

2 Rinse the head, tail and skeleton, and put them in a pot. If the skeleton is too long break it up into sections. Add 2 cups of water, a tiny pinch of sea-salt, 1 thin slice of ginger and 2 of the spring onions, sliced into $2^{1}/_{2}$ cm (1 in) lengths. Bring to a fast rolling boil, then reduce the heat and simmer until 1 cup of liquid is left. Strain the stock and bring back to a simmer.

3 Meanwhile, rinse the fillets, thinly slice them and marinate with a tiny pinch of sea-salt, a dash of freshly ground black pepper, a drop of roasted sesame oil and the remaining spring onion, finely chopped.

4 When the strained stock has come back to a simmer, add the marinated fish slices and simmer for another 1 to 2 minutes or until just cooked. (*Caution*: if you simmer them too long they will become tough and fibrous.) Serve as soon as possible. Cold fish soup has an even stronger fishy odour.

Note: If you do not know how to fillet fish, ask the fishmonger to do it for you. If he is unwilling to fillet a small fish ask him to do a larger fish; use one fillet with the carcass for the soup and keep the other for the next day. If it is not possible to buy whole fish, skin the fillet and use the skin for the stock.

Variations: The following alternatives are appropriate for overheated blood systems, and hot, dry summer days or climates.
1 Add chopped Chinese or English celery.
2 Add chopped fennel bulb.
3 Add 1 cm ($^{1}/_{2}$ in) slices of courgettes, angled luffa or fuzzy melon.
4 Add black wood ears.
5 Add Shiitake mushrooms.

6 Add a small quantity of a seaweed such as *kombu, wakame, hiziki, arame, nori,* purple seaweed, laverbread, dulse, carageen or black hair moss.

The following additions will make the soup more neutral.

1 Add onion.
2 Add carrot.
3 Add snow peas.
4 Add baby sweet corn or sweet corn kernels.
5 Add onion and carrot.
6 Add onion, carrot and snow peas.
7 Add onion, snow peas, and baby sweet corn.

These variations make the soup less cooling.

If it is still not warming enough, stir-fry the carcass with a little cold-pressed sesame oil and some garlic until the garlic is fragrant and golden. Then add water to make the stock.

1 Add a bay leaf.
2 Add 2 black peppercorns.
3 Add 5 coriander seeds and freshly chopped coriander stalks, and discard them with the carcass after the stock is strained. Add finely chopped coriander leaves to the fish marinade with the spring onion.
4 Add a pinch of dill seeds and freshly chopped dill weed stalks, and discard them with the carcass after the stock is strained. Add finely chopped dill weed leaves to the fish marinade.
5 Add a pinch of fennel seeds and finely chopped fennel leaves to the strained stock and simmer for 10 minutes before adding the marinated fish slices.
6 Add 1 heaped teaspoon dried lemongrass to the stock, and discard it with the carcass.

Fish Congee

Fish congee is also very easy to digest. A cooling congee can be made with pot barley or millet, a less cooling variety with brown rice, and a more or less neutral congee with oat groats.

Fish congee with pot barley or millet is good for gall bladder inflammation, cystitis, prostatitis and stomach ulcers due to too much heat in the stomach. People with these ailments should marinate the fish slices in only spring onions, sea-salt and 1 drop of roasted sesame oil, and leave out the freshly ground black pepper.

Brown rice congee is suitable for everyone. Those with overheated blood systems should choose any of the cooling variations listed under White Fish Soup on page 143 and add raw lettuce. Those with cooled blood systems should choose any of the warming variations on this page, or stir-fry the fish carcass before making the stock.

Fish congee made with oat groats is good for people with diabetes, high blood pressure and high blood cholesterol. Choose cooling variations from pages 143-144 and serve with raw lettuce. Oat groat congee is also appropriate for people with cooled blood systems. Again, choose warming variations from this page and leave out raw lettuce.

White Fish Congee

1 small whole white fish
¹/₄ cup whole cereal grains
sea-salt
1 thin slice ginger
3 spring onions
3 cups water
freshly ground black pepper
1 drop roasted sesame oil

1 Prepare the fish as for fish soup (see page 143). Place the carcass, washed whole cereal grains, tiny pinch of sea-salt, ginger, $2^1/_2$ cm (1 in) lengths of 2 spring onions and 3 cups of water in a pot. Bring to a fast rolling boil, then simmer until the grains are cooked. Add more water if necessary. The congee can be thin or thick, as preferred, depending on the water added and the simmering time.

2 Meanwhile, rinse the fillets, thinly slice them and marinate in a tiny pinch of sea-salt, a dash of freshly ground black pepper, a drop of roasted sesame oil and the remaining spring onion, finely chopped.

3 When the whole cereal grains are cooked and the congee has reached the consistency you desire, remove the fish carcass, add the marinated fish slices and simmer until the slices are just cooked, about 1 to 2 minutes. Serve as soon as possible.

Note: Place the fish carcass in a loose-weave muslin bag for easy retrieval.

Steamed Fish

Steamed fish is the Chinese way of presenting fresh fish at its very best – whether in a fine Chinese restaurant or at home. Great care is taken to steam the fish until just cooked. A minute or two longer can render the flesh tough and fibrous. Ideally, the flesh should be smooth, moist, succulent and come away from the bone easily. It does not matter if the bone is slightly pink, as long as the flesh falls away easily.

Steamed Whole White Fish

Steamed whole fish is also very easy to digest. It is suitable for everyone, and especially for young children, the elderly and the sick.

The recipe that follows is very basic. There are many variations on the same theme, as you will see.

1 small whole white fish
tiny pinch sea-salt
1 thin slice ginger
3 spring onions
1 drop roasted sesame oil
tamari

1 Scale and gut the fish. Rinse and drain. Make a few deep cuts on both sides of the fish so the flesh cooks easily and quickly.

2 Place the fish on a heat-proof dish and marinate for 30 to 60 minutes with a tiny pinch of sea-salt, finely sliced ginger, 2 spring onions, finely chopped, and 1 drop of roasted sesame oil.

3 Bring some water to a boil in a wok or large pan, place the steamer inside and rest the heat-proof dish on top. Cover with a lid and steam for 8 to 10 minutes, depending on the thickness of the fish.

4 Garnish with the remaining spring onion, chopped, and a dash of *tamari*.

Note: It is quite an art to know just when to stop steaming. Judge by the thickness of the fish: approximately 8 minutes for a thin fish and 10 minutes for a thick fish. I use the eyes as an indicator most of the time, and it works. When they become white and opaque, the fish is done. Sometimes, you may have to use a fork to test whether the flesh comes easily away from the bone. If it does, the fish is cooked. Remember to place the fish on the steamer when the water has come to a fast rolling boil, and to time the fish from that point.

Variations:

Cooling garnishes

1   Add fine strips of boiled black wood ears.

2   Add fine strips of Shiitake mushrooms.

3   Add finely chopped Chinese or English celery.

Neutral garnishes

1   Add fine strips of boiled black wood ears and finely chopped coriander leaves.

2   Add fine strips of Shiitake mushrooms marinated with a dash of *tamari* and finely chopped coriander leaves.

3   Add sprigs of rosemary leaves.

4   Add *miso* mixed with garlic and finely chopped coriander leaves.

5   Add strips of Chinese red dates and Shiitake mushrooms marinated with a dash of *tamari* and finely chopped coriander leaves.

Warming garnishes

1   Stir-fry minced garlic in as little cold-pressed oil as possible. Add just before serving with the chopped spring onion.

2   Add a stir-fried sauce of minced garlic, fermented black soyabeans, ginger, some thinned out *miso* and some chopped coriander leaves. Spread over the fish before steaming.

3   Add a stir-fried sauce of minced shallots, *miso* and Chinese celery leaves. Pour over the fish before steaming.

4   Add a stir-fried sauce of minced onion, fennel seeds, *miso* and fennel leaves. Pour over the fish before steaming.

5   Add a stir-fried sauce of minced onion, cumin seeds and *miso*. Pour over the fish before steaming.

NEUTRAL COOKING METHODS

Tamari Braised Fish

This is a more neutral way of preparing easily digestible white or oily fish.

110-175 g (4-6 oz) white fish fillet
tiny pinch sea-salt
$^1/_2$ dessertspoon tamari
1 drop roasted sesame oil
1 clove garlic
1 thin slice ginger
cold-pressed sesame oil
1 spring onion

1   Wash and drain the fillet. Slice into 8 x 3 cm (3 x 1 in) slices.

2   Marinate the slices for 30 minutes with a tiny pinch of sea-salt, *tamari,* 2 dessert-spoons of water and 1 drop of roasted sesame oil.

3   Finely mince the garlic and ginger.

4   Heat a wok. When hot, add just enough oil to coat the bottom. When the oil is hot, add the garlic and ginger and stir for 1 minute. Lower the heat and add the fish slices. Then slowly pour in the marinade and simmer gently until the fish slices are just cooked, about 5 to 6 minutes.

5   Garnish with finely chopped spring onion.

Variations:

1   Add a dash of freshly ground black pepper to the marinade to make the dish slightly warmer.

2   Stir-fry 1 small finely minced onion (after the garlic and ginger) until the onion is soft and glassy, then add the fish slices to make a

tastier and thicker sauce. You may need slightly more *tamari* and water.

3 Add a few coriander seeds, fennel seeds or 1 star anise to the minced onion to make the dish more warming and aromatic.

Braised Fish with Vegetables

110-175 g (4-6 oz) white fish fillet
sea-salt
1 clove garlic
1 thin slice ginger
1 small onion
1 small carrot
2 stalks celery
cold-pressed sesame oil
chopped parsley

1 Wash and drain the fillet. Slice into 8 x 3 cm (3 x 1 in) slices and marinate with a tiny pinch of sea-salt.
2 Finely mince the garlic and ginger. Dice the onion, carrot and celery into 1 cm ($^1/_2$ in) cubes.
3 Heat a wok. When hot, add just enough oil to coat the bottom. When the oil is hot, add the garlic and ginger and stir for 1 minute. Add the onion and another tiny pinch of sea-salt and stir until glassy. Add the celery and stir for 2 minutes. Then add the carrot and just enough water to cover the bottom of the wok. Add the fish slices and simmer for 5 to 6 minutes or until just cooked.
4 Garnish with chopped parsley.

Variations:
1 Use fennel bulb instead of celery. Add fennel seeds.
2 Use dill weed and seeds instead of celery.

3 Use coriander leaves and seeds instead of celery.
4 Add snow peas or tender garden peas.
5 Use a vegetable combination of onion, baby sweet corn and snow peas.

Braised Fish with Lemongrass

1 small herring or mackerel
sea-salt
1 clove garlic
1 thin slice ginger
1 small onion
cold-pressed sesame oil
1 teaspoon dried lemongrass
$^1/_2$ dessertspoon tamari
spring onions

1 Scale, gut, wash and drain the fish. Rub with a tiny pinch of sea-salt and leave to marinate.
2 Finely mince the garlic, ginger and onion.
3 Heat a wok. When hot, add just enough oil to coat the bottom. When the oil is hot, add the garlic and ginger and stir for 1 minute. Add the minced onion, another tiny pinch of sea-salt and the lemongrass. Stir on medium heat until the onion is soft and glassy. Then add the *tamari* mixed with 2 dessertspoons of water and simmer gently for 15 minutes. Add the fish and braise until just cooked, about 10 to 15 minutes depending on the size of the fish.
4 Garnish with finely chopped spring onions.

Note: The dried lemongrass is not meant to be eaten. If you do not like it in the dish you can boil the lemongrass beforehand in some water

until only the water is flavoured by it. Then use this lemongrass water to mix with the *tamari* at step 3.

Variations:
1 Use shallots instead of onion.
2 Use tamarind paste or dried tamarind instead of lemongrass to give a slightly sour taste and to further aid the digestion of oily fish.

WARMING COOKING METHODS

Sautéed Fish

Sautéeing is more warming than the previously mentioned cooking methods because it requires less water. It is appropriate for cold autumn, winter and spring days, for the weak, those who feel the cold easily, and those who have or tend to have cooled blood systems. If you sauté a less digestible oily fish, take care to add vegetables, herbs and spices that will aid digestion.

Sautéed White Fish

110-175 g (4-6 oz) white fish cutlet
tiny pinch sea-salt
freshly ground black pepper
1 thin slice ginger
1 clove garlic
cold-pressed sesame oil
herbs

1 Wash and drain the cutlet. Marinate for 30 minutes with a tiny pinch of sea-salt and a dash of freshly ground black pepper.
2 Finely mince the ginger and garlic.
3 Heat a wok. When hot, add just enough oil to coat the bottom. When the oil is hot,

add the ginger and garlic and stir for 1 minute. Then lower the heat and add the cutlet. Brown slowly on both sides until the fish is cooked.
4 Garnish with finely chopped herbs like parsley, chives, fennel leaves, dill leaves or coriander leaves.

Variations: Marinate the cutlet for 30 minutes in $^1/_2$ dessertspoon of *tamari* mixed with 2 dessertspoons of water and some freshly ground black pepper. Drain off the marinade before sautéeing. Boil the marinade for 2 to 3 minutes to use as a sauce. Add some fresh herbs like chopped parsley, spring onions, chives, coriander leaves, fennel leaves or dill weed to the marinade as it boils.

Sautéed Leek and Herring

1 small herring (or mackerel)
sea-salt
freshly ground black pepper
1 thin slice ginger
1 medium leek
cold-pressed sesame oil

1 Scale, gut, wash and drain the fish. Marinate for 30 minutes with a tiny pinch of sea-salt and a dash of freshly ground black pepper.
2 Finely mince the ginger and finely slice the leek.
3 Heat a wok. When hot, add just enough oil to coat the bottom. When the oil is hot, add the ginger and stir for 1 minute. Add the leek and another tiny pinch of sea-salt and stir on medium heat until the leek is limp. Then add the herring and sauté on low heat until just cooked. Remember to

brown both sides slightly.

Baked Fish

Baking is an excellent cooking method for winter. I like to bake fish with plenty of vegetables to add more taste.

Baked White Fish with Fennel

110-175 g (4-6 oz) white fish fillet
sea salt
freshly ground black pepper
1 clove garlic
1 thin slice ginger
1 small fennel bulb
cold-pressed sesame oil
$^1/_8$ teaspoon fennel seeds
fennel leaves

1 Wash and drain the fish and cut into 8 x 3 cm (3 x 1 in) slices. Place in a heat-proof dish and marinate for 30 minutes with a tiny pinch of sea-salt and a dash of freshly ground black pepper.

2 Preheat the oven to 250°C or 500°F. Finely mince the garlic and ginger and dice the fennel bulb into 1 cm ($^1/_2$ in) cubes.

3 Heat a wok. When hot, add just enough oil to coat the bottom. When the oil is hot, add the garlic and ginger and stir for 1 minute. Add the fennel bulb and seeds and stir for 2 minutes. Then add just enough water to cover the fennel and a tiny pinch of sea-salt. Simmer until the fennel is soft, then pour the mixture around the fish slices. Make sure there is enough liquid to keep the food from burning.

4 Bake on the highest rung of the hot oven for 8 to 10 minutes, depending on the thickness of the slices.

Baked White Fish with *Miso*

110-175 g (4-6 oz) white fish fillet
ginger
tiny pinch sea-salt
freshly ground black pepper
1 drop roasted sesame oil
2 spring onions
1 teaspoon genmai miso

1 Wash and drain the fish and cut into 8 x 3 cm (3 x 1 in) slices. Place in a heat-proof dish and marinate for 30 minutes in some grated ginger, a tiny pinch of sea-salt, freshly ground black pepper, 1 drop of roasted sesame oil, the onion whites of 2 finely sliced spring onions, and 1 teaspoon of *genmai miso* thinned out with some warm water. Make sure there is enough liquid in the *miso* sauce to cover the fish slices and the bottom of the heat-proof dish so that the food does not burn. However, do not add so much water that the fish slices float in it.

2 Preheat the oven to 250°C or 500°F. Bake on the highest rung of the oven for 8 to 10 minutes depending on the thickness of the slices.

3 Garnish with the remaining spring onion greens, finely sliced.

> *Variations:*
> 1 Use coriander leaves, chives or parsley instead of spring onions.
> 2 Use $^1/_2$ dessertspoon of *tamari* and 2 dessertspoons of water instead of *miso*.
> 3 Add a bay leaf or other herbs.

Baked Oily Fish

1 small herring (or mackerel) fillet
ginger
tiny pinch sea-salt
juice of 1 lemon
parsley

1 Wash and drain the fillet. Place in a heat-proof dish and marinate for 30 minutes in some grated ginger, a tiny pinch of sea-salt and the lemon juice. (If you like, add the zest of the lemon, but grate it before squeezing the juice.) There should be enough lemon juice to wet the heat-proof dish to prevent the fish from burning. If not, add just enough water to wet the dish and the entire fillet.

2 Preheat oven to 250°C or 500°F. Bake on the highest rung of the oven for 8 to 10 minutes or until just cooked, depending on the thickness of the fillet.

3 Garnish with finely chopped parsley.

> *Variations:*
> 1 Use rice vinegar or cider vinegar instead of lemon juice.
> 2 Use turmeric powder mixed with water instead of lemon juice.
> 3 Use tamarind pulp and water instead of lemon juice.
> 4 Use mustard powder mixed with water and finely minced garlic instead of lemon juice.

Grilled Fish

Grilling is the most heating cooking method and, therefore, not advisable on a daily basis. Grilling once a month is about right for people with overheated blood systems or tendencies towards one.

Whole, small white or oily fish are fun for parties or barbecues and they are easy to prepare. Just marinate them for 1 to 2 hours in herbs or spices such as

- turmeric, ginger, garlic and water
- mustard, ginger, garlic and water
- tamarind, ginger, garlic and water
- lemon juice, ginger and garlic
- lemon juice, ginger, garlic and rosemary
- lemon juice, ginger, garlic and oregano

Try cutting white fish fillets into chunks,

marinating them in one of the above marinades, and skewering them onto *satay* or *kebab* sticks with onions, mushrooms and pumpkin.

OTHER SEAFOOD

Cockles
Crab
Lobster
Mussels
Octopus
Oysters
Periwinkles
Prawns
Scallops
Shrimps
Squid
Whelks

The Chinese eat the above seafood infrequently because they are harder to digest. When they are used they usually make up only one third of the dish; the remaining two thirds are composed of vegetables. Often, they are used merely as flavourers rather than protein sources.

People suffering from high blood pressure, high blood cholesterol, food allergies, skin diseases, infections or inflammations of any kind, migraines, indigestion, arthritis and rheumatism should avoid these foods. They are rich in cholesterol, difficult to digest and have cold energies.

Occasionally, people who are low on energy can have a small amount of prawns, shrimps or squid stir-fried with lots of vegetables to build them up. The Chinese believe that the energy these creatures had when alive can be imparted to the eater.

Stir-fried Prawns with Spring Onions

2 large prawns
sea-salt
freshly ground black pepper
1 clove garlic
1 thin slice ginger
6 large spring onions
cold-pressed sesame oil

1   Trim, wash and drain the prawns. Marinate them for 30 minutes with a tiny pinch of sea-salt and a dash of freshly ground black pepper.
2   Finely mince the garlic and ginger. Cut the spring onions into $2^1/_2$ cm (1 in) lengths.
3   Heat a wok. When hot, add just enough oil to coat the bottom. When the oil is hot, add the garlic and ginger and stir for 1 minute. Add the spring onions and a tiny pinch of sea-salt and stir for 1 minute. Then add the prawns and stir for 1 to 2 minutes. Add a drop or two of water and cover for 2 minutes or until the prawns are cooked. They will turn red.

Variations:
1   Use freshly ground Sichuan pepper instead of black pepper.
2   Use coriander leaves and ground coriander seeds instead of spring onions and black pepper.
3   Use Chinese celery instead of spring onions.

Stir-fried Shrimps with Chinese Flowering Cabbage

75 g (3 oz) fresh shrimps
tiny pinch sea-salt
freshly ground black pepper
1 thin slice ginger
1 clove garlic
225 g (8 oz) Chinese flowering cabbage
cold-pressed sesame oil

1 Shell, devein, wash and drain the shrimps. Marinate them for 30 minutes with a tiny pinch of sea-salt and some freshly ground black pepper.
2 Finely mince the ginger and garlic. Cut the Chinese flowering cabbage into $2^1/_2$ cm (1 in) lengths and separate the stalks from the leaves.
3 Heat a wok. When hot, add just enough oil to coat the bottom. When the oil is hot, add the garlic and ginger and stir for 1 minute. Then add the shrimps and stir for 1 to 2 minutes. Remove them as soon as they turn pink and start to curl. Add the cabbage stalks and stir for 1 to 2 minutes. Add the leaves and stir for 2 to 3 seconds. Then add just enough water to cover the bottom of the wok. Cover and simmer until the greens are just cooked, about 5 to 6 minutes. Add the cooked shrimps and stir for 1 to 2 minutes. Serve immediately.

Note: Add a drop more oil if the wok is too dry after stir-frying the shrimps.

Variations:
1 Use Chinese Peking cabbage or round white cabbage instead of Chinese flowering cabbage.

2 Use freshly ground Sichuan pepper instead of black pepper.
3 Use snow peas and cauliflower instead of Chinese flowering cabbage.

Stir-fried Squid with Leeks

110 g (4 oz) squid
sea-salt
freshly ground black pepper
1 clove garlic
1 thin slice ginger
2 small leeks
cold-pressed sesame oil

1 Remove the skin, ink-sac and transparent backbone from the squid. Cut the tentacles from the eyes and discard the eyes and beaks. Score the body into fine criss-cross patterns to ensure quick cooking, then cut into 2 x 5 cm ($^3/_4$ x 2 in) slices. Wash, drain, and marinate with a tiny pinch of sea-salt and freshly ground black pepper.
2 Finely mince the garlic and ginger and cut the leeks into $2^1/_2$ cm (1 in) diagonal slices.
3 Heat a wok. When hot, add just enough oil to coat the bottom. When the oil is hot, add the garlic and ginger and stir for 1 minute. Add the leeks with a tiny pinch of sea-salt and stir until limp. Then add the squid slices and stir for 1 to 2 minutes or until they begin to turn white and curl. Serve immediately.

Note: Do not overcook the squid or it will become tough and rubbery.

Variations:
1 Use spring onions instead of leeks.

2 Add finely minced fermented black
   soyabeans.
3 Use freshly ground Sichuan pepper instead
   of black pepper.

FISH FOR BABIES AND INFANTS

Fish helps to develop the brain, the central
nervous system, the bones and the teeth.
Moreover, it is very easy to digest – much
more so than eggs – and quick and easy to
prepare.

White fish soups and white fish congees
(cooked without ginger or black pepper) can
be given to babies as soon as they start to
teethe. Add vegetables as desired. Make sure
you remove all bones before giving fish to
babies.

As the baby grows older give him mashed
plain white fish, steamed or braised, without
ginger or black pepper. Braised white fish
with vegetables (see page 147) is also
appropriate for a young child.

By age six, children can have all kinds of
plain white or oily fish prepared in a variety
of cooking methods.

11 Chicken

Chicken is a warming energy food that the Chinese value as a tonic. Since many Chinese cannot afford to have chicken daily they save it for festive days or when a member of the family needs strengthening. The wealthy Chinese, however, take chicken as a protein source along with strengthening herbs.

In Chinese medicine, chicken is not as nourishing as old hen. A chicken is a young bird while an old hen is in its prime in terms of egg-laying capacity. Old hens are boiled or double-boiled for many hours with herbs appropriate for different ailments. The rich would only drink the soup or broth, giving the tough chicken meat to the dogs. Since old hens are not readily available in the West, free-range chickens (or fresh battery-reared chickens) can be used instead.

Free-range chickens are those bred with the freedom to roam the farm to pick and peck up earthworms, insects, etc., to supplement their diet. These chickens are usually not fed antibiotics or hormones. Battery-reared chickens are kept in wire-cages with enough room for them to squat or stand only. They are never let out of their cages and are fed intensively on special feeds containing antibiotics to prevent the spread of diseases and hormones to fatten them up for the table in as short a time as possible.

The black-boned chicken is even more nourishing than old hen. The de-feathered bird has greyish-black skin and bones, and, from my experience, weighs about one to two pounds. (In Singapore, black-boned chickens are the only chickens not battery-reared.)

If possible, black-boned chicken should be used in all tonifying soups, broths or dishes. You will have to make do with free-range chickens where black-boned ones are unavailable in the West.

According to Chinese medical theory, chicken is warming and affects the liver, spleen and stomach. It tonifies the blood, *qi* and *jing* (the vital essence without which there is no life). It warms the middle *jiao* (the spleen and stomach) especially after childbirth, removes blood stagnation and assists *yang* (warming energy). Chicken can be used for anorexia and loss of appetite; fatigue, weakness and thinness; diabetes; oedema; polyuria and frequent urination; rheumatic pains; and blurred vision.

Note: Do not eat if suffering from external diseases, i.e. diseases due to external attacks of wind, cold or damp, like colds, 'flus, bronchitis and pneumonia (because chicken may increase the coughing and mucus).

COOLING COOKING METHODS

Chicken on its own is warming. If chicken is prepared as a soup with cooling ingredients it will become cooling. If it is prepared with tonifying and warming herbs it will be warming.

Cooling chicken soups are ideal for people with overheated blood systems who love the taste of chicken, as well as for people with high blood pressure or high blood cholesterol who find it hard to give up eating meat.

Neutral chicken soups are for everyone, especially young children and the elderly, because they are so nourishing and easy to digest.

Warming chicken soups are for the old, weak, fatigued, anaemic and those who have cooled blood systems. They are usually boiled or double-boiled for 4 to 6 hours to extract the goodness from the chicken and the various herbs.

Basic Chicken Soup

1 drumstick
1 thin slice ginger
sea-salt
2 spring onions

1 Remove the skin and all the fat from the drumstick. Take the flesh off the bone.
2 Place the bone in a pot with 2 cups water, the ginger and a tiny pinch of sea-salt. Finely slice the spring onion whites and add them to the pot. Bring to a fast rolling boil, then simmer the stock until it is reduced to 1 cup of liquid. Skim off any scum and excess oil.
3 Meanwhile, finely slice the chicken flesh and marinate it with a pinch of sea-salt and some finely sliced spring onion greens.
4 When the stock has been reduced, bring it to a fast boil again and add the marinated chicken slices. Cook for 1 to 2 minutes or until the chicken is just cooked. (It will turn white.) Serve immediately.

Note: The Chinese are very particular about not overcooking the chicken. If it is overcooked, it will be tough and fibrous. As with fish, there is an art to cooking chicken.

Variations:
Cooling chicken soups
1 Add black wood ears to help lower high blood pressure and high blood cholesterol, or snow ear fungus to help clear heat from the lungs.
2 Add 3 Shiitake mushrooms to help lower blood pressure and blood cholesterol.
3 Add 1 cm ($^1/_2$ in) slices of courgettes, green cucumber or angled luffa.
4 Add 1 cm ($^1/_2$ in) cubes of marrow, yellow cucumber, fuzzy melon or winter melon.
5 Add some Chinese box thorn leaves and berries for excess liver *yang* conditions, symptoms of which are headaches with red and sore eyes.
6 Add Chinese or English celery to help lower high blood pressure or high blood cholesterol.

Neutral chicken soups
1 Add onion.
2 Add carrot.
3 Add leek instead of spring onions.
4 Add fennel bulb.
5 Add coriander leaves.
6 Add a bay leaf for arthritic and rheumatic pains.

Warming chicken soups

1 Add 6 dried chestnuts which have been soaked overnight in 2 cups of water and use soaking liquid to make the stock. Chestnuts help tonify the *qi*, blood and *jing*, and are good for weakness in the lower back and knees.

2 Add 6 walnuts for the kidneys, especially if you suffer from frequent urination.

3 Add a drop or two of a good quality rice wine just before serving to improve circulation, especially for the elderly during the winter months.

Tonifying Chicken Soup

Do not use just a drumstick for this warming, nourishing soup – it is for the whole family (or at least two people) and should be taken about once a month. I recommend using a one-pound black-boned chicken, old hen or free-range chicken for this recipe as opposed to a battery-reared chicken that was fed on hormones, antibiotics and other artificial feeds. They may negate the healing properties of the herbs and may even be harmful.

450 g (1 lb) whole chicken
3 thin slices ginger
tiny pinch of sea-salt

1 Place 3 cups of water per person in a large pot. (If using a double-boiler, 1 cup per person is sufficient because the evaporating liquid condenses back into the pot.)

2 Bring all the ingredients to a fast rolling boil. Then simmer gently for 4 to 6 hours. Add more water if it looks like there will be less than 1 cup of soup per person.

Variations:

1 Add 1 dried scallop per person. Soak them overnight and tease into fine shreds before adding. Use the scallop soaking water for extra flavour. Scallops help tonify the *qi*, blood and *jing*, and lubricate the joints to prevent stiffness.

2 Add 1 to 2 dried abalone slices per person. Soak them overnight and use the soaking water for extra flavour and goodness. Abalone also tonifies the *qi*, blood and *jing*.

3 Add a herbal combination of: *dang shen, huang shi, shan yao* (see Chapter 8 on Dried Ingredients) and Chinese box thorn berries. Consult the Chinese herbalist for proper amounts of each in proportion to the chicken. These herbs tonify the *qi* and blood and are good for the eyes.

4 Add 1 thumb-sized piece of *dang gui* and 20 Chinese red dates (with all the stones removed). This bitter tonic soup tonifies the *qi* and blood and is good for the old, weak and anaemic and for new mothers, to build up blood and strength after childbirth.

5 Add Korean ginseng for tonifying the *qi* and *yang* of the body. Consult the Chinese herbalist for the correct amount. For this variation you must use only the double-boiling method because the healing properties of Korean ginseng is spoilt by boiling.

Chicken Congee

Congee is easy to digest, suitable for the young and the elderly. Use pot barley and millet for cooling chicken congees, brown rice for a more neutral congee and oat groats for a very warming congee.

Basic Chicken Congee

1 drumstick
¹/₄ cup whole cereal grains
2 spring onions
1 thin slice ginger
sea-salt
1 drop roasted sesame oil
tamari

1 Remove the skin and all the fat from the drumstick. Take the flesh off the bone.
2 Place the bone in a pot with: 3 cups of water, washed whole cereal grains, the whites of the spring onions, finely chopped, 1 thin slice ginger and a tiny pinch of sea-salt. Bring to a fast rolling boil and then simmer until the whole cereal grains are soft and mushy.
3 Meanwhile, finely slice the chicken flesh and marinate with a tiny pinch of sea-salt, 1 drop of roasted sesame oil and finely sliced spring onion greens.
4 Bring the simmering congee to a fast rolling boil again, then add the chicken slices and cook on high heat for 2 to 3 minutes or until the chicken is just cooked. (It will turn white.)
5 Serve immediately with a dash of *tamari*.

Variations: Cooling chicken congee
1 Use pot barley or millet.
2 Add fresh tarragon or sage leaves.
3 Serve with raw lettuce leaves.
4 Add a little fresh lemon juice.
5 Use any of the variations suggested for cooling chicken soups (see page 155).

Neutral chicken congee
1 Use brown rice.

2 Add fresh thyme or parsley.
3 Use any of the variations suggested for neutral chicken soups (see page 155).

Warming chicken congee
1 Use oat groats.
2 Add dried chestnuts or walnuts.

Steamed Chicken

This recipe requires the flesh of a very young spring chicken. A Chinese gourmet would expect the cooked meat to be silky smooth, tender and succulent. (It requires great skill to know just how long to steam the chicken in this dish. In a sense, it is more difficult than steaming fish because the thickness of the meat varies so much more with chicken. Some Chinese claim that the chicken is done even though the bones are still pink.)

Steamed Chicken Breast

110-175 g (4-6 oz) chicken breast
tiny pinch sea-salt
1 thin slice ginger
1 drop roasted sesame oil
2 spring onions
tamari

1 Remove the skin and fat from the chicken breast. Wash and drain and cut the flesh into 2¹/₂ cm (1 in) wide strips. Then slice each strip across the grain of the flesh into 4 cm (1¹/₂ in) lengths with a width of 5 mm (¹/₄ in). The thickness of the flesh should also be 5 mm (¹/₄ in) to ensure quick, even steaming and tender, succulent meat.
2 Marinate the chicken for 30 minutes in a heat-proof dish with a pinch of sea-salt, 1 slice of ginger, 1 drop of roasted sesame

oil and the whites of 2 finely sliced spring onions. Just before steaming, arrange the slices in the dish in one layer with the spring onion whites in between. Place half the spring onion greens, finely sliced, in between the slices to give a lovely contrasting colour and to ensure quick steaming.

3 Bring some water to boil in a wok or a large pot. Place a steamer inside the wok or pot. When it has come to a fast rolling boil, place the dish inside, cover the wok or pot and steam for 1 to 2 minutes or until the flesh turns white. (It should not take long because the chicken has been sliced so thinly.) If you oversteam for 1 or 2 minutes, the flesh will be tough and fibrous.

4 Garnish with the remaining spring onion greens, finely sliced, and a dash of *tamari*.

Variations:

Cooling additions

1 Add finely sliced Chinese or English celery.
2 Add fresh or dried tarragon leaves.
3 Add the peel and juice of half a lemon.

Neutral additions

1 Use minced garlic or shallots instead of spring onions, and garnish with parsley.
2 Add a dash of *tamari* to the marinade.
3 Use coriander leaves instead of spring onions.
4 Add finely sliced strips of baby carrot.
5 Add tender young snow peas.
6 Add thyme to the marinade.

Warming additions

1 Use minced garlic or shallots instead of spring onions and coriander leaves.

---

2 Marinate the slices in freshly ground coriander seeds and steam with coriander leaves.
3 Add freshly ground black pepper.

NEUTRAL COOKING METHODS

Neutral cooking methods are for all types of blood systems – overheated or cooled – as well as for young children and the elderly. This type of preparation also requires a tender young spring chicken.

Chicken Rice

1 small chicken portion (a thigh and leg)
$^1/_3$ cup brown rice
2 cloves garlic
unrefined cold-pressed sesame oil
1 thin slice ginger
tiny pinch sea-salt

1 Remove the skin and all the fat from the chicken. Wash, drain and bone it, but save the bone.

2 Wash the brown rice and drain. Finely mince the garlic.

3 Heat a pot. When hot, add just enough oil to coat the bottom. When the oil is hot, add the garlic and ginger and stir for 1 minute. Lower the heat, add the chicken bone and stir for 1 minute. Add the drained brown rice and stir for 2 minutes. Then add $^2/_3$ cup of water and a tiny pinch of sea-salt and bring the brown rice to a boil. Simmer and cook the brown rice as you would normally (see page 37).

4 Meanwhile, prepare the chicken meat as you would for steamed chicken (see page 157). If you have an overheated blood

system, choose the cooling additions. If you wish to maintain your neutral blood system, try the neutral additions. If you have a cooled blood system, choose the warming additions. Steam the chicken directly on the brown rice.

5   Serve the chicken rice with the steamed chicken and some stir-fried greens. Remember to remove the bones before serving.

Claypot Chicken Rice

This is a popular rice dish among the Chinese. The brown rice is prepared and cooked the normal way and the chicken is added when the rice has absorbed most of its water but is still wet. The steam cooks the rice and the chicken, and the claypot and charcoal fire enhance the aroma and taste of the dish. In modern Chinese homes, gas stoves replace charcoal fires. If you do not have a claypot, use a stainless steel or a cast-iron pot. You can use a charcoal fire or a gas stove to cook this dish.

1 drumstick or 110-175 g (4-6 oz) chicken breast
tiny pinch sea-salt
1 thin slice ginger
1 clove garlic
$^1/_3$ cup brown rice
2 drops roasted sesame oil
tamari
1 spring onion

1   Remove the skin and fat from the chicken. Wash, drain and cut the flesh into $2^1/_2$ cm (1 in) bite-sized pieces to ensure quick cooking. If the drumstick is very thick, score the flesh. If you are using chicken breast, be sure to cut across the grain of the flesh to ensure tenderness.

2   Marinate the chicken with a tiny pinch of sea-salt, 1 thin slice of ginger and 1 finely minced garlic clove.

3   Meanwhile, wash the brown rice and cook it the usual way (see page 37).

4   When the brown rice has absorbed most of the water but is still wet, add the marinated chicken and continue to simmer until the rice and chicken are done.

5   Meanwhile, mix together 2 drops of roasted sesame oil, $^1/_2$ dessertspoon *tamari*, 2 dessertspoons water and 1 finely chopped spring onion.

6   Pour the sauce over the rice and chicken and stir thoroughly. Serve immediately.

Variations:
1   Add 3 Shiitake mushrooms.
2   Add black wood ears.
3   Add freshly ground black pepper.

Braised Chicken

This is another neutral way to prepare chicken for people with all types of blood systems. This dish is easily digested by the young and the elderly and does not require a young spring chicken. The longer cooking time helps tenderise the meat.

1 drumstick
1 clove garlic
cold-pressed sesame oil
1 thin slice ginger
tiny pinch sea-salt
1 spring onion

1   Remove the skin and fat from the chicken. Wash and drain.

2   Finely mince the garlic.

3   Heat a wok. When hot, add just enough oil to coat the bottom. When the oil is hot,

add the garlic and ginger and stir for 1 minute. Then add the drumstick and a tiny pinch of sea-salt. Brown on all sides. Lower the heat and add a little water. Gently simmer until the drumstick is cooked.

4 Garnish with finely chopped spring onion.

Variations:

Cooling additions

1 Add $2^1/_2$ cm (1 in) cubes of courgettes, marrow, angled luffa or fuzzy melon.

2 Add English celery cut into $2^1/_2$ cm (1 in) lengths.

3 Add Chinese Peking cabbage cut into $2^1/_2$ cm (1 in) lengths.

4 Add fresh or dried tarragon leaves.

5 Add fresh mushrooms.

Neutral additions

1 Use $^1/_2$ dessertspoon *tamari* and 2 dessertspoons water and gently simmer.

2 Add $2^1/_2$ cm (1 in) cubes of fennel bulb.

3 Add fresh garden peas, long beans, string beans, runner beans or French beans.

4 Add thyme or parsley.

5 Add baby sweet corn and snow peas.

Warming additions

1 Add onion or leek.

2 Add carrot.

3 Add celeriac.

Warming Cooking Methods

Casserole cooking is more warming than braising because the dish is set in a confined space with a heat source all round (as in an oven). Before the oven, the Chinese made charcoal fires both below and above the casserole to give heat from all sides.

Basic Chicken Casserole

1 small chicken portion (a thigh and leg)
1 clove garlic
1 thin slice ginger
1 carrot
cold-pressed sesame oil
tiny pinch sea-salt
tamari
1 spring onion

1 Remove the skin and fat from the chicken. Wash and drain.

2 Finely mince the garlic and ginger. Cut the carrot into $2^1/_2$ cm (1 in) diagonal sections.

3 Heat a casserole or a heat-proof pot. When hot, add just enough oil to coat the bottom. When the oil is hot, add the garlic and ginger and stir for 1 minute. Then add the chicken and a tiny pinch of sea-salt and brown on all sides. Lower the heat, add the carrot and stir-fry for 1 to 2 minutes. Then add $^1/_2$ dessertspoon *tamari* and enough water to reach half way up the chicken and carrot. Bring contents to a boil, then place in a moderate oven for 30 minutes.

4 Garnish with finely chopped spring onion.

Variations:

1 Add onion or leek.

2 Add onion and 1 bay leaf for arthritis and rheumatism.

3 Add 1 star anise and an onion for a winter warming dish that is good for lower backache.

4 Add a 5 cm (2 in) piece of dried tangerine peel (soaked) to remove mucus in the lungs and to prevent water retention.

5   Add 3 Shiitake mushrooms and an onion or leek.

6   Add 3 Shiitake mushrooms and 1 teaspoon dried Chinese box thorn berries to improve deficient liver blood (when headaches start upon waking up or which wake you up in the middle of the night).

7   Add 6 dried chestnuts (soaked overnight and boiled until soft) and their cooking liquid to the browned chicken before it goes into the oven. Also add $2^1/_2$ cm (1 in) stick of cinnamon and 1 onion. This warming winter variation is good for the liver, spleen, stomach and kidneys, and for lower back pain and weak knees.

8   Add 5 Chinese red dates (with the stones removed), a little black hair moss (soaked), a 5 cm (2 in) piece of dried black wood ear (soaked), 6 to 10 pieces of dried golden needles (soaked) and 1 onion for anaemia.

9   Add a 5 cm (2 in) piece of dried snow ear fungus (soaked) to strengthen the lungs.

10 Add a drop or two of a good quality rice wine just before serving to improve circulation of the old and weak on cold days. (*Note*: elderly people suffering from high blood pressure or high blood cholesterol should not eat this variation.).

Stir-fried Chicken

This is another warming method of preparing chicken. The dish can be made less warming for consumption by those with overheated blood systems by adding cooling vegetables. Such people should have stir-fried chicken only once a week.

Stir-fried Chicken with Mung Bean Sprouts

110 g (4 oz) chicken breast
tiny pinch sea-salt
1 clove garlic
1 thin slice ginger
225 g (8 oz) mung bean sprouts
1 thin slice carrot
1 spring onion
cold-pressed sesame oil

1   Remove the skin and fat from the chicken. Wash, drain and slice the flesh into $2^1/_2$ cm (1 in) strips. Then slice each strip across the grain into very thin 4 cm ($1^1/_2$ in) lengths to ensure quick cooking.

2   Marinate the slices in a tiny pinch of sea-salt.

3   Finely mince the garlic and ginger. Wash and drain the mung bean sprouts thoroughly. Finely slice the carrot. Finely slice the spring onion into diagonal strips.

4   Heat a wok. When hot, add just enough oil to coat the bottom. When the oil is hot, add the garlic and ginger and stir for 1 minute. Then add the chicken and stir for 1 minute or until the slices turn white. Remove the chicken immediately and set aside.

5   If the wok is dry, add another drop of oil. Then add the spring onion with a pinch of sea-salt and stir for 1 minute. Add the carrot and the mung bean sprouts. Stir thoroughly. When the vegetables are just cooked but still crisp add the cooked chicken slices and mix thoroughly. Serve immediately.

Note: The carrot and spring onion are added only for colour contrast.

Variations:

Instead of mung bean sprouts use

Cooling additions

1 Soyabean sprouts
2 Finely shredded celery
3 Finely shredded yam bean
4 Finely shredded green cucumber, courgettes, marrow, angled luffa or fuzzy melon
5 Finely shredded Chinese Peking cabbage
6 Finely shredded lettuce, especially Webb's or Cos or Iceberg
7 Finely shredded asparagus

Neutral additions

1 Chinese flowering cabbage
2 Broccoli
3 Spring cabbage

Warming additions

1 Leek and carrot
2 Onion and carrot

You can also marinate the chicken slices in a mixture of $^1/_2$ dessertspoon of *tamari* and 2 dessertspoons of water for 30 minutes before stir-frying.

Roast Chicken

Roasting is more warming than either casserole cooking or stir-frying because hardly any water is used and no vegetables are added. Oven cooking is very warming as well. This dish is definitely not for people with overheated blood systems or those who tend towards them, and it should not be eaten on hot summer days or in hot climates. It is more suitable for those with cooled blood systems or on cold days.

Tamari Roast Chicken

1 drumstick
tiny pinch sea-salt
$^1/_2$ dessertspoon tamari
1 clove garlic
1 thin slice ginger
$^1/_2$ tsp barley malt extract
parsley

1 Remove the skin and fat from the chicken. Wash and drain. Place in a heat-proof dish and marinate for 1 to 2 hours in a tiny pinch of sea-salt, $^1/_2$ dessertspoon of *tamari*, 2 dessertspoons of water, finely minced garlic and ginger, and $^1/_2$ teaspoon barley malt extract.
2 After 1 to 2 hours cover the heat-proof dish with some aluminium foil. Place it in a moderate oven of 235°C or 450°F. After 10 minutes remove the aluminium foil and turn the chicken over, then roast uncovered for another 10 minutes. Check that it is properly roasted before serving.
3 Serve with finely chopped parsley.

Note: If you remove as much meat off the bone as possible you will marinate the chicken better as well as ensure faster roasting.

Variations: Less warming additions

1 Omit the ginger.
2 Omit the *tamari*, barley malt extract and ginger, and add fresh finely minced sage or tarragon.
3 Omit *tamari* and ginger, and marinate in lemon juice, lemon peel, barley malt extract and fresh parsley.

Grilled and Barbecued Chicken

These two methods of preparation are very heating because the meat is in almost direct contact with the heat source. Use this method of preparation occasionally, at parties for instance, but not on a daily basis.

Be sure to counteract the heating effects of the meat with cooling vegetables, fruits and drinks – salads, lemon juice, pears, peppermint tea, chamomile tea, rosehip tea and chrysanthemum tea.

CHICKEN FOR BABIES AND INFANTS

Clear, oil-free, plain chicken soup cooked without ginger is good for building up weak babies. It can be given to them as soon as they start to teethe. The younger the baby, the more diluted the soup should be. Young babies' digestive systems are not developed enough to cope with the heavy richness of chicken soup. Be careful not to overburden the baby's digestive system with too much richness. It is better to give too little than too much.

Babies who are able to eat mashed foods can have liquidised chicken congee without ginger. Add some vegetables to give extra vitamins and minerals.

As the child grows older, give him steamed, braised and casserole-cooked chicken. Continue to mash the meat up until he can chew properly.

Stir-fried and roast chicken are too heating for children, who are very active and tend to have overheated blood systems. On the other hand, if the child is weak and feels the cold easily, he can have stir-fried or roast chicken occasionally.

12 Fruits

Fruits constitute only 5 per cent of the Tao diet (or a piece of fruit a day for adults). Vegetables, however, constitute 25 per cent of the diet, that is, one quarter of a meal twice a day. Why is this? Vegetables contain more fibre, vitamins and minerals than fruits. Moreover, fruits are generally more cooling than vegetables because of their water content. Fruits are more appropriate for people with overheated blood systems or tendencies towards them to help them cool down or stay cool. They are also suitable for hot climates and hot summer days. People with cooled blood systems should eat fruits only occasionally.

Try to eat fresh, local or seasonal fruits as much as possible. Or buy fresh fruits imported from countries in the same latitude. If you live in temperate zones you should be eating fruits with more neutral or warming energies and less cooling energies. On the other hand, if you live in the tropics, then you will require more cooling fruits to help cope with the heat.

In this chapter, I have listed the fruits of three different zones according to their energies. In the temperate zone, pears are the only cooling fruit but there are 7 types of fruits with warming energies. In warmer climates, e.g. the Mediterranean, you have a choice of 8 cooling fruits but only 2 warming fruits. In the tropics there are 14 cooling fruits and only 3 warming fruits.

When eaten in excess, some fruits – such as clementine, mandarin, orange and lychee – can give rise to a condition known as damp heat in Chinese medicine. Damp heat tends to affect the liver, gall bladder, bladder, large and small intestines, and the urino-genital systems. Symptoms include pain, burning sensations, heat and dampness in the genital area, infections, foul odour and a general feeling of heaviness in the body. People with damp heat can develop hepatitis, gall bladder inflammation, cystitis, pelvic inflammation, ulcerative colitis, leucorrhoea, prostatitis, etc.

When eaten in excess, some cooling fruits may give rise to a condition called 'wind'. In Chinese medicine, wind can cause symptoms like tremors, convulsions, shaking, spasms and pain that travels from place to place. The Chinese believe that epilepsy, arthritis and rheumatism can be aggravated by an excessive consumption of certain cooling fruits.

Other fruits can cause irritations when taken in excess, especially when the individual has a skin disease, insect bite or a healing wound. Such irritating fruits can cause the wound to become septic, or lead to uncontrollable itching.

Fruits with medicinal value will be discussed in this chapter. For a complete list

of fruits and their properties, see Appendix A, at the back of the book.

Try to eat organically grown fruits as much as possible.

> *Note:* Vegans, vegetarians, macrobiotics and wholefooders who eat large quantities of wholegrains, legumes and pulses must NOT finish a meal with fruit. Complex carbohydrates from wholegrains, legumes and pulses take much longer to digest than simple fruit sugars. When taken together the body will digest only the simpler fruit sugars, leaving the others to ferment in the digestive system and give rise to unpleasant and embarrassing flatulence.
>
> To avoid this, eat fruit about one to two hours after a meal as a snack.

TEMPERATE FRUITS

PEARS
(Pyrus communis)
property: cooling

There are several varieties of pears – Conference, Williams, Japanese and Tiensein, to name a few – and all have cooling energies. Pears are good in cases of lung heat where the symptoms are dry hacking cough, dry throat, dry mouth, loss of voice and sometimes coughed up blood with yellow-green sputum. They are also helpful for stomach heat which may cause bad breath, mouth ulcers and pain, especially after eating oily, greasy, deep-fried, and spicy foods.

Try pears for other symptoms such as: spots, pimples, acne, boils, red face, red eyes and mouth, gum and tongue ulcers, general heating feeling, irritability, scanty urination, dark reddish yellow urine and constipation with hard, dry stools.

> *Pears are unsuitable for:*
> 1 People with weak constitutions, cooled blood systems or tendencies towards them
> 2 Women who suffer from menstrual pains
> 3 Pregnant women who suffer from anaemia

Cooked pears can be taken occasionally in small quantities by those with cooled blood systems if they have symptoms like those mentioned above.

> *To make pears less cooling:*
> Stew with raisins and a tiny pinch of sea-salt (try Conference pears).

> *To make pears even less cooling:*
> 1 Bake with cinnamon, raisins and a tiny pinch of sea-salt, especially during the winter.
> 2 Bake with cloves, star anise or caraway seeds.

APPLES
(Malus spp.)
property: neutral

Sweet red apples are neutral, while green, sour ones tend to have more cooling energies. Apples are good for constipation, especially eaten with the peel. Try to eat organically grown apples whenever possible.

> *To make apples more warming:* Stew apples with raisins and a tiny pinch of sea-salt for autumn, winter and early spring.

PLUMS
(Prunus spp.)
property: neutral

Plums are neutral if they are sweet and more cooling if they are sour. They are good for people with sluggish livers who, according to traditional Chinese medicine, have difficulty in getting out of bed in the mornings or take a long time to get adjusted to new situations and environments.

To make plums more warming: Stew with sultanas and a tiny pinch of sea-salt in autumn and winter.

To make plums even more warming: Bake with sultanas, a tiny pinch of sea-salt and either cinnamon, cloves, caraway seeds or star anise. This is warming for autumn and winter.

RASPBERRIES
(Rubus idaeus)
property: neutral

Raspberries are my favourite summer fruit. To me, they are best picked at the end of a hot summer's day in the Swiss Alps or on some remote mountain or hill in the Scottish Highlands. My home-grown raspberries cannot compare in sweetness and flavour to the wild ones I have tasted.

Raspberries are good for the liver, kidneys, and blurred vision due to a condition called deficient liver blood in Chinese medicine. They are also able to help impotence, spermatorrhoea, abundant urine and bed-wetting due to deficient kidney *yang*, another Chinese term. To remedy the latter, stew or bake small amounts of raspberries and eat throughout the season. Eating too much will negate the medicinal values.

Caution: Raspberries are unsuitable for those with scanty, dark urine.

To make raspberries more warming: Stew with barley malt extract and a tiny pinch of sea-salt.

To make raspberries even more warming: Bake with barley malt extract, a tiny pinch of sea-salt, and either cinnamon, cloves, star anise or caraway seeds.

APRICOTS
(Prunus armeniaca)
property: warming

Sweet, ripe apricots are warming; sour ones are less warming. All are supposed to be good for the lungs.

Caution: Apricots are unsuitable for those with spots, pimples, acne, boils, eczema, psoriasis, other skin infections, or lung heat symptoms.

To make apricots more warming: Stew with barley malt extract and a tiny pinch of sea-salt. Add raisins, sultanas or currants, according to preference.

BLACKBERRIES
(Rubus fruticosus)
property: warming

Sweet, ripe blackberries are warming; sour ones are less warming. Because they are rich sources of iron, they are appropriate for anyone with anaemia. If you happen to live in the country you can pick them from the hedgerows in autumn. Stew them with ripe elderberries for an iron-rich fruit stew.

To make blackberries more warming:
1 Stew with barley malt extract and a tiny pinch of sea-salt.
2 Stew with elderberries, barley malt extract and a tiny pinch of sea-salt.
3 Stew with apples or pears and barley malt extract with a tiny pinch of sea-salt.
4 Stew the above variations with any one of these hot, aromatic spices: ginger, cinnamon, cloves, star anise, caraway seeds or nutmeg. A hot stew with blackberries, elderberries, ginger, cloves, cinnamon, barley malt extract and a tiny pinch of sea-salt is said to keep colds and 'flu away.

BLACKCURRANTS
(Ribes nigrum)
property: warming

Blackcurrants are rich in iron and vitamin C. Eat them fresh throughout the season to replenish your iron.

To make blackcurrants more warming:
1 Stew with barley malt extract and a tiny pinch of sea-salt.
2 Stew with apples, barley malt extract and a tiny pinch of sea-salt.

CHERRIES
(Prunus avium)
property: warming

Ripe, sweet, red or black cherries are warming, while sour cherries are less warming.

Caution: Cherries are unsuitable for anyone suffering from vomiting.

PEACHES
(Prunus persica)
property: warming

Peaches are said to help people with lung problems.

Note: You may create internal heat (a Chinese medical term), if you eat too many peaches. Symptoms include: red face and eyes, bad breath, dry mouth and throat, thirst, scanty, dark urine, and constipation with hard, dry stools.

STRAWBERRIES
(Fragaria x ananassa)
property: warming

Sweet, ripe strawberries are warming and sour strawberries are less warming. They are said to help motion sickness and abundant urination.

I prefer to eat fresh strawberries on their own, to better appreciate their delicate, unique aroma and flavour. The best strawberries I have ever had were those I found on the Swiss Alps at the end of summer. They were wild and tiny and had been basking in the hot sun all day. They were

sweet as honey and uniquely flavoured.

If you still dream of strawberries and cream try a healthier version using seed or nut cream from sunflower seeds or almonds.

MEDITERRANEAN FRUITS

GRAPEFRUITS
(Citrus paradisi)
property: cooling

Grapefruits are very cooling. They are said to be a diuretic too.

Most people should not eat half a grapefruit and a cup of tea daily for breakfast to lose weight. Both grapefruit and tea have cooling energies and both are diuretics. If you have a weak constitution, tea and grapefruit may cause cold symptoms such as feeling cold easily; the inability to properly digest food; stools with undigested food; loose stools; diarrhoea; clear, frequent and abundant urination; weak back, legs and knees; water retention; painful periods; arthritis and rheumatism.

Grapefruits are unsuitable for:
1 People with weak constitutions, cooled blood systems and tendencies towards them
2 Pregnant women
3 People who suffer from aches and pains (because sour, cooling foods can aggravate the condition)
4 Women who suffer from menstrual pains

LEMONS
(Citrus limon)
property: cooling

Pure lemon juice diluted with mineral water and sweetened with barley malt extract is a nice cooling drink for anyone with an overheated blood system. The vitamin C helps cool the body.

Lemons are unsuitable for:
1 People with weak constitutions, cooled blood systems and tendencies towards them
2 People who suffer from aches and pains
3 Women who suffer from menstrual pains

MANDARINS
(Citrus reticulata)
property: cooling

Chinese New Year would not be Chinese New Year without mandarin oranges. We greet our friends with gifts of mandarins to signify wealth and prosperity.

When taken in small doses, mandarins are good for the digestion. However, they may create damp heat and phlegm if taken in large quantities, especially in people prone to catarrh, mucus, phlegm and sputum.

Mandarins are unsuitable for:
1 People with weak constitutions, cooled blood systems or tendencies towards them
2 People who suffer from or are prone to catarrh, mucus, phlegm and sputum

SWEET ORANGES
(Citrus sinensis)
property: cooling

Oranges and vitamin C go hand in hand. They are good for people with overheated blood systems or those who tend towards them, but not those who suffer from or are prone to catarrh, mucus, phlegm or sputum. Sour oranges are not suitable for those who suffer from aches and pains because sour, cooling foods can aggravate the pain by contracting the tendons and muscles. Women who suffer from menstrual pains should also stay away from oranges, especially between ovulation and the last day of the period.

JAPANESE PERSIMMONS
(Diospyros kaki)
property: cooling

In China, persimmons are eaten on hot summer days to cool down the body. They are used to treat constipation with hard, dry stools, dry hacking coughs accompanied by a dry throat and mouth, and high blood pressure, especially in people with overheated blood systems or tendencies towards them.

Home remedy for non-stop sneezing. Wash, dice and boil 4 fresh persimmons in some water. Slowly sip the liquid. (This remedy is taken from a Chinese book on diet therapy.)

Persimmons are unsuitable for:
1 People with weak constitutions, cooled blood systems or tendencies towards them
2 Women who suffer from menstrual pains

DATES
(Phoenix dactylifera)
property: neutral

Fresh dates are good for the spleen when taken in small quantities (two to six every now and then). Do not eat them daily, or you may gain unnecessary weight.

Caution: Dates are unsuitable for people who suffer from or who are prone to catarrh, mucus, phlegm and sputum.

FIGS
(Ficus carica)
property: neutral

Because figs are rich in fibre, they are suitable for those who suffer from constipation. Stew them in water to increase their cooling energies and to remedy constipation with hard, dry stools.

Caution: Figs are unsuitable for people who suffer from loose stools and diarrhoea.

GRAPES
(Vitis vinifera)
property: neutral

Green grapes are neutral but red or black grapes are more warming. They are good for constipation sufferers because of their high fibre content. Red or black varieties contain iron so they are appropriate for anaemics.

Caution: Grapes are unsuitable for people who suffer from loose stools and diarrhoea.

LYCHEES
(Litchi chinensis)
property: warming

Fresh lychees are a treat in countries outside China and Hong Kong. They are said to help people who suffer from 'cock's crow diarrhoea', a form of diarrhoea that strikes as early as 5 a.m.!

Too many lychees can create damp heat in the body.

> *Caution:* Lychees are unsuitable for people with overheated blood systems or tendencies towards them.

LONGAN
(Nephelium longana)
property: warming

Fresh longans are another treat outside China, Hong Kong and Thailand. They are suitable for people suffering from anaemia and hair loss due to anaemia.

> *Beware:* Overconsumption of longans can overheat the body.
>
> *Longans are unsuitable for:*
> 1 People with overheated blood systems or tendencies towards them
> 2 People who are prone to catarrh, mucus, phlegm or sputum

TROPICAL FRUITS

BANANAS
(Musa spp.)
property: cooling

This cooling fruit is appropriate for people suffering from heat-caused constipation with hard, dry stools, piles or bleeding piles. Several varieties of bananas are available in Malaysia and Singapore but *pisang hijau* is the coolest variety. *Pisang raja* and *pisang emas* are slightly less cooling. Overconsumption can create wind in the body.

> *Bananas are not suitable for:*
> 1 People who suffer from or are prone to catarrh, mucus, phlegm or sputum
> 2 People with weak constitutions, cooled blood systems or tendencies towards them, arthritis or rheumatism
> 3 Women who suffer from menstrual pains
>
> *To make bananas less cooling:*
> 1 Bake, grill or barbecue in their own skin.
> 2 Mash and bake with one of these hot spices: cinnamon, cloves, nutmeg, star anise or caraway seeds.

CIKU
(Manilkara achras)
property: cooling

This heart-shaped brown fruit has a unique texture and flavour.

COCONUTS
(Cocos nucifera)
property: cooling

Fresh green coconut meat and juice are sweet and cooling for hot sunny days, especially on tropical beaches. Overconsumption can cause wind in the body.

CUSTARD APPLES
(Annona squamosa)
property: cooling

This unusual fruit with its green, scaly skin, white flesh and black seeds is another of my favourites. It is not as cooling as other fruits so it can be taken by anyone in small quantities (e.g. one small fruit per sitting), and not on a daily basis.

JACKFRUIT/NANGKA
(Artocarpus heterophyllus)
property: cooling

This highly aromatic fruit is usually sold in sections because the whole fruit is too large. Take jackfruit only in very small quantities (e.g. not more than two or three 'seeds' per sitting), and not on a daily basis. Overconsumption can cause wind in the body.

MALAY APPLES/JAMBU MERAH
(Eugenia malaccensis)
property: cooling

These light, airy, red fruits are used in Malay *rojak,* a local salad. I prefer them on their own. Their unique texture, taste, flavour and aroma are lost when combined with other fruits, vegetables and sauces. Malay apples should be eaten in small quantities, e.g. five to six small ones at one sitting, but not on a daily basis.

MANGOSTEENS
(Garcinia mangostana)
property: cooling

Mangosteens should always be eaten with durians because their cooling properties balance the heating properties of the durian. Durians and mangosteens are in season at the same time. (Perhaps it is nature's intention for man to eat a warming fruit followed by a cooling fruit to create balance.) Those with weak constitutions, cooled blood systems or tendencies towards them should not eat more than three mangosteens without having at least one durian 'seed'.

PINEAPPLES
(Ananas comosus)
property: cooling

Not many people are aware of the fact that pineapple is very cooling and acidic and can be unhealthy if eaten in excess. In Malaysia and Singapore, ripe pineapples are peeled, sliced and soaked in a sprinkling of sea-salt to neutralise their acidity. Overconsumption can cause damp heat in the body.

Pineapples are unsuitable for:

1   People with weak constitutions, cooled blood systems or tendencies towards them
2   People with stomach or duodenal ulcers
3   People with arthritis or rheumatism
4   People with aches and pains
5   Women with menstrual pains
6   Pregnant women

---

7   People with skin infections or diseases
8   People with healing wounds

To make pineapple less cooling: Peel and slice a sweet, ripe pineapple. Sprinkle with some sea-salt, leave for 1 hour, then drain the liquid. Stew the slices with cinnamon, cloves and barley malt extract until all the juices have evaporated. Then bake until almost dry. Sprinkle with roasted sesame seeds or roll the jam-like pineapple into little balls and coat with roasted sesame seeds or salt-free *gomasio*.

POMELOES
(Citrus grandis)
property: cooling

Ipoh, Malaysia is famous for its pomelo trees. The fruit is high in fibre and suitable, therefore, for heat-caused constipation with hard, dry stools. Pomelo is not as cooling as banana so people with weak constitutions, cooled blood systems or tendencies towards them should only eat an occasional slice or two.

ROSE APPLES/JAMBU MAWAR
(Eugenia jambos)
property: cooling

These cream-coloured fruits do smell a bit like roses. At home, I have to fight with the flying foxes and bats to see who gets them first! Rose apples are not to be eaten on a daily basis – three to four fruits once in a while are fine.

SEA APPLES
(Borassus flabellifera)
property: cooling

Sea apples grow on palm-like trees. They resemble coconuts but they have purple skin. Inside, there are usually three to four jelly-like fruits stuck to a central core. I have only seen them in Penang. Although I like the texture of the sea apple, I have seldom come across a sweet fruit. They are usually bland and surprisingly filling. It would be difficult to eat more than one sea apple in one sitting.

STAR FRUIT/CARAMBOLAS
(Averrhoa carambola)
property: cooling

These crisp, juicy orange fruits are said to help lower blood pressure in people with overheated blood systems or tendencies towards them.

Caution: Star fruits are unsuitable for people with weak constitutions, cooled blood systems or tendencies towards them.

WATER APPLES/JAMBU AIR
(Eugenia aquea)
property: cooling

Similar to Malay apples, water apples are also used in *rojak*. Do not eat them on a daily basis or have more than five to six small fruits in one sitting.

WATERMELONS
(Citrullus lanatus)
property: cooling

When the dry season approaches in Southeast Asia you are sure to see watermelons in the markets. It is almost as if nature times it so that the juicy, cooling watermelon coincides with the hot, dry weather, to quench thirst and cool us down. If you suffer from spots, pimples, acne, boils, thirst, heat-caused constipation with hard, dry stools and scanty dark urine, eat watermelon until your condition clears.

Caution: Watermelon is unsuitable for people with weak constitutions, cooled blood systems or tendencies towards them.

Note: Milk mixed with watermelon may cause diarrhoea.

PAPAYAS
(Carica papaya)
property: neutral

Each zone has its own neutral fruit: temperate countries have apples; the Mediterranean has grapes; and the tropics have papayas (or paw-paws). Papayas are inexpensive and plentiful in Southeast Asia. Almost anyone with a garden has a tree that bears large fruits all year round.

Papayas are good for constipation and digestion because they contain an enzyme called papain found in the white sap on the skin. Years ago, I tasted a dish made of beef

that was marinated in some papaya sap before being stir-fried. It was certainly more tender than normal cuts of beef but the taste was the same. If you have a tough old hen, marinate it in some natural papaya sap before stir-frying.

GUAVAS
(Psidium guajava)
property: neutral

These hard, unattractive fruits have more vitamin C than oranges. People in Southeast Asia should eat them instead of oranges – they are inexpensive and have neutral properties.

> *Note:* Overconsumption can cause constipation.

DURIANS
(Durio zibethinus)
property: warming

These rugby-shaped thorny fruits are extremely popular in Malaysia and Singapore. They are so aromatic you can literally smell them miles away. During the season their aroma hangs over all of Southeast Asia. There are tales about men pawning their *sarongs* to buy durians for their families.

Personally, I do not like durians – not because of the smell but because I find the sweet creamy flesh difficult to digest. Their richness and indigestibility can be harmful to people who overindulge themselves.

Southeast Asian doctors will tell you the

beginning of the durian season signals the beginning of the 'flu season. Durians create heat in the body which gives rise to fever and thick yellow nasal discharges.

Although mangosteens are supposed to accompany durians, many durian lovers do not have room for them after overindulging. Their sour taste helps the body digest the warming durians. If you do not like mangosteen, take plain brown rice congee with raw lettuce to counteract the effects of durian.

Durians can be medicinal too. According to my grandmother, a distant relative of mine who used to suffer from the cold was advised to take durian to warm him up. It worked!

> *Durians are unsuitable for:*
> 1 People with strong constitutions, overheated blood systems or tendencies towards them
> 2 People with high blood pressure
> 3 Anyone with a fever
> 4 People with skin diseases like eczema, psoriasis, red rashes, etc.
>
> *Caution:* Alcohol must not be taken with durians. Alcohol and durians are both warming. The two together can kill.

MATA KUCING
(Nephelium longana)
property: warming

Mata kucing is the Southeast Asian variety of longan (which normally grows in China, Hong Kong and Thailand), but is of a much poorer quality.

MANGOES
(Mangifera indica)
property: warming

All of the many variations of mango – Indian, Thai, Indonesian, Philippine and Malaysian – are warming. They should be eaten in small quantities only. Overindulgence can cause damp heat.

Caution: Mangoes are not suitable for people who suffer from or are prone to hepatitis, gall bladder inflammation, cystitis, prostatitis, leucorrhoea, vaginal infections, pelvic inflammation, skin diseases like eczema, psoriasis, spots, pimples, acne and boils.

RAMBUTANS
(Nephelium lappaceum)
property: warming

These hairy red or yellow fruits are in season about twice a year in Southeast Asia. They are nice to have in small numbers but overconsumption can cause damp heat.

Rambutans are unsuitable for:
1   People with coughs. The fruit juice seems to tickle and aggravate the respiratory tract.
2   People who tend to suffer from or are prone to hepatitis, gall bladder inflammation, cystitis, prostatitis, leucorrhoea, vaginal infections, pelvic inflammation, skin diseases like eczema, psoriasis, spots, pimples, acne and boils.

FRUITS FOR BABIES AND INFANTS

Babies can have a small quantity of fruits once or twice a week as soon as they begin eating mashed food.

In temperate zones, plain stewed apples are best. However, if the baby shows signs of heat (e.g. red, hot rashes, or dark, smelly, scanty urine, or dark, smelly, hard stools), give him plain stewed pears.

In Mediterranean zones, give babies a few mashed, peeled and seeded green or red grapes. Stew them a little to soften, if you prefer. If the child shows signs of heat, give him a small amount of squeezed orange juice.

Note: If the baby suffers from or is prone to catarrh, mucus, phlegm or sputum, do not give him any type of citrus fruit.

In tropical zones, give the baby a little mashed papaya. If baby shows signs of heat, give him a little watermelon juice.

Note: Do not give the baby watermelon juice after milk. The two together can cause diarrhoea.

Caution: Babies or infants who look pale, have weak constitutions, suffer easily from the cold, loose stools, diarrhoea and frequent, clear urination should not be given fruits or fruit juices.

As the child grows older, increase the fruit intake in reference to his blood system. Those who tend towards an overheated blood system should have more fruits than those who tend towards a cooled blood system. Those with weak constitutions and cooled blood systems should not have fruits at all.

Children of three years and older can have two pieces of fruit a day because they are active and growing fast. They need extra vitamins from fruits for their growth. Adults have stopped growing and are generally less active than children, so one piece of fruit a day will be enough.

13 Beverages

The most popular beverages all over the world are tea and coffee, but many people still do not know how harmful they can be.

TEA

Tea is very cooling and therefore injurious to people with weak constitutions, cooled blood systems or tendencies towards them.

> *Caution:* People who drink several cups of tea a day for several years may later suffer from dull headaches, insomnia, depression, loss of appetite, loose stools, frequent clear urination (especially during the night), chills, cold body and limbs, weak back and knees, fatigue, lethargy and, in some women, the inability to conceive.

Tea is not healthy for the strong, robust and active, or those with overheated blood systems or tendencies towards them. Why not – when it can help cool the body?

Tea is a stimulant that can be addictive. A cup of tea gives you a lift. When the lift fades you need another cup to boost you up again. You may rely on it so much that you may not know when your body is overtired. Tea can give you a lift and the mental power to accomplish things, but it can also sap your natural reserves and resources. If you drink tea frequently, for a long period of time, you may suffer from nerves, irritability, depression, anxiety, frustration, insomnia, hair loss or premature greying, and a lack of sexual desire.

Those with strong constitutions, overheated blood systems or tendencies towards them should try to keep their tea intake down to one cup a day, if they are unable to give it up entirely. Cut down your tea intake gradually; sudden cessation of tannin (a substance found in tea and most plants and used in the tanning of hide) and caffeine may cause headaches.

Macrobiotics should not drink large quantities of strong bancha tea because the tannin coats the stomach lining and prevents the absorption of wholefoods which are often much harder to digest. Macrobiotics should chew their food well before swallowing.

COFFEE

Coffee is very heating. It is definitely not suitable for people with overheated blood systems or tendencies towards them.

> *Caution:* Large quantities of coffee can give rise to spots, pimples, acne, boils, eczema, psoriasis, heat rashes, migraines, intense headaches, red eyes, bad breath, insomnia, restlessness,

irritability, nervous anxiety, depression, frustration, and heat-caused constipation with hard, dry stools. Coffee can also give rise to damp heat diarrhoea and other damp heat problems like cystitis, prostatitis, pelvic inflammation, gall bladder inflammation and thrush.

Like tea, coffee is a stimulant. It is especially unhealthy for people who work under stress. It is not surprising that coffee drinkers develop stomach or duodenal ulcers, insomnia, migraines, high blood pressure, high blood cholesterol and heart palpitations.

Modern research has shown that there is a positive link between caffeine consumption and fibrocystic breast disease. This may also apply to tea, because it also contains caffeine. There may also be a link between coffee and cancer of the bladder and the pancreas, but conclusive evidence is still not available. Pregnant women should be aware that large doses of caffeine may cause birth defects.

Everyone should try to give up coffee, especially those with overheated blood systems or tendencies towards them. Those with cooled blood systems or tendencies towards them should have one cup a day, maximum, if it is impossible for them to give it up entirely.

Like tea, coffee intake must be reduced gradually to minimise withdrawal symptoms like restlessness, anxiety and headaches.

Decaffeinated coffee is not the answer. It is just as heating as coffee and, if it has been extracted using a chemical solvent, it can leave a low-grade carcinogen in the system. Make sure the decaffeinated coffee you buy has been made by a water extraction process, not by solvent extraction.

COFFEE SUBSTITUTES

These healthier substitutes do not taste exactly like coffee but very close to it. There are now several varieties available in health food shops. They are usually made from one or more of the following: barley, malted barley, rye, wheat, oats, millet, chicory, figs, acorns or dandelion root. They all have warming properties because they are made from roasted ingredients. Therefore, if you have an overheated blood system or tendencies towards one, do not drink these substitutes too often in a day; about one to two cups is enough.

Dandelion root coffee does not have the same such warming energies as the others because dandelion root has cooling properties. So people with overheated blood systems can drink this more often. Beware, however, of its diuretic properties.

COCOA AND DRINKING CHOCOLATE SUBSTITUTE

In the appendix you will find that cocoa and drinking chocolate are not recommended. There is now a cocoa and chocolate substitute called carob. You can buy this from any health food shop. It is sold in the form of a dark brown powder. It tastes sweeter than cocoa and does not contain caffeine but some minerals. It is made from the seeds of the Mediterranean carob tree. Use it as you would drinking chocolate. (Make it with soya milk or goat's milk or with barley or rice malt extract.)

Carob is not known in China so I do not know what energies it has, whether cooling,

neutral or warming. I suggest that it be taken only occasionally.

MINERAL WATER

Uncarbonated mineral water served at room temperature is good for the active, strong and robust, and those with overheated blood systems or tendencies towards them. Warmed mineral water is better for those with cooled blood systems or tendencies towards them.

Naturally fizzy mineral water should be taken only occasionally because gaseous substances can upset the digestive functions, especially in people with weak stomachs who are prone to indigestion.

TAP WATER

If mineral water is too expensive, tap water is a good substitute. (Note: This only applies to countries where the tap water is safe to drink.) Let the water run a bit before filling up a glass. If you have an overheated blood system let the glass warm up to room temperature before drinking.

Those with cooled blood systems or tendencies toward them should boil water and drink it hot or lukewarm. Anything cold will make your condition worse.

Do not look down on boiled water – it cleanses the system. Many of my patients have told me that their grandmothers advised them to drink boiled water. Hot water is all I drink, whether I am in a temperate country or the tropics. Try it and see how it will benefit you.

Note: Tap water can be filtered to remove chemicals such as lead or copper. For this you will need a Brita Water Filter jug. This German-made filter is available in most health food shops. Fill the upper compartment of the filter with tap water. In a short while the water will flow through to the lower compartment. Use the filtered water for drinking and cooking.

Those who simply cannot drink tasteless water should try the following beverages. The cooling beverages are appropriate for those with overheated blood systems, the neutral drinks are for everyone, and the warming ones for those with cooled blood systems or tendencies towards them. No single beverage should be had too often. Overindulgence can be harmful, even though the ingredients are organically grown. Alternate beverages often for a variety of taste, vitamins and minerals.

COOLING BEVERAGES

Pot Barley Water
Take pot barley water (see recipe on page 30) for all damp heat symptoms and skin diseases. Drink it all day long until your condition improves. Or, drink several glasses a day once or twice a week to maintain the neutrality of your blood system.

Soyabean Milk
Soyabean milk is rich in vegetable protein and soya lecithin, and is good for cooling the body down. Drink 1 to 2 glasses a day about 2 to 3 times a week and no more. (Follow recipe for Black Soyabean Milk on page 63, but do not remove the seed coats.) It is better to drink fresh soyabean milk rather than the

prepacked varieties that may have added sugar.

Borage Tea

Borage tea is good for melancholy or for someone who has had a course of steroids because it helps to restore the function of the adrenal cortex.

Infuse 1 teaspoon of the dried herb in a cup of boiling water in a thermos flask for 10 to 15 minutes. Strain and sip the hot tea. Inhale the steam, especially if you are melancholic. The volatile oils from the borage can give you a lift. Drink a cup a day or every other day for mild cases, and three cups a day if your condition is bad.

Burdock Tea

Burdock tea is a good blood purifier in the spring or for those suffering from eczema, psoriasis and other skin diseases.

Boil 25 g (1 oz) of burdock root in 855 ml (1$^1/_2$ pints) of water until 570 ml (1 pint) is left. Drink a wineglassful four times a day before meals until the condition eases. If your problem is not severe, once a week is sufficient in the spring.

Chamomile Tea

This tea can help you relax if you suffer from migraines, anxiety or insomnia. Insomniacs should drink a cup of hot chamomile tea at night. Migraine sufferers should take a cup or two at lunch. If you are tense or anxious three cups a day is enough. Try to inhale the steam as you slowly sip the tea.

Infuse 1 teaspoon of dried flowers in 1 cup of boiling water in a thermos flask for 10 to 15 minutes. Strain and drink.

Chrysanthemum Tea

Drink chrysanthemum tea several times a day if you suffer from headaches caused by too much heat, red and sore eyes, bad breath, bitter taste in the mouth, spots, pimples, acne, boils, heat rash, eczema and psoriasis. Do this daily until your condition improves. One cup a day or once a week is sufficient for mild cases.

Infuse 3 to 6 whole flowers in 1 cup of boiling water in a thermos flask for 10 to 15 minutes. Strain and drink.

Note: This is a very cooling tea. Please do not use more than 6 whole flowers per cup.

Comfrey Tea

Comfrey tea is good for people with dry hacking coughs, dry mouth and throat, and inflamed gastric or duodenal ulcers.

Boil 1 to 3 teaspoons of the dried comfrey root in a cup of water and simmer for 10 to 15 minutes. Drink 3 times a day until the condition eases.

Corn Silk Tea

Corn silk tea is good for diabetes, nephritis, cystitis, prostatitis and high blood pressure.

Infuse 1 tablespoon of dried corn silk in 1 cup of boiling water for 10 to 15 minutes in a thermos flask. Strain and drink three times a day until the condition eases.

Dandelion Tea

Dandelion tea is suitable for mastitis, sores, chronic gastritis, urinary tract infections, gall bladder inflammations, hepatitis, bronchitis and tonsilitis.

Boil 25 g (1 oz) of the dandelion root in

570 ml (1 pint) of water. Boil down to 275 ml ($^1/_2$ pint). Strain and drink once a day until the condition clears. If you find the root too bitter and strong, you can try using the same amount of dried leaves.

Lemon Balm Tea
Lemon balm tea helps keep you cool on hot summer days. Inhaling the lemon fragrance can be very relaxing.

Infuse 3 to 4 sprays of fresh leaves or 1 teaspoon of dried leaves in 1 cup of boiling water in a thermos flask for 10 to 15 minutes. Strain and drink.

Mint, Cornmint and Peppermint Teas
Try these teas after a meal to aid digestion. You can also combine peppermint with chamomile for headaches.

Infuse 1 teaspoon of the dried herb in 1 cup of boiling water in a thermos flask for 10 to 15 minutes. Strain and drink.

For headaches infuse $^1/_2$ teaspoon of peppermint and $^1/_2$ teaspoon of chamomile in 1 cup of boiling water in a thermos flask for 10 to 15 minutes. Strain and drink.

Vervain Tea
This tea helps relieve stress, tension, gall bladder inflammation and jaundice. It is good for 'flu too.

Infuse 1 teaspoon of the dried herb in 1 cup of boiling water in a thermos flask for 10 to 15 minutes. Drink three times a day until the condition eases.

Fruit Juices (cooling)
The following cooling fruit juices should be taken at least 1 to 2 hours before or after meals. Fruit sugars are easier to digest than complex sugars from wholegrains, legumes, pulses, seeds and nuts, and can upset the digestive system when taken together.

It is not advisable to drink fruit juices all day long; a glass a day for the strong, active and robust is sufficient. Juices from organically grown fresh fruits are best, but you can also use pure, sugar- and additive-free, concentrated fruit juices diluted with mineral water, filtered tap water or hot water. Cartons of pure fruit juices which are sugar-free and additive-free are also acceptable. (See Chapter 12 on Fruits for more specific information.)

In temperate countries, drink: Pear juice

In Mediterranean countries, drink:
1   Clementine juice
2   Grapefruit juice
3   Lemon juice
4   Mandarin juice
5   Orange juice
6   Tangerine juice
7   Melon juice

Note: Citrus fruits are not advisable for people who suffer from or are prone to catarrh, mucus, phlegm or sputum. People who suffer from aches and pains should avoid sour juices.

In tropical countries, drink:
1   Coconut juice
2   Lime juice
3   Pineapple juice
4   Star fruit juice
5   Sugar-cane juice (from the variety with the pale yellow-green skin) juice
6   Watermelon juice

Honey

Pure honey helps soothe dry throats, dry mouths, dry coughs and constipation with hard, dry stools. Drink a cup of mineral water, filtered tap water or hot water mixed with a teaspoon of honey three times a day when the condition is severe. Otherwise, once a day is sufficient. Use only pure honey.

Overconsumption of honey can lead to catarrh, mucus, phlegm or sputum.

NEUTRAL BEVERAGES

Almond Milk

Almond milk is a good substitute for cow's, goat's or soyabean milk. Cow's milk often contains traces of hormones and antibiotics. Although goat's milk rarely contains hormones or antibiotics it has a very strong taste, and it is warming, making it unsuitable for those with overheated blood systems, eczema, psoriasis, etc. And soyabean milk is too cooling for those with cooled blood systems. Almond milk, on the other hand, is neutral and contains calcium and magnesium as well as trace elements like sulphur, sodium, iron, zinc, manganese and copper. It is also rich in vitamins B and E.

Boil and simmer some blanched almonds until they are soft, then liquidise. The amount of water used determines the thickness of the milk. Serve plain or sweetened with barley or rice malt extract. Have a fresh glass daily, for the calcium if you do not drink cow's or goat's milk.

Peanut Milk

Like almond milk, peanut milk is neutral and contains calcium and magnesium. However, it has a higher calorific content than almonds and should be taken sparingly, to break the monotony of almond milk.

Boil and simmer some skinless peanuts until they are soft; then liquidise. Serve plain or sweetened with barley or rice malt extract.

> *Note:* Overconsumption can create catarrh, mucus, phlegm or sputum.

Parsley Tea

Parsley tea is suitable for those with bladder, kidney, gall bladder or liver problems, water retention, painful menstrual periods, delayed periods or amenorrhoea (failure to menstruate).

Infuse 1 teaspoon of the dried herb in 1 cup of boiling water in a thermos flask for 10 to 15 minutes. Strain and drink. Eat the strained leaves – they are rich in iron. Drink three times a day if your condition is severe, once a day if your condition is minor.

Raspberry Leaf Tea

Raspberry leaf tea is good for expecting mothers during the last three months of pregnancy to aid a smooth and quick delivery.

Infuse 1 teaspoon of the dried herb in a cup of boiling water in a thermos flask for 10 to 15 minutes. Strain, and drink, three times a day.

Rosemary Tea

Rosemary tea is good for people with sluggish livers, gall bladder inflammations, jaundice, depression and water retention. It helps digestion following a rich, fatty meal.

Infuse 1 teaspoon of the dried herb in 1 cup of boiling water in a thermos flask for 10 to 15 minutes. Strain, and drink three times a day if your condition is severe, once a day otherwise.

Sage Tea

This tea also aids digestion after fatty rich meals and helps to regulate the menstrual cycle.

Infuse 1 teaspoon of the dried herb in 1 cup of boiling water in a thermos flask for 10 to 15 minutes. Strain, and drink three times a day if your condition is severe, once a day otherwise.

Thyme Tea

Thyme tea is appropriate for those who suffer from or are prone to catarrh, mucus, phlegm or sputum. It also aids digestion and is good for gastritis.

Infuse 1 teaspoon of the dried herb in 1 cup of boiling water in a thermos flask for 10 to 15 minutes. Strain, and drink three times a day if your condition is severe, once a day otherwise.

Japanese Tea

This tea consists of Japanese green leaf tea and roasted rice grains. It is a balanced tea because the cooling green leaves are counteracted by the roasted rice grains. Please do not have this too often because of the tannin content of the green tea leaves.

Fruit Juices *(neutral)*

Drink the following fruit juices 1 to 2 hours before or after meals. If you drink a glass of fruit juice it is not necessary to have a piece of fruit that day.

In temperate countries, drink:
1   Apple juice
2   Plum juice
3   Raspberry juice
4   Redcurrant juice

In Mediterranean countries, drink:
(White or red) grape juice

In tropical countries, drink:
1   Papaya juice
2   Guava juice
3   Sugar-cane juice (only from the variety with deep red-purple skins)

Barley Malt or Rice Malt Extract Drinks

Dilute 2 teaspoons of barley or rice malt extracts with 1 cup of hot water for a nourishing hot drink.

WARMING BEVERAGES

Sunflower Seed Milk

This milk is good for those who are anaemic because sunflower seeds are rich in iron.

Boil and simmer the seeds until they are soft; then liquidise. Serve plain or sweetened with barley or rice malt extract. Drink a glass a day.

Walnut Milk

According to books on Chinese diet therapy, this milk helps keep your complexion smooth and youthful. It is also good for people with weak kidneys, backs, legs and knees.

Boil and simmer the nuts until they are soft; then liquidise. (Blanch them first if you do not like the bitter taste of the skin.) Serve plain or sweetened with barley or rice malt extract. Drink a glass a day.

Caraway Seed Tea

This tea is good for digestion.

Boil 1 teaspoon of the bruised seeds in 1 cup of water for 10 to 15 minutes. Strain and drink.

Cinnamon Tea

Cinnamon tea helps warm up cold hands and feet in winter.

Boil a $2^1/_2$ cm (1 in) stick of cinnamon in 1 cup of water for 10 to 15 minutes. Strain, and drink 1 cup a day every other day. Over-consumption can cause nose bleeds.

Fennel Seed Tea

Fennel seed tea is good for indigestion and helps nursing mothers promote the flow of milk.

Boil 1 teaspoon of bruised seeds in 1 cup of water for 10 to 15 minutes. Strain, and drink three times a day if your condition is severe, once a day otherwise.

Ginger Tea

Ginger tea helps sweat out a cold at the beginning of an attack.

Grate 1 teaspoon of fresh root ginger into a cup and add 1 cup of boiling water. Sip the tea slowly, then go to bed to sweat out the cold under lots of blankets. Repeat three times a day until the cold goes away.

> *Note:* Do not take ginger tea if you are old, weak, or if the cold begins with a sore throat. If you are old and weak and you use ginger tea to sweat out a cold you may deplete your strength. If you have a sore throat, the heat from the ginger will aggravate the condition.

Mu Tea

This invigorating herbal tea was originally developed by George Oshawa, the founder of Macrobiotics. It contains nine mountain-grown herbs: herbaceous peony root, hoelen, Japanese parsley root, cinnamon, liquorice, peach kernels, ginger root, Japanese ginseng and rehmannia.

This tea is especially good for women after menstruation to build up the blood again because most of these herbs nourish the blood. Unfortunately, it is not widely available. The best sources would be macrobiotic shops or some health food shops which stock macrobiotic products.

You will need to decoct this tea because it contains a lot of roots to extract the goodness out of them. Place 1 teaspoon or 1 tea bag in 2 cups of water and boil down to 1 cup. Do this in a Chinese earthenware herbal pot or stainless steel pot. Strain and drink it hot. One decoction a day is sufficient.

> *Note:* This tea is appropriate for those with a cooled blood system. Remember it is not to be drunk when you have a cold or 'flu because it contains Japanese ginseng. Anyone with high blood pressure or tendencies towards it must not drink this tea; the same applies to anyone with an overheated blood system or tendencies towards it.

Mugwort Tea

Mugwort tea helps to promote menstrual flow if a period is delayed. Do not drink too much, however, and do not drink between the end of one period and the next ovulation.

Infuse 1 teaspoon of the dried herb in 1 cup of boiling water in a thermos flask for 10 to 15 minutes. Strain, and drink three times a day if your condition is severe, once a day otherwise.

Spearmint Tea

Spearmint tea helps indigestion. It is more warming than peppermint tea so it will be more suitable for people with a cooled blood system or tendencies towards one.

Infuse 1 teaspoon of the dried herb in 1 cup of boiling water in a thermos flask for 10 to 15 minutes. Strain and drink.

Fruit Juices *(warming)*

The following fruit juices are not meant for those with weak constitutions, cooled blood systems or tendencies towards them. They are only for those with neutral blood systems and, again, they must be taken 1 to 2 hours before or after a meal.

In temperate countries, drink:
1   Apricot juice
2   Blackberry juice
3   Blackcurrant juice
4   Cherry juice
5   Nectarine juice
6   Peach juice
7   Strawberry juice

In Mediterranean countries, drink:
1   Lychee juice
2   Longan juice

Have you noticed there are far more choices than just tea and coffee? Now you have many healthy and wholesome beverages to choose from to suit your blood system and the requirements of your health for the day.

Note: If you prefer vegetable juices to fruit juices, please have them in moderation. Remember to choose vegetables suitable for your blood system. For this please refer to Chapter 6 on Vegetables.

In general it is best to buy fruit and vegetable juices or juice concentrates from health food shops. This is because the quality of the products is usually higher. However, do read the labels to check there are no additives like glucose, citric acid, ascorbic acid, etc. The ideal is to make your own from organically grown vegetables and fruit as soon as they are picked.

BEVERAGES FOR BABIES AND INFANTS

Newborn babies should have mother's milk and some still mineral water or still spring water which has been boiled and cooled to body temperature. You can also supplement mother's milk with grain milks and seed or nut milks. Please see Chapters 2 and 4 on Whole Cereal Grains and Seeds and Nuts.

When they grow older, you can introduce very dilute vegetable or fruit juices once a day. You have to judge which blood system your child has and choose the appropriate vegetables or fruits.

Children can have still mineral water or still spring water or filtered tap water. Tea or coffee is not recommended at all. Have hot barley malt or rice malt drinks instead. Hot pure honey drinks are good for children who tend to have overheated blood systems as long as they are not prone to catarrh, mucus, sputum and phlegm. Vegetable and fruit juices are fine but in moderation. Follow the advice given for adults.

Hot water (from still mineral water, still spring water or filtered water) is the best beverage for all ages.

14 The Importance of Cooking in the Tao Diet

In the West, something called the 'raw food energy' school of thought has gained popularity over the past few years. Its followers eat almost all foods raw because they believe that cooking destroys the vital energy of foods.

There is a similar school of thought in India. It is practised mainly by holy men who believe raw foods can help them attain spiritual awareness.

There is nothing wrong in these beliefs but they are not suitable for everyone. Cold, raw foods are very difficult to digest. They require a great deal of chewing so the saliva can predigest the food in the mouth before it enters the digestive system. A strong digestive system is also required to further digest and assimilate the vital nutrients.

A raw food diet is suitable for someone with a strong constitution, an active life, an overheated blood system or a tendency towards one. Few people should follow it forever. In my opinion, when a person with an overheated blood system goes on a raw food diet he should only eat raw foods until the blood system cools down, or it may become too cooled.

A raw food diet is suitable for holy men because when they have reached a certain level of daily meditation they have created enough heat in their bodies to cope with any raw foods they ingest and so have no problems digesting and extracting the vital nutrients.

> *Note:* A raw food diet is not suitable for most people. This is because as you grow older the digestive system fails to work at its optimum level.

To overcome all these shortcomings we have to cook most of our food. Taoists do not believe that cooking destroys vital energies. On the contrary, they believe that energy from cooking transforms the natural energies of food. It is very difficult to understand how the energy from a cooking fire can be imparted to you by mere cooking. Let me give you an example.

One of my patients used to eat lots of raw salads all year round believing it was good because the vitamins would not be lost or destroyed by cooking. She could not understand why she felt cold all the time and had loose stools several times a day.

This is my explanation. The heat from the cooking fire breaks down the cellulose surrounding each plant cell so that the body's digestive juices can enter to extract the nutrients for body metabolism to keep the body warm. The body's digestive juices cannot break through or digest the cellulose if a vegetable is eaten raw so the cellulose is

passed out through the system undigested. Therefore if a lot of raw salads are eaten the body's digestive juices cannot extract the necessary nutrients from the food hence the cold feeling and loose stools.

Also, traditional Chinese medicine explains that the heat from the cooking fire is necessary to help you keep warm. That is why you eat more cooked foods in winter. It does not matter whether you blanch, steam, stir-fry, bake, roast or grill the food. As long as you have applied some heat you will receive some warming energies. However, the different methods of cooking will give you different degrees of warmth, i.e., blanching and steaming are less warming than baking, roasting or grilling.

After my patient followed my advice to have more cooked meals and to avoid salads in winter she reported that she felt warmer, more energetic and her bowel movements became normal and frequency was reduced to once a day. There was noticeable improvement within a few weeks.

THE ART OF TAOIST COOKING

1   Use wholefood organic ingredients suitable for climate or season

In winter, for example, use winter roots such as onions, carrots, turnips, swedes, celeriac and garlic in higher proportions than leafy greens such as leeks and members of the cabbage family.

In summer, use more leafy vegetables, beans and peas (i.e., lettuce, spinach, Chinese Peking cabbage, watercress, dwarf beans, string beans, snow peas, garden peas, baby carrots, radishes, etc.), rather than roots.

In the tropics, use more cooling vegetables such as cucumbers, fuzzy melon, bitter gourd, angled luffa, Chinese Peking cabbage, Chinese flowering cabbage, Chinese box thorn leaves, and various types of spinach.

2   Select appropriate foods for the blood system

An overheated blood system requires a larger proportion of cooling foods than neutral foods.

A neutral blood system requires foods from the cooling, neutral and warming groups.

A cooled blood system requires more warming foods than neutral foods.

3   Select the appropriate cooking method suitable for the blood system

Cooling methods of cooking are foods blanched, parboiled, bain-maried, hot-tossed (with or without water or stock), steamed, or poached on the stove.

Neutral methods of cooking are foods poached in the grill or in the oven, or boiled.

Warming methods of cooking are foods cooked in a casserole on the stove or in the oven; stewed on the stove or in the oven; braised on the stove or in the oven; sautéed; stir-fried; baked with liquids and/or vegetables; roasted in oil; grilled or broiled; or barbecued.

> *Cooling methods:*
> *raw* – as in salad
> *blanching and parboiling* – vegetables are just dipped into some hot boiling water with a pinch of sea-salt for 2 to 3 minutes or until they just change colour
> *bain-marie cooking* – food is cooked in a pot of hot water without the lid

hot-toss – cooking salad in the barest minimum of boiling water or stock for 1 to 2 minutes to remove the rawness; alternatively, vegetables with a high water content, like cucumbers, Chinese Peking cabbage, Cos lettuce, radishes, etc., can be hot-tossed in a hot stainless steel pan for 1 to 2 minutes to remove the rawness

steaming – food is placed in a steaming basket in a wok or pot with the lid on.

poaching – food is slowly simmered on the stove in water or stock

Neutral methods:

poaching – food can also be simmered in water or stock in the grill or oven on the hottest setting (this method is even warmer because the food is surrounded by heat on all sides)

boiling – I do not mean using lots of water and discarding it at the end, but using just enough water so it evaporates or can be used as a sauce

Warming methods:

casserole/stewing – food is cooked on the stove top, slowly simmered in liquid, with or without vegetables; casseroles or stews can also be made in the oven, which is more warming

braising – cooking on the stove top by sautéing foods in a little oil before adding liquid and/or vegetables and slowly simmering; foods braised in the oven are sautéed and then slowly simmered in the oven to make them even more warming

sautéing – food is cooked on the stove top on low or medium heat

stir-frying – food is cooked on high heat, so it is more warming

baking – as this takes longer than poaching, it is more warming; it is also more warming than

casserole cooking or stewing because less water is used.

roasting in oil – this method is more heating, because water is not used, and roasted food has a drier texture

grilling or broiling – even more heating because the food is nearer to the heat source.

barbecuing – the most heating cooking method because food is very close to the heat source and slightly charred, to give it that authentic smoky taste

4 Combine different cooking methods for different blood systems

For overheated blood systems, use more cooling and fewer neutral methods.

For neutral blood systems, use equal proportions of cooling, neutral and warming methods.

For cooled blood systems, use more warming and fewer neutral methods.

5 Select herbs and spices

Choose herbs and spices to stimulate the senses of smell and taste and, therefore, to improve the appetite and digestion. See Chapter 7 for information on the herbs and spices and their special healing properties.

6 Cook creatively

Combine colours and textures of foods to further stimulate the appetite.

Note: If you eat lots of cold, raw foods and you suffer from or are prone to the following complaints, try the Tao diet to correct your imbalance, and give you more energy and warmth, especially in winter: poor appetite, loose stools, diarrhoea, abdominal distension, oedema, general lassitude, lethargy, cold, weak limbs, sallow complexion, and a dislike of the cold.

15 Meals and Menu-Planning

The following menus are designed for vegans, macrobiotics, vegetarians and wholefooders and anyone wishing to follow the Chang Ming or Tao Diet. If you are a wholefooder trying to cut down on meat products, have the vegetarian menu for lunch and the wholefooder menu for dinner. As you will see, it is not difficult to cook for the odd one out in the family.

COOLING MEALS FOR OVERHEATED BLOOD SYSTEMS

Menu for summer or hot, sunny tropical days

Main menu
1 *Wakame*, onion and *miso* soup (boiled) *neutral*
2 Brown rice (boiled) *neutral*
3 Mixed vegetables (stir-fried) *warming*
4 Lettuce salad (raw) *cooling*

For vegans, macrobiotics and vegetarians
5 *Tofu* (steamed) *cooling*

For wholefooders
6 Pomfret (steamed) *cooling*

As you can see, three dishes out of six are prepared by cooling methods, two dishes by neutral methods and only one by a warming method.

If you look at the ingredients of the individual dishes, you will find that there are more cooling foods than neutral or warming foods. These ingredients are then combined with others and cooked by different methods to create balance.

In *wakame*, onion and *miso* soup, for instance, the *wakame* and *miso* are cooling, the water is neutral, and the onion and coriander leaves are warming. The cooking method – boiling – is neutral. Most of this dish is either cooling or neutral, so the onion and coriander leaves are added for balance, taste and aroma. Without them, the *miso* soup would be flat and unappealing.

In the mixed vegetable dish, the bean sprouts and cucumber are cooling, the carrot and garlic are warming and the sesame oil is neutral. Stir-frying, however, is warming. So, although this stir-fried dish has warming properties, it also has a large proportion of cooling vegetables. The shreds of carrot are added for colour and texture contrast. Garlic is added for smell, taste, to improve digestion, lower blood pressure and blood cholesterol, resolve catarrh, and strengthen the body's immune system to resist colds and 'flus.

Why, you may ask, should you have a warming stir-fried dish in a menu for an overheated blood system? Firstly, most people are used to highly spiced and seasoned foods and they cannot stimulate enough saliva if the food is too bland. The smell and taste of garlic help stimulate the salivary glands. Secondly, a stir-fried dish offers a contrast in preparation method. Steaming and boiling involve too much water and are too bland. Thirdly, the unrefined, cold-pressed sesame oil adds essential polyunsaturated oils to the diet. Fourthly, in terms of *yin* and *yang*, steaming, boiling and eating foods raw are all *yin*, so you need stir-frying, which is *yang*, to create balance.

In lettuce salad, the lettuce is cooling and the spring onion garnish is warming. Even in a raw salad it is essential to create balance for visual, olfactory and taste appeal, as well as for contrast.

In the *tofu*, the *tofu* and *tamari* are cooling, the Shiitake mushrooms are neutral, and the spring onion, coriander leaves and roasted sesame seeds (all garnishes) are warming. Steaming is cooling. This dish is cooling, even though it has small amounts of warming ingredients. They add contrast in colour, taste and smell, and keep the steamed *tofu* from being bland.

In the pomfret dish, the pomfret is cooling, the Shiitake mushrooms are neutral, the spring onion and coriander garnishes are warming and steaming is cooling. Pomfret is less cooling than *tofu*, and therefore does not need any additional roasted sesame seeds. The warming properties of spring onion and coriander leaves not only balance the dish but negate the strong fishy odour.

Fruits – Choose any cooling fruits in season, like pears or star fruit. Refer to Chapter 12 on fruits.

Beverages – Refer to Chapter 13 on beverages to choose a cooling tea that will suit your body condition.

Variations:

Soups – Cooling soups like those below can be made from boiling any of the cooling vegetables with a little warming root vegetable, such as onion or garlic, or some herbs to give taste and create balance.

1   Cucumber, peppermint and onion soup
2   Chinese box thorn leaves and onion soup
3   *Miso*, spinach and onion soup

Mixed vegetables – Stir-fry the following mixtures.

1   Watercress, fresh mushrooms and a few shreds of carrot
2   Angled luffa, black wood ears and fresh baby sweet corn
3   Chinese Peking cabbage, courgettes and a little carrot

Salads

1   Red radishes and spring onion
2   Alfalfa sprouts and roasted sunflower seeds
3   Celery, parsley and roasted sesame seeds

Protein dishes for vegans, macrobiotics and vegetarians

1   *Tempeh* marinated with *tamari* and steamed like *tofu*
2   Mung beans stewed with a pinch of turmeric powder, cumin seeds, a small clove of garlic and a thin slice of ginger.

3 Black-eyed beans stewed with *kombu* and onion.

Protein dishes for wholefooders
1 Bass steamed with *miso*
2 Whiting poached in fennel stock
3 Mackerel poached in lemon juice

LESS COOLING MEALS FOR OVERHEATED BLOOD SYSTEMS

Menu for winter
The dishes are less cooling to warm the body and prevent colds and 'flus.

Soups
1 *Wakame*, onion and *miso* soup
2 Celery, pot barley, garlic and carrot soup
3 Spinach, onion and nutmeg soup

For the *wakame*, onion and *miso* soup, slice the onion and sauté in a little cold-pressed oil until soft. Add water and *wakame* and simmer until the onion softens. Then add *miso* and simmer for another 15 minutes.

For the second soup, use only 1 small clove of garlic, and a few carrot slices for garnish.

The onion in spinach, onion and nutmeg soup should be sautéed in a little cold-pressed oil until soft before adding spinach and water. Add a dash of nutmeg for taste and aroma.

Mixed vegetables – Braise or stir-fry the following combinations.
1 *Arame*, white cabbage, onion and carrot
2 Watercress, carrot and onion
3 Celery, Brussels sprouts and garlic

Salads
1 Alfalfa sprouts and roasted sesame seeds
2 Mustard, cress and roasted sunflower seeds
3 Lamb's lettuce and garlic

Fruits – Use cooling or neutral fruits. Prepare them in one of the following ways.
1 Raw
2 Steamed with dried fruits
3 Stewed with dried fruits

Protein dishes for vegans, macrobiotics and vegetarians
1 Stir-fried or braised *tofu* with vegetables
2 Braised or stewed *fu zhou* with vegetables
3 Boiled or stewed beans with vegetables

Protein dishes for wholefooders
1 Cod poached in the grill or oven
2 Steamed chicken
3 Steamed egg

For rainy monsoon days in the tropics
Prepare the food the same way as for winter but eat the fruits raw. Of course, you must find substitutes for Brussels sprouts, mustard, cress, lamb's lettuce and cod.

NEUTRAL MEALS FOR NEUTRAL BLOOD SYSTEMS

Menu for summer or hot, sunny tropical days

Main menu
1 Carrot, onion, spinach and *miso* soup (stir-fried, then simmered) *neutral*
2 Brown rice (boiled) *neutral*

3 Mixed vegetables (stir-fried) *warming*

4 Greens (blanched) *cooling*

5 Fruit (raw) *cooling*

For vegans, macrobiotics and vegetarians

6 Chick-peas (stir-fried, then simmered) *neutral*

For wholefooders

7 Prawns (stir-fried) *neutral*

This neutral menu consists of three neutral dishes, two cooling dishes and one warming dish.

Note: Use only 1 to 2 thin slices of ginger. Do not eat the ginger.

Let us look at the individual dishes.

In the carrot, onion, spinach and *miso* soup, there is an equal balance of warming and cooling ingredients: the carrot and onion are warming; the spinach, *miso* and water are cooling; the simmering is neutral and the stir-frying is warming. Lightly stir-fry the vegetables with a little unrefined cold-pressed oil before adding the water and simmering until just cooked. Add the *miso* and the soup and gently simmer for another 15 minutes.

In the mixed vegetables, the ginger, garlic and spring onion in this dish are warming and the Peking cabbage is cooling. This warming dish is very quickly stir-fried to retain the crispness of the cabbage leaves and spring onion.

For greens, use neutral ones like broccoli, lamb's lettuce, spring greens, Chinese flowering cabbage, Chinese kale or garland chrysanthemum and blanch for a few minutes with a tiny pinch of sea-salt. The blandness of this dish contrasts the spicy stir-fried main dish.

In the chick-peas for vegans, macrobiotics and vegetarians, pumpkin and parsley are neutral, the garlic and ginger are warming, the simmering is neutral and the sautéing is warming. Since the garlic and ginger are small in proportion to the chick-peas and pumpkin the dish remains neutral. Lightly sauté the garlic, ginger, parsley stalks and pumpkin in a little cold-pressed oil before adding the chick-peas and enough water to cover. Bring to a fast rolling boil, then simmer until the chick-peas are soft. Add sea-salt and simmer for another 15 minutes. Garnish with finely chopped parsley.

The cooling prawns in the dish of stir-fried prawns outweigh the warming effects of the garlic, ginger, spring onions and stir-frying, so the dish remains neutral. Quickly stir-fry the garlic, ginger and spring onions in a little unrefined cold-pressed oil before adding the prawns. Stir-fry for 2 to 3 seconds, add a drop of water and cover the wok until the prawns are just cooked, about 2 to 3 minutes.

People with neutral blood systems can have fruit with all types of energies, but only a small portion of each type. Do not indulge in fruits from only the cold or warm energy group or you will create an imbalance. If you feel overheated, eat a cooling fruit that day. If you feel you are moving towards a cooled blood system or if the day is cooler, choose a warming fruit. Have your fruit at least 1 hour before or after a meal, or as a snack.

Choose a beverage from Chapter 13 to suit your blood system.

Variations: There are countless variations for people with neutral blood systems. All you have

to remember is that each meal must have a balance of cooling, neutral and warming ingredients and methods of preparation.

Menu for winter

In general, winter dishes have more garlic and/or ginger. Omit the ginger on a very hot summer day. In winter, include a bit more ginger in every dish, but do not eat it.

Let us look at our main menu again and make adjustments to individual dishes.

Main menu

1   Carrot, onion, spinach and *miso* soup (stir-fried, then simmered) *neutral*
2   Brown rice (boiled) *neutral*
3   Mixed vegetables (stir-fried) *warming*
4   Greens (blanched) *cooling*
5   Fruit (raw) *cooling*

For vegans, macrobiotics and vegetarians

6   Chick-peas (stir-fried, then simmered) *neutral*

For wholefooders

7   Prawns (stir-fried) *neutral*

Add a thin slice of ginger to the carrot, onion, spinach and *miso* soup and/or stir-fry the vegetables with garlic and ginger.

To mixed vegetables, add a dash of freshly ground black pepper.

Use winter greens such as Brussels sprouts, Savoy cabbage, kale, etc. Add a sauce of roasted sesame oil and *tamari* or a garnish of dry roasted seeds.

For the chick-peas, instead of parsley, add coriander seeds and coriander leaves, and simmer the chick-peas in the oven. If the winter is very cold, bake the chick-peas after they have softened.

Variations: Braise or stew beans, *tofu, fu zhou* or *tempeh*.

Stir-fry prawns with warming coriander leaves, spring onions and a dash of freshly ground black pepper. Alternatively, marinate the prawns in a mixture of sea-salt and ground Sichuan pepper before stir-frying. Or grill the prawns.

Variations: Stir-fry, braise, stew, bake or grill white or oily fish, squid, octopus or chicken.

Stew fresh fruit on cold winter days, or stew a mixture of fresh and dried fruits for colour and texture contrast. Add some chopped nuts or seeds for added texture and extra vitamins.

Hot teas of a neutral or warming nature will be best depending on the weather, your activity, and your blood system.

For rainy monsoon days in the tropics

Prepare food as you would for summer or hot, sunny tropical days, but add slightly more ginger. (Do not eat the ginger – just use it for flavour.) There is no need to add black or Sichuan pepper, or to cook the fruit. You may, if you wish it, but no more than once or twice a week.

WARMING MEALS FOR COOLED BLOOD SYSTEMS

For summer or hot, sunny tropical days

Main menu

1   Red rice (boiled) *neutral*
2   Mixed vegetables (stir-fried) *warming*

3   Greens (braised) *neutral*

For vegans, macrobiotics and vegetarians
4   *Fu zhou* (braised) *warming*

For wholefooders
5   Chicken (braised) *warming*

In this menu, there is an equal balance of neutral and warming dishes. Do not eat too many warming dishes in summer or you will have difficulty coping with the heat. Use about 1 to 2 thick slices of ginger for flavour or mince an equivalent amount to eat to keep you warm only if you require very much warmth in the summer.

Unpolished or unrefined red rice is better than brown rice for weak individuals with cooled blood systems.

In the mixed vegetable dish, the white cabbage, snow peas and baby sweet corn are neutral and the garlic, ginger and stir-frying are warming. If you do not find this dish warming enough add a dash of black pepper. Alternatively, substitute warming spring onions for snow peas.

For the braised greens, quickly stir-fry any neutral greens with warming garlic and ginger, then add a drop or two of water and steam the greens until they are just cooked. Add a sauce of roasted sesame oil and *tamari*, if you prefer, or dry-roasted nuts or seeds for texture and colour contrast.

In braised *fu zhou*, the warming ingredients outweigh the neutral and cooling ones. Stir-fry the following ingredients in this order: garlic (warming), ginger (warming), onion (warming), Shiitake mushrooms (neutral) coriander seeds and stalks (warming), *fu zhou* (neutral) and carrot (warming). Add water

and bring to a fast rolling boil. Then simmer slowly in the oven for even more warmth. Add *miso* (cooling) and slowly simmer for another 15 minutes. Garnish with freshly chopped coriander leaves.

For chicken, too, the warming ingredients outweigh the neutral or cooling ones. Stir-fry warming garlic, ginger, onion, and chicken pieces with neutral Shiitake mushrooms. Then add water and warming chestnuts and Chinese red dates. Bring the lot to a fast rolling boil then simmer 1 to 2 hours in the oven for extra warmth. When the dish is ready, the chicken meat should melt in the mouth. Add cooling *tamari* and warming finely chopped spring onion just before serving.

Fruit, on the whole, is too cooling for people with cooled blood systems. If you cannot do without it, bake neutral or warming fruits with dried fruits and warm spices such as cinnamon, nutmeg, mace, allspice and caraway seeds.

Warming herbal teas and hot water are the best choices of beverage.

Variations:

Rice
1   Brown rice boiled with walnuts
2   Brown rice boiled with sunflower seeds
3   Red rice served with salt-free *gomasio*

Mixed vegetables – Stir-fry one of the following combinations.
1   Garlic, ginger, sage, onion and broad beans
2   Garlic, ginger, onion, carrot and long beans
3   Garlic, ginger, caraway seeds and white cabbage

Greens

Use different neutral greens (see Chapter 6) and cook them as on page 194, Greens.

Vegan, macrobiotic and vegetarian protein

1 Choose any bean. Stir-fry the vegetables, add the bean and simmer slowly in the oven.
2 Use *tofu*. Stir-fry and simmer in *miso* in the oven.
3 Use *tempeh*. Stir-fry and simmer with warming herbs in the oven.

Wholefooder protein

1 Braise or poach fish in the oven or in a casserole.
2 Braise, stew or stir-fry chicken or use a casserole.

For winter

Use more garlic, ginger and other warming herbs and spices in the cooking. Either mince the ginger so you can eat it or use 3 to 4 thick slices.

Variations:

Rice

1 Brown rice boiled with black sesame seeds
2 Red rice boiled with walnuts

Mixed vegetables – Stir-fry a mixture of the following ingredients.

1 Garlic, ginger, caraway seeds, onion, carrot and white cabbage
2 Garlic, ginger, oregano, onion and turnip
3 Garlic, ginger, black pepper, leek and swede

Greens – Stir-fry these vegetables, then braise them until the greens are just cooked and retain their green colour.

1 Garlic, ginger, black mustard seeds and green cabbage
2 Garlic, ginger, coriander seeds and Brussels sprouts
3 Garlic, ginger, nutmeg and Savoy cabbage

Vegan, macrobiotic and vegetarian protein

Add any one of the warming spices (cinnamon, star anise, fenugreek, fennel, 5-spice powder, black pepper, coriander seeds, cumin seeds, etc.) to the following protein-rich dishes.

1 Stir-fry vegetables. Add beans, slowly simmer in the oven until the beans are cooked, then bake.
2 Stir-fry *tofu*, then simmer in the oven with *miso*. Or, marinate *tofu* in *miso*, then grill. Or, just stir-fry plain *tofu*.
3 Marinate *tempeh* in *tamari* and warming spices, then grill or bake.

Wholefood protein

1 Bake, grill or shallow-fry white or oily fish with warming spices and herbs.
2 Bake, roast, grill or stir-fry chicken with warming spices and herbs.

For rainy monsoon days in the tropics

Cook the dishes as for hot, sunny tropical days but use more ginger, and once or twice a week prepare winter dishes using warming spices and herbs. In tropical countries, even though it is slightly cooler in the monsoon season than during the rest of the year, it is not cold enough to eat warming spices and herbs daily.

CONCLUSION

I hope this chapter will help you plan menus according to your blood system and the season or climate you live in. Bear in mind that your blood system can change from day to day, week to week, month to month and year to year. Determine which blood system you have that day before preparing your meals.

If there is no clear-cut division between an overheated blood system and a neutral blood system, or a cooled blood system and a neutral blood system or a bit of all three, then you simply must decide which is the most predominant for you on any particular day.

In fact, it is possible for a person with a cooled blood system to suffer from a sore throat. (If this happens to you, eat more cooling and neutral foods until the throat eases, then return to more neutral and more warming dishes to maintain balance.) A person with an overheated blood system rarely suffers from the cold, but when he does, he must eat more neutral and warming foods.

Remember, health, vitality and longevity depend on:

1 wholesome organic foods
2 balancing foods and cooking methods to suit your blood system, climate and activities
3 chewing well to aid digestion.

Neutral Meal

1 Brown rice
2 Mixed vegetables
3 Greens
4 Chick-peas
5 Prawns
6 Apple, grapes or strawberries
7 Mineral water

Cooling Meal

1 *Wakame,* onion and *miso* soup
2 Brown rice
3 Mixed vegetables
4 Lettuce salad
5 Pomfret
6 Japanese pears or star fruit

Warming Meal

1 Red rice
2 Mixed vegetables
3 Greens
4 *Fu zhou*
5 Chicken

Tea & Snacks

1 Banana couscous
2 Walnuts & Chinese red dates
3 Bananas
4 Pineapple
5 Cooked pineapple
6 Chrysanthemun tea (*cooling*)
7 Japanese tea – green tea leaves
   with roasted rice grains (*neutral*)
8 Mu tea

Legumes, Pulses & Soyabean Products

Cooling
1 Fermented black soyabeans
2 *Miso*
3 *Shoyu*
4 *Tamari*
5 Mung beans
6 Soyabeans
7a *Tofu* (hard)
7b *Tofu* (soft)

8 Soyabean milk
9 *Tempeh*

Neutral
10 Dried *tofu* squares
11 Soyabean sticks (*fu zhou*)
12 Aduki beans
13 *Chi xiao dou*

14 Black-eyed beans
15 Black soyabeans
16 Chick-peas
17 Haricot beans
18 Hyacinth beans
19 Red kidney beans

Warming
20 Brown lentils
21 Green lentils

Seeds, Nuts & Dried Ingredients

Cooling

1 Bitter apricot kernels
2 Ginkgo nuts
3 Buddha's fruit
4 Chinese box thorn berries
5 Figs

6 Golden needles
7 Job's tears
8 Persimmons
9 Snow ear fungus

Neutral
10 Almonds
11 Apricot kernels
12 Lotus seeds
13 Peanuts
14 Black wood ears
15 Dried shrimps

16 Raisins
17 Shiitake mushrooms

Warming
18 Chestnuts
19 Pumpkin seeds
20 Beige sesame seeds

21 Black sesame seeds
22 Sunflower seeds
23 Walnuts
24 Chinese black dates
25 Chinese red dates
26 *Dang gui*
27 *Dang shen*

28 *Huang shi*
29 Longan
30 Silver fish
31 Tangerine peel
32 Hunza apricots

Eastern Herbs & Spices

Cooling

1 Chrysanthemum
2 Mint
3 Tamarind
4 Turmeric root
5 Turmeric powder

Warming

6 Cardamom
7 Chinese cinnamon bark

8 Cinnamon quill
9 Cloves
10 Coriander seeds
11 Cumin
12 Fennel seeds
13 Fenugreek
14 Garlic
15 Ginger
16 Lemongrass

17 Nutmeg
18 Mace
19 Mugwort
20 Black peppercorns
21 Sichuan pepper
22 Spring onions
23 Star anise

Leafy Vegetables

Cooling
1 Chinese box thorn leaves
2 Chinese celery
3 Chinese spinach
4 Chinese white cabbage (big)
5 Chinese white cabbage (small)
6 English celery
7 Spinach
8 Watercress
9 Water spinach

Neutral
10 Chinese flowering cabbage
11 Chinese kale
12 Garland chrysanthemum
13 Sweet potato leaf

Warming
14 Coriander leaves

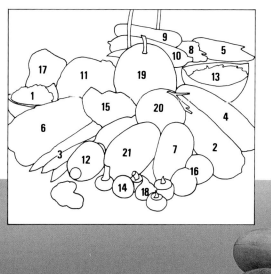

Cooling Vegetables

1 Alfalfa sprouts
2 Angled luffa
3 Asparagus
4 Bitter gourd
5 Chicory
6 Chinese Peking cabbage
7 Chinese radish
8 Courgettes
9 Cucumber
10 Fuzzy melon
11 Lettuce
12 Lotus root
13 Mung bean sprouts
14 Mushrooms
15 Radicchio rosso
16 Radish
17 Swatow mustard cabbage
18 Water chestnuts
19 Winter melon
20 Yam bean
21 Yellow cucumber

Neutral & Warming Vegetables

Neutral
1 Baby sweetcorn
2 Beetroot
3 Broccoli
4 Brussels sprouts
5 Cauliflower
6 Fennel
7 Four-angled beans
8 French beans
9 Long beans

10 Parsnips
11 Pumpkin
12 Snow peas
13 Swede
14 Sweet potato
15 White cabbage
16 Yam

Warming
17 Carrot
18 Chinese chives
19 Chinese leeks
20 Garlic
21 Ginger
22 Leeks
23 Onion
24 Shallots
25 Spring onions

Fruits

Cooling

1 Pears, Williams
2 Pears, Japanese
3 Lemons
4 Japanese persimmons
5 Bananas
6 Bananas
7 Bananas
8 Coconut
9 Jackfruit
10 Mangosteens
11 Pineapple
12 Pomelo
13 Star fruit
14 Watermelon

Neutral

15 Apples
16 Plums
17 Grapes
18 Papaya
19 Guava

Warming

20 Apricots
21 Cherries
22 Peaches
23 Strawberries
24 Lychees
25 Durian
26 Mangoes
27 Pomegranate
28 Rambutans

Whole Cereal Grains

Cooling
1 Buckwheat
2 Millet
3 Pot barley
4 Whole wheat grains

Neutral
5 Short-grain brown rice
6 Long-grain brown rice
7 Red rice
8 Rye
9 Sweet corn (Popping corn)

Warming
10 Oat groats

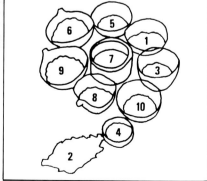

Whole Cereal Grain Flakes

Cooling
1 Millet flakes
2 Pot barley flakes
3 Whole wheat flakes

Neutral
5 Rye flakes
6 Brown rice flakes

Warming
4 Porridge Oats
7 Jumbo Oats

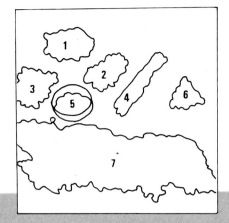

Seaweeds, Fish & Seafoods

1 *Kombu*	3 *Hiziki*	5 *Nori*	7 *Fat choy*
2 *Wakame*	4 *Arame*	6 Purple seaweeds	8 Agar

The Tao of Healing

16 Introduction

The first part of this book dealt with the Taoist philosophy of eating. The second part will deal with the philosophy of living. You cannot have health, vitality and longevity without eating and living well. There is no point in paying great attention to diet, and eating wholesome, organic foods, and then wasting all the goodness by leading a chaotic lifestyle.

You may find the Taoist art of living too simple, especially if you lead a hectic life, but simplicity is the key to health, vitality and longevity. Traditional Chinese medicine says by conserving your energy, you can keep the body going for a long time.

How Do You Conserve this Energy?

1   Adopt a regular eating pattern
The stomach, spleen and the rest of the digestive system work best at regular hours to extract the essential nutrients for building new cells, and to maintain health and vitality.

2   Do not overeat
Overeating places a great strain on the digestive system. Once it is not functioning properly, health will deteriorate.

3   Do not drink excessive alcohol
It is fine to have a glass of wine once or twice a week. (White wine is less warming than red wine.) Drinking excessively can overwork the liver and fill the body with sugar and chemicals. Try to buy alcoholic beverages prepared from organic ingredients; they are now available in some health food shops.

4   Do not smoke
Smoking is not only expensive but very detrimental to health. If you have an overheated blood system or a tendency towards one, you should try to give up smoking immediately, because smoking creates additional heat in the body. A hypnotherapist or acupuncturist can only help if you are mentally prepared to give up smoking.

5   Do not stay up late
Try to go to bed by 11 p.m. after a hard day's work. Between 11 p.m. and 1 a.m., the gall bladder works at its optimum to digest the fatty foods you have eaten throughout the day. If you are awake, the gall bladder cannot function at its optimum.

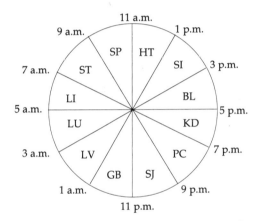

GB – gall bladder	HT – heart
LV – liver	SI – small intestine
LU – lung	BL – bladder
LI – large intestine	KD – kidney
ST – stomach	PC – pericardium
SP – spleen	SJ – *san jiao**

* *San jiao* is the name of a meridian or channel. There is no equivalent Western term. Sometimes it is known as the Triple Heater.

If you refer to the diagram, you can see that:

1 if you suffer from gall bladder problems, you should go to bed at 11 p.m.
2 if you have constipation, try to empty your bowels between 6 and 7 a.m. According to traditional Chinese medicine there is a form of diarrhoea called 'cock's crow' diarrhoea which wakes you up between 5 and 7 a.m.
3 if you have heart problems try to massage the heart reflex area between 11 a.m. and 1 p.m. (See Reflexology in Appendix B.)
4 if you have bladder problems try to massage the bladder reflex area between 3 and 5 p.m. (refer to Reflexology), and so on.

6 Do not exercise excessively

Any exercise which increases the heart beat, dilates the blood vessels or puts excessive pressure on the bones can be bad for health in the long run. When you are young, the blood vessels are elastic, and can dilate and constrict easily. After long-term strain, elasticity wears out and the blood vessels may have difficulty constricting. According to my acupuncture teacher, excessive pounding of the bones (from running, jogging or jumping) can injure the kidneys (in Chinese medical terms). In weak people, it will show up as lower backache and weak knees.

The best exercise involves a lot of postural changes, done at a slow pace, within your own limits. Gentle activities like walking, cycling at a leisurely pace, swimming for pleasure, gardening and housecleaning are fine.

7 Do not have excessive sex

This will horrify most Westerners. Traditional Chinese medicine says sex depletes both men and women of their vital energies. In general it affects men more than women. This vital energy is stored in the reproductive system so that when a child is conceived the vital energy is then transferred to the embryo for growth and development. If casual sex is the norm, you are losing all these vital energies which are not being transferred to a new human being.

When is sex excessive? If you feel drained

of energy afterwards. You have to judge the frequency for yourself.

> **Guide to sexual frequency:** This guide, taken from the *Nei Jing*, gives the correct frequency of sex depending on age, health and the seasons.
> 1 Person of 60 years
>   in good health – once every 10 days
>   in average health – once every 20 days
> 2 Person of 50 years
>   in good health – once every 5 days
>   in average health – once every 10 days
> 3 Person of 40 years
>   in good health – once every 3 days
>   in average health – once every 4 days

Have more sex in spring and summer, less in autumn, least in winter.

ADJUSTING IMBALANCES

We seldom go through life without experiencing some form of aches and pains, even though we have done our best to eat and live correctly. These states of 'dis-ease' are the body's way of telling us to correct imbalances.

'Dis-eases' are not diseases. Traditional Chinese physicians see them only as imbalances that can be corrected by re-balance or re-adjustment.

The second half of this book deals with the re-adjustment of imbalances for different types of dis-eases. Diet is one way to correct imbalances, but it is not the only way. The following chart, from Richard Grossinger's *Planet Medicine* (1982), is helpful in explaining the various ways to achieve balance.

> **Levels of healing:**
>
> **Active role**
> 1st level   – meditation, prayer, self-reflection
> 2nd level – activity, *do-in, taijiquan,* chanting
> 3rd level   – diet (fasting), herbs
> 4th level   – healing by senses
>   (touch, vision, healing, dreams)
> 5th level   – body work (massage, adjustment)
> 6th level   – acupuncture
>
> **Passive role**
> 7th level   – surgery, radiation, drugs

Although Richard Grossinger calls his philosophy the 'levels of healing' it can also be called the 'levels of re-adjustment of imbalances'.

THE FIRST LEVEL

The first level, the highest level of re-adjustment, involves active self-reflection. You do not have to be religious to reflect – just sit quietly for a moment or two and ask yourself: is my dis-ease caused by incorrect eating, incorrect lifestyle, emotional upset or a bit of all three?

Think positively about how to help yourself, at your own pace, according to the severity of your dis-ease. Is self-help enough? Do you need the support of relatives, friends, doctors and alternative practitioners? Each day, reflect on how well you have done to positively re-adjust your life, and how much more you ought to do. Do not be harsh on yourself. Meditation is highly recommended and you may go to meditation classes to learn.

STIMULATING THE **12** MERIDIANS OR CHANNELS* IN THE LIMBS

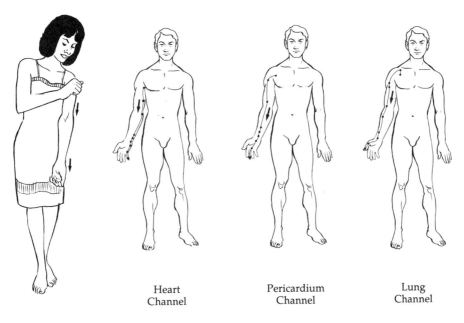

Heart Channel	Pericardium Channel	Lung Channel

FIG 1

* All these channels are bilateral, i.e., on both sides of the body. Only one channel is illustrated for simplicity and clarity.

THE SECOND LEVEL

Activity, the second level in the chart, can also include housework, gardening, *yoga*, *taijiquan* and *qigong*. *Do-in* is a Japanese form of self-massage that is very similar to acupressure. You can learn *do-in* very quickly by attending evening or weekend classes (if available). It helps improve the circulation of *qi* and blood.

Do-in exercises

You can do the following simple *do-in* exercises if you cannot attend a class.

1 *Stimulating the 12 meridians or channels in the limbs*
  This exercise will help to revitalise you first thing in the morning or during short breaks between studying, classes, office work or meetings.

A With a loose fist, gently 'hit' the inside arm from the top of the arm down to the palm. You will stimulate the heart, pericardium and lung meridians or channels. (See FIG 1.)

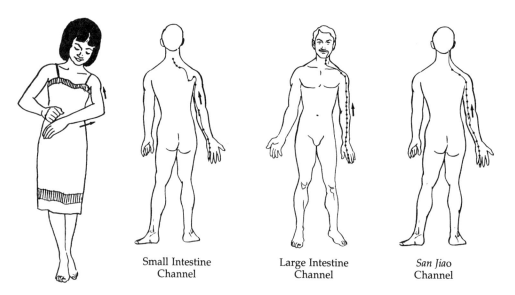

FIG 2. The Small Intestine and *San Jiao* Channels are not complete in these diagrams

Small Intestine
Channel

Large Intestine
Channel

San Jiao
Channel

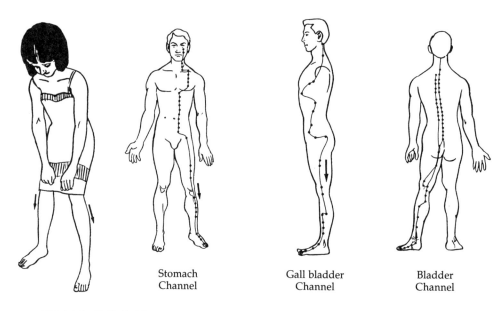

Stomach
Channel

Gall bladder
Channel

Bladder
Channel

FIG 3. The Gall Bladder and Bladder channels are not complete in these diagrams

* All these channels are bilateral, i.e., on both sides of the body. Only one channel is illustrated for simplicity and clarity.

STIMULATING THE 12 MERIDIANS OR CHANNELS* IN THE LIMBS

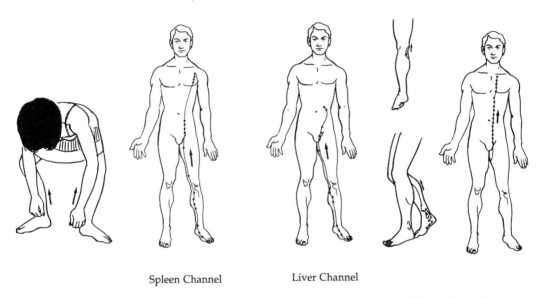

Spleen Channel

Liver Channel

Kidney Channel

FIG 4

* All these channels are bilateral, i.e., on both sides of the body. Only one channel is illustrated for simplicity and clarity.

B Turn the palm downwards and gently 'hit' the outside of the arm from the back of the hand up to the top of the arm. You will stimulate the small intestine, large intestine and *san jiao* meridians or channels. (See FIG 2.)

Repeat: Do steps A and B two more times. Do the same steps three times on the other arm.

C For the legs (you can do both legs at the same time), start 'hitting' gently on the front (to stimulate the stomach meridian or channel); side (to stimulate the gall bladder meridian or channel) and back (to stimulate the bladder meridian or channel) of the legs from the top of the legs down to the ankles. (See FIG 3.)

D Turn the feet outwards and gently 'hit' the inside of the legs from the ankles up to the thighs. You will be stimulating the spleen, liver and kidney meridians or channels. (See FIG 4.)

Repeat: Do steps C and D two more times.

FIG 5. Warming up the kidneys

FIG 6. Warming up the lower abdomen

2 *Warming up the kidneys*
With a loose fist rub on either side of the spine at waist level. Use an up and down movement. (See FIG 5.)

Repeat: Do this 50 times.

This is excellent for keeping your kidneys in good order and preventing backaches. Traditional Chinese medicine says the kidneys store *jing*, the essence for keeping us vital and youthful. So if you do this exercise daily you will benefit.

3 *Warming up the lower abdomen*
Rub the lower abdomen with the palm in a clockwise movement for constipation but an anticlockwise movement for diarrhoea or loose stools. (See FIG 6.)

Taijiquan, qigong and yoga
Taijiquan is a very popular gentle exercise in China among the older generation. It also improves the circulation of *qi* and blood. I highly recommend it daily to anyone who wishes to remain youthful.

Qigong, another form of Chinese exercise, improves the circulation of *qi* and blood. If you practise *qigong* daily, you will be youthful, full of vitality and in good health. In China, there are people who have 'cured' themselves of cancer just by doing *qigong*. Some cancer patients have combined chemotherapy and/or radiotherapy with *qigong* and they have progressed very well. In fact, some of the best *qigong* masters were cancer patients themselves.

Yoga is an Indian exercise which improves the circulation of *qi* and blood, and helps

maintain good health and vitality. People who have been ill have found *yoga* very helpful in improving their health.

Chanting

In chanting, the vibration of the voice helps improve the circulation of *qi* and blood. Personally, I find that chanting lifts the mind and spirit more than *do-in, taijiquan, qigong* or *yoga*. Chanting the simple sound of *su* helps calm the mind, spirit and heart. *Aaaah* helps balance the lower abdomen; *eeeeh* helps balance the liver; *ieeeh* helps balance the spleen and pancreas; and *ooooh* and *uuuuh* help balance the heart. ('Balance' here means that if an organ is underactive or overactive, chanting will bring back the organ's normal working capacity.) *Aum* and *om* help revitalise the spinal column and all the various *chakras* up the spine.

> **Note:** *Chakras* are centres of energy up the spinal column. There are seven *chakras* as illustrated. (See FIG 7.)
>
> First *chakra* or base *chakra* governs the functions of the bladder, rectum and reproductive organs. Second *chakra* or sacral *chakra* governs the functions of the small and large intestines and reproductive organs. Third *chakra* or solar plexus *chakra* governs the functions of the stomach, spleen, pancreas, liver, gall bladder and kidneys. Fourth *chakra* or heart *chakra* governs the functions of the heart and the circulatory systems of blood and lymph. Fifth *chakra* or throat *chakra* governs the functions of respiration and vocalisation. Sixth *chakra* or third eye *chakra* controls consciousness and physical reactions. Seventh *chakra* or crown *chakra* controls consciousness and the higher spiritual consciousness.

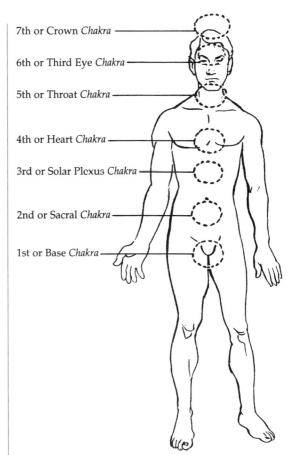

7th or Crown *Chakra*

6th or Third Eye *Chakra*

5th or Throat *Chakra*

4th or Heart *Chakra*

3rd or Solar Plexus *Chakra*

2nd or Sacral *Chakra*

1st or Base *Chakra*

FIG 7. The seven *chakras* of the spine

Chanting is excellent for depression, tension, stress, heart problems and even multiple sclerosis. Chant daily on your own or in a group, about one hour a week, to listen to and absorb other people's vocal vibrations. This interchange of vibrations is a powerful healing tool. Often people come to chanting classes depressed, tired and tense but feel better after a few minutes. After an hour, they know they will have a good night's sleep.

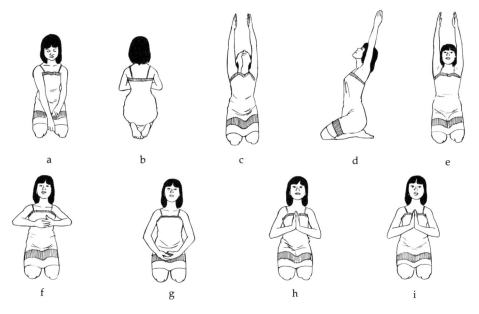

FIG 8. Chanting procedure

Chanting, sitting on heels – This is the best position for chanting because it keeps the spine straight. (See FIG 8.)

a   Make sure your knees are one fist-width apart.

b   Cross your left big toe over your right big toe.

c   Straighten the spine by stretching both arms above the head to form an infinite 'V' shape with the palms of the hands facing each other. Then look up with the arms still above the head.

d   Look straight ahead with the arms still above

e   the head.

f   Relax the shoulders, thus bringing arms down, and rest the palms above the thighs with the eyes still looking straight ahead.

Repeat procedure two more times.

h   Put the palms together in the prayer position and take a deep breath. (Push your abdominal muscles out as you inhale.)

i   Breathe out through the mouth and make the sound of *su*. (Pull in your abdominal muscles as you exhale.) You can do this with eyes open or shut.

Each time you exhale chant the sound of *su*. Repeat until you feel calm. Most beginners can only sit in this position for 3 breaths. With daily practice, you will be able to chant up to 9 breaths without any problem.

If you are unfamiliar with deep breathing, the best way to practise is to lie on your back

with your hands over your navel. When you inhale, push out your abdominal muscles so that the diaphragm is lowered for you to fill your chest with air. Then when you exhale, pull in your abdominal muscles to raise the diaphragm to push the air out of your lungs. Practise this first until you can do it automatically. It will help you relax, improve the circulation of *qi* and blood, and strengthen the lungs.

If you cannot sit on your heels, sit on a chair or stool so both feet are flat on the floor. Make sure the knees are one fist-width apart. Then proceed as described above. Make sure you keep your spine straight. Sitting towards the edge of the chair will help. You can chant to whatever sounds appeal to you.

THE THIRD LEVEL

The third level of re-adjustment, diet and herbs, has already been discussed. Fasting for one or two days is beneficial for some people. Some schools of thought say it will clear the body of accumulated toxins.

THE FOURTH LEVEL

The fourth level of re-adjustment, healing by senses, can include aromatherapy. In France, aromatherapy is accepted by medical doctors. You can even get an aromatogram to see which essential oils help which ailments. Aromatherapists believe that smells can lift the mind and spirit and thereby trigger a very vital part of the body's healing process. That is why fragrant flowers mean so much to hospital patients. (See the Bibliography.)

In traditional Chinese medicine essential oils have been in use for many, many years in balms or embrocation oils for the relief of muscular cramps, aches and pains, sprains, bruises, rheumatism, lumbago, sciatica, headaches and even insect bites. Here are two examples.

White Tiger Balm contains:
camphor, peppermint oil, cajuput oil, menthol crystals, clove oil

Boxing Ring Brand Embrocation contains:
wintergreen oil, cajuput oil, citronella oil, menthol crystals, cassia oil

The essential oils that you come across in this book are used to relieve emotional problems as well as alleviate uncomfortable symptoms.

How to use essential oils
You must not use the essential oil 'neat' if you are going to use it as a massage oil. It must be diluted. You will need four drops of the essential oil in 10 ml of sweet almond oil or any unrefined cold-pressed oil such as sesame seed, sunflower seed or safflower oil. Then store this in a dark glass bottle in a cool dark place.

When you may use essential oil undiluted:
1 Add it to a hot bathful of water (use 4 drops)
2 Add it to a basin of hot water for inhalation (use 8 to 12 drops)
3 Add it to a small basin of hot water for fumigation or as an air-freshener (use 5 drops)
4 Dab it on a piece of tissue or cottonwool ball for inhalation (use 1 drop).

The chapters that follow will give you

more information on the various essential oils and when to apply them. Essential oils are not cheap, so use them sparingly!

> *Note:* The same essential oil must not be used daily for more then 3 weeks. The body may build up a toxic level. Therefore, stop for a month before using it again.
>
> Essential oils are not always readily available in health food stores. You may have to order them by mail. See the back of the book for addresses.

THE FIFTH LEVEL

This level of re-adjustment, body work, includes acupressure, moxibustion, reflexology, osteopathy, chiropractic manipulations, etc. In acupressure, thumb pressure rather than needles is applied to acupuncture points and meridians or channels to relieve specific problems. The chapters that follow will give you more information.

Moxibustion

Moxibustion is the burning of a herb called mugwort at certain acupuncture points to tonify or disperse specific problems. You can buy moxa sticks from Chinese herbalists.

> *Beware:* Use moxibustion with great care. It can be dangerous if used incorrectly. It is not to be used:
> 1 if you cannot stand the heat
> 2 if you feel hot and sweat a lot, especially at night
> 3 if you suffer from or are prone to an overheated blood system
> 4 if you suffer from skin diseases
> 5 if you suffer from ulcers

Moxibustion is most appropriate for people who feel the cold easily for it helps to drive out arthritic or rheumatic pain caused by cold, wind and damp. It is also used in some cases of multiple sclerosis.

> *Using a moxa stick:*
> 1 Remove the colourful wrapper.
> 2 Light the stick. Blow it a bit to get it glowing red hot.
> 3 Place the glowing moxa stick about 2 cm ($^3/_4$ in) to $2^1/_2$ cm (1 in) away from the skin above the tender spot.
> 4 Move the stick slowly backwards and forwards above the spot.
> 5 When the tender spot becomes hot, remove the moxa stick for about 1 minute then come back to it.
> 6 When it is hot again, remove and repeat procedure.
> 7 Repeat this several times until the spot gets hotter faster or the skin turns pink.
>
> *Points to remember:*
> 1 Keep removing the ash.
> 2 Do not use moxa after a bath when the skin is still wet or you may get blisters. Wait for 1 hour for the body to return to normal temperature. Blisters will also result from taking a bath after moxa treatment. Wait for 1 to 2 hours for the body to return to normal temperature.
> 3 Do not use moxa after you have rubbed oil on the skin. This will cause blisters too. You can rub essential oils about four hours after moxibustion.

Reflexology

In reflexology, the feet or hands are massaged to bring all the body organs to work in harmony with one another, to improve

circulation of *qi* and blood, to help the elimination of toxins and help relieve tension. No one knows how reflexology works, but it has been in practice since the days of the Egyptian pharoahs. Reflexology can help relieve tension and improve circulation quickly and it is very simple to learn.

The diagram in Appendix B gives the reflex areas for the various body organs. Give both feet a general massage from toe to heel. (See Appendix B.) If the foot hurts anywhere it could mean that the corresponding organ is not functioning properly. To bring that organ in harmony with the others, massage the tender area for 1 minute, and then give both feet another general massage from toe to heel. Never work more than 2 to 3 minutes on the same area.

> *Note:* Do not rub oil or talcum powder on the feet before reflexology. They may block the pores and so prevent the release of toxins from the soles of the feet during treatment.

If you do not wish to do reflexology with your thumbs, roll a wooden rolling pin or foot roller under each foot daily for about 5 minutes to keep the body organs working in harmony. You can do it standing up or sitting down (see FIG 9). The recommended reading list on reflexology is given at the back. Courses are available in many areas.

I highly recommend reflexology as a supplement to orthodox or alternative medicine. It should not be performed on pregnant mothers, however, as it may harm the mother and foetus.

Osteopathic and chiropractic manipulations help to re-align the vertebrae in the spinal column to correct posture. It also helps to balance body functions which could have been affected when the spine was out of alignment.

THE SIXTH LEVEL

Acupuncture is the least active role of self-healing. It is a method used when the dis-ease is so great that you need help from others.

THE SEVENTH LEVEL

Surgery, radiation and drugs, the seventh level, form the most passive role. Often, if you combine one of these with other positive roles you can pull yourself through. There are many cancer patients in China who have survived through a combination of surgery, radiation and/or chemotherapy and *qigong*.

FIG 9. How to use a wooden rolling pin or foot roller to massage the feet, standing or sitting

BACH FLOWERS

Sometimes people are ill because they are emotionally upset or their illness becomes worse when they are under emotional stress. The Bach Flower Remedies discovered by Dr Edward Bach in the early 1930s help to correct these emotions so that the body can begin to relax and allow good, wholesome organic foods and alternative therapies to aid the body's healing processes.

The Bach Flower Remedies are not scientifically based. There is no history of their use in traditional Chinese medicine. They are mentioned here because in my clinical practice I have used them to help many of my patients in conjunction with the Chang Ming Diet, exercises, reflexology and acupuncture. As the aim of this book is to guide you to a healthy body, mind and spirit, it would be wrong of me not to mention the Bach Flower Remedies. More than that would be departing too much from the subject of this book.

If you are interested in Bach Flower Remedies, refer to Further Reading, which lists an excellent book on the subject by Mechthild Scheffer.

CONCLUSION

If you are healthy and wish to remain healthy, practise the Tao of eating and living and any one of the active roles of balancing the body. Each day, I follow a Taoist diet, do chanting and reflexology in the mornings, and meditation at night. If I am ill, I use essential oils, moxibustion, acupressure, acupuncture or reflexology. I do not let things go too far because I know it will be harder to re-adjust the balance if a dis-ease is ignored for too long.

I treat my patients through a self-help approach, giving them advice on how to adjust their diet and lifestyle to correct imbalances. Then I show them or their family members how to use reflexology or moxibustion as a supplement to their weekly acupuncture treatments. Patients who are not willing to help themselves improve less rapidly than those who try their best.

The chapters that follow, on the different types of dis-eases, are only guidelines to various ways of helping yourself.

Caution: In many cases, it is dangerous to treat yourself – you must see your doctor and/or alternative practitioner as well.

An alternative practitioner is one who practises the healing of the body, mind and spirit, using natural means. The following are some examples of alternative practitioners:

Acupuncturist/Chiropractor/Diet therapist
Herbalist/Homeopath/Hypnotherapist
Osteopath/Reflexologist

In this half of the book you will find many unfamiliar words and phrases which are peculiar to traditional Chinese medicine. I am afraid there is no way in which I can explain them in Western terms without writing in depth about acupuncture and its philosophy. Please accept what you read.

17 Constipation

Constipation is a very common ailment that can affect people of all ages, from toddlers to grandparents. Fortunately, it is an easy problem to correct if one knows the root cause and treats it without delay. Toxic waste matter that remains in the body for more than a day can lead to serious health problems in the future.

According to traditional Chinese medicine there are six types of constipation. I will deal with each type individually in this chapter.

> *Excessive Types:*
> 1   Full heat
> 2   Obstruction of food
> 3   Stagnation of *qi*
>
> *Deficient Types:*
> 4   Deficient *qi*
> 5   Deficient blood
> 6   Deficient kidney *yang*

CONSTIPATION CAUSED BY FULL HEAT

Symptoms and signs
- Hard, dry, small stools
- Hard, painful lower abdomen (especially when pressed)
- Red face
- Pimples, acne or spots on face or body
- A hot, uncomfortable feeling in the body
- Bad breath
- Mouth ulcers
- Frequent sore throats or splitting headaches
- Thirst with the desire for cool drinks
- Scanty dark yellow urine
- Tongue body: red and dry
- Tongue coat: yellow

> *Possible causes:*
> 1   Eating too many hot or warm energy foods and drinks
> 2   Incorrect lifestyle
> 3   Weather
> 4   Past illness (such as high fevers)

To re-adjust the imbalance

1   Correct your diet

> *Avoid these hot or warming energy foods and drinks:*
> Red meats
> Animal fat
> Dairy products, especially hard cheeses, dried (powdered) milk and dried skim-milk
> Baked flour products
> Warming vegetables
> Warming fruits

Deep-fried foods
Baked foods
Roasted foods
Grilled foods
Barbecued foods
Tonic herbs
Coffee
Chocolate
Cocoa
Chocolate and malt-based beverages
Alcohol

Go on a Chang Ming Diet for overheated blood systems. Eat the following foods:

Brown rice – This has seven layers of bran. Do not eat pure bran, which tends to cause bloating and flatulence and may be too harsh for the delicate intestinal lining.

Pot barley soups – Cooling and rich in bran fibre. Add a few grains of pot barley to the brown rice to make it more cooling.

Whole wheat grains – Added to brown rice, they make it more cooling and give it more bran fibre.

Millet – Helps get rid of bad breath and mouth ulcers because of its alkaline qualities and cooling energies.

Fresh sweet corn – When in season, this also provides lots of roughage.

Whole wheat pasta or whole wheat noodles – Easier to digest than baked bread and have more cooling energies than bread.

Mung beans – Stewed or boiled with onions, they cool the body and provide roughage.

Tofu – Excellent cooked with long beans. Tofu is cooling and the long beans provide roughage. Try steaming soft silken tofu with blanched long beans or boiling hard tofu cubes with long beans. Tofu, long beans and onion can also be sautéed. In the West you can use French beans, dwarf beans, string beans, kidney beans, garden peas or marrowfat peas instead of long beans.

Miso – Not only cooling, it also contains bacterial cultures and enzymes which are helpful to the intestinal flora, in preventing and correcting constipation.

Dried beans – All kinds are rich sources of fibre. Use them often in soups and stews.

Linseed – Very appropriate for this type of constipation. It is mucilaginous so it helps lubricate the intestinal wall. Add a dessertspoon or tablespoon of linseed to your breakfast cereal of brown rice flakes, millet flakes or wheat flakes.

Seaweeds – Any kind helps cool the body down and all are rich in fibre. Apple and raisin jelly made with the seaweed agar-agar is very good for this type of constipation. Remember not to eat seaweed in excess or you may lower your blood pressure too much. Seaweeds are excellent for people with high blood pressure and full heat constipation.

Vegetables and herbs – Use mostly neutral and cooling vegetables and herbs. Warm energy vegetables and herbs should be used only in small amounts to create balance and give taste.

Sauerkraut – Very good for this type of constipation. Have a tablespoon daily.

Snow ear fungus – Boiled with honey, it is supposed to help full heat constipation because both ingredients are cooling.

Dried figs – Boiled in water until soft, they are appropriate for full heat constipation because they cool the body, and help moisten and lubricate the intestines.

Dried persimmons – Boiled in water until soft, they also cool the body and lubricate the

intestines.

Fish and chicken – Have fish, both white and oily, steamed, poached, boiled, stewed or made in a casserole, and chicken, steamed, boiled, stewed or made in a casserole.

Fresh fruits – Juicy pomeloes and fresh persimmons are specially good for full heat constipation. Other cooling fruits like bananas, pears, oranges, grapefruits, lemons, clementines, tangerines, mandarins, etc. will help too.

Beverages – Drink cooling or neutral beverages.

> **For breakfast:**
> 1 Cook brown rice flakes with figs and linseed.
> 2 Cook millet flakes with raisins and linseed.
> 3 Cook brown rice flakes with honey and linseed.
> 4 Cook wheat flakes with figs.

2   Correct your lifestyle

> **Note:**
> No smoking – Try to give up smoking on your own first before consulting a hypnotherapist or acupuncturist.
> No late nights – Try to be asleep by 11 p.m.
> No stress or tension – Try *yoga, taijiquan, qigong,* chanting or meditation, or take a lavender bath to help you relax. Add 4 drops of oil of lavender to a hot bath before you get in.
> Do not work or study too hard – Life is meant to be spent both working and playing.

Use acupressure on the Large Intestine 4 (*Hegu*) point on both hands. (See Appendix C, FIGS 1 and 2.) To locate the point, gently move the thumb towards the index finger so they lie alongside one another. The acupressure point is the highest part of the mound on the side of the index finger. (It only appears when the thumb is in this position.) Using the thumb of your other hand (not the nail), press down this point and move in a rotatory motion for 1 to 2 minutes. Then pause. Repeat again 1 to 2 minutes later. Do this when you are in the lavatory or any time of the day if the problem is serious. Most constipation sufferers will find this point very sore – so massage gently.

Use foot reflexology. (See Appendix B.) Massage both feet from toe to heel first before concentrating on the following reflex areas: small intestines, ascending colon, transverse colon, descending colon, Sigmoid flexure and rectum. Repeat the general foot massage, then concentrate on the specific reflex areas again. The whole massage should not take more than one hour. Do this three times a day if the problem is severe, once or twice a day otherwise.

3   Compensate for the weather

Hot, dry weather can lead to full heat constipation because it dries up the body fluids through sweating. Therefore, take lots of cooling drinks and soups whenever you are thirsty.

> **Recommendation of a Chinese herbalist:**
> The following keep the intestines moist during hot, dry weather:
> 1 Boiling Chinese radish with carrots to make a soup.
> 2 Boiling dried figs and dried persimmons to make a sweet soup to be taken as a snack or for breakfast.

4   Compensate for past illness

Past illness such as a high fever can cause full

heat constipation because the body loses fluids during the fever. If they are not replenished, you can develop full heat constipation.

If, after following these guidelines, there is no improvement, see your doctor and/or alternative practitioner as soon as possible.

CONSTIPATION CAUSED BY OBSTRUCTION OF FOOD

Symptoms and signs
- Bloated feeling in the stomach and abdomen
- Belching foul breath
- Flatulence with an unpleasant odour
- Nausea
- Tongue coat: thick, greasy or slippery
- Tongue coat colour: greyish or yellowish

Constipation caused by obstruction of food is due to overeating. The stomach, spleen and the rest of the digestive system cannot digest great amounts of food. The excess stays in the large intestine and rots, giving rise to foul breath and smelly flatulence.

To re-adjust the imbalances

1 Stop overeating

2 Fast
Drink just mineral water for one to two days only. Or, go on a semi-fast of brown rice congee seasoned with *miso*, raw lettuce and spring onion. Eat congee for breakfast, lunch and dinner for two to three days. The brown rice has seven layers of bran to aid constipation and the *miso* will alleviate the

nausea. *Miso* and lettuce help cool down the heat caused by the food in the gut. The spring onion gives taste and colour appeal.

3 Use acupressure
Apply the acupressure point Large Intestine 4 (*Hegu*) as described on page 229.

4 Use reflexology
Just as recommended for full heat constipation on page 229 but concentrate on these reflex areas: stomach, spleen, pancreas, small intestines, large intestines, ascending colon, transverse colon, descending colon, Sigmoid flexure and rectum.

Once you have corrected the imbalances go on the Chang Ming Diet and eat sensibly, at regular intervals, three times a day. If you still cannot clear your bowels within two to three days of following the above guidelines, see your doctor or alternative practitioner.

CONSTIPATION CAUSED BY STAGNATION OF *QI*

Symptoms and signs
- Lots of belching and flatulence
- Discomfort and pain below and near the rib cage
- Pain that comes and goes, starting from below the right rib cage and travelling across the transverse colon and down the descending colon
- Increased pain during emotional stress and tension

According to traditional Chinese medicine, this type of constipation is usually caused by stagnation of *qi* in the liver. When the liver,

which ensures the free flow of *qi*, is impaired, it can affect the digestive system, causing belching and flatulence. Emotional stress can impair the liver function further, making the condition worse.

To re-adjust the imbalances

1 Adopt the Chang Ming Diet
Choose foods appropriate for your blood system. Eat plenty of greens, sprouts and sauerkraut.

2 Avoid stress and tension
Lead a less hectic life. If stress and tension are self-induced, try self-reflection or seek help from a counsellor. Try chanting or meditation.

3 Take a lavender bath
This helps you unwind after a difficult day. See page 229.

4 Practise yoga, taijiquan or qigong
A daily routine helps to improve the circulation of *qi*.

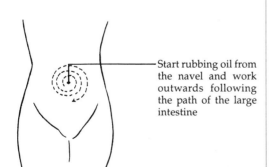

Start rubbing oil from the navel and work outwards following the path of the large intestine

FIG 10. How to rub essential oil for constipation

5 Use oil of rosemary
This helps improve liver *qi*. Mix 4 drops of oil of rosemary in 10 ml of sweet almond oil. Rub the mixture below your right rib cage and all around the lower abdomen about once or twice a day. (See FIG 10 and page 223.)

> *Note:* If you have high blood pressure or tendencies towards it do not use oil of rosemary. It may increase your blood pressure.

6 Use reflexology
Just as described for full heat constipation on page 229 but concentrate on these reflex areas: liver, gall bladder, small intestines, large intestines, ascending colon, transverse colon, descending colon, Sigmoid flexure and rectum.

> *Note:* Do not use oil on the feet because the pores must be kept open for the toxins to come out. See section on reflexology in Chapter 16 for explanation.

If you have no success in self-healing, see an acupuncturist. Continue to carry out the above guidelines throughout the acupuncture treatment so your body can re-adjust faster. It is also advisable to see your doctor.

CONSTIPATION CAUSED BY DEFICIENT *QI*

Symptoms and signs
- Pale face
- Fatigue
- Breathlessness after exertion
- Difficulty in passing stools (this difficulty

is much worse than with other types of constipation)
- Exhaustion after passing stools
- Incomplete evacuation of stools
- Tongue body: pale
- Tongue coat: thin

To re-adjust the imbalances

1   Adopt the Chang Ming Diet
Eat neutral and warming energy foods in equal proportion and avoid cooling energy foods. If you are a vegetarian, eat chicken eggs to tonify the *qi*. If you are a wholefooder, eat chicken flesh.

2   Do not overwork
Make time to relax and to enjoy life.

3   Do simple exercises daily
They may be functional, as in housecleaning or gardening. If there is no movement, the body will find it difficult to transport food.

4   Build yourself up after illness
Look after your body and see a doctor or alternative practitioner as soon as you suspect illness, to prevent your imbalance from becoming excessive.

5   Practise yoga, taijiquan and qigong
These are the best forms of exercise to improve deficient spleen *qi*. Your condition will take time to improve but you should persevere.

6   Try oil of fennel
Mix 4 drops of oil with 10 ml of sweet almond oil and rub on the lower abdomen once a day. (See FIG 10 and page 223.)

7   Use reflexology
Just as described on page 229 but concentrate on these reflex areas: spleen, stomach, pancreas, small intestines, ascending colon, transverse colon, descending colon, Sigmoid flexure and rectum.

Consult an acupuncturist but supplement your treatment with the above guidelines.

CONSTIPATION CAUSED BY DEFICIENT BLOOD

Symptoms and signs
- Pale face
- Dizziness
- Dull headaches
- Insomnia
- Irritability
- Palpitations
- Thirst
- Difficulty in passing the stools, which tend to be dry
- Tongue body: pale and dry

In traditional Chinese medicine, deficient blood is also known as insufficient liver blood. The liver stores blood and regulates the amount of blood that goes to different parts of the body.

To re-adjust the imbalances

1 *Adopt the Chang Ming Diet*
Eat equal proportions of neutral and warming energy foods and avoid cooling energy foods. Include foods rich in iron such as:

Black soyabeans
Aduki beans cooked with carrots
Brown lentils cooked with caraway seeds and
    thyme
Miso braised with *fu zhou*, garlic, ginger,
    onions and carrots
Sunflower seeds
Red beetroot
Beetroot greens stir-fried with garlic and
    ginger
Watercress stir-fried with garlic, ginger and
    carrots
Spinach stir-fried with garlic, ginger and
    nutmeg
Golden needles
Shiitake mushrooms
Longans
Chinese red dates
Chinese black dates
Raisins
Blackcurrants
Blackberries
Raspberries
Strawberries
Red grapes
Red grape juice

For vegans and macrobiotics:
Stir-fry garlic, ginger, onion, black wood ears, golden needles, Shiitake mushrooms, carrot and *fu zhou*. Add some water to make a stew. Simmer until the *fu zhou* is soft, then add *miso* and simmer very gently for 15 minutes. Garnish with coriander leaves.

For vegetarians:
Stir-fry chicken eggs (which are good for tonifying the blood) with onion or shallots, ginger, Shiitake mushrooms.

For wholefooders:
Braise chicken (which is very good for tonifying the blood) with onion, Shiitake mushrooms and Chinese red dates.

2 *Practise yoga, taijiquan or qigong*
At the same time as the above diet is tonifying the blood, practise *yoga, taijiquan* or *qigong* to improve the circulation of blood.

3 *Use reflexology*
Just as described on page 229. Concentrate on these reflex areas: spleen, pancreas, liver, gall bladder, small intestines, ascending colon, transverse colon, descending colon, Sigmoid flexure and rectum.

Acupuncture is the final prescription, in conjunction with the above guidelines. If possible, see a Chinese herbalist as well, for a blood tonifying prescription.

CONSTIPATION CAUSED BY DEFICIENT KIDNEY *YANG*

Symptoms and signs
- Pale face
- Dislike of the cold
- Cold and pain, especially around the abdomen
- Hot water bottles placed over the abdomen relieves the pain and give lots of comfort (although this sounds more like a cure than a symptom, to a traditional Chinese herbalist or acupuncturist, this is a clue as to which syndrome this ailment falls under)
- Tongue body: pale and moist
- Tongue coat: white

> *Possible cause:*
> In deficient kidney *yang* constipation the body does not have enough warmth and energy for peristalsis to take place efficiently. (Peristalsis is repeated contractions and relaxations of the intestinal muscles to move the stools along the length of the intestinal tract.) It is often seen in old, weak patients.

To re-adjust the imbalances

1 *Adopt the Chang Ming Diet*
Eat mainly warming energy foods and use warming methods of cooking. Neutral energy foods can also be included, but cooling energy foods and cooling methods of cooking must be avoided.

> *Note:* Walnuts are especially good for this type of constipation. Boil them with brown rice and eat twice a day at lunch and dinner. Use the following warming spices often to help warm up deficient kidney *yang* conditions – fenugreek seeds, fennel seeds, cinnamon, star anise, dill seeds.

Wholefooders should double-boil chicken with ginger and cinnamon to tonify the kidney *yang*. If you do not have a double-boiler, simmer the dish slowly for several hours in a cool oven or an electric slow-cooker.

2 *Keep warm*
Always keep warm, and protect yourself well in winter when going out of doors.

3 *Use moxibustion*
Ask someone to help you as it is difficult to treat yourself if your hand is unsteady or your grip is weak. Move the glowing moxa stick above the lower abdomen as shown. (See FIG 11.) Make sure the glowing hot end of the moxa stick is about 2 to 2½ cm (³/₄ to 1 in) away from the skin and remember to remove

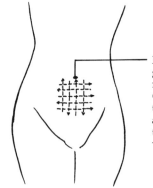

Navel. Move the glowing end of the moxa stick 2 to 2½ cm (³/₄ to 1 in) away from the skin, backwards and forwards horizontally and up and down vertically.

FIG 11. Moxibustion for Deficient Kidney *Yang* Constipation

the ash from the glowing tip as often as possible to prevent it from dropping on the skin. Stop when the abdomen feels warm. Repeat 3 or 4 evenings a week until you feel stronger.

> *Note:* Do not apply any oil before or after moxibustion. Wait for four hours to let the skin go back to normal temperature. This is to prevent blisters. Do not have a bath at least 1 hour before and after moxibustion to prevent blisters.

4 Use oil of fennel
Mix 4 drops of oil of fennel with 10 ml of sweet almond oil and rub over the abdomen (as shown in FIG 10 on page 231) once or twice a day.

5 Consult a specialist
See an acupuncturist to help you tonify the deficient kidney *yang* and follow the above guidelines. If possible, also see a Chinese herbalist.

6 Practise taijiquan or qigong
When you have more energy, practise *taijiquan* or *qigong*.

CONCLUSION

In this chapter, I have described six different types of constipation. In real life, however, you may find that you suffer from a combination of two types or more. In that case, see an acupuncturist.

All constipation sufferers should train themselves to empty their bowels between 5 and 7 a.m., or as soon as they wake up. The large intestines work at their optimum between 5 and 7 a.m. according to the Chinese body clock. If you feel constipated in the morning do not strain yourself. Either apply acupressure to the Large Intestine 4 (*Hegu*) point on both hands, or massage the small and large intestine reflex areas (after giving both feet a general massage from toe to heel) until you feel you have to go. With daily practice in the mornings, your body can learn to work this way.

> *Note:* If the above guidelines, acupuncture treatments and herbal treatments do not relieve the constipation, see an osteopath or a chiropractor. Sometimes a displaced vertebrae may be the cause of your problem. If osteopathic or chiropractic manipulations do not help, consult your doctor.

18 Colds and 'Flus

In traditional Chinese medicine, colds and 'flus are known as 'invasions of wind cold or wind heat'. Wind cold usually affects those with cooled blood systems while wind heat tends to strike those with overheated blood systems. Sometimes an invasion of wind cold can turn into wind heat.

In Chinese medical terms, 'wind' describes a sudden onset of symptoms and signs. It is analogous to real wind, which comes and goes suddenly, but does not necessarily mean colds or 'flus caused by the wind. Wind cold or wind heat can be caused by sudden changes in temperature due to wind, cold, damp or heat when the body is not prepared.

Again, in Chinese medical terms, the body is protected from external factors like wind, cold, damp and heat by the *wei qi* or defensive *qi*. When the *wei qi* is healthy and strong, sudden changes of temperature will not cause wind cold or wind heat. But when it has been weakened, the body is easily attacked by wind cold or wind heat.

If the *wei qi* is only slightly weakened and the person is strong, the wind cold or wind heat will cause mild colds or 'flus. However, if the *wei qi* and the body are very weak, the wind cold or wind heat can enter deeper into the lung, giving rise to colds or 'flus and cough. Such cases are called invasions of lungs by wind cold or wind heat.

WIND COLD

Symptoms and signs
- Itchy throat
- Dislike or fear of the cold
- The need for lots of bedclothes and hot water bottles to keep warm
- No sweating
- Mild fever
- Nasal obstruction with runny, watery discharge or thick, white discharge
- Aching bones (in cases of 'flu)
- Coughing with white, dilute sputum (if the wind cold has entered the lungs)
- Tongue body: pale
- Tongue coat: thin, white

WIND HEAT

Symptoms and signs
- Itchy throat
- Sore, swollen or red throat
- Feeling of heat
- Fever (which may be high)
- Lots of sweating
- Nasal obstruction with thick, yellow purulent discharge
- Aching bones (in cases of 'flu)
- Coughing with thick, yellow purulent sputum if the wind heat has entered the lungs; sometimes this sputum is green or tinged with blood.

- Tongue body: red
- Tongue coat: thin, yellow

Prevention of Wind Cold and Wind Heat

1 Adopt the Chang Ming Diet

If you have a cooled blood system, eat mainly neutral and warming foods and use neutral and warming methods of cooking. Use garlic frequently in stir-fried dishes. Take a *dang shen* and *huang shi* tonic once a week to strengthen the *wei qi*. (See page 133.)

If you have an overheated blood system, eat mainly neutral and cooling foods and use neutral and cooling methods of cooking. Use raw garlic and steam or simmer vegetables with garlic. Cool the blood system at least once or twice a week by drinking pot barley water all day long instead of other beverages.

2 Lead a stress-free life

Stress weakens the whole body's immune system – not only the *wei qi*. Take up *yoga*, *taijiquan*, *qigong*, chanting or meditation.

3 Take lavender baths

Have lavender baths at least once a week to strengthen your immune system and to help you relax. Add 4 drops of oil of lavender to a hot bath just before you get in.

4 Use exfoliators daily

Rub exfoliators like loofahs or rough sponges all over the body to improve circulation of *wei qi*. This is most important in winter when the skin is overprotected and becomes sluggish under many layers of clothing.

5 Protect yourself in an epidemic

If there is a 'flu epidemic going around, soak a $2^1/_2$ cm (1 in) cotton ball with 4 to 5 drops of cypress, eucalyptus or pine oil and hang it over the radiator to purify the air.

6 Protect yourself in winter

In winter, wrap yourself well to avoid catching a chill. If it rains and you get soaked, change into warm dry clothes as soon as possible. It is a good idea to carry an umbrella with you in case of an unexpected downpour or drizzle.

Re-adjusting Imbalances Causing Wind Cold

1 Drink ginger tea

At the first sign of a sneeze, a chill or a runny nose, drink ginger tea and go to bed to sweat out the cold.

> *Recipe for ginger tea:*
>
> Add a cup of hot water to $^1/_2$ to 1 teaspoon of grated fresh ginger and sip it as hot as you can. If you do not feel better after one dose, repeat three times a day.

2 Drink ginger and cinnamon tea

If the sneeze, chill or runny nose is a result of sudden cold weather, sitting in a cold, draughty place or working in a cold, windy place, take ginger and cinnamon tea and sweat out the cold in bed with layers of bedclothes and hot water bottles. There is usually a fear of draughts on top of the fear of cold in this type of wind cold.

3 Eat stir-fried *tofu*

Have a dish of *tofu* stir-fried with spring onions and black pepper with either of the above teas. Also eat some brown rice, and cabbage braised with ginger.

4 Use oil of ginger

Soak for 10 minutes in a hot bath with 4 drops of oil of ginger. Rub yourself thoroughly dry before getting into a warm bed. This remedy is best for people with a very slight sore and itchy throat, who are shivering from the cold. Ginger tea or ginger and cinnamon tea will irritate the throat. It is also appropriate for 'flus with aching bones.

5 Use mustard water

Instead of having a bath, just soak your feet in a bowl of mustard water. According to Western herbalists, this remedy draws the congestion down from the head and out through the pores of the feet. Mix some yellow mustard powder with a little cold water to form a thin paste. Then add hot water to fill the bowl up. Do not use if your feet are sensitive to irritants.

6 Use oil of eucalyptus or pine

Inhale essential oil of eucalyptus or pine to clear nasal and sinus congestion. Add 8 to 12 drops of essential oil to a large bowl of hot water. Then bend your head over the bowl, cover it with a large towel and inhale. Repeat as often as necessary.

7 Use Olbas oil

Every now and then inhale a drop or two of Olbas oil dabbed on a handkerchief or tissue. It is available from health food shops.

8 Use foot reflexology

(See Appendix B.) Give both feet a general massage from toe to heel first before concentrating on the following reflex areas: head, sinus, nose, throat, lymph glands, neck, lungs, bronchial area, solar plexus, diaphragm, small intestines and large intestines. (See chart in Appendix B, especially the details of big toes.)

Twiddle the toes gently, clockwise and counter-clockwise to drain the obstruction in the head. Remember to support the toes before rotating them. Then give both feet another general massage and concentrate again on the reflex areas. The whole massage should not take more than one hour.

9 Apply acupressure
Use the following acupressure points (see Appendix C, FIGS 1, 2, 3, 4 and 6).

Bladder 12 (*Fengmen*) – Located 2 fingers'-width from either side of the lower border of the spinous process of the second thoracic vertebra, this point helps eliminate wind cold.

Bladder 13 (*Feishu*) – Located 2 fingers'-width from either side of the lower border of the spinous process of the third thoracic vertebra, this point helps strengthen the lungs.

Gall Bladder 20 (*Fengchi*) – Located on either side of the neck below the occipital protuberance, this point helps clear the head of sinus congestion and headaches.

To relieve a cold or 'flu in the head, and congestion in the sinus and nasal cavities, use the following points:
Large Intestine 4 (*Hegu*)
Yintang
Bitong
Large Intestine 20 (*Yingxiang*)

Massage the jawline to stimulate the lymphatic glands. (See FIG 12.) You can massage the jawline daily if you do not have a cold or 'flu. This is to keep the lymphatic glands working to prevent infection.

10 Use moxibustion
Apply only over acupuncture points Bladder 12 (*Fengmen*) and Bladder 13 (*Feishu*) if the wind cold symptoms and signs do not change to those of wind heat with yellow, green or blood-tinged nasal discharges or sputum.

Moxibustion is very effective for coughing with lots of watery, diluted, white sputum. See Appendix C, FIG 5.

> *Caution:* Do not use moxibustion on acupuncture points Bladder 12 (*Fengmen*) and Bladder 13 (*Feishu*) if you have heart problems. These points are near enough to the heart points to make it risky if you are inexperienced.

11 Consult an acupuncturist
An acupuncturist can also cure a cold or 'flu. If you go when your cold or 'flu has just started, acupuncture can prevent it from getting worse, but you may need more than one treatment. Acupuncture treatment is best for people who are frail or weak, be they young or old, especially if they have lung problems. Such people must not allow the cold or 'flu to enter the lungs.

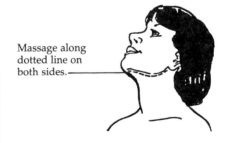

Massage along dotted line on both sides.

FIG 12. Massaging the jawline to stimulate lymphatic glands

RE-ADJUSTING IMBALANCES CAUSING WIND HEAT

1 Use a sea-salt gargle
At the first sign of a sore throat use a sea-salt gargle. Dissolve $^1/_2$ teaspoon of sea-salt in a glass of warm or cold water. Gargle as often as necessary.

2 Use a sage and honey gargle
This is more effective than the sea-salt gargle. Simmer 25 g (1 oz) sage in 570 ml (1 pt) water for 10 minutes. Allow the brew to cool down and strain when it is cold. Add 1 teaspoon of honey for a whole day's gargle.

To soothe the throat, warm half a glassful and use as a hot gargle.

Caution: Never use leftover sage and honey gargle.

3 Drink pot barley water
Drink lots of pot barley water to cool the overheated blood system. Sweeten with a little honey, but do not use too much or you may lose your voice or create mucus in the respiratory tract. Alternatively, flavour the pot barley water with fresh or dried peppermint leaves.

4 Drink a decoction of Buddha's fruit
This clears sinuses with thick, yellow or greenish-yellow mucus or catarrh. Boil $^1/_2$ a Buddha's fruit, which has been broken up into several small pieces, in 2 cups of water, in a Chinese earthenware herbal pot. It is ready when it has boiled down to 1 cup. Strain and drink 2 to 3 times a week. (You may have to acquire a taste for it.)

5 Eat cooling vegetables
During this time eat plenty of cooling vegetables, especially watercress and lotus root. Eat the watercress raw or made into soup, and take the lotus root in soup form. If you cannot find fresh lotus root use slices of reconstituted dried lotus root (available from Chinese supermarkets). Remember to soak the dried variety before using it.

6 Avoid citrus fruits
They tend to create mucus, catarrh, phlegm or sputum. Have pears, melon or guava instead for vitamin C.

7 Drink herbal tea
Use the Western herbal mixture of peppermint leaves, elderflowers and yarrow to make a tea. You will need 1 teaspoon each of dried peppermint leaves, elderflowers and yarrow and 1 cup of boiling hot water. Infuse the herbs in a thermos flask for 10 to 15 minutes. Strain and drink. Take this three times a day until the cold or 'flu eases.

8 Use foot reflexology
See the relevant section on page 238 for wind cold.

9 Apply acupressure
See the relevant section on page 239 for wind cold.

10 Use essential oils
See the relevant section on page 238 for inhalation in the case of wind cold.

11 Do not use moxibustion

12 Consult an acupuncturist
Acupuncture can help bring down an overheated blood system if you see your acupuncturist at the start of a cold. If the cold or 'flu is 2 to 3 days old you may need several treatments.

A FEW WORDS OF CAUTION

The advice in this chapter is applicable only for people who are young, active and fairly

strong. It is not for those of any age who are frail and weak. Such people must see their doctors or alternative practitioners as soon as possible. However, it is all right to follow the advice given in this chapter in conjunction with orthodox medical treatment.

Frequent attacks of wind cold or wind heat can give rise to sinusitis. I have seen many cases of this in Southeast Asia where people live and work in and out of airconditioned homes, cars, offices and shops, thereby subjecting their bodies to sudden temperature changes. This is especially harmful if you were born with a weak constitution or weak lungs.

If you think your sinusitis is a result of wind cold or wind heat, try living in a more natural environment, or build up your body to withstand sudden temperature shifts. *Taijiquan* or *qigong* practised daily over a long period of time can help strengthen the body, as can the Chang Ming Diet for sinusitis (see Chapter 19).

Colds and 'flus can also result from overeating, which puts stress on the whole body. People often fall sick after feasting on rich, spicy, greasy and indigestible foods at Chinese New Year, Christmas and Easter, as well as during the durian season. To remedy this, eat only brown rice congee cooked with dried tangerine peel for a day or two if you have a cold or 'flu caused by wind cold. Serve brown rice congee with raw lettuce leaves if you have a wind heat cold or 'flu. See page 40. If the condition does not improve, see your doctor or alternative practitioner as soon as possible.

Beware: If your fever is high, especially in cases of wind heat, see your doctor immediately for antibiotics to suppress the infection. This is very important for people of all ages who are weak and frail.

Avoid: The following should be avoided if you have cold or 'flu caused by wind cold or wind heat.

1   Chicken, which can create more mucus, catarrh, phlegm and sputum

2   Ginseng, which can drive external factors deeper into the body and make you ill years later

Note: It is not advisable to work while you are fasting, especially if you are old. For best results, take a few days off.

19 Sinusitis and Hay Fever

According to traditional Chinese medicine, the root causes of sinusitis and hay fever are 'deficient spleen *qi*' and 'deficient lung *qi*'.

The spleen digests, assimilates, transforms and transports all food and drink. If this function is impaired, as in deficient spleen *qi*, the food and drink turn into mucus instead of being transformed and transported.

According to traditional Chinese medicine, the lung has the function of dispersing the essence of food and drink which the spleen has transformed and transported. If this lung function (lung *qi*) is strong, the mucus can be dispersed and there will be no pathological consequences. However, if this function is impaired, as in deficient lung *qi,* mucus accumulates in the lungs, respiratory tract, throat, nose and sinus cavities.

> *The 3 types of sinusitis:*
> 1   Deficient lung *qi*
> 2   Stagnation of *qi* and blood
> 3   Liver and gall bladder damp heat

SINUSITIS CAUSED BY DEFICIENT LUNG *QI*

Symptoms and signs
- Pale face
- Weak voice
- Frequent fatigue
- Recurrent cough with diluted, watery sputum
- Cold or 'flu caught easily
- Increased nasal discharge during cold weather
- White, or clear and watery nasal discharge
- Tongue body: pale
- Tongue coat: thin and white

> *Possible causes:*
> 1   Hereditary lung weakness (often characterised by a white face).
> 2   Severe lung illness – whooping cough, bronchitis, pneumonia, etc. – when young.
> 3   Overwork. Too much studying or bending over a desk or drawing board can weaken the lungs.
> 4   Great sadness and grief. (Traditional Chinese medicine explains that sadness and grief injure the lungs.)

To re-adjust the imbalances

1   Adopt the Chang Ming Diet
Eat mainly neutral and warming energy foods and use neutral and warming methods of cooking.

> *Avoid:*
> Sugar of any kind and foods prepared with it

To strengthen the spleen, eat:

Brown rice

Red rice

Hyacinth beans – The stir-fried variety which is available only from a Chinese herbalist. Stir-fried hyacinth beans look as if they have been scorched

Peas (all types) – Cook with basil, spearmint or savory

Black-eyed beans

Black soyabeans

Note: To aid digestion of foods and prevent mucus formation, use the following herbs and spices.

    Garlic

    Ginger

    Sage

    Thyme

    Basil

To strengthen the spleen and lungs:

1   Boil a decoction of *dang shen* with *huang shi* (see page 133 in Chapter 8, Dried Ingredients). Consult the Chinese herbalist for the correct amount.

2   Boil 10 Chinese red dates (stones removed) and 1 thin slice of ginger in 2 cups of water. Boil down to 1 cup. Sweeten with a little barley malt extract and drink once a week.

2   *Practise yoga, taijiquan, qigong or deep breathing*

This should be done daily.

3   *Apply acupressure*

Use either thumb or finger and massage in a circular movement for 1 to 2 minutes. Pause for 1 to 2 minutes, then repeat the massage two more times. Do this hourly if the condition is bad, three times a day otherwise. See Appendix C, FIGS 1, 2, 3 and 6, and use the following points.

Large Intestine 4 (*Hegu*) – Apply acupressure on both hands.

Bladder 13 (*Feishu*) – Located about 2 fingers'-width away from the lower border of the spinous process of the third thoracic vertebra, this point helps strengthen the lungs.

Yintang – Located between the eyebrows, this point helps clear the sinus cavities.

Bitong – Located on either side of the nose midway between the tip and the bridge of the nose, this point helps clear the nasal passage.

Large Intestine 20 (*Yingxiang*) – Located on either side of the nostrils, this point also helps clear the nasal passage.

4 Use essential oils

One of these is oil of pine. Add 8 to 12 drops of essential oil of pine to a large bowl of hot water. Bend the head over the bowl and cover with a large towel. Inhale for 10 to 15 minutes until the sinuses clear. Repeat as often as necessary.

Alternatively, mix 4 drops of oil of pine with 10 ml sweet almond oil. Massage a drop of the mixture on acupressure points *Yintang*, *Bitong*, Large Intestine 20 (*Yingxiang*). See Appendix C, FIG 6. Repeat as often as it is necessary.

Try essential oils like eucalyptus or tea tree. (Use them as described above for oil of pine.) Remember to dilute them if using them on the face.

Olbas oil and Kwon Loong Foong Yau can be purchased from health food shops and Chinese herbalists respectively. They are too strong to apply directly on the face, especially if you have sensitive skin. Just put a few drops on a handkerchief or tissue and inhale for as long as you get the vapour.

5 Use foot reflexology

(See Appendix B.) Give both feet a general massage from toe to heel before concentrating on the following reflex areas: big toes (as illustrated in Appendix B); all the other toes, especially the stems; lungs on the soles and tops of the feet; bronchial area; throat; small intestines; ascending colon; transverse colon; descending colon; Sigmoid flexure and rectum.

Give both feet another general massage, then return to the specific areas. This time, gently rotate all the toes clockwise then counter-clockwise to help to drain the sinuses and release tension. Please make sure you support the toes first. The entire massage should not take more than 1 hour. If your condition is severe repeat the procedure three times a day. Otherwise, once or twice a day is sufficient.

6 Exercise

Do gentle exercises with deep breathing. Walking in the fresh air is good. If you can take a walk in a pine forest or among eucalyptus trees, so much the better.

7 Consult an acupuncturist

Acupuncture treatment is very good for tonifying the lungs and clearing the sinuses but it will not be successful if you do not follow the above guidelines, especially the diet.

SINUSITIS CAUSED BY STAGNATION OF *QI* AND BLOOD

Symptoms and signs
- Sticky yellow discharge
- Sinus pain
- Nasal polyps
- Tongue coat: thick, yellow, greasy or slippery

Possible cause: Repeated attacks of cold and 'flu.

To re-adjust the imbalances

1 Adopt the Chang Ming Diet

Eat mainly neutral energy foods. Have a few cooling energy foods but balance them with warming energy foods. Use neutral methods of cooking most of the time.

Avoid the same foods as for sinusitis caused by deficient lung *qi*. (See page 243.)

Use the same foods to strengthen the spleen.

Do not use the tonic brews. They may be too warming for you.

> *To clear sinuses congested with sticky yellow discharge:* Boil $^1/_2$ a Buddha's fruit (which has been broken up into several small pieces) in 2 cups of water in a Chinese earthenware herbal pot. Boil down to 1 cup of liquid. Strain and drink 2 to 3 times a week. (You may have to acquire a taste for it.)

2 Practise yoga, taijiquan, qigong or deep breathing
Do it daily to strengthen the lungs.

3 Apply acupressure
Use the same points as for sinusitis caused by deficient lung *qi*.

4 Use essential oils
Use them for inhalation or massage as described for sinusitis caused by deficient lung *qi*.

5 Use foot reflexology
Just as described for sinusitis caused by deficient lung *qi*.

6 Exercise
Take frequent walks in the fresh air, if possible among trees like pine or eucalyptus.

7 Take a lavender bath
To prevent catching a cold or 'flu, have a lavender bath at least once or twice a week to build up the immune system. Add 4 drops of oil of lavender to a hot bath just before you get in. Inhale and breathe in the lovely scent while you are in the bath. If you do catch a cold or 'flu, build yourself up as soon as you recover.

8 Consult an acupuncturist
Acupuncture is excellent for getting rid of a cold as soon as it starts. It is also very good for tonifying the lungs and relieving stagnation of *qi* and blood. Herbs are very good for getting rid of colds at the very start.

SINUSITIS CAUSED BY LIVER AND GALL BLADDER DAMP HEAT

Symptoms and signs
- Recurrent attacks which worsen under emotional stress
- Attacks triggered by pollen, house dust, etc.
- Itchiness in the nasal passage
- Yellow or white discharge
- Red eyes
- Anger and irritability
- Tongue body: red around the edges
- Tongue coat: thick, yellow, greasy or slippery

> *Possible causes:*
> 1 Excessive greasy, spicy foods, red meats and other hot or warming energy foods
> 2 Mental, emotional or physical stress and/or tension

To re-adjust the imbalances

1 Adopt the Chang Ming Diet
Eat mainly neutral and cooling energy foods until the blood system is balanced. Then eat mainly neutral energy foods.

Eat the following foods to get rid of damp heat.

Pot barley

Job's tears

Cream-coloured hyacinth beans which have
    not been stir-fried

To make pot barley water more effective:
Add a few grains of Job's tears to the pot barley and boil together with 7 to 8 parts water. Sweeten with barley malt extract and drink throughout the day instead of tea or coffee. Take daily if your condition is severe, 2 to 3 times a week otherwise.

Note: Take a decoction of Buddha's fruit (see page 245).

2 *Alleviate stress*

Do something positive to remedy your mental, emotional or physical stress. Learn to relax by taking up *yoga, taijiquan, qigong,* chanting or meditation. Please refer to Chapter 16.

3 *Take a lavender bath*

This helps you relax at the end of a day. Add 4 drops of oil of lavender to a hot bath just before you get in. Inhale the lovely aroma.

4 *Apply acupressure*

Use the procedure described for sinusitis caused by deficient lung *qi.*

5 *Use essential oils*

Their use for inhalation or massage is described on page 244, for sinusitis caused by deficient lung *qi.* The same applies in this case.

6 *Use foot reflexology*

Follow the procedure on page 244 for sinusitis caused by deficient lung *qi* but add the following reflex areas: liver, gall bladder, solar plexus and diaphragm. See the chart in Appendix B for the location of these reflex areas.

7 *Exercise*

Walk, if possible among trees in the park, forest or woods, to strengthen the lungs and to relax.

8 *Consult an acupuncturist*

Acupuncture can help release tension but you must still learn to relax on your own and to avoid the forbidden foods.

Further consultation: In addition to following the guidelines above, see an osteopath or chiropractor to make sure your spinal column is not out of place. It is possible for one or more displaced cervical vertebrae to cause congestion in the sinuses.

HAY FEVER

This chronic summer condition is a combination of the three types of sinusitis. If one type is predominant follow the guidelines for the symptoms and signs of that type. If all three are equally predominant, please see an alternative practitioner to help you re-balance your body.

To prevent hay fever in the summer, begin a course of acupuncture treatment 1 to 2 months before the start of the hay fever season, then weekly during the season. If you are strong and follow the above guidelines you may need treatment only before the season.

20 Asthma

In traditional Chinese medicine, three organs are mainly responsible for asthma: the spleen, lungs and kidneys. The spleen digests, assimilates, transforms and transports purified food essence to the lungs. The lungs disperse this food to all parts of the body in the form of a 'mist'. The kidneys provide the 'fire' or *yang* energy which the spleen uses to digest, assimilate, transform and transport food. The kidneys also help the lungs by 'receiving' the 'mist'.

When the above organs fail to function, the food becomes mucus, which is transported to the lungs. If the lungs are weak, the mucus becomes stuck in the chest. If the kidneys cannot provide the *yang* energy to help the already impaired spleen, then there will be more mucus formation. And, if the kidneys cannot 'receive' the mucus, asthma results.

> *Kinds of asthma:* There are four main types of asthma in traditional Chinese medicine. In real life, it is possible to have a combination of types.
> 1 Asthma caused by external wind cold entering the lungs
> 2 Asthma caused by an accumulation of mucus (cold and heat types)
> 3 Asthma caused by deficient lung *qi*
> 4 Asthma caused by deficient kidney *qi*

ASTHMA CAUSED BY EXTERNAL WIND COLD ENTERING THE LUNGS

This type of asthma results from an attack of wind cold (see Chapter 18, Colds and 'Flus) that has entered the lungs.

Symptoms and signs
- Fear or dislike of the cold
- No sweating
- Mild fever
- Headache
- Aching bones
- Shortness of breath with rough breathing
- Feeling of tightness in the chest
- Tongue coat: white

> *Possible causes:*
> 1 Weak lungs
> 2 Repeated attacks of wind cold (colds or 'flus)
> 3 Exhaustion from overwork, especially due to too much studying or work which involves long hours of bending over something, e.g. a drawing board, desk, etc.
> 4 Sadness or grief

When the lungs are weakened, they become very susceptible to attacks by sudden changes in temperature, for example: when an unusually hot day suddenly turns icy cold; when a cold winter season suddenly turns

warm for a few days; when you go in and out of airconditioned places; when you sweat in the heat, then enter a draughty, airconditioned place; when you sweat in bed in an airconditioned room; when you go from a cold storage room to a centrally heated room.

Prevention

1 Avoid sudden temperature changes where possible

2 Protect yourself from the elements
Wrap up warmly when you go outdoors in winter. During the rainy season, carry an umbrella for sudden drizzles, showers or downpours.

3 Keep chest and throat warm
Always keep the chest, throat and neck warm with a woollen scarf in winter. Wear a polo- or turtle-necked jumper or a collared shirt to protect the throat and neck.

4 Do not smoke

5 Avoid dusty or smoky environments

6 Do not prolong grief
Do not grieve for too long over the loss of a close relative or friend.

To re-adjust the imbalances

1 Adopt the Chang Ming Diet
Asthma caused by external wind cold tends to affect those with cooled blood systems. Therefore, the diet should consist of mainly neutral and warming foods made with neutral and warming cooking methods.

Avoid raw, cold food and drinks, i.e., food and drinks out of a refrigerator or freezer. Try to have as little fruit as possible. If you must have fruit, stew or bake it.

The following foods are recommended:

Fresh ginger – Excellent in dispelling wind and cold from the body, especially from the lungs. It also helps resolve mucus in the lungs in this type of asthma. Use a little ginger in every dish, particularly when cooking cabbage. Should you catch a cold, drink ginger tea as soon as possible to sweat it out. (See Chapter 18, Colds and 'Flus.)

Members of the *Allium* family – Garlic, shallots, onions, spring onions, leeks, chives and Chinese chives are good for respiratory problems. Have some of these daily. Stir-fry, stir-fry and braise, steam or bake them.

Thyme – Use thyme in your cooking as it aids digestion and helps get rid of catarrh.

Cinnamon – Helps warm up the body and is appropriate for this type of asthma. Use Chinese cinnamon bark rather than western cinnamon quill in your cooking once or twice a week.

For vegans, vegetarians and macrobiotics:
Braise *tofu* or *fu zhou* with Chinese cinnamon bark, onions, carrots and *miso*. For one person, a $2^1/_2$ by 1 cm (1 by $^1/_2$ in) piece of cinnamon bark or quill per 175 to 225 g (6 to 8 oz) of *tofu* is sufficient. Alternatively, braise or stir-fry the *tofu* with 5-spice powder, which contains ground Chinese cinnamon bark.

For wholefooders:
Braise white fish or chicken with cinnamon bark,

cinnamon quill or 5-spice powder. Or stir-fry squid with 5-spice powder.

Cinnamon tea: This is also good, but more appropriate for winter. Infuse a $2^1/_2$ cm (1 in) piece of Chinese cinnamon bark or cinnamon quill in a cup of boiling water in a thermos flask for 10 to 15 minutes. Drink once or twice a week. Remember, do not take too much cinnamon – it can cause nosebleeds.

Chinese apricot kernel tea – Use 10 parts sweet Chinese apricot kernels to one part bitter Chinese apricot kernels, e.g. about 110 g (4 oz) sweet Chinese apricot kernels to about 10 g ($^1/_2$ oz) bitter Chinese apricot kernels. Boil in water with a pinch of ground Chinese cinnamon bark, liquidise, and drink warm, about once a week.

Snow ear fungus – Double-boiled for 4 to 6 hours with garlic, ginger and chicken (skin and fat removed), this helps strengthen the lungs. Skim any fat or oil floating on the surface of the soup before serving. Take once a week.

Cooling Buddha's fruit – This becomes more neutral if made with Chinese cinnamon bark.

Buddha's fruit with cinnamon: Boil $^1/_2$ a Buddha's fruit, which has been broken into pieces, with a $2^1/_2$ by 1 cm (1 by $^1/_2$ in) piece of cinnamon bark in 2 cups of water in a Chinese earthenware herbal pot. Boil down to 1 cup of liquid, strain and drink once a week to remove excessive catarrh, phlegm, sputum or mucus. (You may have to acquire a taste for it.)

Dang shen and *huang shi* – These Chinese herbs help strengthen the spleen and lungs. (If possible, see a Chinese herbalist for the right dosage. He may add other herbs to benefit your general body condition too.)

2 Practise yoga, taijiquan, qigong or deep breathing

Do this daily to strengthen the lungs.

3 Use foot reflexology

(See Appendix B.) Give both feet a general massage from toe to heel. Then concentrate on the following reflex areas: lungs (top of feet and soles), bronchial, diaphragm, solar plexus, ileocecal valve, ascending colon, transverse colon, descending colon, Sigmoid flexure, rectum, spleen, pancreas, adrenals and kidneys.

Next, give both feet another general massage from toe to heel and again, concentrating on the specific reflex areas. This massage should not take longer than an hour. Do it three times a day if your condition is serious, once or twice a day otherwise.

FIG 13. How to massage the diaphragm to ease breathing

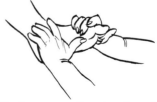

FIG 14. How to massage the solar plexus to relax an asthma patient during an asthmatic attack

4 Apply acupressure

(See Appendix C, FIGS 7 and 8.) Massage on the following points daily:

Dingchuan – Located half *cun* (body inch) lateral to the lower border of the spinous process of the 7th cervical vertebra, this point dispels wind cold, subdues ascending *qi* and soothes asthma.

Bladder 12 (*Fengmen*) – Located two fingers'-width lateral to the lower border of the spinous process of the second thoracic vertebra, this point dispels wind cold, helps the lungs disperse mucus, strengthens the lungs, and soothes asthma and coughing.

Bladder 13 (*Feishu*) – Located two fingers'-width lateral to the lower border of the spinous process of the third thoracic vertebra, this point dispels wind, strengthens the lungs, helps lungs disperse mucus, subdues ascending *qi*, and soothes asthma and coughing.

Bladder 43 (*Gaohuangshu*) – Located three *cun*, four fingers'-width lateral to the lower border of the spinous process of fourth thoracic vertebra, this point strengthens the lungs and tonifies the *wei qi*.

Ren 17 (*Shanzhong*) – Located on the midline of the sternum between the nipples, this point strengthens the body's *qi*, subdues ascending *qi*, clears the lungs when they feel tight, and resolves phlegm.

Lung 1 (*Zhongfu*) – Located one *cun* below the lower border of the acromial extremity of the clavicle and six *cun* lateral to the middle of the sternum, this point strengthens the lungs, and clears them when they feel tight.

5 Use moxibustion

Although moxibustion is very good for this type of asthma, the appropriate points are very near to the heart, so this method should not be used by people with high blood pressure, high blood cholesterol, heart problems or serious medical histories.

Apply the glowing end of the moxa stick to the acupuncture points mentioned above. Keep the glowing end of the moxa stick 2 to $2^1/_2$ cm ($^3/_4$ to 1 in) away from the skin and remove the ash as often as possible to prevent it dropping on the skin.

For *Dingchuan*, Bladder 12, Bladder 13 and Bladder 43, move the glowing end of the moxa stick backwards and forwards across the spine about 2 to $2^1/_2$ cm ($^3/_4$ to 1 in) away from the skin until the skin turns slightly pinkish. Then move down to the next acupuncture point.

For *Ren 17*, move the glowing end of the moxa stick slightly up and down the sternum, about 2 to $2^1/_2$ cm ($^3/_4$ to 1 in) away from the skin. If the chest is hairy, hold the stick higher,

or you will singe the hair. Repeat until the skin turns slightly pinkish.

For Lung 1, move the glowing end of the moxa stick in a rotatory movement about 2 to $2^1/_2$ cm ($^3/_4$ to 1 in) away from the skin. Repeat until the skin turns slightly pinkish.

> *Do not overdo moxibustion:* Use moxibustion only once a week, preferably at night when the air is cooler and when the chest tends to get tight and coughing increases.

6 Consult an acupuncturist
Acupuncture is also very helpful in relieving asthma, especially when the chest is tight. Do not wait until you have an attack to see your acupuncturist. The older you are the more important it is for you to consult an acupuncturist to help balance the spleen, lungs and kidneys and strengthen the body to prevent recurring attacks. It is advisable to follow the above guidelines while consulting a doctor or alternative practitioner.

ASTHMA CAUSED BY AN ACCUMULATION OF MUCUS – COLD TYPE

Symptoms and signs
- Fear or dislike of the cold
- Cold limbs
- Tightness in the chest
- Coughing with copious, thick white sputum
- A feeling of dryness in the mouth without the desire to drink
- Poor appetite
- Loose stools
- Tongue body: pale
- Tongue coat: thick and white

> *Possible causes:*
> Asthma caused by an accumulation of mucus is more pronounced than the first type because the spleen is working even less efficiently. The spleen can be weakened by any of the following.
> 1 Eating too many cold, raw foods, refrigerated foods, and cooling energy foods when you already have a cooled blood system or a tendency towards one
> 2 Overeating
> 3 Irregular eating
> 4 Eating too many rich foods which are hard to digest
> 5 Eating too much red meat or animal fat
> 6 Not chewing thoroughly before swallowing
> 7 Exposure to cold and damp environments over a long period of time, e.g. living in a cold, damp basement or in areas always shrouded by mist or fog

Prevention

1 Eat more cooked foods
Do not, however, overcook them. Use neutral and warming cooking methods.

2 Do not overeat

3 Eat regularly
Adopt a regular eating pattern of three meals a day.

4 Chew your food well before swallowing

5 Live in a healthy environment
Do not live in cold, damp places. Houses must be warm and dry, especially in winter.

6 Wear dry clothes

Do not wear sweaty or rain-soaked clothes. Change into clean, dry ones as soon as possible.

7 Avoid damp and cold surfaces

Do not sit, kneel, lie, sleep or walk barefoot on bare cement floors, damp earth and wet grass.

To re-adjust the imbalances

1 Adopt the Chang Ming Diet

Eat mostly neutral and warming energy foods and use mainly neutral and warming cooking methods. Do not eat anything that has been chilled in the refrigerator or freezer. Try the dietary suggestions given for asthma caused by external wind cold (see pages 249-250).

> *Dried tangerine peel cure:* This is said to be good for resolving mucus. Add a small piece to boiling brown rice or to a pot of *tofu* or *fu zhou* braised with garlic, ginger, leeks, carrots and *miso*. Alternatively, boil beans with a small piece of dried tangerine peel for an unusual flavour. Add dried tangerine peel to food about 2 to 3 times a week.
>
> *Herbal cure:* See a Chinese herbalist for herbs to strengthen the spleen and lungs.

2 Practise yoga, taijiquan, qigong or deep breathing daily

3 Use foot reflexology

Follow the advice given in the section on asthma caused by external wind cold, pages 250-251.

4 Apply acupressure

(See Appendix C, FIGS 9 to 12.) Do this daily, following the procedure for asthma caused by external wind cold (page 251), and also these points to strengthen the spleen and prevent the formation of mucus.

Bladder 20 (*Pishu*) – Located two fingers'-width lateral to the lower border of the spinous process of the eleventh thoracic vertebra.

Stomach 36 (*Zusanli*) – Located three *cun* below the patella, one finger's-width from the anterior crest of the tibia.

Stomach 40 (*Fenglong*) – Located halfway between the patella and the ankle, about three fingers'-width lateral to the lateral border of the tibia.

Spleen 6 (*Sanyinjiao*) – Located three *cun* directly above the tip of the medial malleolus, on the posterior border of the tibia.

5 Use moxibustion

Apply moxibustion on acupuncture points Stomach 36 and Bladder 13 (see Appendix C, FIGS 3 and 10) once a week, in the evening, when the air is cooler.

For Stomach 36, hold the glowing end of the moxa stick about 2 to $2^1/_2$ cm ($^3/_4$ to 1 in) away from the skin for 1 to 2 seconds, withdraw for 1 to 2 seconds, then come close to the skin again. Repeat this 'sparrow pecking' method until the skin turns slightly pinkish. It helps drive energy into the body to strengthen the spleen's digesting, assimilating, transporting and transforming capabilities.

For Bladder 13, hold the glowing end of the moxa stick about 2 to $2^1/_2$ cm ($^3/_4$ to 1 in) away from the skin and move backwards and forwards across the spine until the skin turns slightly pinkish.

6 Consult an acupuncturist
Acupuncture helps tonify the spleen better than the above self-help guidelines. See an acupuncturist for a course of treatment.

ASTHMA CAUSED BY AN ACCUMULATION OF MUCUS – HEAT TYPE

Symptoms and signs
- Red face
- Mental restlessness (e.g. nothing pleases, cannot concentrate, etc.)
- Dislike of the heat
- Spontaneous sweating
- Dry mouth, thirst and the desire to drink cold liquids
- Tightness in the chest
- Fast, coarse breathing
- Coughing with yellow sticky sputum
- Tongue body: red
- Tongue coat: thick and yellow

Possible causes:
1. Repeated attacks of the 'wind heat' type of cold or 'flu that has gone to the lungs.
2. Prolonged retention of mucus in the respiratory tract after a 'wind heat' type of cold or 'flu.
3. Excessive intake of rich, greasy, spicy and hot energy foods and drinks.

Prevention

1 Strengthen your immune system
Build up your immune system to prevent recurrent attacks of wind heat colds or 'flus.

2 Consult a medical practitioner
See a doctor or alternative practitioner as soon as you get a wind heat cold or 'flu, to get rid of mucus, catarrh, sputum or phlegm.

3 Avoid heating foods and drinks
These include all warming and hot energy foods and drinks and those cooked by warming methods: greasy and spicy foods, curries, chillies, coffee, durians, mangoes, pineapples, chocolates, cheeses, dried milk powder, alcohol, and foods which are deep-fried, baked, roasted, grilled and barbecued.

To re-adjust the imbalances

1 Adopt the Chang Ming Diet
Eat mostly neutral and cooling energy foods and use neutral and cooling methods of cooking.

Recommended foods and cooking methods:
1. Use raw garlic, or steam or boil it with vegetables
2. Stir-fry garlic only occasionally with vegetables
3. Use only very thin slices of ginger in your cooking and pick them out before serving
4. Use thyme often
5. Do not use cinnamon or dried tangerine peel because they have warming energies.

The following are foods that will help to adjust the imbalance.

Buddha's fruit – Helps get rid of this type of yellow sputum because it has cooling energies.

> *Buddha's fruit decoction:* Boil $^1/_2$ a Buddha's fruit which has been broken up into pieces, in 2 cups of water in a Chinese earthenware herbal pot. Boil down to 1 cup of liquid. Strain and drink the tea twice a week. (You may need to acquire a taste for it.)

Snow ear fungus – Boiled in water and sweetened with barley or rice malt extract, this helps cool and strengthen the lungs.

> *Snow ear fungus decoction:* For one person, you will need 2 pieces of dried snow ear fungus, each $2^1/_2$ cm (1 in) in diameter. Soak the fungus until it has swelled before bringing to a boil in 2 cups of water. Boil it down to 1 cup of liquid, then add the barley or rice malt extract. Drink the decoction warm, 2 to 3 times a week and remember to eat the snow ear fungus.

Ginkgo nuts – Boiled with *fu zhou* and sweetened with barley or rice malt extract, ginkgo nuts also help cool and strengthen the lungs and get rid of mucus. Have this no more than once or twice a week – ginkgo nuts must not be taken in excess.

2 Exercise the lungs
Practise *yoga*, *taijiquan*, *qigong* or deep breathing daily, and go for long walks to strengthen the lungs.

3 Use foot reflexology
Follow advice given for asthma caused by external wind cold on pages 250-251.

4 Apply acupressure
Follow advice given for asthma caused by external wind cold on page 251.

5 Do not use moxibustion

6 Consult an acupuncturist
Repeated acupuncture treatment can also help cool the body, dispel mucus, and strengthen the spleen and lungs. Supplement it with the above guidelines.

ASTHMA CAUSED BY DEFICIENT LUNG *QI*

Symptoms and signs
- Bright, white face
- Low, weak voice
- Short, quick breathing
- Difficulty in exhaling
- Weak cough with difficulty in expectorating
- Spontaneous sweating
- Poor appetite
- Easily fatigued
- Tongue body: pale and flabby

> *Note:* The causes, prevention, re-adjustment, dietary advice, etc. for this type of asthma are the same as for asthma caused by deficient kidney *qi*. See below.

ASTHMA CAUSED BY DEFICIENT KIDNEY *QI*

Symptoms and signs
- Pale face
- Breathlessness that becomes worse upon exertion

- Difficulty in inhaling
- Improvement after resting or when lying down
- Frequent urination
- Oedema
- Cold limbs
- Loose stools
- Little appetite
- Tongue body: pale, flabby and wet

Asthma caused by deficient kidney *qi* usually involves the spleen, lungs and kidneys equally. The kidneys fail to provide the *yang* energy that the spleen needs to digest, assimilate, transform and transport food, and the lungs fail to disperse the 'mist'.

Women may have asthmatic attacks more frequently between ovulation and menstruation because, in traditional Chinese medicine, the spleen and kidneys are involved in the menstrual cycle. Between ovulation and menstruation the spleen finds it even more difficult to carry out its normal function of transforming and transporting food, because the *yang* energy from the kidneys is being used for ovulation.

Possible causes:
These apply to asthma caused by both deficient lung and kidney *qi*.
1   Weak constitution from birth, or hereditary asthma
2   Overwork, e.g. too much bending over a desk, can weaken lung *qi*, while too much bending at the waist or lifting heavy objects can weaken the kidneys.
3   Prolonged coughing
4   Excessive sex
5   Old age

Prevention

1   Do not study too much
Take breaks between study periods. Do not spend hours bent over a drawing board – take walks around the room, straighten the spine and take deep breaths.

2   Avoid carrying heavy loads
Do not carry heavy objects, especially if you are weak.

3   Consult a medical practitioner
See a doctor or alternative practitioner to get rid of coughs, or you will weaken the lungs.

4   Do not smoke

5   Avoid smoky and dusty environments

6   Avoid sudden temperature changes

7   Keep warm all the time
Carry extra clothing with you when you go out in case the temperature drops suddenly. In winter, protect the neck and chest well.

8   Do not have excessive sex
See Chapter 16, which discusses this subject on pages 215-216.

9   Be extra careful during pregnancy
Women must take great care of their health, and eat nutritious, natural, wholesome foods before, during and after pregnancy. If not, they may weaken their health, especially if there is a family history of lung weakness or asthma.

10 Have a longer birth interval
Do not have too many children close together, but leave a gap of 3 to 4 years between them.

To re-adjust the imbalances

1 Adopt the Chang Ming Diet
Eat mostly neutral and warming energy foods and use neutral and warming methods of cooking. Try to avoid cooling energy foods and drinks as much as possible, especially fruit. If you crave fruit, stew or bake it with cinnamon, nutmeg, cloves or allspice.

For these two types of asthma, follow the dietary advice given for asthma caused by external wind cold and try these foods.

Walnuts – Especially good for asthma caused by deficient kidney *qi*. Have about 6 walnut halves a day cooked with brown rice, vegetables, *tofu* or *fu zhou*.

Fenugreek seeds – Help strengthen the kidneys. Have them 3 to 4 times a week, with any kind of beans in a stew or casserole.

Warming spices – Other warming spices that are good for the kidneys include fennel seeds, star anise, cumin seeds and cardamom seeds.

> *From the Chinese herbalist:* The following are supposed to help deficient lung or kidney *qi*, but consult a Chinese herbalist before taking them.
>   Korean ginseng
>   Powdered placenta
>   Processed *Rehmannia glutinosa* (*shu di huang*)

2 Practise yoga, taijiquan, qigong or deep breathing
Daily practice strengthens the spleen, lungs and kidneys. Massage to warm up the kidneys is also helpful. Do it as often as you like. (See the *do-in* massage on page 220 and FIG 5.)

3 Use foot reflexology
(See Appendix B.) Follow the procedure for asthma caused by external wind cold on pages 250-251.

4 Apply acupressure
(See Appendix C.) Follow the procedure for asthma caused by external wind cold and add these points. (See also page 251.)

Bladder 20 (*Pishu*) – Located two fingers'-width lateral to the lower border of the spinous process of the eleventh thoracic vertebra, this point helps strengthen the spleen. (For this and Bladder 23, see Appendix C, FIG 9.)

Bladder 23 (*Shenshu*) – Located two fingers'-width lateral to the lower border of the spinous process of the second lumbar vertebra, this point helps strengthen the kidneys.

Stomach 36 (*Zusanli*) – Located three *cun* below the patella, one finger's-width from the anterior crest of the tibia, this point helps strengthen the immune system and improves vitality. (See Appendix C, FIg 10.)

Spleen 6 (*Sanyinjiao*) – Located three *cun* directly above the tip of the medial malleolus, on the posterior border of the tibia, the point also strengthens the spleen (See Appendix C, FIGS 11 and 12.)

Kidney 3 (*Taixi*) – Located in the depression

between the medial malleolus and tendo calcaneus, level with the tip of the medial malleolus, this point strengthens the kidneys. (See Appendix C, FIG 11.)

5 Use moxibustion

See Appendix C, FIGS 7 to 12 and use moxibustion on the following acupuncture points:

> *Dingchuan*
> Bladder 13
> Bladder 20
> Bladder 23
> *Ren* 17
> Lung 1
> Stomach 36
> Spleen 6
> Kidney 3

For *Dingchuan*, Bladder 13, Bladder 20 and Bladder 23, move the glowing end of the moxa stick about 2 to $2^1/_2$ cm ($^3/_4$ to 1 in) away from the skin, backwards and forwards across the spine, until the skin turns slightly pinkish.

For *Ren* 17, move the glowing end of the moxa stick about 2 to $2^1/_2$ cm ($^3/_4$ to 1 in) away from the skin, up and down the sternum, about 2 cm ($^3/_4$ in) above the point and 2 cm ($^3/_4$ in) below the point, until the skin turns slightly pinkish.

For Lung 1, move the glowing end of the moxa stick about 2 to $2^1/_2$ cm ($^3/_4$ to 1 in) away from the skin in a rotatory movement, until the skin turns slightly pinkish.

For Stomach 36, use the 'sparrow pecking' method as described for asthma caused by an accumulation of mucus, cold type (page 253). Do the same for Spleen 6 and Kidney 3.

A FEW WORDS OF CAUTION

People stricken with asthma caused by deficient kidney or lung *qi* are usually weak and/or old. They should see a doctor or alternative practitioner regularly as well as follow the above guidelines.

If possible, combine traditional Chinese acupuncture treatments with Chinese herbs. The herbs slowly build up deficient *qi*, while acupuncture helps relieve congestion in the chest.

> *Avoid these foods:* No matter which type of asthma you have, stay away from the following mucus-forming foods.
>
> Sugar
> Dairy products
> Coconut products
> Red meats
> Animal fats
> Eggs – eat no more than 2 or 3 free-range eggs a week, scrambled with shallots, onions, leeks, spring onions, chives, Chinese chives, parsley or thyme
> Baked flour products
> Almonds
> Peanuts, peanut butter, *tahini* and other nut or seed butters
> Citrus fruits
> Chinese Peking cabbage, Chinese white cabbage, lady's fingers (okra) and slippery spinach
> Tropical fruits, especially *ciku*, banana, durian, *rambutan* and avocado
> Chicken – cook only without the skin or fat, and skim floating oil or fat from soups and stews; cook with the following ingredients to help

digestion and prevent mucus formation: Shiitake mushrooms, black wood ears, snow ear fungus, garlic, shallots, onions, spring onions, leeks, chives, Chinese chives, ginger, thyme, sage, rosemary and tarragon.

If you are still suffering from asthma after following these guidelines, your thoracic vertebra may be out of alignment. Please see an osteopath or chiropractor to have it adjusted and supplement your treatment in accordance with the above guidelines.

Note: When any vertebra is out of alignment it can press on a nerve or obstruct a meridian or channel to give rise to all kinds of problems like constipation, sinusitis, hay fever, asthma, etc.

GUIDELINES FOR BABIES AND INFANTS

To ease baby's breathing, gently massage acupuncture points *Dingchuan*, Bladder 12 and Bladder 13. Prop the baby up against your chest so that he can feel your breathing and be reassured of your presence, especially during an attack, which can be very frightening. Hold the baby up with one hand and gently massage the acupuncture points with the other hand. Do not remove the baby's clothes or he may catch a chill. Because babies are very sensitive to pressure, massage them for only five minutes, three times a day or during attacks.

Take the baby to the doctor or alternative practitioner for regular check-ups.

Note: Moxibustion is not suitable for babies or young children.

21 Headaches and Migraines

eadaches and migraines are common complaints that can affect people of all ages and make life miserable. Is it possible to prevent headaches or migraines? Yes, but only if you understand their root causes in terms of traditional Chinese medicine.

According to traditional Chinese medicine, there are more than 50 types of headache and 5 types of migraine. The most common varieties of headache as well as the 5 types of migraine will be explained in this chapter.

HEADACHES

Headaches can be classified according to:

1 *Location* – top of head
front of head or forehead
sides of head or temples
back of head
whole head

2 *Intensity* – dull, heavy
full, bursting
tight, boring
varying from dull to sharp
continuous
needle-like pain

3 *Differentiation of syndromes*
– dysfunction of internal
organs
deficiency of *qi*
wind cold
wind heat
wind damp
summer heat

4 *Aggravations*
– worse when lying down
worse when tired
worse in the morning
worse in the afternoon or
evening
worse in the cold
worse in the heat
worse in the damp
worse when there is a change
in weather, e.g. before a
thunderstorm
worse with tension
worse after eating certain
foods
worse before menstruation
worse during menstruation
worse after menstruation

The location, intensity, differentiation of syndromes and aggravations are all equally important in helping to diagnose the root

cause of the headache. This will be clear to you as you read on.

LOCATION OF HEADACHE: TOP OF HEAD

intensity: dull, heavy

Causes:

1 Deficiency of *qi*
2 Deficiency of blood
3 Deficiency of heart
4 Stagnation of liver *qi*

1 Deficiency of *qi*

This type of headache occurs because the body does not have enough vital energy (or *qi*) to reach the top of the head. It is worse when you are tired or when you suddenly get up from a sitting or lying position. After resting, the headache disappears.

Prevention
- Do not overwork.
- Have enough sleep.

To re-adjust the imbalances

- Try acupuncture
Acupuncture treatments revitalise the *qi*. Supplement the treatments with the Chang Ming Diet and practise *yoga, taijiquan* or *qigong* daily to improve *qi* circulation.

- Use foot reflexology
Give both feet a general massage from toe to heel, then concentrate on the head reflex area. (See Appendix B.) Do not spend more than 1 hour on the massage. Do it three times a day, if you find it helps, once a day otherwise.

- Use acupressure
Massage the acupuncture point Large Intestine 4 (*Hegu*) for no more than 5 to 10 minutes. (See Appendix C, FIGS 1 and 2.) Repeat as often as necessary.

2 Deficiency of blood

Deficiency of blood is more than anaemia: it means that the body does not have enough blood to reach the top of the head. A headache of this type is worse when you are tired or when you get up suddenly from a sitting or lying position. For women, it may be worse during menstruation or just at the end of the cycle because the body loses blood during these times. Rest should relieve the headache.

Prevention
- Do not overwork.
- Have enough sleep.
- Have plenty of rest and avoid doing heavy work when you are menstruating.

To re-adjust the imbalances

- Adopt the Chang Ming Diet
Eat foods according to your blood system. Concentrate on foods with a high iron or B_{12} content or foods which the Chinese classify as blood-building, for example:

Red rice
Millet – Only if you have an overheated blood system or a tendency towards one
Aduki beans – Cooked with carrots or pumpkin
Black soyabeans – Boiled with dried squid
Brown lentils – Cooked with thyme and caraway seeds
Miso
Tempeh

Sunflower seeds

Seaweeds, especially *hiziki* and *arame* – Only if you have an overheated blood system or a tendency towards one

Beetroot greens – If you have a cooled blood system or a tendency towards one, stir-fry with garlic, ginger and black pepper

Mushrooms, fresh – If you have a cooled blood system or a tendency towards one, stir-fry then braise with garlic, ginger and coriander seeds

Nettles – If you have a cooled blood system or a tendency towards one, stir-fry then braise with garlic, ginger and black pepper

Spinach – If you have a cooled blood system or a tendency towards one, stir-fry with garlic, ginger and grated nutmeg

Watercress – If you have a cooled blood system or a tendency towards one, stir-fry with garlic, ginger, onion, carrot and black pepper

Beetroot

Cabbage – Cook with ginger, coriander seeds or leaves, cumin seeds, oregano, marjoram, caraway seeds or dill seeds to aid digestion and prevent flatulence

Parsley

Golden needles – Stew with black wood ears and black hair moss

Dried oysters – Stew with black hair moss

Shiitake mushrooms

Chinese black dates

Chinese red dates

Dang gui

Longan, or *long yan rou*

Raisins

Eggs – Use only free-range eggs, not more than 2 or 3 per week, cooked with onions, shallots, spring onions, leeks, Chinese chives, chives, thyme or parsley

Dried squid – Boiled with lotus root and

Chinese red dates

Chicken – Use only free-range chicken, with skin or fat removed, cooked with black hair moss, black wood ears or Shiitake mushrooms

Red grapes or red grape juice

Blood building soup – See Chapter 8, Dried Ingredients

Vitality tea – See Chapter 8

Blood building tonic at the end of menstrual period – See Chapter 8

Blood tonic for the old, weak and anaemic – See Chapter 8

> *Note:* If you do not have a cooled blood system or a tendency towards one, take Floradix, a liquid extract of foods rich in iron and B vitamins that is easily absorbed into the bloodstream. It is available at health food shops.

• Practise *yoga, taijiquan* or *qigong*
Do this daily to improve the *qi* so the body can absorb the goodness from wholesome, natural foods and turn it into blood.

• Use foot reflexology
(See Appendix B). Follow the guidelines for deficiency of *qi* on page 261.

• Use acupressure
Follow the guidelines for deficiency of *qi*, page 261.

I would recommend using acupuncture treatments to supplement the above guidelines. If possible, also see a Chinese herbalist for a prescription to tonify the blood.

3 Deficiency of heart
In this type of headache the heart is too weak to pump the blood to the top of the head. This

condition is more serious than the first two and should not be remedied only through self-help. See a doctor or alternative practitioner regularly for treatments to strengthen the heart.

Supplement your treatments with foot reflexology massage. Give both feet a general massage from toe to heel, then concentrate on the heart and head reflex areas. (See Appendix B.) Spend no more than 30 minutes on the massage, three times a day, if it does not tire you. If it does, once a day is sufficient.

If you are strong enough, try gentle daily *taijiquan* exercises.

4 Stagnation of liver *qi*

In traditional Chinese medicine, the liver ensures that the *qi* flows smoothly throughout the body. If this function is impaired, aches and pains will result. In this type of headache the liver has failed to ensure a smooth flow of *qi* to the top of the head. It may be worse before a thunderstorm.

Prevention

Try to avoid emotional upset. The liver is easily affected by anger, frustration, anxiety and tension.

To re-adjust the imbalances

• Adopt the Chang Ming Diet
Eat foods according to your blood system. Concentrate on leafy greens and sprouts like mung bean sprouts, soyabean sprouts, alfalfa sprouts, mustard and cress.

Reduce your intake of tea or coffee immediately. These two stimulants tend to cause anxiety and tension.

• Practise *yoga*, *taijiquan* or *qigong*
Do this daily to ensure a smooth flow of *qi*. Daily chanting and meditation are excellent for relieving tension, anger, frustration and anxiety.

• Use aromatherapy
Oil of rosemary is very good for liver *qi* stagnation. Dilute 4 drops of essential oil of rosemary in 10 ml of sweet almond oil. Then rub the oil below the right rib cage over the liver once or twice a day or when you have a headache. Store in a dark glass bottle in a cool, dark place.

> *Note:* Oil of rosemary may raise blood pressure. Do not use frequently if you suffer from hypertension.

• Use reflexology
Give both feet a general massage from toe to heel, then concentrate on the following reflex areas: liver, diaphragm, solar plexus, neck and head. (See Appendix B.) It is important to twiddle the big toes to release tension in the neck in this kind of headache. Do not spend more than 1 hour doing this massage. Massage one to three times a day.

• Use acupressure
To relieve headaches, massage acupuncture points Large Intestine 4 (*Hegu*) and Gall Bladder 20 (*Fengchi*) several times a day for no more than 5 to 10 minutes. (See Appendix C, FIGS 1, 2 and 4.)

Acupuncture is also very good in giving quick relief to this type of headache.

LOCATION OF HEADACHE: TOP OF HEAD
intensity: full, bursting

> **Causes:**
> 1 Too much hot sun beating on the head
> 2 Blow on the head

This type of headache should be treated by a doctor or alternative practitioner as soon as possible. The best self-help exercises you can do to supplement treatment are reflexology and acupressure. Follow the guidelines for deficiency of *qi,* page 261.

Personally, I believe that acupuncture is the best form of treatment for a blow on the head because acupuncture needles can remove the obstruction of *qi* and blood in the channels very quickly. However, see a doctor first to make sure you have not damaged the skull.

LOCATION OF HEADACHE: TOP OF HEAD
intensity: tight, boring

> **Causes:**
> 1 Liver *yang* rising
> 2 Cold obstruction

1   Liver *yang* rising
In traditional Chinese medicine, 'liver *yang* rising' means there is too much heat in the liver. This heat 'flares up' and goes to the top of the head causing tight, boring headaches. The other symptoms can be red eyes, red face, a general feeling of heat, restlessness, and a desire for cool drinks and cool air.

Prevention
- Do not overwork.
- Try to avoid emotional upset.

To re-adjust the imbalances

- Adopt the Chang Ming Diet

Eat mostly neutral and cooling energy foods and use neutral and cooling methods of cooking.

Stop drinking tea or coffee as soon as possible. Try chamomile or chrysanthemum tea, mineral water or cooling fruit juices to cool down the blood system.

> *Note:* Do not use more than 6 whole chrysanthemum flowers per cup of chrysanthemum tea.

- Practise *yoga, taijiquan, qigong,* chanting or meditation daily to calm the emotions.

- Use reflexology

See stagnation of liver *qi,* page 263.

This type of headache is most common among people who suffer from high blood pressure, hyperthyroidism and menopausal problems. See your doctor or alternative practitioner regularly for check-ups.

2   Cold obstruction
This type of headache usually occurs in winter, or if you happen to work in a cold storage place or in the direct blast of an airconditioner.

Prevention
- Avoid exposing your head to the cold.
- In winter, wear a scarf or hat.

To re-adjust the imbalances

- Adopt the Chang Ming Diet

This makes your body strong enough to resist the cold. Eat mainly neutral and warming energy foods and use neutral and warming methods of cooking.

- Practise *yoga, taijiquan* or *qigong*

Done daily, it improves the circulation of *qi*, and builds up *wei qi* or defensive *qi* to help you resist the cold.

- Use aromatherapy

Dilute 4 drops of essential oil of ginger in 10 ml of sweet almond oil. (Never use the oil undiluted.) Rub oil on top of the head to drive out the cold and clear obstruction. Place a hot water bottle over the spot. The heat from the bottle opens the pores on the scalp and aids penetration of the oil as well as provides warmth to the head. If you cannot get oil of ginger, place a few slices of fresh ginger under the hot water bottle.

- Use foot reflexology

See the procedure given for deficiency of *qi*, page 261.

- Use acupressure

See the procedure given for deficiency of *qi*, page 261.

Acupuncture is also effective in driving cold from the head.

LOCATION OF HEADACHE: TOP OF HEAD
intensity: varying between dull and sharp

This headache is due to too much worrying, thinking or lack of sleep.

Prevention
- Try to avoid worrying.
- Give yourself little time to ruminate by keeping busy.
- Get more sleep.

To re-adjust the imbalances

- Adopt the Chang Ming Diet.

- Practise *yoga, taijiquan, qigong,* chanting or meditation daily.

- Use reflexology

Give both feet a general massage from toe to heel, then concentrate on the following reflex areas: head, neck, diaphragm and solar plexus. (See Appendix B.) Twiddle the big toes gently clockwise and counter-clockwise. Do this once a day, for no more than 1 hour.

- Use acupressure

Massage acupuncture point Large Intestine 4 (*Hegu*) as often as necessary. (See Appendix C, FIGS 1 and 2.)

In addition to the above, you may try a Bach Flower Remedy. (See page 226.)

LOCATION OF HEADACHE: FRONT OF HEAD OR FOREHEAD
intensity: dull, heavy

> **Causes:**
> 1 Deficiency of stomach *qi*
> 2 Deficiency of stomach blood
> 3 Catarrh, mucus or phlegm

1 Deficiency of stomach *qi*

This headache is similar to the dull, heavy kind on the top of the head caused by deficiency of *qi*, except it is caused by a lack of *qi* in the stomach and its subsequent inability to digest food.

Prevention
- Do not eat too many cold, raw or cooling energy foods, especially if you have a cooled blood system or a tendency towards one.
- Do not overeat.
- Do not have irregular meals.
- Do not do heavy manual jobs immediately after a meal. Wait at least 2 hours.

To re-adjust the imbalances

- Adopt the Chang Ming Diet
Eat foods appropriate to your blood system and cook them accordingly.

- Practise *yoga*, *taijiquan* or *qigong*
If done daily, it improves the circulation of *qi*.

- Use reflexology
Give both feet a general massage from toe to heel, then concentrate on the stomach and head reflex areas. (See Appendix B.) For frontal headaches, concentrate more on the

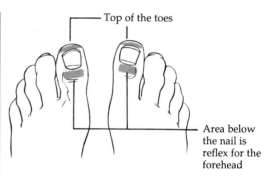

FIG 15 Reflexology for frontal headaches

tops of the big toes and the areas just below the nails. (See FIG 15.) Do it once or twice a day and do not spend more than one hour on each massage.

- Use acupressure
Apply acupressure at points Large Intestine 4 (*Hegu*), *Yintang* and Stomach 36 (*Zusanli*) once a day and spend no more than 5 minutes on each point. (See Appendix C, FIGS 1, 2, 6 and 10.) Large Intestine 4 (*Hegu*) and *Yintang* can be done whenever you have a headache.

Acupuncture and Chinese herbs are also very good for tonifying the stomach *qi*. See your alternative practitioner.

2 Deficiency of stomach blood

This type of headache is similar to the dull, heavy headache on the top of the head caused by deficiency of blood (see page 261). It is best treated immediately by acupuncture and/or Chinese herbs and will involve more treatments than deficiency of stomach *qi*. Supplement the treatments with the dietary advice given on page 261 for deficiency of blood.

Use reflexology. Follow guidelines given for deficiency of stomach *qi*, this page.

Use acupressure. Massage Large Intestine

4 (*Hegu*), *Yintang*, Stomach 36 (*Zusanli*), Spleen 6 (*Sanyinjiao*) and Bladder 20 (*Pishu*) once a day for no more than 5 minutes on each point. Large Intestine 4 (*Hegu*) and *Yintang* can be massaged whenever you have a headache. (See Appendix C.)

3   Catarrh, mucus or phlegm

Some people produce a lot of catarrh, mucus or phlegm when the spleen's food transformation function is impaired. This type of headache may be worse in damp weather or in hot, humid countries where you walk in and out of airconditioned rooms. The catarrh, mucus or phlegm may not be visible and you may feel dull, heavy and muzzy, as if there were cotton wool inside the head.

Prevention
- Do not eat too many raw, cold or cooling energy foods, especially if you have a cooled blood system.
- Do not overeat.
- Do not have irregular meals.

To re-adjust the imbalances

- Adopt the Chang Ming Diet

Eat foods appropriate to your blood system and cook the foods accordingly.

Eat foods or herbs that will aid digestion like garlic, shallots, onions, leeks, spring onions, chives, Chinese chives, thyme, sage and ginger.

Avoid these mucus forming foods:
Sugar
Dairy products
Baked flour products
Red meats
Animal fats
Almonds
Peanuts
Bananas
Avocados
Eggs (no more than 2 or 3 free-range eggs a week)

- Practise *yoga*, *taijiquan* or *qigong*

Done daily, this improves *qi* circulation and aids the spleen in transforming food.

- Use reflexology

Give both feet a general massage from toe to heel, then concentrate on the following reflex areas: stomach, spleen and head. (See Appendix B.) For frontal headaches, concentrate more on the tops of the big toes and the areas just below the nails. (See FIG 15.) Massage for no more than 1 hour, once or twice a day.

- Use acupressure

Massage Large Intestine 4 (*Hegu*), *Yintang*, Stomach 36 (*Zusanli*), Spleen 6 (*Sanyinjiao*) and Stomach 40 (*Fenglong*) once a day for no more than 5 minutes on each point. Massage Large Intestine 4 (*Hegu*) and *Yintang* whenever you have a headache. (See Appendix C, FIGS 1, 2, 6, 10 and 12.)

I would strongly advise anyone with this type of headache to see an acupuncturist or Chinese herbalist to tonify the spleen and resolve the phlegm. Follow the above guidelines along with the treatments.

LOCATION OF HEADACHE: FRONT OF HEAD OR FOREHEAD
intensity: full, bursting

> *Causes:*
>
> 1   Stomach full heat
> 2   Too much sunlight

1   Stomach full heat

This type of headache can be due to a high fever. See a doctor or alternative practitioner as soon as possible to bring the fever down.

This headache can also result from eating too many hot or warming energy foods like curries, chillies, durians and mangoes, and foods that are deep-fried, baked, roasted, grilled, barbecued or smoked.

Prevention

Do not eat hot or warming energy foods in excess, especially if you have an overheated blood system or a tendency towards one.

To re-adjust the imbalances

• Adopt the Chang Ming Diet
Eat mainly neutral and cooling energy foods and cook them accordingly. Fast for 1 to 2 days on only brown rice congee, *miso* and some raw lettuce. Drink plenty of peppermint tea to bring down the heat in the stomach.

• Use aromatherapy
Mix 4 drops of essential oil of peppermint with 10 ml sweet almond oil. Store in a dark glass bottle in a cool, dark place. Rub a few drops of the mixture on the forehead and over the stomach area. Or, add 4 drops of diluted oil of peppermint to a bowl of cold water and immerse your feet to draw the heat down from the forehead. Use the diluted oil as often as necessary.

It is a good idea to see an acupuncturist for this type of headache. Acupuncture can quickly relieve the intensity of the headache and cool down the heat in the stomach at the same time. Combine the above guidelines with the treatments for faster relief.

2   Too much sunlight

Too much sunlight can affect the eyes and give rise to frontal headaches.

Prevention

Avoid the glare of the sun as much as possible. Wear sunglasses or a wide-brimmed hat.

To re-adjust the imbalances

As far as I know, only acupuncture can give quick relief. However, after I started eating a carrot a day my eyes could withstand the glare without giving me headaches. Eat a carrot a day for 6 months to a year and see if it works for you.

> *Caution:* Eat no more than one carrot a day. Carotene taken in excess can turn your skin yellow and poison your system.

LOCATION OF HEADACHE: FRONT OF HEAD OR FOREHEAD
intensity: tight, boring

> *Causes:*
>
> 1   Wind
> 2   Stomach cold
> 3   Sinusitis

1 Wind

Wind refers to wind cold. Please see Chapter 18, Colds and 'Flus.

2 Stomach cold

Stomach cold is due to eating too many cold, raw foods and drinking too many ice-cold drinks. It affects people with cooled blood systems more than those with overheated blood systems.

Prevention

Avoid cold, raw foods and drinks.

To re-adjust the imbalances

- Adopt the Chang Ming Diet

Eat foods which have neutral or warming energies and cook them accordingly. Eat the following vegetables, herbs and spices to warm up the stomach: spring onions, leeks, ginger, garlic, black pepper, coriander leaves or seeds, fennel seeds, basil and nutmeg.

- Practise *yoga*, *taijiquan* or *qigong*

Daily practice improves *qi* circulation and strengthens and warms up the stomach.

- Use aromatherapy

Mix 4 drops of essential oil of black pepper with 10 ml sweet almond oil and store in a dark glass bottle in a cool, dark place. Rub a drop or two of the mixture on the stomach area and place a hot water bottle on top. Wrap the bottle in a towel to retain the heat and to avoid burning the skin. Do this once or twice a day depending on the severity of the headache.

- Use moxibustion

Hold the glowing end of the moxa stick about 2 to 2$\frac{1}{2}$ cm ($\frac{3}{4}$ to 1 in) above the acupuncture point *Ren* 12 (*Zhongwan*) for 1 second, then remove it. (See Appendix C, FIG 13 for the correct position.) Repeat this 'sparrow pecking' method until the point turns slightly pinkish. Repeat this procedure once every 2 days in the evening until the condition improves.

> *Caution:* Read the precautions to observe in moxibustion, in Chapter 16. Do not use moxibustion after aromatherapy or you will cause blisters. Do not use aromatherapy and moxibustion on the same day. Remember not to use moxibustion immediately before and after a bath. Please wait for at least 1 to 2 hours for the body temperature to return to normal.

3 Sinusitis

Please see Chapter 19, Sinusitis and Hay Fever.

LOCATION OF HEADACHE: FRONT OF HEAD OR FOREHEAD
intensity: varying between dull and sharp

This type of headache is usually due to some obstruction of *qi*. Practise *yoga*, *taijiquan* or *qigong* daily to relieve it.

LOCATION OF HEADACHE: SIDE OF HEAD OR TEMPLES
intensity: dull, heavy

> *Causes:*
> 1   Deficiency of blood
> 2   Too much reading

1   Deficiency of blood

Refer to page 266, the section on deficiency of stomach blood.

2   Too much reading

Too much reading can strain the eyes and cause headaches. See Chapter 29, Failing Eyesight.

LOCATION OF HEADACHE:
SIDE OF HEAD OR TEMPLES
intensity: full, bursting

Causes:
1   Liver *yang* rising
2   Heat in the gall bladder
3   Wind heat

1   Liver *yang* rising

This type of headache is usually due to high blood pressure. Those who suffer from them should not rely on self-help only. See a doctor or alternative practitioner for regular check-ups.

2   Heat in the gall bladder

This type of headache is usually caused by eating fatty, greasy foods over a long period of time. Often such headaches are a sign of gall bladder inflammation or gall bladder stones. See your doctor or alternative practitioner as soon as possible to confirm this before starting self-help treatments.

3   Wind heat

See the section on wind heat in Chapter 18, Colds and 'Flus.

LOCATION OF HEADACHE:
SIDES OF HEAD OR TEMPLES
intensity: tight, boring

This type of headache may result from exposing the shoulders and neck to draughts.

Prevention
Do not sit in draughts. Protect yourself well.

To re-adjust the imbalances
Use aromatherapy. Mix 4 drops of essential oil of ginger with 10 ml of sweet almond oil. Rub the mixture on the neck and shoulders and massage. Use a few drops of diluted oil of cinnamon if oil of ginger is not available. Never use the oils undiluted.

Combine the above guidelines with daily *yoga*, *taijiquan* or *qigong* to start the *qi* moving and to dispel wind from the body.

Acupuncture also gives excellent relief to this type of headache.

LOCATION OF HEADACHE:
SIDES OF HEAD OR TEMPLES
*intensity: varying between
dull and sharp*

This type of headache is usually due to too much worrying, reading or a combination of the two.

Prevention
Try to read less. Exercise and rest the eyes at intervals when you read. See Chapter 29, Failing Eyesight, for the eye exercises.

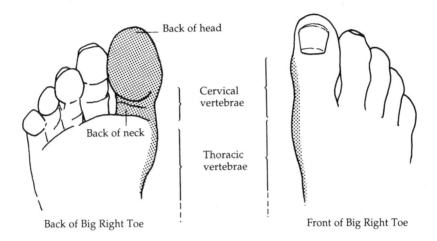

Back of head

Cervical vertebrae

Back of neck

Thoracic vertebrae

Back of Big Right Toe

Front of Big Right Toe

FIG 16. Reflexology for spondylosis

LOCATION OF HEADACHE: BACK OF HEAD
intensity: dull, heavy

This type of headache is usually due to deficiency of kidney *qi*. In Chinese medicine, the kidneys nourish the brain and spinal column. If this function fails, parts of the spinal column (the cervical vertebrae, in this case) may be damaged.

Acupuncture and/or Chinese herbs are best for this type of headache. If treated in the early stages, they may help prevent further degeneration of the cervical vertebrae. Go on the Chang Ming Diet and practise *yoga*, *taijiquan* or *qigong* daily to supplement the treatments.

Use reflexology. Give both feet a general massage from toe to heel, then concentrate on the following reflex areas: spine (especially the cervical vertebrae), kidneys, adrenals, back of neck and head. (See Appendix B and FIG 16.)

LOCATION OF HEADACHE: BACK OF HEAD
intensity: full, bursting

This type of headache is often seen in cases of nephritis (or inflammation of the kidneys). See your doctor or alternative practitioner as soon as possible.

LOCATION OF HEADACHE: BACK OF HEAD
intensity: tight, boring

Causes:

1 Wind

2 Bone *bi*

3 Attack of cold in the bladder channel

1 Wind

This is the same as exposure to draughts. See 'prevention' on page 270.

2 Bone *bi*

In Western terms, bone *bi* refers to arthritis with bone degeneration and/or deposits, or spondylosis. This type of headache starts from the nape of the neck, travels up the back of the head and may go to the eyes.

A few acupuncture treatments can relieve the headache but you may need several treatments to stop further bone degeneration or deposits. Supplement acupuncture treatments with the Chang Ming Diet and practise *yoga*, *taijiquan* or *qigong* daily.

Use reflexology. Give both feet a general massage from toe to heel, then concentrate on the following reflex areas: spine (especially the cervical vertebrae), kidneys, adrenals, back of neck and head. (See Appendix B.) Concentrate on the cervical vertebrae and the beginnings of the thoracic vertebrae. The side of the neck is also very important. (See FIG 16.)

3 Attack of cold in the bladder channel

This type of headache is uncommon and usually strikes people who are very weak. Symptoms include a cold feeling down the spine.

Prevention

Do not expose yourself to the elements if you have a weak constitution. Always wrap up well.

To re-adjust the imbalances

Use moxibustion. Have someone run the glowing end of a moxa stick about 2 to 2^1/$_2$ cm (^{3}/$_4$ to 1 in) away from the skin, up and down the spine, as illustrated in FIG 17, until the skin turns slightly pinkish and you no longer feel cold down the back.

Caution: Do not use moxibustion when the body is wet. To prevent blisters, perform moxibustion 1 to 2 hours before or after a bath or shower, when the body has returned to its normal temperature.

Follow the Chang Ming Diet and practise *yoga*, *taijiquan* or *qigong* daily to strengthen the immune system.

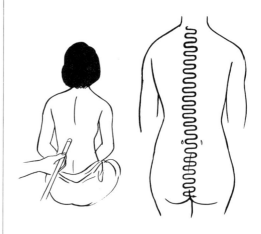

FIG 17. Moxibustion for tight, boring headache at the back of the head. Move the glowing end of the moxa stick down the spine as indicated by the arrow.

LOCATION OF HEADACHE: BACK OF HEAD
*intensity: varying from
dull to sharp*

This kind of headache is due to obstruction of *qi* or the displacement of the cervical vertebrae. See an osteopath or chiropractor for treatment.

Location of Headache: Whole Head

This type of headache is more serious than all the others described above. See a doctor and/or alternative practitioner as soon as possible to check that it is not a symptom of a more serious illness. Similarly, headaches with needle-like sensations must be checked with a doctor and/or alternative practitioner. They may be a sign of a serious problem.

Migraines

> *Causes:*
> 1 Stagnation of liver *qi*
> 2 Stomach heat
> 3 Deficiency of liver blood
> 4 Deficiency of *yin*
> 5 Deficiency of both *yin* and *yang*

1 Migraine due to stagnation of liver *qi*
This type of migraine can be extremely painful and can become worse with worry, anxiety and tension, or before a thunderstorm or a menstrual period.

Prevention
- Try not to worry or be anxious.
- Try to be more relaxed.

To re-adjust the imbalances

- Adopt the Chang Ming Diet
Eat foods appropriate to your blood system and cook the foods accordingly. Eat mainly leafy greens and sprouts like mung bean sprouts, soyabean sprouts, alfalfa sprouts, mustard and cress.

Decrease your intake of tea or coffee immediately and slowly learn to do without it. Drink chamomile tea, mineral water or hot water instead. Tea and coffee are stimulants which can cause anxiety and tension. Also try to cut out sugar, red meats and dairy products.

- Practise *yoga, taijiquan, qigong,* deep breathing, chanting or meditation daily to improve *qi* circulation and to help you to relax.

- Use aromatherapy, reflexology and acupressure. Follow guidelines on page 263 for stagnation of liver *qi*.

Acupuncture can bring almost instant relief for this type of migraine. See also the Bach Flower Remedies, in Chapter 16, page 226.

2 Migraine due to stomach heat
This type of migraine is worse after eating foods like cheese, chocolate, coffee, cocoa, chocolate flavoured drinks, dried milk, prawns, crabs, lobsters, red wine, cow's milk, eggs, red meat, animal fats, sugar, curries and other spicy foods, oranges, mangoes, durians, other hot or warming energy foods, and foods which are baked, grilled, roasted, deep-fried, barbecued and smoked.

Prevention
Avoid hot and warming energy foods, especially if you have an overheated blood system or a tendency towards one.

To re-adjust the imbalances

• Adopt the Chang Ming Diet
Eat foods appropriate for your blood system and cook them accordingly. Drink peppermint tea to help digestion and cool the stomach. Go on a semi-fast of brown rice congee, *miso* and raw lettuce leaf for 1 to 2 days, to clear the system of heat.

• Practise *yoga, taijiquan* or *qigong*
This brings balance and harmony to the stomach.

• Use aromatherapy
Mix 4 drops of essential oil of peppermint with 10 ml of sweet almond oil. Rub on the stomach area and sides of the head where it hurts. Or soak the feet in a bowl of cold water mixed with 4 drops of oil of peppermint as often as necessary.

Acupuncture can also bring relief for this type of migraine, but not as quickly as it would for the first type, because the body is still full of heating foods. Combine acupuncture treatment with the guidelines above to prevent recurrent attacks.

3 Migraine due to deficiency of liver blood

This migraine is most common among women. It gets worse during or just after menstruation (because blood has been lost), first thing in the morning, when lying down for extended periods and when you are tired.

Prevention
• Do not overwork during menstruation.
• Have enough sleep, and, if possible, try resting between 1 and 3 p.m.

To re-adjust the imbalances

• Adopt the Chang Ming Diet
Concentrate on foods which are rich in iron and vitamin B$_{12}$, and foods that the Chinese classify as blood-building. See page 261, the section on deficiency of blood, for dietary and other advice.

Acupuncture and Chinese herbs are best for this type of migraine. They may take some time to take effect because the body needs extensive building up. Follow the guidelines given above during the treatment for faster improvement.

4 Migraine due to deficiency of *yin*

This type of migraine can result from neglecting to treat a migraine due to stomach heat or to overwork. It is different from the other types of migraine in that it is usually worse in the afternoons or evenings.

Prevention
• Treat any type of migraine as soon as possible or it might develop into this type.
• Do not overwork.
• Learn to relax.

I would advise anyone with this type of migraine to see an alternative practitioner as

soon as possible. If left untreated, it can become serious.

5 Migraine due to deficiency of *yin* and *yang*

This type of migraine may be treated only by the patient. It is a direct result of working too hard. It is often at its worst on Fridays but disappears by Sunday.

To prevent this type of migraine you need rest for a prolonged period – 3 to 6 months – and a complete change of lifestyle so that you work 50 per cent of the time and relax 50 per cent of the time.

Follow the Chang Ming Diet and study *yoga*, *taijiquan*, *qigong*, deep breathing, chanting or meditation to build the body up and aid relaxation.

Have acupuncture treatments during your extended rest to speed up the body's healing process but note: acupuncture treatment is useless if you are still working.

22 Pains of Joints, Muscles and Nerves

**Arthritis, Rheumatism, Sciatica, Lower Back Pain,
Trigeminal Neuralgia, Gout and Muscular Spasms**

Arthritis, rheumatism, sciatica, lower back pain, trigeminal neuralgia and gout are all painful conditions that often strike people over 40 years of age. At times the pain can be so intense that people resort to having the nerves frozen or surgically removed.

Traditional Chinese physicians believe that this pain is not caused by nerve dysfunction or damage to the nervous system. Rather, it is a sign that there is a blockage or obstruction of the flow of *qi* and blood in the channels. Nerves are the body's information carriers and should not be surgically removed; they should be nourished so they can inform us if the body is in danger.

To Chinese physicians, the blockage or obstruction of the flow of *qi* and blood in the channels is caused by the elements: wind, cold and damp. According to a Chinese saying, 'The wind is the cause of a hundred dis-eases.' Wind is the most pernicious of the four elements because it can combine with cold and damp and give rise to wind cold and wind damp. Wind cold and wind damp, however, are the more common causes of arthritis and rheumatism, especially in damp countries like Britain. Wind can also drive the elements deeper into the body, especially if the *wei qi* (or defensive *qi*) is weak. To avoid this the Chinese always wrap themselves in long silk or cotton padded jackets with high collars in the winter.

ARTHRITIS AND RHEUMATISM

These dis-eases can be divided into 5 syndromes:

1 Wandering *bi* where wind predominates
2 Painful *bi* where cold predominates
3 Fixed *bi* where damp predominates
4 Febrile *bi* where heat predominates
5 Bony *bi* with extra deposits of bone

Note: Bi means the obstruction of the flow of *qi* and blood by wind, cold, damp and heat. It is possible to suffer from a combination of the above *bi* syndromes.

1 Wandering *bi* where wind predominates

Symptoms and signs
- Wandering pain (characteristic of the nature of wind which moves constantly)
- Widespread pain involving many joints
- Sore, painful or hot muscles and joints
- Attacks can be brought on from exposure to wind, draughts and sudden temperature changes

2   Painful *bi* where cold predominates

Symptoms and signs
- Severe, biting or stabbing pain
- Limitation of movement
- Pain decreases with hot applications
- Pain increases when cold
- No local inflammation

This type of arthritis often occurs after exposure to cold, e.g. from working in cold storage rooms, near freezers, outdoors in winter, or even from washing hands often in cold water.

3   Fixed *bi* where damp predominates

Symptoms and signs
- Stiffness and numbness more than pain
- Fixed pain
- Heavy body and limbs
- Swelling or oedema around the affected joint

This type of arthritis is usually brought on by damp, humid weather, living in damp places (like basement flats), living in misty or foggy places (near ponds, lakes, streams, etc.), or sleeping, lying, sitting, kneeling or walking barefoot on marble, tiled or cement floors, damp ground or wet grass.

4   Febrile *bi* where heat predominates

Symptoms and signs
- Painful, red, hot and swollen joints
- Pressure makes pain more severe
- More than one joint affected
- Limitation in movement

This kind of arthritis is usually a result of other types of *bi* syndromes that have been neglected. After a long period of time, wandering, painful and fixed *bi* can turn into febrile *bi* because accumulated wind, cold or damp can turn into heat.

5   Bony *bi* with extra deposits of bone

Symptoms and signs
- Deformity of joints
- Limitation of movement
- Swelling of joints
- Muscular atrophy

This is usually a result of long-term untreated *bi* syndromes where the obstruction of *qi* and blood to the joints has allowed toxins and mucus, catarrh or phlegm to accumulate and cause pain and deformity.

Prevention for all *bi* syndromes

1   Do not expose yourself to the elements
Take precautions, especially if you have weak *wei qi* (or defensive *qi*). Wrap up well in winter with a cap, scarf, jacket with a collar, and a three-quarter length coat which is long enough to protect the back. If you have arthritis or rheumatism in the joints, wrap them up in 100 per cent knitted woollen leg warmers to keep them warm.

2   Stay home in bad weather
It is better to be in a dry, warm place when it is misty or foggy outdoors. Do not do any outdoor activities like gardening when the weather is windy, cold, damp, misty or foggy.

3 Stay dry

During the monsoon or rainy season try not to get caught in the rain. Always carry an umbrella for sudden drizzles, showers or downpours. If you do get caught in the rain, change into warm, dry clothes as soon as possible.

4 Do not stand in the direct blast of an airconditioner or aircooler.

5 If you must work in a cold storage place or near a freezer, wrap up well.

6 Avoid cold water

If you must do work in cold water, wear gloves. Similarly, if you go fishing, wear Wellington boots and thick socks to keep the legs and feet warm and dry.

7 Damp-proof your home

Consider installing damp-proofing, central heating, etc., if your house is damp.

8 Do not sleep, lie, sit, kneel or walk barefoot on marble, tile or cement floors, earth or grass.

9 Do not sleep in damp, sweaty clothes

In the tropics lay a cooling rattan or rice straw mat over the mattress. Try not to use an airconditioner or fan, both of which create wind and cold. Avoid red meat, dairy products, coconut products, hot spices, curries, sugar and animal fats and eat more *tofu*, beans, vegetables and fruits to feel cooler.

10 Avoid showers during yin hours

Do not take baths or showers or wash your hair, even though the water is hot, after sunset during the *yin* or cooling part of the day. Even after a thorough drying, droplets of water can cling to your skin and cause dampness. Do not soak in a bath or dampness can enter the body.

11 Dry hair thoroughly before curling

Use the towel vigorously before rolling hair in curlers to set or the skull and nape of the neck can become damp, leading to arthritic or rheumatic headaches. Then use a hairdryer.

12 Do not wear out your joints

Do not jog, run or play tennis, squash, football, rugby, golf, or sports that require constant pounding or the use of specific joints. Sports like these will not bother you when you are young, but after several years the wear and tear will weaken the joints, making them more susceptible to wind, cold and damp.

13 Dry yourself after exercise

Dry yourself thoroughly after *yoga*, *taijiquan*, *qigong* or any exercise and do not sit in a draughty environment, i.e., near a fan, aircooler, airconditioner or natural breeze. When you sweat, the pores open, allowing the wind to enter and cause aches and pains, especially if you are weak. Be sure to dry your hair and body completely after swimming.

14 Try your best not to catch a cold

Have at least one lavender bath weekly (see page 237) or take *miso* soup daily to strengthen the immune system. If you do catch a cold, try to get rid of it as quickly as possible (see Chapter 18, Colds and 'Flus). A prolonged cold can add more wind, cold or damp to your *bi* syndrome and make it more difficult to prevent aches and pains.

To re-adjust the imbalances for all *bi* syndromes

Try to avoid the initial causes of arthritis and rheumatism (wind, cold and damp) and follow the Chang Ming Diet. Wind, cold and damp cause obstruction of *qi* and blood to the joints. If your diet is rich in mucus-forming foods or toxins they will accumulate in the joints and aggravate the aches and pains. After many years, the mucus can harden to form extra bone deposits such as in bony *bi*.

In Chinese medicine, obstruction of *qi* and blood to the joints does not mean complete blockage. (If that happens the limbs will atrophy.) Rather, it means that circulation to and from the joints is decreased and that the blood flows more slowly when bringing nourishment to the joints and removing waste products. It is this slowness which allows the build-up of mucus and toxins in the joints.

Foods to avoid

Sugar
Replace white sugar with good quality brown sugar like Barbados or Muscovado sugar. Try giving up sugar completely if your arthritis or rheumatism is due to fixed *bi*, febrile *bi* or bony *bi*. Sugar creates dampness, which becomes mucus, in the body. If you recall, fixed *bi* and febrile *bi* are caused by external dampness, and bony *bi* by long-term accumulation of mucus which has hardened.

Use the following in moderation instead of sugar: barley or rice malt extract, and dried fruit like Hunza apricots, other apricots, raisins and sultanas (cook before eating).

Foods to avoid when aches are severe

Dairy products
All dairy products are hard to digest, especially for the Chinese who do not have the enzyme, galactase, to digest milk sugar, galactose. Foods that are difficult to digest become mucus, get lodged in the joints, and obstruct *qi* and blood circulation. In addition, cows are often given hormones and antibiotics and fed grass or hay that has been sprayed with chemical fertilisers and pesticides. There are bound to be traces of these toxins in the milk products that can also become lodged in the joints.

Red meats
All red meats are marbled with saturated fats, even the leanest joints or cuts. Like dairy products, saturated fats are hard to digest and can become mucus. Meat, like milk, can contain toxins, too.

Animal fats
These fats are the most difficult to digest and can easily become mucus.

Coconut products
Besides being rich in saturated vegetable fats (which are also difficult to digest), these products create wind in the body because of their cooling energies. Anyone with wandering *bi* should avoid them so as not to add to the external wind already in the body. Southeast Asians are fond of using coconut products and glutinous rice to make sweet cakes called *kuih-muih* – the worst food for arthritics or rheumatics. Coconut products have wind and cold energies, and sugar and glutinous rice have damp energies.

Other wind-causing foods
Avoid other wind-causing foods – soyabean milk, silken *tofu*, fresh mushrooms, Shiitake mushrooms, seaweeds, mung bean sprouts, soyabean sprouts, water spinach, rhubarb, seafood (like shrimps, prawns, crabs, cockles, whelks, mussels, lobsters and oysters), and bananas (especially *pisang hijau* or Jamaican banana). The Chinese believe that leftovers can also create wind in the body. Avoid them if you have wandering *bi*.

Avoid other damp or mucus forming foods like deep-fried foods, eggs, wheat, oats, rye, barley, potatoes, almonds, peanuts and bananas.

Frozen foods
Macrobiotics believe that if you eat frozen foods you will get frozen muscles and joints. Frozen foods have cold energies even if they previously had hot or warming energies.

Tea, coffee and all soft drinks
Tea and coffee contain caffeine which can accumulate in the joints and muscles, cause obstruction of *qi* and blood and give rise to aches and pains. All soft drinks have sugar, chemicals, colourings, flavourings and preservatives which are toxic when taken in excess over long periods of time.

Convenience foods
These are bound to contain colourings, flavourings, chemicals and preservatives.

Alcohol
Alcoholic beverages are made with sugar and all kinds of chemicals. Imbibe only occasionally.

Foods to eat

Grains
Eat brown rice, red rice, or brown rice flakes. Instead of porridge oats or jumbo oats, use brown rice flakes in porridge for breakfast. Because millet is cooling, use only if you have an overheated blood system or an acid stomach. Use only fresh and seasonal sweet corn.

Legumes and pulses
Use the neutral and warming varieties. Avoid those with cooling energies unless you have febrile *bi*.

Seeds and nuts
Eat in small amounts; their high oil content makes them difficult to digest.

Seaweeds
Because they are cooling, use seaweeds only if you have an overheated blood system or high blood pressure.

Vegetables
Have mainly neutral vegetables cooked with ginger. Combine small amounts of cooling vegetables with warming vegetables and ginger to make them less cooling.

Herbs and spices
Have mainly neutral energy varieties. Add warming energy herbs and spices to cooling vegetables.

> *Note:*
> For wandering *bi* use – cinnamon or ginger
> For painful *bi* use – bay leaves, nutmeg, black pepper or ginger

For fixed *bi* use – Sichuan pepper, garlic, ginger, black pepper or a tiny amount of chilli or cayenne. If you live in a cold, damp country like Britain, use chillies and cayenne medicinally, once or twice a week, in tiny amounts, cooked with food.

Eggs

Eat only 2 or 3 free-range eggs per week. (They are mucus-forming but high in protein.) Cook with onions, shallots, leeks, spring onions, chives, Chinese chives, ginger, parsley, thyme or mushrooms. Eat with vegetables to aid digestion.

Fish

All kinds of fish are appropriate because they are very easy to digest. If you suffer from bone degeneration or creaking joints, try cod liver oil.

Chicken

Eat only fresh free-range chickens without the skin and fat. Season with herbs like sage, thyme, tarragon, parsley or bay leaves to aid digestion, or cook with members of the onion family.

Fruit

Eat mainly neutral and warming energy fruits. On a cold day, stew or bake them. Do not have more than one piece of fruit a day because fruit acids can aggravate aches and pains. If you have severe pain avoid fruit for a couple of days until the pain goes away.

Note: Do not eat sour fruits – the sour taste can aggravate aches and pains.

Beverages

Drink boiled water or warm mineral water all day long. If you dislike plain water, drink some diluted herbal tea once a day for variation.

Note:

For wandering *bi* – drink cinnamon tea or ginger tea

For painful *bi* – drink fennel tea

For fixed *bi* – drink ginger tea

For febrile *bi* – drink comfrey tea or pot barley water sweetened with a little barley or rice malt extract

For bony *bi* – drink fennel tea.

Most fruit juices are too cooling or acidic for arthritis and rheumatism. Red or white grape juice is the most neutral if you crave fruit juice. Remember, fruit juices must only be taken in small quantities, no more than half a glass per day.

Effective exercises

Practise *yoga*, *taijiquan* or *qigong* daily to gently exercise all the joints and improve circulation of *qi* and blood. Daily practice over a long period of time can slowly unblock the obstruction to the joints. Do not expect overnight success.

Gentle walking is also another very good exercise. Use proper shoes and wrap up well, especially if you walk in the hills and moorlands.

Swimming can also help the joints. Remember to dry yourself thoroughly after a swim. Do not swim after sunset when the day is getting more *yin*, i.e., cooler. Gentle dancing of any kind where there is not much bouncing up and down of the whole body is fine, e.g. ballroom dancing. It is good to do this several times a week.

Use aromatherapy

For painful *bi* or fixed *bi*, rub diluted oil of ginger or diluted oil of black pepper on joints to ease the pain and dispel cold or damp. Mix 4 drops of essential oil with 10 ml unrefined, cold-pressed safflower oil and store in a dark glass bottle in a cool, dark place.

For fixed *bi*, try a mixture of juniper, cypress and lavender oil. Combine 2 drops oil of juniper, 1 drop oil of cypress and 1 drop oil of lavender with 10 ml unrefined, cold-pressed safflower oil. Mix together and store in a dark glass bottle in a cool, dark place.

For febrile *bi*, diluted oil of comfrey is very soothing. Mix 4 drops essential oil of comfrey with 10 ml unrefined, cold-pressed safflower oil and store in a dark glass bottle in a cool, dark place. If oil of comfrey is unavailable. use fresh comfrey leaves. Rub some vegetable oil (e.g. olive oil) on the painful joint, then wrap a comfrey leaf or several leaves over the joint. Use a large handkerchief or bandage to hold the leaf in place.

For painful *bi* and fixed *bi*, take a hot bath with 3 drops of essential oil of ginger. (Add it just before stepping in.) Do not soak too long – be sure to get out before the temperature drops.

For wandering *bi* (where the joints are not hot), add 2 drops essential oil of ginger and 1 drop essential oil of cinnamon to a hot bath just before you get in. Do not linger in the bath, and dry yourself thoroughly after getting out. A long soak may allow the dampness to enter the joints.

If essential oil of ginger is unavailable, use freshly grated ginger. Add about 1 handful to a large hot bath. Or, save your ginger peelings and dry them in a warm dry place. Use 2 handfuls per hot bath.

If essential oil of cinnamon is unavailable, gently brew 1 long cinnamon quill or several pieces of Chinese cinnamon bark in 570 ml (1 pint) water for 30 minutes to extract the goodness. Add this to the hot bath just before you step in. Cinnamon can drive wind out of the body, hence its use in wandering *bi*.

> *Note:* Please remember all baths must be taken before sunset when the day is more *yang*, i.e., hot.

If only the fingers are affected, dip them in a bowl of hot water and only 1 drop of essential oil. All aromatic oils can be used daily for 3 weeks. After 3 weeks, refrain from using them for 1 month to prevent a possible build-up of toxicity. During this time, use other self-help methods.

Use reflexology

Give both feet a general massage from toe to heel, then concentrate on the following reflex areas: diaphragm, solar plexus, pituitary, thyroid, thymus, pancreas, adrenals, kidneys and the areas that correspond to your specific pain, e.g. spine, hips, knees, shoulders, etc. (See Appendix B.) Then give both feet another general massage from toe to heel again before going back to the specific areas. Do not spend more than 1 hour per massage and do the massage once or twice a day.

Use moxibustion

> *Note:* Moxibustion is only applicable when the joints do not feel hot.

Apply the glowing end of the moxa stick about 2 to $2^1/_2$ cm ($^3/_4$ to 1 in) away from the skin above the painful joint. Move the stick backwards and forwards or around the joint

For shoulder pains

For elbow pains

For knee pains

FIG 18. Moxibustion for pains due to wind, cold or damp

to drive away the wind, cold or damp. Treat the joint until it feels warm or the skin turns slightly pinkish. Do moxibustion in the cool of the evening, once a day if your condition is severe. As you begin to feel better, do it once every other day, then slowly decrease the frequency. (See FIG 18.)

> *Note:* Do not use aromatic oils immediately before or after moxibustion or you may cause blisters. And do not have a shower or bath 1 to 2 hours before or after moxibustion. Wait 1 to 2 hours for the body to resume normal temperature. Do not do moxibustion on wet or sweaty skin.

From my own experience, I have found that arthritic and rheumatic pain can be relieved through acupuncture. If you have been suffering for a long time you will need many treatments, but each treatment can relieve more and more pain.

Summary of advice for arthritis and rheumatism

To sum up, arthritis and rheumatism can be relieved by following the various guidelines discussed in this chapter.

- The Chang Ming Diet helps prevent accumulation of toxins and hardened mucus and this, in turn, prevents aches, pains or deformity.

- Exercise helps improve the circulation of *qi* and blood.

- Aromatic oils help drive away the wind, cold, damp or heat.

- Reflexology helps improve the circulation of *qi* and blood, and releases tension.

- Moxibustion helps drive out the wind, cold and damp.

Pains of Joints, Muscles and Nerves 283

- Acupuncture releases tension, relieves pain, improves circulation of *qi* and blood, removes wind, cold, damp or heat, strengthens the spleen to prevent mucus formation, resolves mucus, halts the degeneration of bones and, if seen to in time, may rectify the deformity.

SCIATICA

Sciatica is pain that originates from the lower back, usually of the sacral-iliac joint. This pain may or may not radiate down the back or side of the legs to the toes.

Sciatica is very similar to arthritis and rheumatism. The three types of sciatica described below are best treated by acupuncture and/or osteopathic or chiropractic treatments. I recommend having the spine adjusted first by an osteopath or chiropractor, then seeing an acupuncturist to relieve the pain, expel the wind, cold or damp or to clear blood stagnation. Sometimes, you may not need acupuncture treatments after the spinal adjustments. You should also consider the following advice.

In sciatica there are 3 syndromes:
1 Obstruction of wind cold
2 Obstruction of wind damp
3 Stagnation of blood

1 Obstruction of wind cold
In this type of sciatica, the pain is intense, wandering, and aggravated by cold, windy weather. To remedy:

Use aromatherapy
Mix 2 drops of essential oil of ginger, 2 drops of essential oil of cinnamon and 10 ml of unrefined cold-pressed safflower oil. Rub the mixture along the sciatic nerve or along the path of pain. Store in a dark glass bottle in a cool, dark place. Use the oil daily for 3 weeks, then stop for 1 month to prevent possible toxicity.

Have a ginger and cinnamon bath. See the aromatherapy section for arthritis and rheumatism, page 282.

Use reflexology
Give both feet a general massage from toe to heel, then concentrate on the following reflex areas: diaphragm, solar plexus, spine and sciatic nerve. (See Appendix B.) Give the feet another general massage before returning to the special reflex areas. Do this once or twice a day, for no more than 1 hour.

Use moxibustion
Apply the glowing end of the moxa stick about 2 to $2^1/_2$ cm ($^3/_4$ to 1 in) above the skin along the path of pain. Keep moving the glowing end down the leg along the path of pain until the skin turns slightly pinkish and the leg feels nice and warm. Use moxibustion daily, in the cool of the evening, when the pain is severe. Decrease the frequency when the pain eases. (Follow precautions given in Chapter 16, page 224.)

2 Obstruction of wind damp
In this type of sciatica, the pain wanders, but is less intense than in the first type. It is aggravated by windy, damp weather or damp environments.

To remedy:

Use aromatherapy
Mix 1 drop of essential oil of cinnamon, 1 drop of essential oil of ginger and 2 drops of

essential oil of juniper with 10 ml of unrefined cold-pressed safflower oil. Rub the mixture along the path of pain. Store in a dark glass bottle in a cool, dark place. Use the oil daily for 3 weeks, then stop for 1 month to prevent any possible toxicity.

Or, have a ginger and cinnamon bath. (See page 282.)

Use reflexology
See sciatica caused by obstruction of wind cold.

Use moxibustion
See page 284, under sciatica caused by obstruction of wind cold.

3 Stagnation of blood
This type of sciatica is chronic, and usually results from neglecting to treat sciatica caused by obstruction of wind cold and wind damp. It will need prolonged osteopathic, chiro-practic or acupuncture treatments to correct it. To remedy:

Re-adjust the imbalances
Add turmeric to some of your dishes; it is said to help resolve blood stagnation. If you have a cooled blood system, balance the cooling turmeric with warming ginger and garlic or even a tiny pinch of cayenne to activate the circulation of stagnated blood.

Use aromatherapy
Oil of safflower (or what the Chinese call red flower oil) is excellent in relieving stagnation of blood. Unlike unrefined, cold-pressed safflower oil, it is very aromatic and has a very deep reddish-brown colour. It is available in India and from Chinese herbalists.

Use reflexology and moxibustion
See page 284 for sciatica caused by obstruction of wind cold.

LOWER BACK PAIN

Lower back pain also has 3 syndromes:
1 Invasion and retention of wind, cold or damp
2 Deficiency of kidneys
3 Stagnation of *qi* and blood

1 Invasion and retention of wind, cold or damp
If lower back pain is caused by the elements, the pain will be aggravated by windy, cold or damp weather. Follow the advice and guidelines given for arthritis and rheumatism, pages 276 to 283.

2 Deficiency of kidneys
This type of lower back pain is usually characterised by a dull ache, weakness in the knees, and the tendency to get up several times during the night to urinate. Although the elements are not responsible for this type of pain, wind and cold can make the condition worse.

See an acupuncturist and/or Chinese herbalist immediately to strengthen the kidneys. To remedy:

Re-adjust the imbalances
Follow the Chang Ming Diet. Eat foods appropriate to your blood system. (Usually people with deficiency of kidneys have a cooled blood system so eat more neutral and warming foods.) Look at your tongue and urine first thing in the morning to determine the nature of your blood system before eating

anything or brushing your teeth. The following warming foods and spices are good for the kidneys: walnuts, fennel, fenugreek, cinnamon and star anise.

Exercise
Practise *yoga*, *taijiquan* or *qigong* daily to strengthen the kidneys. Use the exercise 'Warming up the Kidneys' daily (see *do-in* in Chapter 16 and FIG 5).

Use reflexology
Give both feet a general massage from toe to heel, then concentrate on the following reflex areas: kidneys, adrenals, and spinal column, especially the lumbar area. (See Appendix B.) Do reflexology once a day, for 30 minutes to an hour.

3   Stagnation of *qi* and blood
This type of lower back pain is usually a result of a neglected injury. See an osteopath or chiropractor first to have the spine properly re-aligned, then consult an acupuncturist to improve the circulation of *qi* and blood. And, keep the self-help guidelines that follow in mind.

Re-adjust the imbalances
Use turmeric in your cooking to help resolve the blood stagnation. If you have a cooled blood system, balance the cooling turmeric with warming garlic and ginger, or even a pinch of cayenne.

Use reflexology
See above, under lower back pain caused by deficiency of kidneys.

Use moxibustion
Apply the glowing end of the moxa stick 2 to $2^{1}/_{2}$ cm ($^{3}/_{4}$ to 1 in) away from the skin above the painful area. Keep moving the glowing end backwards and forwards across the spine until the skin turns slightly pinkish and the area feels nice and warm. Use moxibustion daily, in the cool evening. Slowly decrease the frequency as the pain eases. (Follow the precautions on page 224.)

> *Note:* See a doctor for all types of lower back pain. You could have kidney stones, kidney prolapse, nephritis or pyelonephritis.

TRIGEMINAL NEURALGIA

This is a spasm of the facial muscles due to pain in the trigeminal nerve. It can affect the forehead, side of the head, the cheek and upper and lower jaws. Usually only one side of the face is affected.

> *Syndromes include:*
> 1   Invasion of wind and heat
> 2   Excessive heat in the liver and stomach that 'flares upward'
> 3   Deficient kidney *yin*

1   Invasion of wind and heat
This type of trigenimal neuralgia is brought on by wind and/or heat, or exposure to draughts or heat. It can be relieved quickly with acupuncture.

2   Excessive heat in liver and stomach that 'flares upwards'
This type of neuralgia is usually caused by a sudden rise in blood pressure. See a doctor

first to check your pressure, then see an acupuncturist to bring the pressure down and to relieve the pain. You should go on the Chang Ming Diet and avoid all hot and warming energy foods. (See Chapter 26, High Blood Pressure.)

3 Deficient kidney *yin*

This type of trigeminal neuralgia may be accompanied by restlessness, night sweats, a hot feeling in the palms, soles, and the area between the breasts and a flush in the cheeks. See an acupuncturist to correct the imbalance, and try to relax and take things easy.

> *Note:* Trigeminal neuralgia can also be caused by traumatic dental surgery or arthritis in the neck. If you have had dental surgery, see an osteopath or chiropractor to have the jaw and cervical vertebrae re-adjusted. Then see an acupuncturist to improve the circulation of *qi* and blood.
>
> If you have an arthritic neck, acupuncture is the best therapy. If you have had neck pain for many years, you will probably need extensive treatment.

GOUT

Unlike arthritis, rheumatism, lower back pain and trigeminal neuralgia, gout is not caused by the elements. Rather, it is the result of many years of eating rich, greasy, spicy foods and drinking alcohol. Smoking also adds to the problem.

According to traditional Chinese medicine, the stomach and spleen cannot cope with a rich diet of hard-to-digest foods. After several years, the stomach and spleen's ability to digest, assimilate, transform and transport food fails, and the undigested food becomes mucus which eventually hardens. Furthermore, heat from alcohol and smoking helps dry up the body fluids, causing the mucus to dry up and harden faster. The mucus eventually forms uric acid deposits which obstruct the flow of *qi* and blood to the joints, causing pain and discomfort.

Take the following measures to re-adjust the imbalances.

1 Adopt the Chang Ming Diet

Avoid the following:
Coffee
Beans – They are hard to digest and contain small amounts of uric acid
Animal fats
Red meats
Dairy products
Coconut products
Sugar
Almonds
Peanuts
Bananas
Citrus and other sour fruits
Durians
Alcohol
Hot spices and curries
Chemicals – Some examples are saccharine, preservatives, colourings, flavourings
All hot and warm energy foods and drinks

To make the body less acidic and more cooling, eat:
Millet
Brown rice
Celery
Alfalfa sprouts
Beansprouts

Soyabean milk

Chinese Peking cabbage

Miso

Courgettes

Marrow

Lettuce

Watercress

Tofu, silken and hard

Fish

Seaweeds – But check your blood pressure regularly; as soon as it normalises eat seaweeds only once a week or once a fortnight

Lots of mineral water to flush out the system

Use herbal teas

Comfrey tea – Helps bring the inflammation down

Peppermint tea – Cools down the digestive tract

Nettle tea – Purifies the blood system

2 Use herbal tea foot baths

Soak the feet in cold comfrey tea to cool the inflamed joint. If you can get fresh comfrey leaves, mash them, mix with flour, and bind the poultice around the inflamed joint.

3 Consult an acupuncturist

Acupuncture can also help improve the circulation of *qi* and blood, provided you accompany your treatments with a bland Chang Ming Diet of wholegrains, vegetables, fish, chicken and a small amount of non-acidic fruits.

MUSCULAR SPASMS

Muscular spasms can be from various causes. Muscular spasms caused by draughts or sudden exposure to the wind, cold or damp can be extremely painful. The muscles go into spasms every few minutes and they feel rock hard.

The best way to alleviate this problem is to use moxibustion. Make sure the skin is dry. Then move the glowing end of the moxa stick 2 to $2^1/_2$ cm ($^3/_4$ to 1 in) away from the skin above the painful area. Do this until the skin turns pinkish or the person feels the warmth of the moxa stick.

After 4 hours, if the muscles are now bearable to the touch, you can rub some oil of lavender or Bach Flower Rescue Cream (see our reference to Bach Flowers on page 226) to ease the tension in the muscles. (For the oil of lavender, mix 4 drops of essential oil of lavender with 10 ml of sweet almond oil.) Next day if the spasm is still there repeat moxibustion and the application of oil of lavender or Bach Flower Rescue Cream. Do this until not a trace of spasm or pain remains to make sure the draught or elements are completely out of the system. It may take up to 3 or 4 days. However, the relief can be tremendous after the first moxibustion.

If you can see an acupuncturist as soon as the problem arises you will get much faster relief.

Note: If you have high blood pressure or tendencies towards one or suffer from night sweats, do not use moxibustion. See an acupuncturist as soon as possible.

23 Cystitis, Prostate Gland Problems and Prostatitis

Cystitis is an inflammation of the membrane lining the urinary bladder. It affects both men and women, but women seem to suffer from it more because their urethra is shorter. Men can suffer from cystitis as a secondary disease due to an enlargement of the prostate gland or paralysis of the bladder.

Although urine is normally sterile and contains antibacterial properties, and the bladder membrane is resistant to infections, people can still contract cystitis. The external sites of the urinary passage (urethra) in both males and females are teeming with bacteria. These bacteria are kept out of the urinary passage by the downward flow of urine. In men, cystitis can develop when they are unable to completely empty the bladder because of an enlarged prostate gland, or when there is paralysis of the bladder. In women, frequent intercourse and the use of tampons can introduce bacteria in the urethra. Also, not urinating after sex, a stricture in the bladder and anything that prevents you from emptying your bladder completely can cause the presence of bacteria in the bladder.

Symptoms and signs
- pain upon urinating
- pain in the lower part of the abdomen
- lower back pain
- frequent desire to urinate
- inability to pass urine
- urinating in painful dribbles
- hot and/or acidic urine (which gives a burning sensation)
- cloudy or blood-stained urine
- dark coloured urine
- smelly urine

In acute cases there may be fever, but in chronic cases there is usually no fever.

Causes
According to traditional Chinese medicine, cystitis is caused by damp heat in the lower abdomen which provides the right environment for the growth of bacteria. What can cause damp heat in the lower abdomen?

1 Too many hot or warming energy foods and drinks when your blood system is overheated
2 Emotional upsets, stress and tension
3 Smoking
4 Too many late nights
5 Wearing nylon underwear
6 Wearing tight jeans

Prevention
1 Learn to relax.
2 Give up smoking.
3 Sleep by 11 p.m. nightly.

4 Wear 100 per cent cotton underwear.
5 Wear loose clothing to allow free circulation of air.
6 Wash the genitals after urinating and dry yourself thoroughly each time.
7 If you perspire a lot, change to a fresh pair of underpants at mid-day.
8 Wash yourself after sexual intercourse.
9 Do not use tampons because the tampon string can harbour or transfer bacteria. Change your sanitary towels as often as possible.
10 Do not use scented or coloured soaps, vaginal talcum powder, deodorants or 'freshener' tissues, or coloured toilet paper. The chemicals in these products may upset the natural pH of the genital area and allow bacterial growth.
11 Do not wash your underpants with biological washing powders.
12 Do not swim in chlorinated water. This is more applicable to people who have chronic cystitis or frequent attacks of it because their genitals may be irritated by the chlorine, and the pH in their genitals may easily be altered by the chlorine, too.

To re-adjust the imbalances

1 Adopt the Chang Ming Diet

Include the following foods:

Wholegrains – Brown rice, pot barley, millet, wheat, rye and buckwheat
Legumes and pulses – Mung beans, black-eyed beans, *tofu, tempeh, miso,* etc.
Fresh neutral and cooling vegetables – Cabbages, swedes, turnips, watercress, Chinese radish, nettle leaves, dandelion leaves, mung bean sprouts, soyabean sprouts, alfalfa sprouts, cucumbers, lettuce, etc.
Seaweeds – Have daily only if you have high blood pressure, once or twice a week if your blood pressure is normal; check your blood pressure regularly
Sauerkraut – This sour, naturally fermented product is very good for eliminating damp heat
Thyme – This is one of nature's best anti-biotics; use it raw in salads, boiled in stews, or steamed with vegetables
Eggs – Have no more than 2 or 3 free-range eggs a week
Fish – Eat mainly white fish
Chicken – Eat fresh and free-range chicken without the skin and fat about 2 or 3 times a week
Fresh fruits – Eat mainly neutral and cooling varieties

Beverages:

Pot barley water – Cooked with a few grains of Job's tears, this is excellent in eliminating damp heat from the body; drink instead of tea or coffee, and prepare fresh pot barley daily until the condition clears
Corn silk tea – Helps relieve acute and chronic cystitis; use corn silk from a Chinese or Western herbalist instead of pot barley water and prepare fresh tea daily

Mild dose: Add 1 cup of boiling water to 1 heaping teaspoon of finely cut dried corn silk in a thermos flask. Infuse for 10 minutes then strain and drink warm.

Stronger dose: Add 570 ml (1 pint) of boiling

water to 2 heaping tablespoons of cut dried corn silk in a thermos flask. Infuse for 1 hour and then strain.

Note: Corn silk tea lowers the blood pressure and the blood sugar level.

Chamomile or chrysanthemum tea – Helps you relax; use no more than 3 to 4 chrysanthemum flowers per cup of water
Nettle tea – Helps purify the blood system
Dandelion tea – This is a diuretic and helps cool the body
Peppermint tea – Aids digestion
Mineral water
Pear juice
Watermelon juice

Avoid:

Sugar
Dairy products
Coconut products
Red meats and organ meats
Animal fats
Certain cooking methods – Foods that are deep-fried, dry-roasted, roasted, baked, grilled, smoked or barbecued
Sour and/or acidic foods
Chemicals such as saccharine, other artificial sweeteners, preservatives, colourings, flavourings, monosodium glutamate, etc.
Tinned foods
Alcohol
Foods that are irritating, have hot energy or create damp heat

Foods with hot energy, or creating damp heat:
chicken fat, black-boned chicken, curries, turkey, carp, clams, cockles, whelks, shrimps, crabs, lobsters, prawns, duck eggs, duck gizzard, duck, roe, geese, sea cucumber

sweet fermented rice, hot pickles, peanuts, peanut butter, *tahini*, sesame seeds, pepper (white or black), roasted sesame oil, Sichuan pepper, fennel, ginger, cumin seeds, fenugreek, cardamom, oyster sauce, fish sauce, star anise, ginseng, fermented soyabean cheese, vinegar

lychees, longans, chestnuts, sunflower seeds, taro, walnuts, watermelon seeds, asparagus, bamboo shoot (fresh, dried, tinned or frozen), spiced pickled cabbage, celery (Chinese and English), mango, pineapple, rambutan, *langsat*, *bacang*, durian, *mata kucing*, pomegranate, potatoes, tomatoes, aubergines, sweet peppers

2   Exercise
Practise *yoga, taijiquan, qigong*, deep breathing, chanting or meditation daily to help you relax and eliminate damp heat from the body.

3   Use reflexology
Give both feet a general massage from toe to heel, then concentrate on the following reflex areas: diaphragm, solar plexus, spinal column, adrenals, kidneys, ureter tubes, bladder and the lymphatic glands in the groin. (See Appendix B.)

A word of caution
You may need antibiotics during an acute attack to suppress the bacterial growth or you can become very ill. After finishing the course of antibiotics, repopulate the intestinal flora with the right kinds of friendly bacteria like *miso* and/or sauerkraut.

Always see a doctor to have a thorough check-up. If you suffer from chronic cystitis, see an alternative therapist as soon as possible to help balance your body to avoid recurrent attacks. Supplement the alternative therapy

with the above guidelines to help you get better faster.

PROSTATE GLAND PROBLEMS

The prostate gland surrounds the urethra (the tube that connects the bladder with the penis) where it joins the bladder. Ducts run from the prostate gland into the urethra where fluids from the seminal vesicles and prostate gland mix with sperm cells to form semen.

As men approach middle age, most have a gradual enlargement of the prostate gland. As the gland enlarges, it presses on the neck of the bladder, interfering with the discharge of urine. The urine then tends to build up in the bladder, which becomes strained and weakened. This may lead to infection in the kidneys, bladder or prostate gland.

Symptoms and signs
The enlarged prostate gland causes
- frequent urination (especially at night)
- slow or intermittent flow of urine
- dribbling at any time but usually just after urination because the bladder is not fully emptied

According to Dr W. Derient (of Berlin, Germany) there is practically no incidence of prostate gland disorder in men that eat pumpkin seeds daily. Pumpkin seeds contain large amounts of phosphorus, iron, an abundance of B vitamins, a small amount of calcium, zinc, vitamins A and E, magnesium, 30 per cent protein, 40 per cent fat (which is rich in unsaturated fatty acid), curcurbitin, albumin, lecithin, resin and phytosterin. Hungarian gypsies, Bulgarians, Anatolian Turks, Ukrainians and Transylvanian

Germans ate them regularly to prevent the prostate gland problems later on in life, but nobody knows how they work.

It cannot hurt to chew 10 pumpkin seeds a day to help prevent or even heal prostate gland problems.

To re-adjust the imbalances

1 Adopt the Chang Ming Diet
Eat and cook foods according to your blood system.

2 Practise yoga, taijiquan or qigong daily
This improves and maintains health and vitality.

3 Use reflexology
Give both feet a general massage from toe to heel, then concentrate on the following reflex areas: diaphragm, solar plexus, spinal column, pituitary, thymus, thyroid, adrenals, kidneys, ureter tubes, bladder, prostate gland, vas deferens, testicles, and the lymphatic glands in the groin area and the area between the prostate gland and the bladder. See Appendix B and FIG 19.

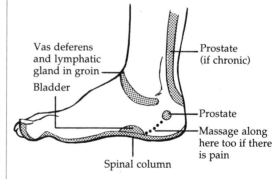

FIG 19.   Reflexology for prostate gland problems and prostatitis. Massage shaded areas and where indicated.

Seek professional help
See your doctor before starting on the above self-help guidelines. Some prostate gland troubles are caused by cancerous growths.

Prostatitis

Prostatitis is an inflammation of the prostate gland. It can be due to an enlarged prostate gland, a gonorrhoea infection or non-specific causes.

Symptoms and signs
These include slight fever, pain in the perineum (the area between the genital organs and the anus) and pain in the lower back.

Chronic prostatitis is characterised by: no fever, dull ache in the perineum, itching in the urethra and pain in the lower back.

According to traditional Chinese medicine, prostatitis, like cystitis, is caused by damp heat in the lower abdomen.

To re-adjust the imbalances
Follow all the advice given for cystitis (page 289) but also eat boiled pumpkin seeds. For convenience, add 10 to 15 pumpkin seeds to 1 cup of brown rice and cook both together.

Use reflexology. See page 292, the section on prostate gland problems.

See your doctor or an alternative therapist before using the above self-help guidelines.

24 Acne

Acne is an unsightly condition that affects people of all ages. It is more prevalent in hot countries and/or when the diet is rich in hot, spicy, greasy foods. Western physicians believe that acne is connected with the hormonal system and occurs during puberty. Western herbalists, on the other hand, see acne as a condition of impure blood. They recommend a diet rich in watercress and nettles to cleanse the blood of impurities.

Naturopaths see acne as a condition of both impure blood and stress, and would prescribe a diet rich in watercress, nettles and foods rich in vitamin B such as wholegrains, legumes, pulses, seeds and nuts.

Chinese herbalists or acupuncturists see acne as caused by too much heat in the blood and would advise a diet of more cooling foods and the avoidance of hot energy foods.

Re-adjust the imbalances with the following measures.

ADOPT THE CHANG MING DIET

Avoid these foods

Sugar
White or brown, rock sugar, *gula melaka*, sweets and chocolates – all these cause heat in the body. Chocolate is an especially hot food. All sugars deplete the body of precious B vitamins so the body has difficulty coping with stress.

Dairy products
Milk, milk powder, condensed milk, skim-milk, cream, butter, ice-cream, cheese, cottage cheese, cream cheese and yogurt. Because milk powder is dried it has hot energies. All dairy products are difficult to digest, and full of hormones, antibiotics and chemicals that can make the blood impure.

Coconut products
Coconut milk, coconut oil, *kuih-muih* made with coconut cream, and curries made with coconut milk – all these foods are too oily for the body and are eliminated in the form of pimples and/or acne.

Red meats
Veal, beef, mutton, lamb, pork, duck, ham, bacon, sausages, and much more belong to this category. Veal, beef, mutton and lamb are hot energy foods. Duck is said to be an irritating food and should not be eaten by people with skin problems. In addition, most animals are fed hormones, antibiotics and chemicals that can make the blood impure.

Fat

Beef dripping, pork fat, chicken fat, goose fat, etc. all have hot energies and are very difficult to digest.

Certain cooking methods

Foods which are curried, deep-fried, grilled, barbecued, baked, roasted and smoked have hot energies.

Flour products

Bread, *chapati*, *nan*, *roti*, biscuits, cakes, *kuih-muih*, etc. belong to this category. Baked products have hot energies, and biscuits, cakes and *kuih-muih* contain too much sugar and/or animal fats.

Breakfast cereals

Cornflakes, muesli, instant porridge oats, and a host of other breakfast cereals, are usually laden with sugar which robs the body of precious B vitamins to cope with stress. Check the labels before buying.

Beverages

Tea, coffee, cocoa, drinking chocolate of various brand names, all soft and aerated drinks, and other artificial beverages. Tea and coffee are stimulants and, with prolonged use, may damage the central nervous system. Coffee, cocoa, several popular brands of chocolate and malt-based beverages and drinking chocolate have hot energies. Soft and aerated drinks, and other artificial beverages contain sugar and chemicals.

Chemicals

Saccharine, other artificial sweeteners, preservatives, colourings, monosodium glutamate, etc. add toxins to the blood.

Vegetables

Tomatoes, potatoes, aubergines, sweet peppers, chillies, cayenne and tabasco should be avoided. They belong to the Deadly Nightshade family and are said to contain a poison called solanin. Chillies, cayenne and tabasco have very hot energies.

Tropical fruits

Durian, *mata kucing*, longans, mango, pomegranate, nutmeg and lychees have hot energies. Rambutans, *bacang* and pineapple have damp heat energies. *Langsat*, *bacang*, pineapple and mango are said to be irritating to the blood system and should be avoided by anyone with skin problems.

Citrus fruits

Oranges, mandarins, tangerines, clementines, and other citrus fruits have damp heat energies when eaten in excess.

Alcohol

Alcohol has hot energies.

Frozen and tinned foods

They usually contain sugar.

Adopt the Chang Ming Diet

The Chang Ming Diet is excellent in providing the body with vitamins A, B, C, D and E, all kinds of minerals, complex carbohydrates, polyunsaturated fats and proteins.

> *A Chang Ming Diet should be made up of:*
> 50 per cent wholegrains
> 25 per cent fresh and seasonal vegetables
> 15 per cent protein in the form of beans, peas, lentils, bean products, eggs, fish or chicken

5   per cent seeds and nuts
5   per cent fresh, local and seasonal fruits

Wholegrains
These are brown rice, pot barley, millet, whole wheat grains, rye and fresh sweet corn. Add a few grains of Job's tears to a cup of brown rice to help eliminate heat and damp heat.

Legumes and pulses
Aduki beans, mung beans, black soyabeans, black-eyed beans, lentils, chick-peas, broad beans, red kidney beans, soyabean products like *tofu*, soyabean milk, *fu zhou*, *tempeh*, *miso*, *tamari*, *shoyu*, fermented black soyabeans and fermented soyabean cheese.

Seeds and nuts
Sesame, sunflower, pumpkin and lotus seeds, peanuts, chestnuts, almonds, Chinese bitter and sweet apricot kernels, walnuts and ginkgo nuts. Seeds and nuts tend to have hot energies, but when they are boiled with water they become less hot. Try cooking them with brown rice.

Fresh vegetables
Eat mainly neutral and cooling energy vegetables, especially: mung bean sprouts, soyabean sprouts, alfalfa sprouts, lettuce, lamb's lettuce, endive, bitter gourd, cucumber, marrow, courgettes, fuzzy melon, winter melon, angled luffa, Chinese radish, radish, yam bean, lotus root, watercress, peppermint leaves, nettles, dandelion and chickweed.

Seaweeds
Hiziki, *kombu*, *wakame*, *arame*, *nori*, purple seaweed, black hair moss and *agar-agar*.

Note: Seaweeds should only be taken by people with strong constitutions, especially those with high blood pressure and high blood cholesterol. The weak should avoid seaweeds altogether. Check your blood pressure regularly if you eat seaweeds daily.

Fish
Eat mainly white fish, steamed or poached.

Chicken
Eat once or twice a week, in moderation. Steam or boil without the skin and fat.

Fresh local and seasonal fruits
In the tropics: papaya, banana, pomelo, mangosteen, watermelon, *ciku*, *jambu*, rose apple, guava, sea apple, star fruit, custard apple and sugar apple. In temperate and Mediterranean countries: pear, grapefruit, lemon, melon, persimmon, plum and apple.

Pure, fresh fruit juices
In the tropics: sugar cane, coconut, lemon, lime, papaya and watermelon. In temperate and Mediterranean countries: pear, grapefruit, lemon and melon.

Cooling herbal teas
Chamomile, chrysanthemum, nettle, dandelion, comfrey, peppermint, rosehip, lemon balm, mixed fruits and a prepacked cooling herbal mixture like Ho Yan Hor tea.

How to cook
The best cooking methods for acne sufferers are: steaming, quick boiling, blanching, poaching, braising, stewing, quick stir-frying in hot stock or water, and occasional quick stir-frying in a little unrefined cold-pressed

oil. (Use just enough oil to coat the bottom of the wok or pan to prevent burning.)

Meal suggestions

Tofu and miso
These are especially good for people with acne.

> **Try the following soups:**
> Watery *tofu*, spinach *miso* soup
> Watery *tofu*, watercress *miso* soup
> Watery *tofu*, Shiitake mushroom and onion soup
> Watery *tofu*, black wood ears and onion soup
> Watery *tofu*, carrot and snow pea soup
> Watery *tofu*, onion and snow pea soup
> Onion *miso* soup
> Watercress *miso* soup
> Spinach *miso* soup
>
> **Note:** Substitute dwarf beans, string beans, French beans or long beans for snow peas.

Seaweed soups
These soups are very cooling and only appropriate for people with strong constitutions and those with high blood pressure or high blood cholesterol.

> **Here are some suggestions:**
> Onion, *wakame* and *miso* soup
> *Arame, tofu* and carrot soup
> *Kombu* and fish bone stock soup
> *Kombu, tofu* and fish head soup
> *Kombu* and chicken bone stock soup
> *Kombu*, onion, carrot and chicken bone stock soup
> *Tofu, nori* and onion soup
> *Hiziki, tofu* and snow pea soup
> Carrot and *hiziki* soup

Other cooling soups
For variety, try the following soups.

> **Some more suggestions:**
> Fresh lotus root and dried octopus soup
> Fish and Chinese radish soup
> Fuzzy melon and dried squid soup
> Winter melon and chicken bone soup
> Spinach and chicken bone or fish bone stock soup
> Chinese box thorn leaves and Chinese box thorn berries soup
>
> **Note:** Substitute angled luffa, marrow, courgette or cucumber for fuzzy or winter melon.

Brown rice congees
As brown rice congees are also cooling, make up one-pot meals with brown rice, varying the other ingredients.

> **Try these variations:**
> Fish and raw lettuce brown rice congee
> *Fu zhou* and brown rice congee
> Ginkgo nut and brown rice congee
> Shiitake mushroom and onion brown rice congee
> Chicken and Shiitake mushroom brown rice congee
> Brown rice congee served with fermented soyabean cheese

Have salads at least once a day in the summer or hot tropical countries to cool the blood system and for extra vitamin C.

KEEP CLEAR OF STRESS

Besides following the Chang Ming Diet, you must also learn to relax and live a stress-free

life. Smoking, drinking and late nights can also heat up the blood system.

Daily *yoga*, *taijiquan*, *qigong*, chanting or meditation can help remove stress and tension, and help eliminate toxins by sweating.

Use *Aloe Vera*

The juice of the *Aloe vera* plant is excellent for acne when applied directly to the skin. Cut a leaf from the base and apply the oozing gel-like juice directly on the acne. Keep the leaf in a brown paper bag in a cool, dark place and re-use twice a day until the gel dries up. Cut away the dried end each time you use it so the gel will ooze freely.

In countries where you cannot get fresh *Aloe vera* plants, buy *Aloe vera* gel from stores like The Body Shop. The product they sell is 98 per cent *Aloe vera* gel. Remember that fresh *Aloe vera* juice or gel only treats the symptoms; it does not heal the root cause of the problem – too much heat in the blood system.

Use Reflexology

Reflexology helps relieve acne due to stress, tension and hormonal imbalance. Give both feet a general massage from toe to heel, then concentrate on the following reflex areas: diaphragm, solar plexus, spinal column, pituitary, thyroid, thymus, pancreas, adrenals, prostate gland or uterus, testicles or ovaries, vas deferens or Fallopian tubes, liver, large and small intestines. (See Appendix B.) Do this daily for no more than 1 hour. If you are pressed for time, roll a wooden foot roller under each foot from toe to heel for 5 minutes each day.

Use Beauty Aids

Apply mud face-packs or similar aids once or twice a week to cleanse the facial skin. Try to use the type which contains seaweed extract for extra minerals. Use a facial steam bath of chamomile or peppermint tea to cool the skin once or twice a week. The smell may also help you relax.

25 Adult Onset Diabetes

CAN DIABETICS EVER LIVE WITHOUT INSULIN?

Dr James Anderson of the University of Kentucky (USA) and Nathan Pritikin of the Longevity Centre (Santa Monica, California) seem to think so. They advocate that daily exercise and a diet high in complex carbo-hydrates and low in proteins and fats will reduce insulin intake.

Within one and a half months, patients on a Pritikin diet of 80 per cent complex carbohydrates, 13 per cent protein and 7 per cent fat (accompanied by daily exercise) were able to reduce their insulin intake, and some were able to do without insulin altogether.

In the 1930s, a British doctor, Dr Himsworth, also found that a diet rich in fat blocks the action of insulin and, eventually, exhausts the pancreas so it is unable to produce insulin. Therefore, a diet low in saturated fats and cholesterol is not only appropriate for those suffering from high blood pressure and high blood cholesterol but for diabetics too.

Researchers at Stanford University have shown that sucrose (sugar) can reduce insulin efficiency in controlling glucose in the blood. They also noticed that some form of dietary fibre will diminish the harmful effects of sucrose a little but not enough to prevent diabetes. Dr Anderson has also shown that fibre plays an important role in regulating blood sugar. He discovered that bran consists of a special fibre called *beta glucan* that can stabilise blood sugar levels and stop the liver from making cholesterol. In his experiments Dr Anderson noted that eating 50 g (2 oz) of oat bran daily was sufficient to lower insulin intake. In some cases patients were able to live without insulin altogether. The bran in pot barley shares this special medicinal property.

Haricot beans and red kidney beans contain soluble fibres too. Beans in general contain a special gum called guar gum which helps reduce the post-meal rise in the blood sugar level and the consequent insulin demand.

The Chang Ming Diet, with its emphasis on whole cereal grains and beans, is ideal for diabetics. Non-insulin-dependent diabetics (Type II) can be healed fairly readily with this type of diet but Type I diabetics often respond readily at first, (with a fairly rapid decrease in insulin requirements) but are more difficult to heal completely. Dr Anderson has had some success with juvenile diabetics too on the same diet and exercise regime.

Caution: Diabetics wishing to follow the Chang Ming Diet must consult their doctors and keep a regular check-up on their blood sugar levels. A sudden cessation of insulin therapy can be very dangerous.

Take the following measures to re-adjust the imbalances.

FOLLOW THE CHANG MING DIET

Avoid these foods

Sugar
In all its forms – white, brown or rock sugar, *gula melaka*, molasses, honey, maple syrup, barley malt extract and hidden sugars in sauces, preserved foods, tinned, frozen foods and other processed foods, breakfast cereals, sweets and chocolates.

Dairy products
Milk, skim-milk, milk powder, butter, cream, cheese, yogurt, ice-cream and hidden dairy products in biscuits, cakes and sauces.

Flour products
Bread, *chapati, nan, roti*, biscuits, cakes, *kuih-muih*, noodles, pastas, dumplings, etc.

Red meats
Beef, veal, lamb, mutton, pork, goose, duck and all their products.

Animal fats
Beef dripping, lamb and mutton fat, pork lard, goose, duck and chicken fat.

Coconut products
Coconut oil, milk, cream and meat.

Deep-fried foods

Oil
As in salad dressing.

Beverages
Coffee, all chocolate-based beverages, cocoa, all soft and aerated drinks and other artificial beverages.

> *Note:* Coffee is believed to cause pancreatic cancer. In diabetics the pancreas is already under stress; coffee can hinder the healing process.

Chemicals
Monosodium glutamate, saccharine and other artificial sweeteners, preservatives, colourings, etc.

Vegetables
Potatoes, tomatoes, aubergines, sweet peppers, chillies, yams and sweet potatoes.

Fruit
Especially durians.

Alcohol

Foods to eat

Wholegrains
Brown rice, oat groats, pot barley and fresh seasonal sweet corn.

Legumes and pulses
Aduki beans, haricot beans, red kidney beans, black-eyed beans, brown or green lentils, chick-peas, black soyabeans, broad beans, butter beans, marrowfat peas and soyabean products, e.g. *tofu, tempeh, fu zhou, miso, tamari, shoyu* and fermented soyabean cheese.

Fresh vegetables
Especially round ones like pumpkin, white cabbage, onions, yam bean and small leafy greens like watercress, landcress, Chinese box

thorn leaves, garland chrysanthemum, coriander leaves and Chinese celery.

Seaweeds
Kombu, wakame, arame, hiziki, nori.

> *Note:* Eat seaweeds only if the body system is not cooled and you do not have a weak constitution.

Seeds and nuts
Sesame seeds, sunflower seeds, pumpkin seeds, lotus seeds, peanuts, Chinese apricot kernels, almonds and Chinese box thorn berries.

Oil
Unrefined cold-pressed sesame, sunflower or corn oil.

Salt
Sea-salt or sesame salt (*gomasio* made of 1 part sea-salt and 15 parts roasted sesame seeds).

> *Caution:* Take salt in moderation only.

Eggs
Eat free-range eggs occasionally (about 2 or 3 eggs a week), steamed or scrambled with water, ginger and other vegetables like spring onions, leeks, Chinese chives, watercress, landcress and celery.

Fish and other seafood
Mainly white and oily fish. Squid, octopus, prawns, etc. may be taken occasionally.

Chicken
Eat fresh and free-range varieties, cooked without the skin or fat, about once or twice a week. Steam with ginger, spring onions, Shiitake mushrooms, black wood ears, snow ear fungus, black hair moss or seaweeds.

> **Main meals should consist of:**
> 50 per cent wholegrains like brown rice, pot barley or oat groats
> 25 per cent fresh vegetables
> 20 per cent beans, bean products, peas, lentils, eggs, fish, seafood or chicken
> 5 per cent *miso* soup, seeds or nuts
> Choose foods suitable for your blood system.

How to cook and eat
The following methods of cooking are suitable for diabetics: steaming, boiling, blanching, sautéing, stir-frying in hot stock or water, stir-frying in just enough unrefined cold-pressed oil to coat the bottom of the wok or pot, grilling and roasting. The dishes should be light and easy to digest. Heavy, fatty, greasy, sticky, and rich foods are difficult to digest and may put stress on the pancreas.

Diabetics should chew their food very thoroughly before swallowing. Saliva pre-digests the food in the mouth, oesophagus and stomach before it reaches the duodenum, where the pancreatic juices are secreted.

Saliva is medicinal for diabetics because it is very alkaline. Therefore, diabetics should try to produce saliva by chewing their food thoroughly to prevent acidosis or too much acid in the blood. (Often diabetics suffer from acidosis, or too much acid in the blood.) A small bowl of *miso* soup daily with or without seaweed can help reduce blood acidity because *miso* soup is alkaline. Grated raw Chinese radish will also help but since it is very cooling, it must be taken with care. Sesame seed salt (*gomasio*) is also good.

Helpful dishes, condiments and snacks

The following dishes, condiments and snacks are said to help diabetics:

1 Sweet corn and brown rice congee. The sweet corn must be fresh and seasonal.
2 Aduki beans cooked with *kombu* and pumpkin (or carrots).
3 A dish of stir-fried or sautéed onions, white cabbage and carrots. (The addition of ginger and/or garlic is optional.)
4 *Miso* soup with or without seaweed.
5 Grated raw Chinese radish.
6 Sesame seed salt (*gomasio*).
7 Dry roasted peanuts or sunflower seeds. Eat in very small amounts and chew thoroughly before swallowing. If you have an overheated blood system or a tendency towards one eat small quantities of raw peanuts or sunflower seeds instead.

Dr Anderson recommends eating 50 g (2 oz) of oat bran daily to reduce insulin intake. If you are unable to obtain oat bran use porridge oats, jumbo oats or oat groats. Oat groats and pot barley are better for you because they are not processed and therefore retain their vitality. Oat groats are suitable for people with cooled blood systems in winter because they are warming. Pot barley is for those with overheated blood systems in summer or in the tropics, because it is cooling.

In China during the Japanese occupation when insulin was in short supply, an ancient method of regulating the blood sugar level in diabetics was unearthed. One *liang* (31.2 g or 1 oz) of dried corn silk was boiled with one pig's pancreas, and the soup was taken daily. The pig's pancreas provided the insulin while the corn silk quenched the person's thirst and maybe even healed the pancreas.

When I was home in Penang, a diabetic friend of mine gave me a very simple recipe for reducing blood sugar.

> *Bitter gourd juice:* You need 605 g (21 oz) of bitter gourd (the thin, dark green, very bitter variety with very close grooves). Cut, remove the seeds, and pound the bitter gourd until you can squeeze out the juice with a muslin cloth (or use a juice extractor). Drink the juice once a day, one hour after a meal. When the condition improves, reduce to once or twice a week.
>
> *Note:* Bitter gourd is very cooling, so eat with care.

Periwinkle (*Vinca rosea*), with its pinkish-white flowers and dark green oval leaves, has been used by South African natives for many years as a cure for diabetes. This plant is very common in Southeast Asia too. It is said to have the ability to strengthen the pancreas but must be used with caution because its property has yet to be determined. Infuse 25 g (1 oz) of the herb in 570 ml (1 pint) of boiling water. Allow to stand for 30 minutes and drink a wineglassful before meals. Children should have less.

Those with cooled or weak blood systems should use the Chinese herb, *dang shen* (*Codonopsis tangshen* Oliv.), or the root of *Campanumaea pilosula* Franch. Boil 1 small root in a cup of water until the water tastes of the root, about 10 to 15 minutes. Drink a small cup daily and slowly reduce the frequency as the blood sugar level normalises.

Dang shen is said to strengthen the pancreas, fortify the central energy, promote salivation and quench thirst. Diabetics with cooled or weak blood systems should try a *dang shen* and *huang shi* double-boiled chicken soup. (See page 133.)

Meal suggestions

Diabetics can also choose from the following suggestions for daily meals.

Breakfast

The variations of oat groats, jumbo oats, porridge oats, brown rice, pot barley and sweet corn are endless, but here are a few suggestions.

1 Wholegrain porridge (oat groats or pot barley) or brown rice congee with roasted seeds or nuts, or with *miso* and fresh herbs.
2 Oat groats porridge or brown rice congee with Shiitake mushrooms.
3 Oat groats porridge or brown rice congee with dried shrimps.
4 Oat groats porridge or brown rice congee with silver fish or *ikan bilis*.
5 Wholegrain porridge (oat groats or pot barley) or brown rice congee with raw lettuce leaves, endive or other vegetables.
6 Sweet corn on the cob.
7 Brown rice and sweet corn congee.
8 Brown rice and aduki bean congee.

Miso soups

1 Watercress or landcress and onion *miso* soup
2 Watercress or landcress and carrot *miso* soup
3 Carrot, onion and cabbage *miso* soup
4 Chinese radish *miso* soup
5 Onion, *wakame* and *miso* soup
6 Carrot, *hiziki* or *arame miso* soup

Other soups

1 Chinese box thorn leaves and Chinese box thorn berry soup
2 Bitter gourd and onion soup
3 *Tofu* and sweet corn soup
4 Marrow or courgettes and leek soup

5 Pumpkin and black-eyed bean soup

Dishes

1 Bitter gourd stir-fried with fermented black soyabeans, garlic and ginger.
2 Bitter gourd stir-fried with dried shrimps and garlic.
3 Bitter gourd stuffed with minced fish and steamed.
4 Bitter gourd stir-fried, then braised with onions or leeks.
5 Haricot beans stewed with onions and pumpkin or onions, carrots and celery and different herbs.
6 Red kidney beans boiled, then stir-fried with other vegetables like:
celery and carrots
white cabbage and watercress or landcress
white cabbage and oregano or marjoram
leeks
watercress or landcress
celeriac and leeks
fennel bulbs
7 Red kidney beans stewed with:
onions, carrots and celery
onions and celeriac
leeks and celeriac
leeks and celery
onions and fennel
pumpkin and leeks
8 Pumpkin steamed, baked or grilled, or stir-fried or sautéed with other vegetables and herbs.
9 Dishes made with soyabean products like *tofu*, *fu zhou*, *miso*, *tempeh* and fermented soyabean cheese:
   - *tempeh* marinated in ginger, roasted sesame oil and *tamari*, then steamed
   - hard *tofu* marinated in *miso* and roasted sesame oil, then steamed
   - soft or watery *tofu* steamed with

minced garlic, ginger and fermented black soyabeans or roasted sesame oil, *tamari* and spring onions or coriander leaves
- *fu zhou* braised with Shiitake mushrooms, onions, carrot and coriander leaves
- hard *tofu* cubes stir-fried with assorted cubed vegetables
- *tofu* and fish soup

MORE THAN THE CHANG MING DIET

Diabetics should supplement the Chang Ming Diet with the following measures.

Exercise regularly
Regular exercise improves blood and *qi* circulation, and accelerates the body's healing process. The best exercises are *taijiquan, qigong* or *yoga*. Walking or swimming are also good.

Use reflexology
Roll a smooth wooden rolling pin or broomstick handle under your feet twice a day to stimulate points on the soles of the feet. Then concentrate on the reflex areas for the pancreas, spleen, stomach, liver, gall bladder, adrenals, thyroid, kidneys, and pituitary. (See Appendix B.)

Use a ginger compress
Place a ginger compress over the pancreas to help blood and *qi* circulation and to further aid the healing process.

> *Ginger compress:* Boil a pot of hot water, switch off the heat, and squeeze out the ginger juice from a handful of freshly grated old ginger in a muslin bag. Dip in an old towel and wring dry. Place over the pancreas area and cover with a thick dry towel to retain the heat. Meanwhile, dip another old towel and place over the pancreas when the first towel begins to cool. Carry on until the hot ginger water begins to cool. Do this 2 to 3 times a week, in the cool of the evening.

Adjust your lifestyle
Diabetics should not have long, hot baths or showers, which may lead to the loss of precious minerals. They should refrain from overeating and eat frequent small meals to allay hunger pangs.

Diabetics should go to bed early (by 11 p.m.). Late nights exhaust the body and hinder the healing process. Rising early to do *yoga, taijiquan, qigong* or reflexology is an excellent way to start the day.

Above all, diabetics must learn to cultivate a strong sense of discipline, moderation and practicality. This is the only way they can learn to follow the Chang Ming Diet and live without insulin.

A WORD OF CAUTION

Diabetics must see their doctors regularly to check the blood sugar level. Do not stop taking insulin without consulting a physician!

26 High Blood Pressure and High Blood Cholesterol

High blood pressure and high blood cholesterol are the direct results of eating highly refined and fat-laden foods, not getting enough exercise and leading a stressful life.

Both Dr James Anderson and Nathan Pritikin (who are mentioned in Chapter 25, Adult Onset Diabetes) independently discovered that these diseases can be remedied by a diet rich in unrefined wholegrain cereals, beans, bean products, peas, lentils, fresh vegetables and fruits, and plenty of exercise. Their diet and exercise regime do not depart too far from the Chang Ming Diet and lifestyle, which recommends the following advice to help those who suffer from high blood pressure and high blood cholesterol.

It would help to take these measures to re-adjust the imbalances.

FOLLOW THE CHANG MING DIET

Avoid these foods

Red meats
Veal, beef, lamb, mutton, pork, goose, duck and red meat products like sausages, burgers, salami, ham, bacon and organ meats, Chinese wind-dried duck, Chinese sausages, etc.

Dairy products
Milk, skim-milk, powdered milk, condensed milk, butter, cream, yogurt, cheese, ice-cream and hidden dairy products in biscuits, cakes and beverages.

Animal fats
Beef dripping, pork lard, goose, duck, chicken fat, etc.

Coconut products
Coconut milk, cream, oil, *kuih-muih* and ice-cream.

Sugar
Especially white sugar, sweets and chocolates, and hidden sugars in biscuits, cakes, *kuih-muih*, tomato ketchup, chilli sauce, etc.

Eggs

Flour products
Especially baked flour products like bread, *chapati, nan, roti*, biscuits, cakes, etc. (Whole-wheat noodles and pastas are acceptable because they are easier to digest.)

Breakfast cereals
Especially those with added sugar and milk.

Beverages
Coffee, tea, cocoa, chocolate-based beverages

and all drinking chocolate, all soft drinks and other artificial beverages laden with sugar. Avoid coffee and tea especially, because they are stimulants.

Deep-fried foods

Chemicals
Saccharine, other artificial sweeteners, preservatives, flavourings, colourings, monosodium glutamate, etc.

Spices
Hot spices like pepper (white or black), chillies, cayenne, tabasco.

Fruit
Especially durians.

Alcohol

Foods to eat
The Chang Ming Diet recommends the following foods for people with high blood pressure and/or high blood cholesterol.

Wholegrain cereals
Brown rice, pot barley, oat groats, millet, buckwheat and fresh sweet corn. Cook the brown rice with pot barley, oat groats, millet, buckwheat or sweet corn kernels to vary the taste and texture.

Legumes and pulses
Mung beans, black-eyed beans, black soyabeans, red kidney beans, lentils, chickpeas, haricot beans, butter beans, broad beans, marrowfat peas, *tofu*, *tempeh*, *fu zhou*, *miso* and other naturally fermented soyabean products

Fresh vegetables
Especially bitter gourd, Chinese radish, radish, Chinese or English celery, watercress, lettuce, all members of the cabbage family and all members of the garlic and onion family

Seaweeds
Kombu, *wakame*, *arame*, *hiziki*, *nori*, purple seaweeds, dulse, carageen and *agar-agar*

Fish
Both white and oily fish. Eat them steamed, poached, or occasionally fried in a little oil or gently grilled.

Chicken
If possible eat fresh and free-range varieties cooked without the fat or skin. Steam or stew chicken with garlic, onions, Shiitake mushrooms, black wood ears, snow ear fungus or seaweeds.

Note: A very strict Chang Ming Diet does not allow fish and chicken. If you wish to follow the regime strictly, but at the same time feel you cannot do without them, eat them only in small quantities.

Beverages
Herbal teas like chamomile, chrysanthemum, lemon balm, peppermint, dandelion, nettle and rosehip are much healthier than regular tea. Fruit juices and mineral water are far better than coffee.

Lunch and dinner meals should consist of:
50 per cent brown rice, cooked on its own or mixed with pot barley, oat groats, millet, buckwheat or fresh sweet corn kernels
25 per cent fresh vegetables

15	per cent protein in the form of beans, bean products, peas, lentils, gluten, fish or chicken
5	per cent seaweeds
5	per cent fresh seasonal fruit

Foods that lower blood pressure/cholesterol
These include the following.

Oat groats

Dr James Anderson, in his experiments with diabetics on a high-carbohydrate and low-fat diet, noticed that oats helped diabetics regulate their blood sugar levels and reduced their serum cholesterol. Oat fibres, it seems, bind with the cholesterol and bile acids, and all three are excreted in the faeces.

Oat groats can also influence the type of cholesterol in the blood stream. They encourage the presence of high density lipo-protein (which is good for the body) and they bind to the bad, low density lipo-protein (which is eventually excreted).

Soyabeans and soyabean products

Soyabeans contain an abundance of an unsaturated fatty acid called lecithin, which the scientific world now realises can reduce cholesterol. Processed soyabean products like *tofu*, *fu zhou*, fermented soyabeans and fermented soyabean cheese retain much of their lecithin. *Tempeh*, discovered by the Indonesians, is highly nutritious and very cheap. And black soyabeans can be used in their whole forms, especially to make soup.

Soyabeans and soyabean products are cooling, so they are suitable for people with high blood pressure and high blood cholesterol who tend to have a more overheated blood system.

Mung beans

Mung beans are very cooling, and mung bean sprouts and mung bean threads are excellent in helping lower high blood pressure and high blood cholesterol. The husks of mung beans are used to stuff pillows instead of the usual *kapok*, cotton or feathers to lower the heat in the head.

Chinese radish

Chinese radish is very cooling and suitable for people used to a diet rich in fatty animal meats and meat products. Chinese radish helps in the removal of accumulated fatty animal deposits, and the digestion of fatty foods, especially those that are deep-fried. The Japanese always serve deep-fried *tempuras* with a dish of grated raw Chinese radish. Sometimes they serve grated radish with mackerel, an oily fish.

Garlic, Shallots, Onions, Leeks, Spring Onions, Chives and Chinese Chives

It has been scientifically proven that these vegetables are excellent in reducing blood pressure and blood cholesterol.

> **How to use garlic:**
> Garlic, especially, is excellent but not if it is stir-fried. Just add finely chopped garlic to soups or stews after adding the water. Stir-frying adds a lot of heat to an already warm energy food. This heat then goes to the liver and head, and can make you quick-tempered and irritable. People with high blood pressure and high blood cholesterol should avoid this kind of stress.

Seaweeds

Seaweeds are very cooling and excellent in reducing blood pressure. Use them with caution or you may lower your blood

pressure too much. Have it checked weekly.

Black wood ears
This cheap black fungus caused quite a stir some years back when scientists discovered that it was good for activating blood circulation and lowering blood cholesterol. For years the Chinese have cooked black wood ears with fatty meats like chicken and pork to aid digestion.

Shiitake mushrooms
These mushrooms have the same medicinal property as black wood ears but they are tastier, so the Chinese tend to use them more often.

Watercress
This vegetable is excellent in purifying the blood and cooling an overheated blood system.

Chinese and English celery
Both types of celery are said to be very good for lowering the blood pressure.

Members of the Solanaceae family
Potatoes, tomatoes, aubergines, sweet peppers, Chinese box thorn leaves and berries are all said to help lower blood pressure caused by a condition called liver *yang* rising in traditional Chinese medicine. Symptoms include tightness in the chest, headaches, dizziness, sudden tinnitus (noises or ringing in the ears), anger, irritability, red face and eyes, a feeling of heat in the head and body, constipation, and the desire for cold foods and drinks.

Although I previously advised you to avoid foods of the *Solanaceae* family (Deadly Nightshade), they can help people with high blood pressure caused by liver *yang* rising if eaten in moderation, about 3 to 4 times a week. Following is a recipe believed to help the condition.

> **Singaporean tomato recipe:**
> 1 big tomato
> 1 medium onion or several shallots
> 1 large Chinese celery with roots and leaves
> 3 cups water
> Make a deep cut halfway down the tomato. Skin the onion and chop finely. Wash the Chinese celery thoroughly and cut into 2$^1/_2$ cm (1 in) lengths.
>
> Boil all the ingredients in a stainless steel pot and simmer down to 1 cup of liquid. Eat 2 to 3 times a week if your blood pressure is very high, once a week otherwise.

People with high blood pressure caused by liver *yang* rising and an overheated blood system should use Chinese or English celery. Those with high blood pressure not caused by liver *yang* rising, a weak constitution or a cooled blood system should substitute coriander leaves and roots for the celery. If coriander is unavailable use parsley leaves and roots. Take this remedy no more than once a week.

Bitter gourd
According to the *Nei Jing*, the bitter taste of bitter gourd is good for the heart and for the blood circulation. See the recipe for bitter gourd juice in Chapter 25, page 302.

Fish
Oily fish like mackerel and herring contain two types of fatty acids that can help prevent

heart disease. White fish like cod, haddock, plaice, sole, whiting and coley are also healthy.

Dried scallops
According to a Chinese herbalist, dried scallops cooked with *kombu* are excellent for lowering high blood pressure.

Star fruit
In Malaysia people with high blood pressure are advised to have at least one fresh star fruit a day. They can help cool an overheated blood system.

How to cook
The most suitable methods of cooking for high blood pressure and high blood cholesterol are: blanching, steaming, poaching, boiling, sautéing, stir-frying in hot water or hot stock, stir-frying in a little oil (only enough to coat the bottom of the pan or wok to prevent the food from burning), stewing, braising and the occasional grilling or baking. Raw salads are also acceptable.

Use unrefined, cold-pressed oils and only tiny pinches of sea-salt. *Tamari, shoyu* and *miso* should be used sparingly as too much sea-salt in the system may create water retention and increase the blood pressure.

> *Note:* To curb your craving for salty foods, just cut out sweet foods. To stop eating sweet foods, just stop eating salty foods!

Meal suggestions

Breakfast (savoury)
- Dry-roasted buckwheat simmered in water and served with roasted sesame seeds
- Additional savoury breakfast ideas are given on page 303; the list is given for diabetics

Breakfast (sweet)
- Porridge oats sweetened with honey, barley or rice malt extract
- Porridge oats with raisins, sunflower seeds, sesame seeds and pears
- Pot barley flakes and porridge oats with sultanas, sesame seeds and apples
- Millet with raisins, caraway seeds and sesame seeds
- Brown rice flakes with Hunza apricots and apricot kernels
- Brown rice and dried persimmon congee
- Couscous steamed with bananas (especially with *pisang raja*)
- Fresh seasonal fruits for hot summer days or hot tropical countries

Dishes with soyabeans and soyabean products
Try the following dishes for all types of high blood pressure and cholesterol.
- Black soyabeans boiled with onions, carrots and *kombu*; use a $2^1/_2$ cm square (1 in square) piece of *kombu* and 25 g (1 oz) of beans per person
- Black soyabean and onion soup
- Watery *tofu* steamed with minced garlic and *tamari*, and garnished with spring onions
- *Tofu* cubes stir-fried with spring onions and a dash of *tamari*
- *Tofu* slices stir-fried with Shiitake mushrooms and snow peas
- *Tofu* braised with Shiitake mushrooms and Chinese chives or leeks
- *Tofu* braised with Shiitake mushrooms, spring onions and *miso*

- *Tofu* and snow pea soup in onion stock
- *Tofu*, snow peas and black wood ear soup in onion stock
- *Tofu* and fresh sweet corn kernel soup in onion stock, garnished with chopped coriander leaves
- *Tofu* and lettuce soup in garlic stock
- *Tempeh* marinated in *tamari* and steamed with spring onions or finely minced garlic
- *Tempeh* instead of *tofu* in the above suggestions
- *Fu zhou* braised with onions, carrots and angled luffa, marrow or courgettes
- *Fu zhou* braised with garlic, Shiitake mushrooms, black wood ears, black hair moss, golden needles and *miso*
- Soyabean sprouts and chicken bone stock soup
- Soyabean sprouts stir-fried with minced chicken, Shiitake mushrooms and spring onions
- Mung bean sprouts stir-fried with spring onions or chives
- Mung bean sprouts stir-fried with spring onions and Shiitake mushrooms
- Mung bean threads stir-fried with minced chicken, Shiitake mushrooms and spring onions
- Mung bean threads stir-fried with fuzzy melon, carrots, Shiitake mushrooms and onion soup (use angled luffa, marrow or courgettes instead of fuzzy melon)

Beans
- All kinds of beans boiled with *kombu*; use 25 g (1 oz) dried beans and 2$^1/_2$ cm square (1 in square) piece of dried *kombu* per person.

- Beans stir-fried with vegetables
- Beans stewed with vegetables

Vegetables
- Bitter gourd stir-fried with fermented black soyabeans and garlic
- Bitter gourd soup (with a stock made from chicken or fish bones, garlic or onion)
- Chinese or English celery braised with black hair moss, gluten and *miso*
- Raw salads of lettuce, endive, lamb's lettuce and radicchio rosso
- Raw salads of cucumbers, baby carrots and celery with minced garlic and *tamari* or *shoyu* dressing
- Blanched salads like French beans, sweet corn kernels and yam bean; sweet corn kernels, yam bean and spring onions; French beans, sweet corn kernels and boiled red kidney beans; use a dressing of minced garlic, rice vinegar and olive oil and baby sweet corn instead of sweet corn kernels

Seaweeds
- *Kombu* and fish bone stock soup
- Brown rice *sushi* (brown rice wrapped in *nori* sheets)
- Black hair moss braised with oysters
- *Kombu* braised with dried scallop soup
- Black hair moss and dried scallop soup

Fish
- White fish steamed with spring onions, ginger shreds and a dash of *tamari* (the ginger is not to be eaten)
- Mackerel or herring marinated in lemon juice for half a day, then steamed with

spring onions, finely chopped fennel or dill leaves
- White fish steamed with fine strips of black wood ears or Shiitake mushrooms, spring onions and ginger shreds (do not eat the ginger)
- Mackerel fish ball soup with spinach and garlic (use fish bones for stock)
- *Wonton* soup with minced mackerel, garnished with shreds of toasted *nori*
- *Tofu* or bitter gourd slices stuffed with minced mackerel, steamed or boiled in fish bone stock, and served with minced garlic and *tamari* sauce.

Chicken
- Chicken, cucumber and Shiitake mushroom soup (or use fuzzy melon, angled luffa, marrow or courgettes instead of cucumber)
- Chicken and watercress soup
- Chicken and winter melon soup
- Chicken, black wood ears, Shiitake mushrooms (or black hair moss) and spring onion soup
- Steamed chicken with minced shallots

Sweet dishes
- Boil *fu zhou*, ginkgo nuts and pot barley to make a soup, then sweeten with barley or rice malt extract. Use a few grains of Job's tears too, to make the sweet soup more cooling.
- Chinese apricot kernel jelly (made with apricot kernels and *agar-agar*) and Chinese red dates
- Soyabean milk sweetened with barley or rice malt extract
- Raisin *agar-agar* (use sultanas, Hunza apricots, or regular apricots instead of raisins, and add fresh apples, pears or plums)
- Dried persimmon stew

EXERCISE REGULARLY

Besides following the Chang Ming Diet, you must also exercise to improve blood and *qi* circulation. The exercises should be gentle, and involve a lot of calf muscle action, e.g. walking, swimming or *taijiquan*. Strenuous exercises like tennis, squash, running, jogging and aerobics are not advisable.

Tao meditation is also excellent for lowering the blood pressure, as is *yoga*.

USE REFLEXOLOGY

It helps you relax and relieves tension and stress. Each day, give both feet a general massage from toe to heel, then concentrate on the following reflex areas: diaphragm, solar plexus, spinal column, heart, adrenals, kidneys, pituitary, thyroid, thymus and liver. (See Appendix B.) Do not spend more than 1 hour per massage.

Use Acupressure

Massage along the heart meridian, from top of arm to little finger, as illustrated, to improve the circulation of blood and *qi*. (See FIG 20.)

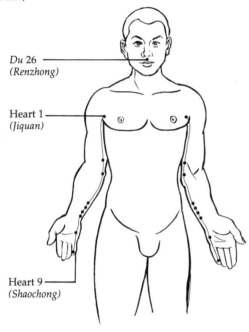

Du 26
(*Renzhong*)

Heart 1
(*Jiquan*)

Heart 9
(*Shaochong*)

FIG 20. How to massage along the heart meridian, on both arms. Massage from Heart 1 to Heart 9 on both arms twice a day. Each massage should take not more than 5 minutes.

Use Aromatherapy

Essential oil of rose is said to strengthen the heart. Dilute 4 drops of essential oil of rose with 10 ml sweet almond oil. Use as a perfume, or massage one or two drops along the heart meridian, as illustrated.

It is important also to learn to relax and stay calm. Oil of lavender can help you unwind. Place a drop of essential oil of lavender on a ball of cotton wool in a place where you can inhale it all day long. Or, buy a small packet of dried lavender flowers, place them in a pot-pourri container with holes in it and add a drop of essential lavender oil to scent the air around you. You can also rub diluted oil of lavender on your shoulders to help you relax and have a restful night's sleep. Dilute 4 drops of essential oil of lavender with 10 ml sweet almond oil. Store in a dark glass bottle in a cool, dark place.

In Case of Heart Failure

People with a history of high blood pressure or high blood cholesterol can suddenly have a heart attack. An attack can be brought on by stress and shock, among other things. Here are some useful steps to take when someone suffers a heart attack.

Four vital steps
1   Phone the ambulance, or ask someone to phone the ambulance while you take care of these other steps.
2   Massage *Du* 26 (*Renzhong*). See FIG 20. This is a very strong massage to bring the patient back to his/her senses. Press your thumb upwards towards the root of the nose. Do this several times. This action will send an 'electric shock' to the brain.
3   Remove the false teeth, dentures, etc.
4   Press Heart 9 (*Shaochong*) on both little fingers as hard as possible to stimulate the heart and heart meridian. See FIG 21. If you do not have the nerve to press so hard, then rub the heart meridian on the little finger as hard as possible.

saliva which was drooling out. I massaged the heart meridian on the little fingers as hard as possible. She came round before the ambulance arrived.

> *Note:* If you know the heart resuscitation technique as taught by the St John's Ambulance or Red Cross, you can still use the above steps with it. It would be excellent if there were three persons on the scene: two to perform the heart resuscitation while the third goes through the above steps.

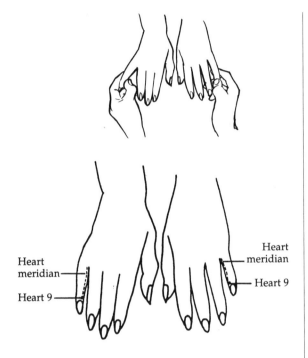

Heart
meridian

Heart 9

Heart
meridian

Heart 9

FIG 21. How to press Heart 9 in case of a heart attack, before help arrives. Note the location of Heart 9.

I had to put the procedure to work once during my talk to a group of old-age pensioners. An 80-year-old lady passed out. I massaged *Du* 26 (*Renzhong*) strongly several times until I felt her breath on my thumb. I was very lucky in that there was a retired ward sister who promptly removed the old lady's false teeth while I massaged *Du* 26 (*Renzhong*) and someone phoned for the ambulance. It also helped that she was still sitting upright and her friend was holding her upright so that she was not choking on her

SEEK MEDICAL ADVICE

The advice given in this chapter is mainly for high blood pressure caused by liver *yang* rising with symptoms of an overheated blood system. It is possible for someone with a cooled blood system and normal or low blood pressure to have a sudden rise in pressure due to tension and worry. Such people must see a doctor and/or alternative practitioner as soon as possible.

Anyone with high blood pressure or high blood cholesterol, for that matter, should see their doctor regularly for frequent check-ups. Supplement your medication with the advice in this chapter. Only when your blood pressure and/or blood cholesterol drops, and remains steady, should you consult your doctor on how to decrease your medication. Never stop your medication without consulting a doctor!

27 Psoriasis

According to Western medicine, psoriasis is due to a disturbance in skin enzymes or linked to mental stress. Some sufferers may also have arthritis.

Psoriasis is not contagious and the lesions can vary enormously. Some may appear along the hairline, others on the elbows and knees, and others all over the body. The lesions vary in appearance from chronic scaling plaques, ringed lesions, smooth red areas, acute pustules and droplike lesions.

Should a patient with psoriasis consult an acupuncturist or Chinese herbalist, the therapist would immediately attribute the disease to too much heat in the blood system. (The heat is much more intense than that seen in acne.)

If the patient only has smooth red areas, it is most likely that he has a great dislike of heat or the sun, often feels hot inside, loves the coolness of the evening, autumn, winter or airconditioned places, and craves cold food and drink.

CAUSES

This very intense heat in the blood can be caused by:

Weather

In the tropics, the heat of the sun is tremendous, especially around mid-day and during the dry season, even in the shade.

Occupational hazards

If you are a restaurant cook, an outdoor labourer or road repairer, a construction worker in the tropics; a smith or steel worker who works by a hot furnace; a travelling salesman in the tropics, etc. you may be exposing yourself to a great deal of heat.

Smoking

Most smokers do not realise that smoking creates heat within the body, as well as damages the lungs.

Too many late nights

Going to sleep after 11 p.m. does not allow the body to rest and rejuvenate itself properly.

Stress

Diet

The most important cause of heat in the blood system is wrong diet. Eating too many hot and warming energy foods for many years can eventually cause an imbalance within the body.

TO RE-ADJUST THE IMBALANCES

To overcome psoriasis, you must watch your diet, prevent stress, stop smoking, go to sleep by 11 p.m. and try to keep out of the sun as much as possible. As the weather and your occupation are the most difficult to change, amending the diet to overcome the disease would appear to be the first course.

Avoid these foods
The following foods – as well as those listed on pages 294-295 in Chapter 24, Acne – should be avoided.

Red meats
Organ meats and Chinese sausages

Poultry
Duck, black-boned chicken, chicken eggs, chicken soup, chicken liver, goose, goose eggs, goose liver, Chinese wind-dried duck and other wind-dried products

Seafood
Salmon, smoked fish, abalone, oyster sauce

Vegetables
Chillies, onions, shallots, Chinese chives, spring onions, leeks, garlic, ginger, carrots and coriander leaves

Fruits
Tropical fruits – durian, mango, guava, pineapple, rambutans; temperate and Mediterranean fruits – pomegranate, oranges, mandarins, tangerines, clementines, straw-berries, blackcurrants, blackberries, black cherries, red or black grapes and raspberries

Miscellaneous foods
Beef lard, pork lard, pork fat, chicken fat, whisky, wine (rice and grape), milk (especially powdered milk), butter, cheese, fermented soyabean cheese, roasted sesame oil, all seeds and nuts especially roasted chestnuts, black sesame seeds and peanut butter, chocolate, drinking chocolate, cocoa, chocolate-based beverages, coffee, white sugar, brown sugar, hot, spicy pickles and chutneys, curries, black pepper, fenugreek, fennel, star anise, coriander seeds, nutmeg, lychees, longans, bread, biscuits, cakes, and all hot or warming energy foods.

Avoid irritating foods
Psoriasis sufferers must also avoid irritating foods that hinder the healing process and aggravate or irritate the skin condition. Following is a list of such foods.

Red meats
Beef and beef products (sausages, minced meat and burgers; marrow; calf and ox liver, kidney, brain and heart; calf's head and foot; ox cheek, tongue, tail and tripe), veal, veal products and pig's head

Poultry
Duck, duck eggs, duck gizzard, goose, goose eggs, goose fat, cockerels and old cocks

Seafood
Crabs, prawns, shrimps (fresh, dried, paste, sauce and crackers), lobsters, cockles, mussels, clams, sea cucumber, fish roe (eggs), fish sauce, carp, mackerel, yellow fish, *ikan bawal hitam*, *ikan kembong* and sardines.

Vegetables
Yam, taro, potato, tomato, aubergine, sweet

pepper, chillies, asparagus, bamboo shoots (fresh, dried or tinned), carrots, garlic, leeks, mushrooms, onions, pumpkin, celery (English and Chinese)

Fruits
Durian, mango, pineapple, *bacang* and *langsat*

Miscellaneous
Whisky, wine, bread, ginseng, mustard, sweet fermented rice, fermented soyabean cheese, wheat flour, vinegar (light or dark), cheese and chocolate.

Adopt the Chang Ming Diet

> *The Chang Ming Diet for psoriasis consists of:*
> 50 per cent wholegrains
> 25 per cent fresh vegetables
> 15 per cent protein in the form of beans, peas, lentils, bean products or fish
> 5 per cent seaweeds and 5 per cent fruits

Wholegrains
Brown rice, pot barley, millet, whole wheat grains, rye and fresh sweet corn. A few grains of Job's tears added to brown rice several times a week is very good for eliminating heat from the body.

Legumes and pulses
Mung beans, black soyabeans, black-eyed beans, lentils, marrowfat peas, butter beans, broad beans, chick-peas, red kidney beans and soyabean products like *tofu*, watery *tofu*, silken *tofu*, soyabean milk, *fu zhou*, *tempeh*, *miso*, *tamari*, *shoyu* and fermented black soyabeans.

Fresh vegetables
Neutral and cooling vegetables like mung bean sprouts, soyabean sprouts, alfalfa sprouts, lettuce, lamb's lettuce, chicory, endive, radicchio rosso, Chinese box thorn leaves, Chinese radish, radish, cucumber, marrow, courgette, fuzzy melon, angled luffa, Chinese Peking cabbage, Chinese white cabbage, peppermint leaves, bitter gourd, yam bean, lotus root and watercress

Seaweeds
Hiziki, *kombu*, *wakame*, *arame*, *nori*, purple seaweed, black hair moss, *agar-agar*, carageen, dulse and laverbread

Fish
Mainly white fish, steamed or poached

Chicken
Only fresh and free-range, and in moderation, about once or twice a week. Steam or braise with cooling vegetables or serve with salads.

Fresh local and seasonal fruits
Tropical fruits – watermelon, banana, papaya, *ciku*, custard apple, mangosteen, *jambu*, pomelo, rose apple, sea apple, star fruit, lemon and lime; temperate and Mediterranean fruits – pear, plum, apple, grapefruit, lemon, persimmon and melon

Beverages
Mineral water, fresh pure fruit juices and cooling herbal teas

> *Tropical juices:* sugar cane, coconut, lemon, lime, papaya and watermelon
> *Temperate and Mediterranean juices* – pear, apple, plum, grapefruit, lemon and melon
>
> *Cooling herbal teas:* chamomile, chrysanthemum, nettle, dandelion, comfrey, chickweed,

peppermint, rosehip, lemon balm, mixed fruit and a prepacked herbal mixture like Hor Yan Hor tea (available at any Chinese supermarket or herbalist)

Here are two special teas for cooling an overheated blood system. The ingredients are available in the East, and in large Chinese supermarkets in the West.

Swatow mustard cabbage and sweet potato tea: Cut a medium-sized Swatow mustard cabbage into bite-sized pieces. Wash and skin 2 medium-sized sweet potatoes, then cut into bite-sized pieces. Bring 6 to 7 cups of water to a boil. When it is boiling vigorously, add the cabbage and sweet potatoes. (This method prevents bitterness.) Bring to a boil again. Then simmer for 2 hours or until about 3 cups of liquid remain. Drink between noon and 3 p.m. when the day is at its most *yang* (i.e., its hottest).

Dried Chinese white cabbage and unsweetened Iraqi date tea: This tea is not as cooling as the first. Soak 18 g ($^3/_4$ oz) of dried Chinese white cabbage (*caigan*) in water, then cut into bite-sized pieces. Bring 8 cups of water to a boil. When the water is boiling vigorously, add the cabbage and 10 unsweetened Iraqi dates. Bring to a boil again and simmer for 2 hours. Drink between noon and 3 p.m. when the day is at its most *yang*.

How to cook

Psoriasis sufferers should use the following cooking methods: steaming, quick boiling, blanching, poaching, braising, stewing, quick stir-frying in hot stock or water and, occasionally, quick stir-frying in a little unrefined cold-pressed oil (just enough to coat the bottom of the wok to prevent burning).

Raw salads are the best. In summer and in hot tropical countries, have salads twice a day. In winter, have salads for lunch. For the evening meal, have a hot protein dish accompanied by raw and lightly steamed vegetables. Have plenty of green leafy vegetables and light soups, especially those made with *tofu* and/or *miso* and white fish. (See the suggestions given in Chapter 24, Acne.)

Exercise regularly

Practise yoga, *taijiquan*, *qigong*, chanting or meditation daily to overcome stress. These exercises help eliminate heat from the body and bring about the balance of *yin* and *yang*.

Use *Aloe vera*

Apply the fresh juice or gel over the affected areas.

Use chickweed ointment

Apply over the affected areas. Chickweed ointment is available from some Western herbalists.

Use reflexology

See Chapter 24 on Acne, page 298.

Use aromatherapy

Put a drop of essential oil of lavender on a ball of cotton wool to scent the air and relax you.

Mix 2 drops of essential oil of rose with 2 drops of essential oil of chamomile and 10 ml of sweet almond oil. Store in a dark glass bottle in a cool, dark place. Rub one or two drops of the mixture on the dry, cracked skin twice a day.

If oil of rose is too expensive, mix 4 drops of essential oil of lavender with 10 ml of sweet almond oil and rub one or two drops of the

mixture on dry, cracked skin 2 to 3 times a day. Oil of lavender is used to treat burns, so it will soothe and heal psoriasis.

Like *Aloe vera*, oils are only symptomatic treatments. For results, rely on dietary and lifestyle changes.

The Tao of helping psoriasis is slow. However, if you accompany dietary and lifestyle changes with acupuncture and Chinese herbs you will heal faster. Western herbal cures may also prove helpful.

A Word of Caution

Those who are taking medication for psoriasis should continue treatment. If you wish to stop, consult your physician first.

28 Multiple Sclerosis

Multiple sclerosis is a disorder of the brain, spinal cord and nerves and leads to destruction of the protective myelin sheaths which insulate nerve fibres. It can occur in patches throughout the central nervous system, giving rise to the formation of plaque. The cause is unknown.

SYMPTOMS

The symptoms are:
- Stiffness, heaviness, weakness, even paralysis of one or more limbs in whole or in part
- Inability to arrest a muscular movement at the desired point, tremor, loss of muscular tone, jerky muscular movements, abnormalities in the limbs
- Nystagmus (rhythmical oscillation of the eyeballs, either horizontal, vertical or rotary), facial weakness, and vertigo (often accompanied by nausea)
- Feeling of numbness, tingling or deadness, usually in the limbs
- Urinary urgency or retention of urine in the early stages of the disease, incontinence and constipation in the later stages

- Blurring of vision or double vision (which comes and goes with remission)
- Memory and abstract reasoning may be affected
- Mood changes
- Extreme fatigue
- Stages of remission and relapse, the intervals of which can vary

INCIDENCE AND PRECIPITATING FACTORS

Multiple sclerosis affects women more than men, and incidence of the disease is rare or does not occur in the tropics.

In northwestern Europe, the northern United States, Canada, the northern hemisphere, south Australia and New Zealand the prevalence is high – 40 cases per 100,000 people. In Great Britain, there are about 50 cases per 100,000. In northern latitudes, like northeast Scotland, there are approximately 100 cases per 100,000, but in Shetland and Orkney the figure can reach 300 per 100,000, the highest known incidence in the world.

There is no relationship between latitude and incidence of multiple sclerosis, however, as the disease is rare among the Chinese, Japanese and Eskimos. Some authorities on

the subject have found a more obvious relationship between prevalence and indigenous or colonising Europeans.

The precipitating factors which trigger initial onset of multiple sclerosis or subsequent relapses seem to be:
- Infections (major or minor)
- Injections (vaccinations or inoculations)
- Trauma
- Surgical operations
- Pregnancy
- Exertion
- Fatigue
- Stress
- Temperature changes

CAUSES

In traditional Chinese medicine, multiple sclerosis is a type of *wei* or 'withering' syndrome. The possible causes of withering in the muscles, in Chinese medical terms, are deficient spleen, deficient kidneys or deficient liver blood.

If the spleen is deficient it cannot digest, assimilate and transform food into useful nourishment and energy to be transported to the muscles to prevent withering. If the kidneys are deficient, they cannot provide enough kidney 'fire' to help the spleen transform and transport food. If the liver does not store enough blood to nourish the tendons and muscles, muscular spasms and withering may result.

What brings about these conditions?

Weak constitution
If the health of one or both parents was bad at conception, or if the mother's diet was poor during pregnancy and nursing, the spleen, kidneys and liver can be affected.

Invasion of damp cold or damp
What the Chinese call 'damp' or 'damp cold' can affect the health of the internal organs, especially the spleen and kidneys. This can happen if you live in a damp country, near a cold, swampy area which has been reclaimed or drained, in a damp basement flat, beside a body of water, near a hill or mountain shrouded in early morning or evening mist or fog, or if you work outdoors near water in a cold, damp country. These cold, damp conditions can slowly injure the spleen and kidneys after several years.

Taking showers or baths or swimming frequently at night can also be harmful, especially if you have a weak constitution. This is because the night is more *yin*, and the dampness tends to cling to the body. During the *yang* daylight hours, dampness evaporates more quickly because the body is more active.

Poor diet
Irregular food intake: The body organs can only work at their optimum at regular intervals. Irregular meals place the stomach and spleen under a lot of stress.

Excessive eating places strain on the stomach and spleen. After many years they can lose the ability to efficiently digest, assimilate, transform and transport food to the limbs.

Malnourishment: Eating too little can be disastrous. Dieting or living on junk foods can also be dangerous.

Raw foods can put stress on the stomach and spleen, especially in people with cooled blood systems. The heat from the cooking helps break down cellulose fibres in

vegetables so they are easier to digest. It also warms the blood system and kidneys, so the kidney fire can help the spleen digest, assimilate, transform and transport food.

Hot spicy, greasy rich foods are very difficult to digest, and after many years, can put strain on the stomach and spleen. They also tend to create mucus in the body.

Excessive sex
Too much sex can drain the kidneys of their fire, which supports the spleen. In traditional Chinese medicine, the kidneys also help keep the brain, spinal cord, bone marrow and the urino-genital organs healthy.

Accidents or surgery
An accident or a surgical operation can block meridians or channels, causing obstruction of blood and *qi* flow to various parts of the body. After many years, or when the body is fatigued, symptoms may arise.

Shock and emotional problems
A shock can affect the internal organs. If the heart is affected, then circulation may be poor. Damaged kidneys may also give rise to multiple sclerosis symptoms. Prolonged tension and stress can eventually affect the liver, giving rise to tremors, spasms, blurred vision and mood changes.

TYPES OF MULTIPLE SCLEROSIS

In traditional Chinese medicine, there are basically two types of multiple sclerosis:
1 Deficient spleen and invasion of damp in the channels and stomach
2 Deficient liver and kidneys

Deficient spleen and invasion of damp in the channels and stomach

Symptoms and signs
- Stiffness, heaviness, weakness and even paralysis of the limbs
- Impaired walking
- Numbness in the limbs
- Feeling of pins and needles
- Swelling of the joints in damp weather
- Blurred vision
- Dizziness
- Extreme fatigue

Causes
- Living or working near cold and/or damp places
- Excessive eating
- Malnourishment
- Irregular food intake
- Excessive intake of raw, cold foods

Deficient liver and kidney

Symptoms and signs
- Weak legs
- Dragging legs (if able to walk)
- Muscle atrophy
- Blurred vision
- Nystagmus (a spasmodic movement of the eyes)
- Jerky muscular movements
- Urinary urgency or retention, incontinence and bowel retention
- Bad memory
- Mood changes
- Pain
- Cramps

Causes
- Excessive sex
- Overwork
- Shock
- Having too many children and/or having them too close together, and not nourishing the body after each childbirth

In practice, most of my patients have symptoms from both types. From their case histories I concluded that multiple sclerosis results from a combination of all or some of the following:
- Poor diet
- Cold, damp climate
- Emotions – many years of stress, tension, shock, grief, unhappiness and negative thoughts
- Lifestyle – late nights, excessive sex, inability to relax, overwork, excessive water sports, playing outdoor games in the rain
- Weak constitution

Note: The symptoms of multiple sclerosis may get worse before, during or after menstruation. This is because the spleen, kidneys and liver are involved in the menstrual cycle.

TO RE-ADJUST THE IMBALANCES

Go on a Chang Ming Diet

50 per cent wholegrains
Brown rice, oat groats and pot barley are the best nerve foods. Try whole wheat pasta instead of brown rice.

25 per cent fresh vegetables
Eat organically grown vegetables such as cabbages, beans and peas, carrots, beetroot, etc.

15 per cent protein
Eat beans, peas, lentils, bean products (like *tofu, tofu* burgers, *tempeh, miso, tamari, shoyu*), free-range eggs, fish (white or oily) and fresh, free-range chicken.

5 per cent seeds and nuts
Have sesame seeds, sunflower seeds, pumpkin seeds, almonds and hazelnuts. (Avoid nut or seed butters and *tahini* which are very difficult to digest.) Use unrefined, cold-pressed oils for cooking. They are rich in polyunsaturated fatty acids.

$2^1/_2$ per cent herbs and spices
To aid digestion, use the following often in your cooking: parsley, sage, rosemary, thyme, oregano, marjoram, chives, basil, caraway, savory, dill, coriander leaves, fennel leaves, garlic and ginger. If you have a cooled blood system, in winter add cinnamon, fenugreek, star anise, cloves, nutmeg, black pepper, black mustard seeds, coriander seeds, fennel seeds, cumin and cardamom.

$2^1/_2$ per cent fresh fruits
In autumn, winter and spring, eat mainly neutral fruits like apples. In summer, eat mainly strawberries, redcurrants, black-currants, raspberries, cherries, apricots, peaches and grapes. In autumn, have blackberries and elderberries. Fruits comprise a small portion of the Chang Ming Diet

because they contain mainly water, some vitamins and a little fibre. Vegetables, on the other hand, are much higher in vitamins, minerals and fibre. Also, organically grown vegetables are now more readily available than organically grown fruits.

Avoid certain foods

Sugar – Especially white sugar, which depletes the body of precious B vitamins

Dairy products – Difficult to digest and may contain hormones and antibiotics

Red or organ meats – Difficult to digest and may contain hormones and antibiotics

Animal fats, deep-fried foods, coconut products, and baked flour products – Very difficult to digest

Chemicals – Sweeteners, flavourings, colourings, preservatives, monosodium glutamate and additives are harmful to the body

Tea and coffee – Prolonged use of these nerve stimulants can wear out the nerves

Most beverages – Many brands of chocolate based beverages, cocoa, drinking chocolate, all soft and aerated drinks, and other artificial beverages contain too much sugar

Alcohol – Slows down the brain function and contains a lot of chemicals

Vegetables – Some of them, like potatoes, tomatoes, sweet peppers, aubergines, chillies, cayenne and tabasco, belong to the Deadly Nightshade family and contain small doses of solanin

Convenience foods – Tinned and frozen foods tend to contain sugar and additives

Adopt good eating or cooking habits

Eat easily digested foods and chew each mouthful well before swallowing. If you do not have an appetite, use the herbs suggested above to stimulate the olfactory nerves, taste buds and salivary glands.

Use a wide range of cooking methods: blanching, steaming, boiling, stewing, casserole-cooking, braising, stir-frying in hot water or stock, stir-frying in a minimum amount of unrefined, cold-pressed oil, baking, roasting and grilling.

Meal suggestions

Breakfast

- Brown rice flakes cooked with raisins and sunflower seeds; this dish may help those with sluggish bowel movements
- Brown rice flakes cooked with raisins and walnuts; this version may help those who have urinary urgency, incontinence and frequent nightly urination

> *Variations:* Try the following substitutions.
> 1 Porridge oats for brown rice flakes
> 2 A combination of porridge oats and pot barley flakes for brown rice
> 3 Sultanas or Hunza apricots for raisins
> 4 Sesame seeds or pumpkin for sunflower seeds

Main meal – Winter menu 1

- Brown rice boiled with sesame seeds
- Black-eyed beans stewed with onions, carrots, *miso* and winter savory
- Stir-fried garlic, ginger and Savoy cabbage

Main meal – Winter menu 2
- Brown rice boiled with a few grains of oat groats
- Eggs stir-fried with ginger and leeks
- Brussels sprouts lightly boiled with oregano or marjoram

Main meal – Winter menu 3
- Brown rice
- Chicken braised with garlic, ginger, fresh mushrooms and leeks
- Stir-fried kale with caraway seeds

Main meal – Summer menu 1
- Brown rice boiled with a few grains of pot barley
- Black-eyed beans boiled alone, then gently simmered for 5 to 10 minutes with chopped spring onions, diced baby carrots, finely chopped carrot leaves and parsley
- Stir-fried garlic, ginger and Webb's lettuce

Main meal – Summer menu 2
- Brown rice
- *Tofu* stir-fried with garlic, string beans and a dash of *tamari*
- White cabbage and baby carrots steamed with fresh thyme

Main meal – Summer menu 3
- Brown rice cooked with sunflower seeds
- Fish steamed with fennel leaves or dill leaves
- Stir-fried spring cabbage with garlic

More protein dish ideas
- Lentils stewed with thyme, caraway seeds, carrot and onion
- Haricot beans stewed with onions, pumpkin, coriander leaves and seeds

- Red kidney beans stir-fried with white cabbage and thyme
- Chick-peas stir-fried with garlic, ginger, onion and mushrooms
- Butter beans stewed with beetroot and cardamom
- *Tofu* (or *tempeh*) stir-fried with garlic, ginger and broccoli, with a *miso* sauce
- Eggs steamed with grated ginger, chopped spring onion and parsley
- Eggs stir-fried with onions and a dash of *tamari*
- Eggs stir-fried with onion and thyme
- Fish marinated in minced garlic and a dash of *tamari*, then grilled
- Fish stir-fried with vegetables, garlic and ginger
- Fish baked with vegetables and bay leaf
- Fish poached with fennel leaves and baby carrots
- Fish soup
- Chicken marinated in minced garlic, minced ginger and a dash of *tamari*, then roasted or grilled
- Chicken steamed with minced garlic and coriander leaves
- Chicken steamed with spring onions or parsley
- Chicken braised with beetroot and cumin seeds
- Chicken stewed with onions, carrots, celery and bay leaf
- Chicken stir-fried with onion and sage

Exercise regularly
Try yoga, *taijiquan*, *qigong*, chanting or meditation if you suffer from multiple sclerosis. For those who are able to walk, the first three are most applicable because they improve the circulation of *qi* and blood. For

those in wheelchairs, chanting and meditation are more suitable. The vibrations in chanting are said to revitalise the brain and spinal column. Crawling on all fours is also good to maintain coordination, especially if you have a fear of falling.

Walking, cycling, swimming and dancing can also prove helpful, if you do not strain yourself. If the weather is wet, cold or windy, try to swim in a heated indoor pool and when you have finished, dry yourself thoroughly before going outdoors. Because multiple sclerosis sufferers are more susceptible to cold and damp, swimming at night is not advisable, even if the pool is heated and indoors. The same is true with taking hot showers or baths after dark.

Do reflexology

For best results, have somebody else do the massage, so you can relax and receive the full benefit of the treatment. Reflexology improves circulation, and encourages the body organs to work at their optimum, in harmony with each other.

Give both feet a general massage from toe to heel, then concentrate on the following areas: brain, spinal column, diaphragm, solar plexus, liver, spleen, kidneys, endocrine system, lymphatic system and those points that correspond to the areas that are not functioning properly. (See Appendix B.)

Try acupuncture

It usually brings faster results than reflexology. Acupuncture treatments have been known to arrest the debility (if diagnosed in its early stages), to prevent relapses or to reduce symptoms.

Try aromatherapy

Lavender oil baths are said to help the immune system resist infections. Three or four times a week add 3 to 4 drops of the essential oil of lavender to the bath just before you get in. Inhale the scent and relax.

In addition, Bach Flower Remedies (see page 226), especially gorse or gentian, gives you a more positive approach to healing yourself of multiple sclerosis. This is especially so during periods of relapse when you have feelings of despair and despondency.

29 Failing Eyesight

In Chinese acupuncture, the eyes are the windows to the state of health of the liver. If the eyesight is failing, it could mean that the liver is not functioning at its optimum.

Fortunately, the liver can gradually improve through dietary changes, *taijiquan*, *qigong*, yoga, or meditation and reflexology.

Failing eyesight can also be caused by too much reading, too much TV watching, or playing too many video games, which puts strain on the eye muscles. In old age, failing eyesight can be due to the condition of the kidneys after years of use and possibly misuse.

ADOPT THE CHANG MING DIET

Accompanied by daily eye exercises, the Chang Ming Diet may help prevent the progression of failing eyesight.

The Chang Ming Diet is made up of wholesome, nutritious food that is full of vitality. It provides the body with the necessary complex carbohydrates, polyunsaturated fats, proteins, vitamins A, B, C, D and E, minerals and dietary fibre. It consists of wholegrains, legumes and pulses, seeds and nuts, fresh vegetables, seaweeds, free-range eggs, fish and chicken.

Remember to select foods and cooking methods appropriate to your blood system. Black soyabeans, in particular, are good for the eyesight. Boil them with onion in a soup or stew or make black soyabean and lotus root soup. Alternatively, stew them with onions and carrots (or pumpkin) and garnish with spring onions or coriander leaves. Or use fermented black soyabeans with *tofu*, *tempeh*, vegetables, fish or chicken, or make black soyabean milk.

Eyesight can be affected by diet through the liver, which detoxifies food and drugs so they do not harm the body. The following foods can overwork the liver.

Sugar
Sugar, as in white sugar, sweets, chocolates, etc. does not exactly harm the body as do antibiotics or hormones, but it gives the liver extra work in converting it to glycogen for storage.

Dairy products
These contain traces of antibiotics, hormones and saturated fats that also overwork the liver.

Coconut products
These are high in saturated fats.

Red meats
They contain traces of antibiotics and

hormones, and are laden with saturated fats.

Animal fats
These are saturated fats that also contain traces of hormones, and possibly of oil-soluble insecticides or pesticides from the chemicals sprayed on the grasses or hay fed to the animals.

Deep-fried foods
They put extra strain on the liver, making it work harder to emulsify the fat by producing more bile.

Eggs
Those from battery hens contain chemicals.

Flour products
All biscuits, cakes, *kuih-muih*, etc. contain sugar and/or saturated fats.

Breakfast cereals
These contain too much sugar.

Beverages
Tea, coffee, chocolate-based beverages, cocoa, drinking chocolate, all soft and aerated drinks and other artificial beverages contain too much sugar and/or chemicals, and, in the case of tea and coffee, can overstimulate the central nervous system.

Chemicals
Saccharine and other artificial sweeteners, preservatives, colourings, monosodium glutamate, etc. can overstrain the liver's detoxification function.

Vegetables
Some vegetables, like tomatoes, potatoes, aubergines, sweet peppers, cayenne, tabasco and chillies, belong to the Deadly Nightshade family and contain a poison, solanin, which the liver must work hard to detoxify.

Alcohol
Alcohol contains many different chemicals used in the brewing process and can be particularly damaging to the liver.

Tinned and frozen foods
These contain sugar and possibly other chemicals.

Harmful hot energy foods
According to Chinese acupuncture theory, the liver is easily overheated by hot energy foods like coffee, chocolate, cheese, chillies, black pepper, Sichuan pepper, curry, cinnamon, cumin, coriander, cardamom, durian, pineapple, mango, greasy or fatty foods, and foods that are grilled, baked, roasted, barbecued and smoked.

My grandmother used to say that chillies can be harmful to the eyes. I have heard stories of people suffering momentary blurred vision from eating very hot chillies. It is said that people who eat chillies daily tend to fall victim to cataracts in old age.

EXERCISES TO IMPROVE EYESIGHT

If failing eyesight is due to old age then daily *taijiquan*, *qigong*, yoga or meditation can help prevent further deterioration. In all these exercises, emphasis is placed on stimulating and rejuvenating the kidneys, especially in *taijiquan* and Tao meditation. In *taijiquan* all the movements involve the waist (not the hips), thereby massaging the kidneys. Tao meditation improves the quality of the *jing*

which in turn rejuvenates the kidneys.

If failing eyesight is due to a malfunctioning liver, then daily foot reflexology, *taijiquan*, *qigong*, yoga or meditation is recommended. Foot reflexology need not take long. Just roll a wooden foot roller or rolling pin beneath the feet from the toes to the heels for 5 minutes, concentrating more on the areas between the second and third toes on both feet (the reflex areas for the eyes). Then concentrate on the liver reflex area, which is on the right foot below the ball of the foot, in line with the third, fourth and fifth toes. (See Appendix B.) If the liver or gall bladder is not functioning properly this area will feel very tender. Finally, concentrate on the kidney reflex area, which is situated in the middle of each foot.

Daily eye exercises are essential for people with failing eyesight, no matter what the cause. Students should do eye exercise too between study periods, to relieve eye strain and rest the brain.

Eye exercises 1

With the head facing forwards:

1 Move the eyes from left to right. Repeat 10 times.
2 Move the eyes from top to bottom. Repeat 10 times.
3 Move the eyes diagonally from bottom left to top right. Repeat 10 times.
4 Move the eyes diagonally from top left to bottom right. Repeat 10 times.
5 Move the eyes around clockwise. Repeat 10 times.
6 Move the eye around counter-clockwise. Repeat 10 times.
7 Rub the eyelids to improve circulation.
8 Place both palms over the eyes to rest them. This is called palming and can be

FIG 22. Palming

done as long as and as often as you like. (See FIG 22.)

Note: If you are old or have a tendency to become giddy or faint, do these exercises lying down.

Eye exercises 2

The following eye massage was shown to me by my *taijiquan* master. It has helped my father, who suffers from tunnel vision due to radiation damage to his optic nerve. (He is also on the Chang Ming Diet and does *taijiquan* daily.) You can do it after meals, during the commercial breaks while watching TV, or as often as you like.

With eyes closed:

1 Using the middle fingers, massage the bone of the eye sockets. Move the fingers outwards and upwards, then down to the bridge of the nose, as indicated by the arrows in FIG 23. Repeat 8 times.
2 Using the middle fingers, massage the hollows in the temples on either side of the face in an up and down movement. Repeat 8 times. (See FIG 23.)

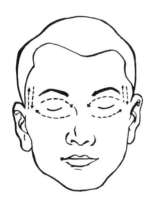

FIG 23. Eye exercises 2

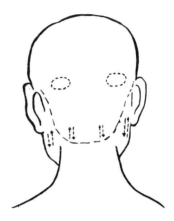

FIG 24. Eye exercises 2 and 3

3 Use the thumbs to massage the bones behind the ear lobes in an up and down movement. Repeat 8 times. (See FIG 24.)

4 Use the thumbs to massage the bones behind the head on either side of top of the neck, in an up and down movement. Repeat 8 times. (See FIG 24.)

5 Finish with some palming. (See FIG 22.)

Eye exercises 3

This set of exercises is excellent for students during intensive study periods.

1 With the fingers, gently massage the areas in the back of the skull directly behind the eyes. These may be very tender. (See FIG 24.)

2 Rotate the big toes clockwise and counter-clockwise, then massage them thoroughly, on the front, back and top, to improve blood supply to the brain and optic nerves, and to relax the neck muscles.

3 Massage the eye reflex areas on the soles directly below the second and third toes on both feet.

4 Massage the eye reflex areas directly below the nails of the big toes.

NO MIRACLE CURE

People who wear glasses should go without them for a few hours each day (and increase the time gradually). There is no miracle cure for failing eyesight – it is a matter of hard work and patience.

30 Balding

THE PATH TO A BALD PATE

Balding can be caused by:
- Eating too much meat, animal products, salt and dried foods. In this type of balding, the hair tends to fall out at the top of the head round the hair spiral.
- Drinking too many beverages containing artificial sweeteners, colourings, flavourings and alcohol, and eating too much sugar, sugar-laden foods, sweets, fruits, monosodium glutamate, and taking hard drugs and some medicines. In this case, the hair starts to fall from the front hairline.
- Eating too much of all the above foods. This combination can cause hair to fall out from the forehead to the back of the head.
- Anaemia.
- Thyroid problems.
- Lack of minerals in the diet.
- Lack of circulation in the scalp.
- Radiotherapy and chemotherapy.
- Exposure to radioactive materials.
- Excessive sex.
- Emotional stress, for example, shock.
- Ill health.
- Old age.

TO PREVENT LOSS OF HAIR

Avoid certain foods
For all types of balding, avoid the following foods:
- Sugar
- Dairy products
- Red meats
- Animal fats
- Deep-fried foods
- Baked flour products
- Breakfast cereals
- Beverages – Tea, coffee, chocolate-based beverages, cocoa, drinking chocolate, etc.
- Chemicals
- Vegetables – Tomatoes, potatoes, aubergines, sweet peppers, cayenne, tabasco and chillies which belong to the Deadly Nightshade family and contain small traces of solanin.
- Alcohol
- Tinned and frozen foods

Adopt the Chang Ming Diet
The Chang Ming Diet is the best way to prevent further loss of hair. It may take time to replenish the loss but with patience it will

happen gradually. The Chang Ming Diet consists of foods that provide complex carbohydrates, polyunsaturated fats, proteins, vitamins A, B, C, D and E, and minerals. All these ingredients are necessary for new growth and vitality. The diet consists of the following foods.

Wholegrains
These include brown rice and fresh sweet corn. Those with overheated blood systems should use pot barley, millet, whole wheat grains, rye and buckwheat. Those with cooled blood systems should use oat groats.

Legumes and pulses
Aduki beans, mung beans (only for those with overheated blood systems), black-eyed beans, lentils, chick-peas, broad beans, butter beans, marrowfat peas, red kidney beans, and soyabean products like *tofu*, soyabean milk, *tempeh*, *fu zhou*, *miso*, *tamari*, *shoyu*, fermented black soyabeans and fermented soyabean cheese.

Seeds and nuts
Sesame, sunflower, pumpkin and lotus seeds, peanuts, walnuts, chestnuts, almonds, Chinese bitter and sweet apricot kernels and ginkgo nuts.

It is best to boil the seeds or nuts if your blood system is overheated. If your blood system is on the cool side, eat them dry-roasted.

Fresh vegetables
All kinds of leafy greens and roots. Those with overheated blood systems should eat mainly neutral and cooling energy vegetables. Those with cooled blood systems should eat mainly neutral and warming energy vegetables.

Seaweeds
Hiziki, wakame, kombu, arame, nori, black hair moss, laverbread, dulse, carageen and *agar-agar.*

> **Caution:** Seaweed is appropriate only for those who are active, robust, strong in constitution or those with overheated blood systems. They are not for the weak or those with cooled blood systems.

Eggs
Eat no more than 2 or 3 free-range eggs per week.

Fish
White or oily fish may be eaten. Those with overheated blood systems should steam, poach or boil fish. Those with cooled blood systems can have fish grilled, baked and, occasionally, fried in a little unrefined cold-pressed oil.

Chicken
Eat in moderation, without the skin and fat. Those with overheated blood systems should steam, boil, braise or stew chicken. Those with cooled blood systems can have chicken braised, stewed, grilled, baked, roasted and, occasionally, stir-fried in a little oil with plenty of vegetables.

Sugar substitutes
Those with overheated blood systems can use barley or rice malt extract, raisins, sultanas, Hunza apricots, pure red grape juice or concentrated apple juice in moderation.

Those whose blood systems are on the cooled side can use Chinese red or black dates or longan in moderation.

Beverages
Mineral water, herbal teas, fruit juices, hot water, etc. See Chapter 13, Beverages.

Diet for the anaemic
If you are anaemic, eat more of the following foods:
- Aduki beans cooked with carrots or pumpkin
- Lentils cooked with caraway seeds and thyme
- *Miso*
- *Tempeh*
- Fermented black soyabeans and fermented soyabean cheese
- Dark green leafy vegetables
- Sunflower seeds
- Raisins
- Pure red grape juice
- Chinese red and black dates
- Longan
- Mu tea
- Floradix (a liquid vegetable and fruit extract that is rich in organic iron and vitamin B)

Those who are anaemic with an overheated blood system should eat cooling vegetables like watercress, spinach, beetroot leaves, nettle leaves, Chinese box thorn leaves, black hair moss, *hiziki*, and *wakame*. They can also take Floradix.

Anaemic women with cooled blood systems should have *dang gui* cooked with chicken, or tea made from 1 small finely sliced *dang gui* root boiled in 2 cups of water with 15 Chinese red dates and 5 Chinese black dates. Boil down to 1 cup. Anaemics can also have chicken cooked with a Mu tea bag.

Note: Dang gui and Mu tea have warming properties, so they are only appropriate for those who have cooled blood systems. *Dang gui* can be taken once a week either with chicken or with Chinese red and black dates. *Dang gui* with chicken has more warming properties than *dang gui* with Chinese red and black dates. Similarly, Mu tea cooked with chicken is more warming and nourishing than Mu tea on its own.

Diet for mineral deficiency
If your diet lacks minerals, use sea-salt in moderation, mineral water and seaweeds. All these foods have cooling properties, however, so if your blood system is on the cooled side, take in small amounts only. Try to eat as many organically grown foods as possible to supplement the lack of minerals in the diet.

Diet for those on radio/chemo therapy
Those who are receiving radiotherapy or chemotherapy treatments or those who work with radioactive materials should take *miso* daily to counteract the effects. *Miso* can be taken in the form of soups, added to stir-fried *tofu* or vegetables at the last minute and then very gently simmered for 5 minutes, or spread over fish, *tofu* or vegetables and steamed.

EXERCISES

To improve blood circulation
To improve blood circulation in the scalp so the hair follicles are well nourished, move the scalp backwards and forwards for a minute or two with your fingertips, then move to another part of the scalp. Continue until you have massaged the whole scalp. Do this daily,

or more often if you like. Avoid scratching the scalp. (See FIG 25.)

Further stimulation of circulation

Rub ginger oil into the scalp to further stimulate the circulation. Mix 1 teaspoon fresh ginger juice with 1 teaspoon unrefined cold-pressed sesame oil and rub into the scalp. Then do the scalp massage as described above. (See FIG 25.) Use the ginger oil only once a day.

Using essential oils

Massage a combination of the essential oils of rosemary, lavender and juniper into the scalp, then wrap the head in a warm, thick towel for 1 hour to aid penetration. After 1 hour, rub in some seaweed and rosemary shampoo and wash the hair. Rub in the shampoo without wetting the hair or you will not be able to wash off the oil.

> ***To prepare the essential oil combination:***
> Mix 2 drops oil of rosemary, 1 drop oil of lavender, 1 drop oil of juniper and 10 ml sweet almond oil. Store in a dark glass bottle in a cool, dark place. Use this treatment once or twice a week.

FIG 25. Scalp massage

For stress, ill health, old age

Yoga, *taijiquan*, *qigong* or meditation may help those whose baldness is caused by emotional stress, ill health and old age.

For thyroid problems

If your baldness is due to a thyroid problem, you must see a doctor. You can also use reflexology in conjunction with orthodox medical treatment. For reflexology, the areas to concentrate on after giving both feet a general massage from toes to heels are: thyroid, pituitary, pancreas and adrenals.

31 Brain Nourishment and Poor Memory

The brain needs three types of nourishment: from wholesome natural foods rich in B vitamins, polyunsaturated fatty acids (PUFA), ribonucleic acids (RNA), carbohydrates, proteins, minerals and vitamins; air and vital essence or *jing*.

Traditional Chinese medicine explains that *jing* is the vital essence formed when the sperm fertilises the egg at conception. It is essential for growth and development throughout life. It is said to be stored in the kidneys. *Jing* is considered to be more fluid in nature compared to *qi* which is more rarefied and immaterial. *Jing* and *qi* are inseparable, because one cannot survive or exist without the other.

THE DIET THAT NOURISHES THE BRAIN

If you go on a Chang Ming Diet your brain will be well nourished because it is made up of wholesome, natural foods such as brown rice.

Foods of the Chang Ming Diet

Wholegrains
Brown rice, pot barley, oat groats, millet, buckwheat, whole wheat grains, rye and fresh sweet corn. If you have an overheated blood system, use the neutral and cooling wholegrains. If you have a cooled blood system, use neutral and warming wholegrains. Otherwise, have a variety of different wholegrains on different days.

Legumes and pulses
Aduki beans, mung beans, black soyabeans, black-eyed beans, brown or green lentils, chick-peas, red kidney beans, and soyabean products like *tofu*, *fu zhou*, *tempeh*, *miso*, *tamari*, *shoyu*, fermented soyabean cheese, fermented black soyabeans, etc.

Fresh vegetables
If possible, have organically grown, leafy greens and root vegetables. If you have an overheated blood system, eat more neutral and cooling vegetables. If you have a cooled blood system, eat more neutral and warming energy vegetables. Otherwise, have a balance of cooling, neutral and warming vegetables.

When cooking leafy greens, add a thin slice or two of ginger, or some oregano or marjoram to aid digestion.

Seeds and nuts
Sesame, sunflower, pumpkin and lotus seeds, peanuts, almonds, Chinese apricot kernels, walnuts and hazelnuts.

Fish
White and oily fish cooked with ginger, fennel or dill. Have seafood like prawns, crabs, squid, octopus, clams, cockles, etc. only occasionally.

Eggs
Have no more than 2 or 3 steamed free-range eggs a week. Always beat them with half an eggshell or more of water and some grated ginger. Omelettes with onions, leeks, Chinese chives, chives, spring onions or shallots are good too. The use of water, ginger and onions aids digestion and helps prevent a build-up of cholesterol, mucus or phlegm.

Chicken
Eat free-range, fresh varieties cooked without skin or fat.

Fresh local and seasonal fruits
Eat organically grown fruits in moderation. If you have an overheated blood system, eat more cooling fruits. If you have a cooled blood system, eat fruits occasionally and choose those with neutral and warming energies. Try to avoid fruits in winter, but if you crave them, bake with warming spices like cinnamon, cloves, nutmeg, allspice, etc. Otherwise, have a balanced selection of cooling, neutral and warming fruits.

Special food for the brain

Wholegrains
Brown rice (neutral), pot barley (cooling) and oat groats (warming) – these three whole-grains have their germ intact, plus vitamins B and E, PUFA and RNA.

When buying grains, examine them to make sure the germ (found at the pointed end) is intact.

Processed wheatgerm is not recommended because all processed foods lose their vitality. In hot climates wheatgerm tends to go rancid very quickly, so beware.

Soyabeans, black soyabeans and soyabean products
Soyabeans are rich in B vitamins such as choline and inositol. Choline is needed to enhance the work of a chemical transmitter which passes impulses from one nerve-ending in the brain to another. Both choline and inositol are necessary for memory.

Yellow soyabeans have one drawback, they are very difficult to digest. Hence from ancient times, the Chinese always processed them into more easily digested products like *tofu*, silken *tofu*, soyabean milk, *fu zhou*, fermented soyabean cheese, etc. Choline and inositol are present in processed soyabean products.

Miso, a naturally fermented soyabean and wholegrain product from Japan, and *tempeh*, from Indonesia, are rich in digestible carbohydrates, proteins, PUFA, RNA, B vitamins including choline and inositol, bacterial enzymes, minerals and sea-salt.

Black soyabeans are easier to digest and can be used in their whole form. Boil them with fish heads and bones, to make a brain nourishing soup, or with dried squid to make soup that nourishes the brain and the blood. You can also stew them with onions and carrots. Fermented black soyabeans are also good for the brain.

Walnuts, sesame seeds, sunflower seeds and peanuts
These seeds and nuts are rich in vitamins B and E, PUFA and RNA. Do not have too

much, however, or you can create catarrh, mucus or phlegm in the body.

Walnuts have a long tradition in Chinese medical history as a good brain food. Young children were given walnuts and Chinese red dates at Chinese New Year to make them smarter and sweeter.

Walnuts contain a large proportion of linoleic acid, a PUFA required for brain function. Sesame seeds and peanuts contain choline and inositol to help memory. Sunflower seeds also contain essential PUFAs for the brain.

A sweet creamy tea (called *woo* in Cantonese) made of walnuts, sesame seeds or peanuts is thought to be good for the brain. Boil the seeds or nuts with a few grains of cooked brown rice until soft, then liquidise into a cream. Warm up the cream again and sweeten with barley or rice malt extract.

Note: This tea is very fattening, so drink only once a week.

Oily fish
Oily fish like herring and mackerel contain a brain-nourishing PUFA called *docosahexaenoic* (DHA), which is also very good for blood pressure, arthritis and rheumatism.

Oily fish are difficult to digest, so cook them with ginger, garlic, onions, leeks, spring onions, Chinese chives, chives, shallots, lemon grass, coriander leaves, fennel leaves, fennel bulb, fennel seed, dill leaves, dill seeds, rosemary or bay leaves.

Fish soups made with the head and bones are helpful too. Try an oily fish head soup with ginger, onions and *tofu*, garnished with chopped spring onions, coriander leaves or celery leaves. The longer you boil the soup the more goodness is extracted out of the heads and bones, and the more delicious it is. Use a stainless steel pressure cooker if you do not have time to watch over the soup.

Fish roe
Roe from white or oily fish is rich in RNA, another memory aid. Cook roe with ginger, garlic or different members of the onion family to aid digestion. Try other herbs like bay leaves, rosemary, fennel or dill.

Longan
According to ancient Chinese herbalists, longan is good for the mental faculties, and for forgetfulness. Do not eat too much, however, as it can create catarrh, mucus or phlegm in the body.

Longan vitality tea helps remedy forgetfulness and anaemia. Boil 10 pieces longan meat, 10 Chinese red dates (stones removed), 10 whole lotus seeds (or 20 lotus seed halves) in 2 cups of water until 1 cup remains. Have this once or twice a week.

Foods to avoid

Sugar
White sugar, sweets and chocolates, etc. come in this category. Sugar depletes the body of B vitamins, slowing down the brain's metabolism.

Dairy products
Milk, milk powder, condensed milk, skimmilk, cream, butter, ice-cream, cheese, cottage cheese, cream cheese and yogurt form a diet high in saturated fats. Such a diet slows down the brain metabolism.

Coconut products
Coconut milk, coconut oil, *kuih-muih* made with coconut cream and curries made with coconut milk – all coconut products are high in saturated fats.

Red meats
Veal, beef, lamb, pork, duck, ham, bacon, sausages, etc. are examples of red meats. Red meats are naturally high in saturated fats. Often people feel sleepy after a heavy meaty meal because all the body's energy is centred in the stomach.

Animal fats
Beef dripping, pork fat, chicken fat and goose fat, etc. are animal fats full of saturated fats.

Deep-fried foods
High cooking temperatures change unsaturated fats to saturated fats.

Breakfast cereals
Cornflakes, muesli, instant porridge oats, and many popular cereals are laden with sugar. Please check the labels before buying.

Beverages
Tea, coffee, chocolate-based beverages, cocoa, drinking chocolate, all soft and aerated drinks and other artificial beverages are included here. Tea and coffee overstimulate the central nervous system and the others are laden with sugar, milk or chemicals.

Chemicals
Saccharine, other artificial sweeteners, preservatives, colourings, monosodium glutamate, etc.

Alcohol
Alcohol can increase the amount of saturated fats in the blood. Alcohol also needs B vitamins for its digestion, especially the memory-aiding B vitamin choline, and also slows down brain functions.

Tinned foods
Tinned foods may contain sugar and other chemicals.

Frozen foods
Sugar may be added to frozen foods during processing.

PREVENT BRAIN DETERIORATION

Adopt good dietary habits
Besides adopting the Chang Ming Diet, take note of the following.
- Avoid milk and do not give it to young babies. It encourages bone growth at the expense of brain development. Breast feeding is best for baby's health and vitality.
- Do not overeat. Eating too much uses up all the body's energies to digest food, leaving little for brain functions.

Ensure adequate oxygen supply
Do not spend all day over a desk studying. In a bent position the lungs and diaphragm do not function properly so the body does not have an abundant supply of oxygenated blood. This will affect brain function as the brain only works at its optimum level in well oxygenated blood.

Do not smoke
Smoking depletes the body of precious B vitamins and vitamin C.

Do not indulge in too much sex
Every time a man or woman has sexual intercourse they lose *jing*, the vital essence, much needed for brain function.

IMPROVE CIRCULATION AND *JING*

To keep the brain well oxygenated with a continuous fresh blood supply, and to improve the quality of *jing*, the following are recommended:
- Reflexology
- Deep breathing
- Exercise
- Meditation

Reflexology
This improves blood circulation to the brain, especially if you study a lot or spend much time working over a desk. Studying over a desk tenses up the muscles, which restricts a free flow of blood to the brain, building up deoxygenated blood.

To prevent this, rotate your thumbs and big toes clockwise and counter-clockwise to relax the neck muscles. Then massage the brain reflex area of the thumbs (fleshy pad of thumbs) and big toes (fleshy pad of big toes). Rotate your fingers and toes to relax the neck and shoulder muscles.

These exercises are most appropriate for students. The brain can only concentrate well for no more than $1^1/_2$ to 2 hours, after which you should take a 30-minute break to relax your neck and shoulder muscles, and to take

in deep breaths to oxygenate the blood and nourish the brain.

Deep breathing
Start in a prone position, in case you hyperventilate and feel faint. Lie on your back and relax your whole body. Put your hand over your navel. As you inhale, try to push your abdominal muscles out, raising your hands. As you slowly exhale your abdominal muscles will fall back in place. Repeat this procedure slowly four times. Once the exercise becomes automatic, do it sitting up with the spine straight.

To increase your breath up to your upper lungs, you have to do this: place one hand over the navel and the other over the chest. As you inhale, push out the abdominal muscles and then the thoracic muscles, so both hands are raised. As you slowly breathe out, the abdominal muscles should fall back in place before the thoracic muscles. Repeat this four times sitting up with the spine straight. When you can do the exercises automatically, do them as many times as you like.

Exercise and meditation
Try walking for exercise. Leisurely walks in a park or botanical garden full of green trees is excellent because all plants give off oxygen during daylight hours. Keep houseplants by your desk to supply you with fresh oxygen all day.

Do yoga, *taijiquan*, *qigong*, chanting or meditation daily to improve the flow of *qi* and blood to the brain. Chanting also revitalises the brain and the central nervous system.

Meditation not only improves the flow of *qi* and blood, but also improves the quality of

jing. In Chinese acupuncture and herbalism, doctors look for a person's *jing shen* in the eyes. The eyes tell them a great deal about the patient's alertness and vitality, i.e., the quality of *jing.* The more brilliant the eyes, the more vital the *jing.*

Meditation used to be practised only in monasteries and convents as part of spiritual awareness. Now we have realised that by stilling the mind one not only attains spiritual awareness, but heals the body and nourishes the brain.

To meditate, sit with your spine straight so your brain and spinal column act as a symbolic acupuncture needle to connect heaven's energy with earth's energy. Once the mind is still, energies can flow freely to heal and nourish. After each meditation session the quality of the jing is improved. This improvement is cumulative.

> *Note:* After having sex you should wait another 24 hours before resuming meditation. In men, the *jing* is stored in the semen. In women, it is stored in the eggs, genital secretions and organs.

Begin meditating for 5 minutes then increase it to 10 minutes and so on, until you can meditate for 1 hour. Do not force yourself to meditate for too long and take your time getting used to the meditating position.

When you can meditate for 1 hour, you have achieved the healing, nourishing and spiritual awareness of meditation. Meditating for less than 1 hour is not wasted; relaxing the mind and body for even 5 minutes can relieve tension and stress.

Regular meditation brings peace from within. You will be amazed how calm you will become and how clear your mind will be. According to some, meditation also helps

keep the facial skin moist and youthful.

> *Note:* Learn to meditate with a qualified master. Meditation should not conjure up strange or frightening images. If it does, *stop immediately.*

POOR MEMORY

When *shen* is in place
According to traditional Chinese medicine, forgetfulness, loss of memory or senility can be due to a malfunction of the heart and kidneys. The heart houses the *shen* (or spirit). If this function is intact, we experience
- Normal mental activities
- Consciousness
- Clear, keen thinking
- Good memory
- Sleep at the appropriate time

When *shen* is absent
If the heart fails to house the *shen*, the following symptoms may result:
- Abnormal mental activities
- Loss of consciousness as in a coma
- Clouded thinking
- Poor memory
- Insomnia or somnolence (sleepiness)

Why is *shen* absent?
The heart can become incapable of housing the *shen* due to the following reasons.

Shock or trauma
This is easily seen in people after they have had an accident, a bad fright or the shock of hearing some bad news.

Deficient blood
In traditional Chinese medicine, deficient

blood signifies an imbalance in the spleen and heart. The spleen must be balanced to digest, assimilate, transform and transport food into useful nourishment and energy for the heart, which circulates the blood. If this harmony between the spleen and heart is impaired, forgetfulness, loss of memory and insomnia can result. And if this condition is not corrected, further symptoms and signs like the following can result.

- Palpitation – More in the evening, or at rest, accompanied by a feeling of anxiety or uneasiness in the chest
- Dream-disturbed sleep
- Anxiety
- Restlessness
- Dull, pale complexion

> *Note:* Some women may find that they suffer from some of these symptoms just before each menstruation. This is due to deficient blood.

Correcting poor memory

Acupuncture and Chinese herbs can help correct this imbalance. If you suffer from poor memory, see an alternative therapist as soon as possible. Vitality tea can help (see pages 132-133) but not as well as acupuncture or a prescription containing stronger Chinese herbs.

DEFICIENT KIDNEY *JING*

The kidneys, according to traditional Chinese medicine, are the source of *jing*. If the *jing* deteriorates, the eyes will lack vitality. Causes include:

- Weak constitution
- Old age
- Poor diet

- Overwork
- Excessive sex
- Having many children close together without nourishing the body in between

In deficient kidney *jing*, poor memory is often accompanied by:

- Ringing in the ears
- Deafness
- Premature greying
- Falling hair
- Loose teeth
- Weakness in the back, legs and knees
- Osteoporosis
- Osteomalacia
- Arthritis in the neck and/or lumbar region

Is it possible to rejuvenate the *jing*? *Jing* that is already lost cannot be recovered, but the quality of *jing* that is left can be improved by:

- Adopting a Chang Ming Diet
- Yoga, *taijiquan*, *qigong*, chanting or meditation
- Chinese herbs
- Acupuncture

This type of poor memory takes a long time to heal and requires patience, perseverance and determination.

> *Note:* In cold, damp countries like Great Britain it is common for people to feel a bit muzzy in the head, especially in winter. They may have clouded thinking or the inability to concentrate properly. This condition may be caused by the climate and an imbalance in the spleen. A diet rich in catarrh, mucus or phlegm-forming foods can aggravate it. Do not confuse this with an imbalance in the heart. Both dis-eases can be corrected with acupuncture.

32 Women's Problems

oday, women work both inside and outside the home, leaving themselves open to exhaustion, illness and women's problems. It is important for women to spend an hour or two each day relaxing, exercising, doing reflexology or any calming activity that helps rejuvenate their inner reserves.

Women are most delicate between ovulation and menstruation. During this period, they should not expose themselves to the elements or extreme temperature changes, or they may be more susceptible to colds or 'flus, especially if they have a weak constitution or are under great stress. At this time other conditions may become worse, like asthma, eczema, cystitis, constipation, diabetes, high blood pressure, arthritis, rheumatism and kidney problems.

Traditionally, all Chinese women drink *dang gui* tonic soup or tea at the end of the period to build themselves up. If you dislike *dang gui* or if it is not available, a bottle of Guinness Stout is just as good. (The hops used in the brewing is the key ingredient.) Drink sage tea, Mu tea or use sage in your cooking for the same purpose.

Chinese women are particularly careful about their bodies during and after pregnancy. During pregnancy it is typical for the mother-in-law to fuss over her daughter-in-law's diet. After childbirth, the mother stays in bed for 40 days, during which time she is not supposed to bathe, shower, wash her hair or do any work except breastfeed the baby, eat nourishing food, be massaged, rest and sleep. Usually, the mother-in-law and other relatives are on hand to cook and care for the family, leaving the mother to rest and rebuild her strength. These days, of course, it is often impossible for a new mother to have her 40-day rest period and, often, women's problems can result.

CRITICAL ORGANS AND CHANNELS

According to traditional Chinese medicine, the spleen, liver, kidneys, uterus and two other channels, the *ren mai* and *chong mai*, are involved in all gynaecological processes. If any one of them is not functioning properly, the system will be out of balance and gynaecological problems like premenstrual tension, dysmenorrhoea, mittleschmerz, menopause, leucorrhoea, thrush and prolapsed uterus can arise.

The spleen and the stomach convert food into *qi* and blood. The spleen has the added function of 'keeping blood within the blood vessels' so that there is no haemorrhage, and 'raising' the central organs so that they do not 'drop' to cause prolapse.

The liver stores blood and ensures that the *qi* flows smoothly to all parts of the body. The kidneys store the vital essence called *jing*. Without *jing*, there is no vitality, reproduction or sexual desire. The kidneys also provide the 'fire' with which the spleen converts food, and the 'water', in the form of *jing*, to ensure the body does not dry out.

The Chinese characters for uterus, 子宫, are literally translated as the 'palace of the child'. It is nourished by *qi*, blood, the kidneys and the *ren* and *chong mai* channels. In menstruation, the uterus stores and discharges blood. In pregnancy, it nourishes and protects the foetus.

The *ren mai* channel which runs up the front of the body to the cleft in the chin, is sometimes called the 'conception vessel'. It allows *qi* and blood (during menstruation) to flow freely. In pregnancy, it nourishes the uterus, ensuring that the foetus will be carried to full term.

The *chong mai* channel is the reservoir of blood for menstruation, and in pregnancy it nourishes the uterus.

PREMENSTRUAL TENSION (PMT)

PMT affects females of all ages between ovulation and menstruation. The symptoms can vary from mild discomfort to acts of crime or even suicide. In traditional Chinese medicine, there are three causes of PMT.

Three causes of Premenstrual Tension (PMT):

1 Stagnation of liver *qi*
2 Deficiency of spleen *yang* and kidney *yang*
3 Deficiency of blood and *yin*

PMT DUE TO STAGNATION OF LIVER *QI*

Symptoms and signs
- Irritability
- Anger
- Depression
- Distension or swelling of the breasts, or water retention
- Distension or swelling of the lower abdomen, or water retention
- Headaches or migraines before the period
- Lower abdominal pain before the period and on the first day
- Lack of appetite
- Aching joints, and aching or swelling eyeballs due to water retention

The above symptoms and signs and their intensity can vary from month to month and are very much linked to the emotions.

PMT due to stagnation of liver *qi* is the most common, especially today when women work outside the home, and lead more stressful lives.

To re-adjust the imbalances

1 Go on a Chang Ming Diet
Eat and cook foods appropriate to your blood system. Choose foods rich in B vitamins, especially B$_6$, like sunflower seeds, cod and sardines.

Eat magnesium-rich foods like almonds, walnuts, raisins, oat groats and fish, to prevent depression. Use little or no sea-salt between ovulation and menstruation to prevent distension in the breasts and lower abdomen due to water retention. To prevent irritability and anger, avoid tea and coffee:

they cause tension and depression.

Eat plenty of greens and sprouting seeds like alfalfa and mung bean sprouts between ovulation and menstruation.

> *Note:* If you have a cooled blood system or tendency towards one, please cook the alfalfa sprouts and mung bean sprouts before eating.

For loss of appetite, drink parsley or sage tea. For water retention, drink 1 to 2 cups of dandelion tea a day. Also use parsley and sage in your cooking.

> *Note:* If you have a cooled blood system or tendency towards one, please drink only 1 cup of dandelion tea a day, preferably in the mornings.

2 Exercise and meditate

Practise yoga, *taijiquan*, *qigong*, deep breathing, chanting or meditation daily to improve liver *qi* stagnation and to lift the mind and spirit. Do gentle exercises like walking, swimming or dancing. Singing, listening or playing soothing music can also help.

3 Use aromatherapy

Oil of lavender is good for irritability and anger. Oil of neroli helps anxiety and nervous depression. Oil of clary sage helps get rid of depression. Massage a few drops of oil on both sides of the wrists and behind the ears.

Oil of juniper is excellent for water retention. Massage a few drops on the breasts, lower abdomen or aching joints. Oil of rosemary is good for headaches or migraines due to stagnation of liver *qi*, and for lower abdominal pain. Massage a few drops over the liver area and lower abdomen.

Never use any oil neat. Mix 4 drops of essential oil with 10 ml sweet almond oil before using.

> *Note:* Oil of rosemary may increase blood pressure, and must not be used by anyone with hypertension.

4 Use reflexology

Give both feet a general massage from toe to heel, then concentrate on the following reflex areas: diaphragm, solar plexus, spinal column, pituitary, thyroid, thymus, pancreas, adrenals, liver, gall bladder, kidneys, uterus, ovaries, Fallopian tubes and breasts. (See Appendix B.) Do this daily for about an hour.

5 Seek expert help

Those who suffer from acute PMT symptoms should see an alternative therapist (like an acupuncturist, homeopath or herbalist) as soon as possible as well as follow the advice given. Do not use self-help alone.

PMT DUE TO DEFICIENCY OF SPLEEN *YANG* AND KIDNEY *YANG*

Symptoms and signs
- Lack of appetite or excessive or compulsive eating, especially of sweet things
- Nausea
- Fatigue
- Lethargy
- Poor memory
- Poor circulation
- Difficulty in thinking due to a feeling of stuffiness in the head
- Tendency to oedema
- Backache and weak knees

- Cold feeling
- Asthma attacks (if the person suffers from the type of asthma that gets worse with exertion)
- Inflammation of the mucus membrane of the nose (if the person suffers from rhinitis)

Possible causes
- Weak constitution
- A diet of too many cold, raw foods, or cooling energy foods
- Having too many children too close together, without resting or nourishing the body back to health after each childbirth
- Excessive sex

This type of PMT is quite common among raw food eaters, vegans, macrobiotics who eat lots of seaweed, and those who live on convenience foods or snacks.

To re-adjust the imbalances

1   Go on a Chang Ming Diet
In this type of PMT, a change in diet can reduce suffering. Eat mainly neutral and warming energy foods and use neutral and warming cooking methods. To warm up the deficient kidney *yang* condition eat:
- Walnuts cooked with brown rice, about 3 to 4 times a week
- Chestnuts boiled or stewed with chicken and Chinese red dates
- Cinnamon, fenugreek seeds and fennel seeds with other cooked ingredients or brewed in herbal tea
- Black-boned chicken, boiled or double-boiled with cinnamon
- *Dang shen*, boiled or double-boiled with regular or black-boned chicken

- Ginseng, double-boiled with longan or chicken once a month (take one week after menstruation)
- Mu tea, 2 to 3 times a week.

2   Drink special tonics and teas
After menstruation, build yourself up with the following tonics:
- Blood building tonic after the menstrual period (see Chapter 8, pages 133-134)
- Blood building tonic for the old, weak and anaemic (see Chapter 8, page 134)
- *Dang gui* and longan tonic tea

Dang gui and longan tonic tea:

1 thumb-sized *dang gui* root
20 pieces dried longan
2 cups water
Boil all the ingredients in a Chinese earthenware herbal pot until only 1 cup of liquid is left. When half cooked, remove the *dang gui* root, slice very thinly, and return to the pot. Drink the liquid and eat the root and longan.

This bitter brew should be taken once, when the period ends, or once every 1 to 2 weeks, if you are anaemic.

Dang gui, longan and egg tonic tea:

1 thumb-sized *dang gui* root
20 pieces dried longan
1 free-range egg
2 cups water
Boil the egg until the white just hardens. Remove the shell and put the egg in a Chinese earthenware herbal pot with the *dang gui*, longan and water. Boil until 1 cup of liquid is left. When half cooked, remove the *dang gui* root, slice very thinly, and return to the pot. Drink the liquid

and eat the root, longan and egg.

Drink this bitter tea once a month after the period ends, or once every 1 to 2 weeks, if you are anaemic.

3 Exercise daily
Practise yoga, *taijiquan* or *qigong* daily to warm up the kidneys. Do the exercise called 'warming up the kidneys' as often as necessary.

4 Use foot reflexology
(See Appendix B.) See PMT caused by stagnation of liver *qi* (page 343).

5 Use moxibustion
(See Appendix C.) Apply the glowing end of the moxa stick about 2 to 2$^1/_2$ cm ($^3/_4$ to 1 in) away from the skin above the following acupuncture points until the skin turns slightly pinkish or feels nice and warm.
- Bladder 20 (*Pishu*) tonifies the spleen which transforms and transports food (Appendix C, FIG 14)
- Bladder 23 (*Shenshu*) tonifies the kidneys to support the spleen, prevent oedema, poor memory, poor circulation and to strengthen the back and knees (Appendix C, FIG 14)
- *Ren* 4 (*Guanyuan*) tonifies the body (Appendix C, FIG 15)
- *Ren* 6 (*Qihai*) tonifies the body (Appendix C, FIG 15)
- Spleen 6 (*Sanyinjiao*) tonifies the spleen (Appendix C, FIGS 10, 11, 12)
- Stomach 36 (*Zusanli*) tonifies the spleen and the body (Appendix C, FIGS 10, 11, 12)

Use moxibustion each night if your condition is severe, once every 2 to 3 days otherwise.

Note: Do not use moxibustion before or after a bath or when the skin is wet. Wait 1 to 2 hours until the body returns to normal temperature to prevent blisters.

6 Consult specialists
This type of PMT syndrome is best treated by following the guidelines given above and through acupuncture. If possible, also see a Chinese herbalist.

PMT DUE TO DEFICIENCY OF BLOOD AND *YIN*

Symptoms and signs
- PMT symptoms increase towards the end of the period
- Great weakness at the end of the period
- Dizziness
- Disturbed sleep
- Palpitations
- Night sweats
- Hot feeling in the palms, soles, and the area between the breasts
- Increased nervousness, edginess
- Tendency to weep easily
- Dull headaches, usually at the top of the head
- Argumentativeness
- Symptoms aggravated by mental work and anxiety
- Symptoms decrease in relaxed environment

Possible causes of PMT
- Anaemia
- Poor diet
- Irregular eating
- Stress, or years of pushing yourself without rest or relaxation

This last PMT syndrome can be more serious than the others if not treated as soon as possible. Most importantly, the patient must learn to relax.

To re-adjust the imbalances

1   Go on a Chang Ming Diet
Eat mainly neutral energy foods and cook cooling foods with warming foods to create balance. Steam, boil or sauté foods. Eat foods with a high iron and B$_{12}$ content, and foods that the Chinese classify as blood-building. See page 261, but *do not* use warming tonics such as:
- Chinese black dates
- Chinese red dates
- *Dang gui*
- Longan
- Blood building soup
- Vitality tea
- Blood building tonic at the end of the menstrual period and tonic for the old, anaemic and weak

> *Note:* Use Floradix (available at health food shops) instead.

2   Exercise or meditate daily
Practise yoga, *taijiquan, qigong*, chanting, deep breathing or meditation daily to help you relax and to bring the body back in harmony.

3   Use aromatherapy and acupressure together
(See Appendix C.) Oil of clary sage is good for weepiness and depression. Oil of rose can help insomnia, palpitations and jumpiness.

Mix 4 drops of essential oil with 10 ml sweet almond oil and store in a dark glass bottle in a cool, dark place. Massage the diluted oil on the acupressure points given below.

Use oil of clary sage for Pericardium 6 (*Neiguan*), for weepiness and depression. (See Appendix C, FIG 16.)

Use oil of rose for
- *Yintang*, to improve sleep (Appendix C, FIG 17)
- Heart 7 (*Shenmen*), for insomnia (Appendix C, FIG 16)
- Heart 6 (*Yinxi*), for insomnia (Appendix C, FIG 16)
- Spleen 6 (*Sanyinjiao*), to help the spleen transform and transport food, and for insomnia (Appendix C, FIGS 10, 11, 12)
- Stomach 36 (*Zusanli*), to strengthen the body (Appendix C, FIGS 10, 11, 12)

4   Use foot reflexology
(See Appendix B.) See also PMT caused by stagnation of liver *qi,* and add the reflex areas for the spleen and heart.

5   See specialists
This type of PMT should be treated by an acupuncturist and, if possible, a Chinese herbalist. The above advice is only to be used as a supplement to acupuncture treatment.

> *Note:* It is possible to suffer from the three types of PMT syndromes at different times. PMT symptoms can also occur after a hysterectomy. If this is the case, seek the advice of an alternative therapist.

DYSMENORRHOEA

Dysmenorrhoea is another word for painful menstruation. Some people only suffer from dull aches in the lower abdomen before the

menstrual flow starts and/or on the first day. Others are not as fortunate – they get severe cramps for almost 24 hours before the flow begins, or they are bedridden for the first two days of the period.

In traditional Chinese medicine, a normal period is described as a discharge of blood at regular intervals, lasting between 3 and 7 days, occurring every 21 to 35 days. The flow should be light red with few clots and there should not be any discomfort or pain.

> ### Four causes of dysmenorrhoea:
> According to traditional Chinese medicine, there are four causes of dysmenorrhoea, and they come into two categories:
> - Dysmenorrhoea with severe pain:
>   1 Stagnation of liver *qi*
>   2 Stagnation of blood
>   3 Stagnation of *qi* and/or blood due to cold
> - Dysmenorrhoea with dull aches
>   4 Deficiency of *qi* and blood
>
> In each type of dysmenorrhoea, avoid sour foods – they can aggravate the pain.

DYSMENORRHOEA DUE TO STAGNATION OF LIVER *QI*
character: severe pain

Symptoms and signs
- Distension and pain, which can radiate from the lower abdomen to the lower back and thighs
- Distension and pain, which becomes worse on pressure
- Pain occurs before the onset of the period and eases when the flow starts

- Irregular flow that is not necessarily heavy
- Dark blood, with occasional clots
- Distension and pain in the breasts, hypochondrium and costal region
- Tightness in the chest
- Belching or vomiting bile
- Irritability and anger
- Frustration, depression
- Heightened sensitivity
- Fainting

This type of dysmenorrhoea usually occurs following PMT caused by stagnation of liver *qi*. Although the list of symptoms and signs is extensive, often the cause of this type of dysmenorrhoea is emotional upset, tension and stress.

To adjust the imbalances
For best results, follow the advice given for PMT caused by stagnation of liver *qi*.

Massage the lower abdomen with oil of clary sage. Dilute 4 drops of the essential oil in 10 ml of sweet almond oil and use as soon as you feel pain.

In between periods, see an alternative therapist to help you cope with stress and tension, and to prevent recurrent attacks. During an acute attack, see an acupuncturist for quick relief.

DYSMENORRHOEA DUE TO STAGNATION OF BLOOD
character: severe pain

Symptoms and signs
- Very severe, fixed pain
- Fainting
- Pain becomes worse on pressure

- Possible masses in the lower abdomen
- The most severe pain occurs at onset of period
- Irregular, hesitant or light flow
- Dark blood that is full of clots

Possible causes
- Stagnation of liver *qi* from emotional upset, tension and stress
- Accident in the lower abdominal area
- Past operation in the lower abdominal area

If the cause is emotional upset, tension and stress, follow the advice given for PMT caused by stagnation of liver *qi*. If it is due to an accident or an operation, see an alternative therapist to help clear up the stagnation of blood and *qi*.

Use reflexology (see Appendix B) in all three instances to improve the circulation of *qi* and blood in the uterus. (See PMT caused by stagnation of liver *qi*, page 343.)

Do yoga, *taijiquan* or *qigong* daily to improve the circulation of *qi* and blood in the uterus.

DYSMENORRHOEA DUE TO STAGNATION OF *QI* AND/OR BLOOD DUE TO COLD
character: severe

Symptoms and signs
- Cold, sore feeling in the lower abdomen
- Dragging, contracting pain in the lower abdomen
- Pain aggravated by touch, relieved by warmth
- Pain increases at onset or just before the period starts

- Pain may radiate to the lower back and legs
- Dislike of the cold
- Cold limbs
- Scanty or very thin, watery flow
- Dark, clotted blood

Possible causes
- Diet consisting of too many cold, cooling energy, raw, frozen, or refrigerated foods
- Exposure to the cold

To adjust the imbalances
In this type of dysmenorrhoea, avoid all cold, cooling energy, raw, frozen, or refrigerated foods between ovulation and menstruation. Eat neutral and warming energy foods and use neutral and warming methods of cooking.

During an attack do any of the following:

1 Use a hot water bottle
Place it over the lower abdomen.

2 Use moxibustion
(See Appendix C, FIG 15.) Hold the glowing end of the moxa stick about 2 to $2^1/_2$ cm ($^3/_4$ to 1 in) above acupuncture points *Ren* 6 (*Qihai*), *Ren* 4 (*Guanyuan*) and *Ren* 3 (*Zhongji*) until the skin turns slightly pinkish or until the point feels nice and warm. Then move to the next point.

> *Caution:* Do not use moxibustion before or after a bath or shower or if the skin is wet. Allow the skin to dry out for 1 to 2 hours before using moxibustion to prevent blisters.

3 Use essential oil
Dilute 4 drops of essential oil of ginger in 10 ml sweet almond oil. Rub over the lower

abdomen. (Do not use moxibustion with this method.)

Alternatively, dilute 4 drops of essential oil of black pepper in 10 ml sweet almond oil. Rub over the lower abdomen. (Do not use moxibustion with this method also.)

4 Exercise
Practise *yoga*, *taijiquan* or *qigong* daily to remove the stagnation of *qi* and/or blood, and cold from the lower abdomen.

5 Use reflexology
See PMT caused by stagnation of liver *qi* (page 343).

6 Consult specialists
I would strongly advise anyone who suffers from this type of dysmenorrhoea to have a course of acupuncture treatment as soon as possible to prevent further weakening of the body.

DYSMENORRHOEA DUE TO DEFICIENCY OF *QI* AND BLOOD
character: dull aches

Symptoms and signs
- Dull pain that can be gnawing, continuous or intermittent
- Dull pain which gets worse when fatigued
- Pain in a generalised location
- Pain improves with warmth and pressure
- Pain at the later stages or after the period
- Scanty, delayed flow
- Light red blood
- Fatigue
- Sallow complexion
- Dizziness
- Tinnitus

- Palpitations
- Poor appetite
- Cold feeling
- Sore back

Possible causes
- Weak constitution
- Overwork
- Anaemia
- Having too many children too close together, without resting or nourishing the body after childbirth

Those who suffer from this type of dysmenorrhoea should rest during and one to two days after menstruation.

To re-adjust the imbalances

1 Go on a Chang Ming Diet
Eat mainly neutral and warming energy foods and use neutral and warming methods of cooking. Avoid cold and cooling energy foods and drinks.

Eat foods high in iron and B_{12} content and blood-building foods. (See the list in Chapter 21, page 261.)

Drink *dang gui* and longan tonic tea, and *dang gui*, longan and egg tonic tea. (See page 344.)

Use the following herbs in your cooking to aid digestion or stimulate the appetite: basil, sage, parsley, thyme, caraway seeds, marjoram, oregano and fennel seeds.

2 Exercise
Practise yoga, *taijiquan* or *qigong* daily to improve *qi* and blood.

3 Use moxibustion
(See Appendix C, FIG 15 for *Ren* and FIGS 10,

11, 12 for Spleen 6 and Stomach 36.) Do this only when you feel pain. Apply the glowing end of the moxa stick about 2 to $2^1/_2$ cm ($^3/_4$ to 1 in) above the skin over the following acupuncture points until the skin turns slightly pinkish or feels nice and warm:
- *Ren 6 (Qihai)*
- *Ren 4 (Guanyuan)*
- *Ren 3 (Zhongji)*
- Spleen 6 (*Sanyinjiao*)
- Stomach 36 (*Zusanli*)

Caution: Do not use moxibustion before or after a bath or shower or when the skin is wet. Wait one to two hours.

Note: If moxa sticks are unavailable, place a hot water bottle over the lower abdomen.

4 Use reflexology
This improves the circulation of *qi* and blood. (See PMT caused by stagnation of liver *qi*, page 343.)

5 Consult an acupuncturist
See an acupuncturist as soon as possible to tonify the *qi* and blood. Use the advice here to supplement the acupuncture treatments.

Note: It is possible for someone to suffer from four different types of dysmenorrhoea at different times. If this is the case, see an alternative therapist as soon as possible.

MITTLESCHMERZ (OVARALGIA)

Sometimes women begin to get pains at ovulation when they reach 30 years of age or over. It does not happen every month, and may affect only the ovary that is ovulating at that time. Sometimes, if the woman has ovulation pain, she may not have menstrual pain.

Symptoms and signs
- Pain and swelling in the lower abdomen
- Pain and swelling of the breasts
- A particular smell in the breasts
- A milky, sticky vaginal discharge, sometimes thick enough for a sanitary towel to be necessary
- Depression
- Lack of appetite

Possible causes
In traditional Chinese medicine, the *ren mai* and *chong mai* channels work at their optimum during ovulation and menstruation. If there is disharmony in the *ren mai* and/or *chong mai*, the *qi* will not flow smoothly and may give rise to the above symptoms and signs.

Certain types of asthmatics (those who feel worse upon exertion) may have increased attacks at ovulation due to disharmony in the *ren mai* channel. Emotional upset, stress and tension can also trigger ovulation pain (due to stagnation of liver *qi*), as can a combination of an imbalance in the *ren mai* channel and stagnation of liver *qi*.

To re-adjust the imbalances

1 Go on a Chang Ming Diet
Eat foods appropriate to your blood system and cook them accordingly. Build yourself up at the end of menstruation.
- *If you have an overheated blood system, take:*
  Floradix, a herbal extract rich in organic iron and vitamin B
  Purple sage tea, or cook with sage daily

- *If you have a neutral blood system, take:*
  Sage tea or cook with sage daily
  Guinness Stout – just 1 small bottle a day
- *If you have a cooled blood system, take:*
  Mu tea
  Blood-building tonic at the end of a period (see Chapter 8, pages 133-134)
  Blood-building tonic for the old, weak and anaemic (see Chapter 8, page 134)
  Dang gui and longan tonic tea (see this chapter, page 344)
  Dang gui, longan and egg tonic tea (see this chapter, page 344)

2 Exercise daily
Practise yoga, *taijiquan* or *qigong* daily to harmonise the body.

3 Use aromatherapy
Mix 4 drops of essential oil of clary sage with 10 ml sweet almond oil before massaging it on the lower abdomen when there is pain.

4 Use reflexology
See PMT caused by stagnation of liver *qi* (page 343) and add the spinal reflex area.

5 Consult specialists
Supplement the above advice with treatment by an alternative therapist.

MENOPAUSE

Menopause can occur in women in their late thirties to early sixties and can last from one to five years. It happens to every woman. However, menopausal problems do not affect every woman.

Symptoms
The symptoms vary and may include:
- Depression
- Hot flushes
- Night sweats
- Palpitations
- Inability to cope physically or mentally

Women who have had a hysterectomy may experience some of these symptoms earlier than other women. The condition takes different forms and can be due to diet, lifestyle and emotional state. Distressing menopausal symptoms can be helped by alternative therapies.

See a therapist as soon as possible.

LEUCORRHOEA

Leucorrhoea is characterised by a vaginal discharge in between periods but not during ovulation. It is not debilitating, like PMT or dysmenorrhoea, but it is unpleasant nevertheless.

Possible causes
According to traditional Chinese medicine, leucorrhoea can be due to:
- Deficiency of *qi* and blood
- Damp heat

LEUCORRHOEA DUE TO DEFICIENCY OF *QI* AND BLOOD

Symptoms and signs
- Thin, white discharge
- Excessive fatigue

- Lethargy
- Weakness
- Dysmenorrhoea with symptoms caused by deficiency of *qi* and blood
- PMT symptoms caused by deficiency of spleen *yang* and kidney *yang*, and deficiency of blood and *yin*

Possible causes
- Weak constitution
- Overwork
- Anaemia
- Having too many children too close together, without resting and/or nourishing the body after childbirth
- Too much sex

Treatment
Leucorrhoea due to deficiency of *qi* and blood is best treated by an acupuncturist or an alternative therapist as soon as possible after detection.

LEUCORRHOEA DUE TO DAMP HEAT

Symptoms and signs
- Yellow, green or red discharge
- Offensive odour
- Dry mouth and thirst
- Hot feeling
- Dark yellow urine with an offensive odour
- Constipation with dry, hard stools

Possible causes
- Too many hot or warming energy foods and drinks
- Heated emotions, stress and tension
- Smoking
- Too many late nights

To re-adjust the imbalances

1 Go on a Chang Ming Diet
Eat mainly neutral and cooling energy foods and use neutral and cooling methods of cooking.

> *Avoid the following foods:*
> Sugar
> Dairy products
> Red meats
> Animal fats
> Foods that are deep-fried, baked, roasted, grilled, smoked or barbecued
> Warming or hot energy foods like chillies, curries, spices, durian, mango, etc.
> Vinegar
> Alcohol
> Coffee and other hot energy drinks, and warming herbal teas and tonics

Eat the following foods to eliminate damp heat from the body:

Job's tears – Add a few grains to pot barley to make pot barley water, or cook with brown rice daily until the condition clears

Pot barley – Drink pot barley water daily to cleanse the system

Millet – Cook with brown rice instead of Job's tears

Miso – Use in soup or as a sauce

Sauerkraut – This sour, fermented product contains the right bacterial enzymes to eliminate damp heat in the gut; use in salads

Watercress – Eat raw or use to make a clear soup to purify the blood

Tender nettle leaves – Like watercress, they purify the system

Thyme – Besides *miso*, this is one of the best natural antibiotics; use it often in your cooking

Garlic – Use raw or boiled, not stir-fried

Try these beverages:
- Chamomile tea
- Chrysanthemum tea
- Dandelion tea
- Nettle tea
- Peppermint tea
- Mineral water
- Pear juice
- Watermelon juice
- Coconut water from a young coconut

2 *Exercise daily*
Practise yoga, *taijiquan*, *qigong*, deep breathing, chanting or meditation daily to eliminate damp heat through sweating. These exercises also help you relax, making it easier to cope with emotional upset, tension and stress.

3 *Consult an acupuncturist*
If the discharge is heavy and accompanied by an offensive odour, consider undergoing a few acupuncture treatments.

THRUSH (*CANDIDA ALBICANS*)

Vaginal thrush is due to damp heat in the lower abdomen. *Candida albicans*, a yeast-like fungus, can only live and thrive in such an environment.

Symptoms and signs
- Thick discharges with offensive odour
- Intense itching

Possible causes
Damp heat in the vaginal area may be due to:
- Too many hot or warming energy foods especially if you have an overheated blood system
- Heated emotions, stress and tension
- Smoking
- Too many late nights
- Wearing nylon panties or briefs with tights
- Wearing tight jeans with or without nylon tights

Prevention
- Learn to relax.
- Stop smoking.
- Go to bed by 11 p.m.
- Wear 100 per cent cotton panties or briefs and change them daily. If you sweat a lot, change to a fresh pair at mid-day.
- Wear tights with a cotton gusset, tights with a gap in the crotch or use suspenders (garters) and stockings instead. Change once or twice daily.
- Wear loose 100 per cent cotton jeans.
- Wash and thoroughly dry the genital area after urination and defaecation

To re-adjust the imbalances
Go on a Chang Ming Diet. Eat mainly neutral and cooling energy foods and use neutral and cooling methods of cooking.

Follow the dietary advice given for leucorrhoea caused by damp heat.

In a severe attack
During a severe thrush attack, do one of the following once or twice daily:
1 Wash the genital area with some cold water mixed with a pinch of sea-salt. Sea-

salt is cooling, healing and it soothes itches.

2 Wash the area with cold chamomile and/or marigold (Calendula) tea to soothe and cool it.

3 Use rose water, another cooling agent. Or add a few drops of rose water to the cold chamomile tea.

4 Wash the area with a large bowl of cold water mixed with 1 drop of essential oil of lavender. It heals the skin and soothes hot, inflamed skin.

Note: Alternatively, mix 1 drop of oil of chamomile and 1 drop of oil of rose with a large bowl of cold water. Bathe the area once or twice daily until the condition clears, and once or twice a week for several months after, to prevent recurrence.

PROLAPSED UTERUS

Traditional Chinese medicine says this is a result of the spleen's failure to 'raise' the central organs. In layman terms, the spleen is supposed to ensure that the central organs, i.e., stomach, kidneys, intestines and uterus, are kept in their normal position within the body. If the spleen's function of 'raising' the central organs is disturbed then prolapse of any one of the organs may occur.

Possible causes
- A forceful forceps delivery during childbirth
- Having too many children too close together without resting or nourishing the body between pregnancies
- Doing hard manual labour (especially lifting heavy objects) immediately after meals

Symptoms and signs
- The feeling that something is dropping down
- Aches radiating from the lower back to the insides of the upper thighs
- Posture tilts forwards at the lower abdomen
- A tipping feeling when walking

Treatment
A prolapsed uterus must be examined first by a doctor to make sure there are no tumour growths. Next, consult an osteopath or chiropractor to rule out spinal problems. Then, see an acupuncturist to balance the spleen and improve its function of 'raising' the central organs.

HELP FOR WOMEN'S PROBLEMS

If you have any of the women's problems detailed in this chapter, I strongly advise that you seek a doctor's opinion first before embarking on any self-help methods. Then, see an alternative therapist to help bring your body back into balance.

Traditional Chinese physicians can also be helpful with cases of amenorrhoea, irregular periods, menorrhagia, abnormal uterine bleeding, pelvic inflammation, endometriosis, menopausal symptoms, infertility, morning sickness, difficult childbirth, mastitis and insufficient lactation after childbirth. Consult your doctor first before seeking help from alternative therapists.

33 Cancer

CAUSES OF CANCER

The word cancer is usually linked with despair and death. Some traditional Chinese physicians think cancer may be caused by weakness of *qi*, stagnation of *qi*, obstruction of blood; or phlegm. However, they are still developing their theories.

In my opinion, cancer may be due to any or many of the following factors:
1. Weak constitution
2. Virus
3. Radiation
4. Chemicals
5. Diet
6. Lifestyle
7. Emotions
8. Trauma

1 Weak constitution
If you were born with a weak constitution you are more susceptible to disease, and should adopt a Chang Ming Diet as well as take up yoga, *taijiquan* or *qigong* to maintain your health, and improve the flow of blood and *qi*. Try to lead a moderate lifestyle and avoid emotional upset.

2 Virus
Viruses are everywhere – in the air, water, and your body. Their presence is not known until your immune system fails to keep them at bay. The cancer virus can strike if you are weak, or suffering from weakness of *qi*.

3 Radiation
You do not have to work with radioactive substances in a scientific laboratory or an X-ray department, or live in an area near nuclear power stations to be exposed to radiation. We get bombarded by radiation when we watch TV, use computers, fluorescent lighting, sun-tanning lamps, microwave ovens, etc. These radiation levels are not dangerous but minute amounts of radiation received daily can accumulate and then it may be dangerous to us if we are weak and under stress.

It takes a tragic disaster like the Chernobyl incident in 1986 to make us aware of the dangers of radiation. Now that the outcry has died down, we tend to forget about it. You should be aware of radiation constantly and make an effort to avoid things that emit even small amounts of it.

In my opinion, radiation affects the *qi* within the body, and disturbs its relationship with the body, mind, spirit and the cosmos. This disturbance creates chaos within the body, disrupts the balance of *yin* and *yang*, and leaves the body prone to attack.

4 Chemicals
We ingest chemicals daily in the form of additives, hormones and antibiotics that have

been fed to animals, and insecticides, pesticides, fungicides, nitrates, etc. that have been sprayed on grains, vegetables and fruits. Make a point to eat organically grown foods as much as possible.

5 Diet

Diet may also cause cancer. If you eat mainly refined foods or junk foods you may develop cancer of the bowels. In my opinion, the following may also trigger the beginnings of cancer:

- Foods difficult to digest or forming mucus – dairy products, greasy and/or spicy foods, sugar, baked flour products, saturated fats, red meats, coconut products and citrus fruits
- Excessive intake of cold and cooling energy foods
- Excessive intake of hot and warming energy foods

According to traditional Chinese medicine, diets such as these create phlegm which can accumulate over the years to contribute to or cause cancer.

Follow a Chang Ming Diet based on wholesome natural foods selected for your particular blood system. Maintain a neutral blood system to keep a balance of *yin* and *yang* in the body.

Briefly, the Chang Ming Diet consists of:

- 50 per cent wholegrains
- 25 per cent fresh organically grown vegetables
- 15 per cent protein in the form of legumes, pulses, soyabean products, free-range eggs, fish or fresh, free-range chicken
- 5 per cent *miso*
- $2^1/_2$ per cent seeds and nuts
- $2^1/_2$ per cent fresh, organically grown fruits

Note: These are the proportions for cancer patients and anyone wishing to prevent cancer.

The percentages indicate that at least one meal – usually the main meal – should be made up of 50 per cent wholegrains, 25 per cent fresh organically grown vegetables, 15 per cent protein, 5 per cent *miso* and 5 per cent seeds, nuts or fruits.

For a balanced blood system
Follow the Chang Ming Diet outlined above.

For an overheated blood system
If you have such a system or tendencies towards one, eat more cooling and neutral energy foods.

For a cooled blood system
Eat more warming and neutral energy foods. Once you have achieved neutrality, maintain it as described above.

Use different cooking methods to make warming or cooling energy foods more neutral. Refer to the first chapters of the book for more details. Avoid the foods listed on pages 16 to 20.

A Chang Ming Diet helps harmonise *yin* and *yang* within the body, and keeps it healthy, full of vitality, and able to withstand attacks.

6 Lifestyle

Lifestyle has a lot to do with health. If you are overworked, under a lot of stress, or if you smoke, drink, sleep late, have excessive sex and no exercise, even a Chang Ming Diet will

not be able to keep your body in balance. These excesses tax the body to its limits, weakening it so it succumbs to all kinds of attacks, and making the healing process difficult. Lack of exercise prevents the smooth flow of *qi* and blood.

7 Emotions

Grief, depression, frustration, irritability, greed, obsession, etc. can cause an imbalance of *yin* and *yang* within the body. In traditional Chinese medicine, such emotions are due to stagnation of *qi*. Seek the advice of an alternative practitioner or a counsellor for your particular emotional upset, and take up yoga, *taijiquan* or *qigong* to prevent stagnation of *qi*.

8 Trauma

Traumatic accidents can cause obstruction of blood in the body. Traditional Chinese medicine explains that if blood is not allowed to flow smoothly, it and/or phlegm may slowly accumulate and trigger the beginnings of cancer.

Surgery can also cause obstruction of blood and *qi* in the body. In Chinese medical terms, obstruction of blood can imply bruising, which impedes the flow of blood, or scar tissue, which obstructs the flow of blood. A herbalist would prescribe comfrey to help heal the wound, and possibly other herbs specific to your condition. A homeopath might prescribe arnica and an acupuncturist would try to improve the circulation of *qi* and blood in that area to prevent obstruction.

COPING WITH CANCER

What about cancer patients? Do they have any hope of getting better? Here are three possible healing programmes, each of which is suited to people with varying degrees of the disease.

Method 1
- Surgery
- Radiotherapy
- Chemotherapy
- Reflexology
- Chang Ming Diet
- *Taijiquan, qigong*, yoga, *do-in*, chanting and meditation

Method 2
Same as Method 1, without the surgery

Method 3
- Bach Flower Remedies
- Aromatherapy
- Healing with crystals
- Self-reflection
- Creative visualisation
- Prayers
- Chanting
- Meditation
- Spiritual healing
- Chang Ming Diet
- *Taijiquan, qigong*, yoga or *do-in*
- Reflexology

COPING: METHOD 1

This method is the most passive. It is to be used if:
- the patient is too ill to think positively
- the physician thinks the cancer may spread if not removed
- the patient has fear of the cancer itself as negative thinking impedes healing
- the cancer has been detected early

In such cases, surgery is best. Although most people feel a great relief after the cancer has been removed they must still go through a course of radiotherapy and chemotherapy which thoroughly knock the body out of balance.

Reflexology is excellent after the operation, during radiotherapy and chemotherapy, and while you are in the hospital. Reflexology will restore harmony among the various organs, help you relax, and improve circulation to excrete toxins.

Do not rub the feet with talcum powder or oil before the massage, or you will clog the sweat pores. At first, the reflexology treatment should be very gentle and not last more than 10 to 15 minutes on each foot. Slowly increase the massage time to 30 minutes on each foot. Do reflexology daily to aid the body's natural healing process.

Go on a Chang Ming Diet

Once released from the hospital, you should try to go on a Chang Ming Diet. Because there are different types of cancer, and because we have different blood systems (that can be altered through radiotherapy and chemotherapy), you must be aware of your body and choose a Chang Ming Diet according to your blood system at that particular time. The best guide I can give is as follows:

50 per cent wholegrains

If you have a neutral blood system, eat brown rice and fresh sweet corn. For an overheated blood system, take pot barley and millet. Oat groats are appropriate for a cooled blood system.

Eat mostly brown rice to maintain a neutral blood system, add a few grains of the others (e.g. 25 per cent pot barley to 75 per cent brown rice for an overheated blood system, or 25 per cent oat groats to 75 per cent brown rice for a cooled blood system).

25 per cent fresh vegetables

If possible, eat organically and locally grown varieties.

If you have a neutral blood system, eat:
- 100 per cent neutral vegetables
- a mixture of 50 per cent cooling and 50 per cent warming vegetables
- a mixture of 33 per cent cooling, 33 per cent neutral and 33 per cent warming vegetables and herbs

If you have an overheated blood system, eat:
- 75 per cent cooling vegetables and 25 per cent neutral vegetables
- 50 per cent cooling vegetables and 50 per cent neutral vegetables (occasionally)
- 80 per cent cooling vegetables and 20 per cent warming vegetables or herbs

If you have a cooled blood system, eat:
- 75 per cent warming vegetables, herbs and spices and 25 per cent neutral vegetables
- 50 per cent warming vegetables, herbs and spices and 50 per cent neutral vegetables (occasionally)
- 80 per cent warming vegetables, herbs and spices and 20 per cent cooling vegetables

15 per cent protein

This consists of:
- Legumes
- Pulses
- Soyabean products
- Free-range eggs (no more than 2 or 3 eggs per week)

- Fish (mainly white fish; eat as often as you like)
- Fresh, free-range chicken (eat no more than twice a week, and cook without skin or fat)

For an overheated blood system, choose these proteins:

    Legumes and pulses
    Black-eyed beans
    Black soyabeans
    Marrowfat peas
    Broad beans
    Butter beans
    Haricot beans
    Red kidney beans
    Chick-peas
    Lentils
Boil them, then mix with other lightly steamed or blanched vegetables to make a hot salad.

    Soyabean products
    Tofu (hard and silken)
    Fu zhou
    Tempeh
    Fermented black soyabeans
Steam, braise or stir-fry with other vegetables.

    Free-range eggs
Steam with a little water and finely minced Webb's or Cos lettuce and spring onion. Or, scramble with a drop of water, finely minced watercress, parsley, spring onion or mushrooms.

    Fish
Steam, poach or boil white fish with parsley, rosemary, fennel leaves, dill leaves or lemon juice to negate the fishy odour.

    Fresh free-range chicken
Serve steamed chicken with plenty of vegetables. Lightly poach it with tarragon, or boil with seaweeds (*kombu, wakame, arame* or *hiziki*) and root vegetables (like onions and carrots).

For a cooled blood system, choose these proteins:

    Legumes and pulses
    Black-eyed beans
    Black soyabeans
    Marrowfat peas
    Lentils
    Aduki beans
    Chick-peas
    Broad beans
    Butter beans
    Haricot beans
    Red kidney beans
Boil with garlic, ginger and other warming vegetables, herbs and spices, like onions, leeks, carrots, basil, caraway seeds, fennel seeds, cumin seeds, etc.

    Soyabean products
    Tofu (hard only)
    Fu zhou
    Tempeh
    Fermented black soyabeans
Stir-fry with garlic and ginger and other neutral and warming vegetables, herbs and spices.

    Free-range eggs
Scramble with a drop of water, finely minced ginger and any of the following vegetables and herbs: onions, leeks, spring onions, parsley or thyme.

    Fish
Steam, poach, boil, bake, casserole or grill with minced ginger and garlic, or bay leaf, rosemary,

fennel seeds and leaves, coriander seeds and leaves, and cumin seeds.

Fresh free-range chicken
Braise, stew, stir-fry, grill or roast, and serve with plenty of vegetables.

5 per cent miso soup

Have one small bowl of *miso* soup a day with or without seaweeds. Why?

1 The drugs used in chemotherapy are cytotoxic (toxic to cells). They are not selective only in their destruction – they kill all fast growing cells including those that line the digestive tract. Hence, patients undergoing chemotherapy have no appetite and cannot digest their food properly. *Miso* is easily digested.

2 The drugs may also upset the intestinal flora, causing constipation. *Miso*, which contains beneficial enzymes and bacteria, can repopulate or bring back a happy balance of intestinal flora to prevent or correct constipation.

3 According to macrobiotic teachers, *miso* can prevent radioactive damage by removing heavy metals from the body.

For a neutral blood system:
Make *miso* soup with *genmai* or *mugi miso* and ingredients such as
    Onion, carrot and thyme
    Leek, carrot and parsley
    White cabbage, carrot and oregano
    Brown rice, onion, carrot and spring onion
    Brown rice, leek and rosemary
    Brown rice, black-eyed beans, onion, carrot and parsley
    Fish, leek, ginger and parsley

For an overheated blood system:
Use *mugi miso* with ingredients such as
    Watercress and onion
    Spinach and onion
    Kombu, onion, carrot and parsley
    Chinese radish, carrot and spring onion
    Spinach, onion and *tofu*
    Watercress, carrot and *tofu*
    Fish, *arame*, carrot and coriander leaves

For a cooled blood system:
Use *genmai miso* with the following ingredients.
    Onion, carrot and coriander leaves
    Black-eyed beans, leek, carrot and parsley
    Brown rice, onion, carrot and coriander leaves
    Fu zhou, Shiitake mushroom, onion, carrot, cinnamon and spring onion
    Fu zhou, leek, carrot and star anise
    Fish, leek, carrot and fennel leaves
    Fish, onion, carrot and bay leaf

5 per cent seeds and nuts or fresh, organically and locally grown fruit

People with neutral blood systems should have $2^1/_2$ per cent seeds and nuts (which are warming) and $2^1/_2$ per cent fresh fruits (which are cooling). People with overheated blood systems should avoid seeds and nuts for the most part. Once or twice a week they can have sesame seeds or sunflower seeds boiled with brown rice. People with cooled blood systems must avoid all fruits.

Note: Cancer patients should avoid seed or nut butter and *tahini*. The oil often separates from the nuts, making them very difficult to digest. It is advisable to eat whole seeds and nuts; they are less greasy and contain more vital energies.

Menu ideas

Here are some menu ideas for different blood systems.

For a neutral blood system
- 50 per cent brown rice boiled with sesame seeds
- 25 per cent stir-fried ginger, kale and oregano
- 15 per cent protein, or any one of the following
    1. Stewed black-eyed beans, onion, carrot and parsley
    2. Free-range egg steamed with minced spring onion and parsley
    3. White fish marinated in minced garlic and *tamari*, and steamed with a thin slice of ginger, spring onions and parsley
    4. Fresh, free-range chicken steamed with minced garlic and thyme, and served with a dash of *tamari*
- 5 per cent leek and *genmai miso* soup
- 2¹/₂ per cent fruit – an apple or any other neutral energy fruit should be taken one hour after finishing the above meal, so as not to upset the digestion of the complex carbohydrates, protein and polyunsaturated fatty acids
- 2¹/₂ per cent seeds and nuts

For an overheated blood system
- 50 per cent brown rice boiled with pot barley (75 per cent brown rice and 25 per cent pot barley)
- 25 per cent lightly steamed or blanched or raw vegetables such as
    1. Carrot, white cabbage, watercress and spring onion
    2. Celery, carrot, chives and parsley
    3. Beetroot and spring onion
    4. White cabbage, spring onion, carrot and alfalfa sprouts
    5. Carrot, mung bean sprouts and spring onion
- 15 per cent protein, or any one of the following
    1. Chick-peas boiled with sunflower seeds, and served with a dash of lemon juice and parsley
    2. Free-range egg steamed with minced mung bean sprouts and spring onion
    3. White fish steamed with lemon slices and parsley
    4. Fresh free-range chicken steamed with garlic and tarragon
- 5 per cent *mugi miso* soup made with *arame*, spinach and garlic
- 5 per cent fresh, organically grown fruits, to be taken one hour after the meal

For a cooled blood system
- 50 per cent brown rice
- 25 per cent green vegetables (e.g. kale, cabbage, Brussels sprouts or Chinese flowering cabbage, steamed with garlic and ginger)
- 15 per cent protein, or any of the following
    1. Lentils boiled with garlic, ginger, cumin seeds and onions
    2. Free-range egg scrambled with onion and ginger
    3. White fish marinated in ginger juice and *tamari*, then grilled with fresh herbs like coriander leaves or fennel leaves
    4. Fresh, free-range chicken stir-fried with garlic, ginger, Shiitake mushrooms and carrots, with a dash of *tamari*.
- 5 per cent *genmai miso* soup made with leek and ginger

- 5 per cent lightly dry-roasted sesame seeds, sprinkled over the cooked brown rice before serving

Meals for the nauseous

If you find these meals too heavy or if you feel nauseated during your radiotherapy or chemotherapy treatments, drink *miso* soup instead. If you have difficulty chewing or swallowing, just liquidise the solid contents of the soup. Make sure each bowl contains complex carbohydrates, protein, polyunsaturated fatty acids, vitamins and minerals. Here are some examples for the different blood systems:

For a neutral blood system

- Brown rice, black-eyed beans, leek, carrot, parsley and *genmai miso*
- Brown rice, one free-range egg, ginger, leek, parsley and *genmai miso*
- Brown rice, white fish, ginger, spring onion and *genmai miso*

For an overheated blood system

- Brown rice, marrowfat peas, celery and *mugi miso*
- Brown rice, *kombu*, black-eyed beans, onion, carrot, parsley and *mugi miso*
- Brown rice, white fish, celery and *mugi miso*

For a cooled blood system

- Brown rice, lentils, garlic, ginger, caraway seeds, thyme, onion, carrot and *genmai miso*
- Brown rice, one free-range egg, leek, ginger, parsley and *genmai miso*
- Brown rice, white fish, garlic, ginger, fennel leaves or bulb and *genmai miso*

If you are a small eater and find the main meal too heavy, have only the brown rice, vegetables and protein. The *miso* soup can be eaten as a light meal if it consists of complex carbohydrates, protein, polyunsaturated fatty acids, vitamins and minerals. Your body needs all these nutrients to repair the damage done by radiotherapy and chemotherapy.

> *Note:* According to macrobiotic theory, all cooking must be done by charcoal, coal, wood or gas fires. Electricity or microwaves must be avoided.

Determining your type

Throughout the course of your radiotherapy and chemotherapy treatment, your blood system may swing from overheated to cooled. Radiotherapy and drugs can create heat in the body. Other drugs can cool the body down. You must determine the nature of your blood system and then eat the appropriate foods and use the appropriate cooking methods.

If you cannot determine the nature of your blood system, use mainly neutral energy foods and methods of cooking and balance cooling foods with warming foods to achieve neutrality. Eat a wide variety of foods to obtain different vitamins and minerals.

Exercise

Once you feel better, exercise is the best form of therapy. It improves the circulation of blood and *qi* and aids the healing process. Exercise seems to help patients who have had radiotherapy and chemotherapy feel less nauseated and depressed. Perhaps exercise releases endorphins in the brain, bringing about a feeling of well being. Or maybe the 30 minutes of moving and concentrating on

coordination helps patients forget their depression.

In China, cancer patients who do *qigong* often fare much better than those who do not. From personal observation of a close relative, I feel *taijiquan* can help as well. Exercise improves vitality, blood and *qi* flow, harmonises the body, provides relaxation, and enables healing to take place. Yoga and *do-in* can also help, and they are easier to perform. Yoga teachers are more readily available than *qigong* or *taijiquan* masters. Classes in *do-in*, or self-massage, are offered by macrobiotic centres all over the world.

Cancer patients should also include gentle walking in their exercise programme.

Other therapy
Chanting and meditation may also prove helpful. (See Chapter 16.) Most importantly, however, you must keep active and try to forget cancer and its consequences and live life to its fullest. Do things that bring happiness, like singing, playing musical instruments, gardening, sailing, swimming, playing with your children or grandchildren, dancing, going to the theatre, visiting museums, etc. Try to do things that make you laugh. It has been scientifically proven that laughter and a positive attitude can help cancer patients.

> *Note:* Please get in touch with a cancer centre which practises alternative therapies to give you moral support and help in your fight to overcome cancer.

COPING: METHOD 2

In some cases where the cancer has spread and surgery is impossible or of little use, radiotherapy and chemotherapy may be the only alternatives. If such is the case, combine the treatments with alternative therapy to aid the healing process. Follow all the suggestions given for Method 1.

COPING: METHOD 3

When method 3 applies
This method – the most active – is appropriate if:
- the patient does not wish to have orthodox treatment
- the fear of surgery, doctors and hospitals is far greater than the cancer and its consequences, and the patient is prepared to fight it alone
- the patient thinks the cancer can be overcome by changing his emotional outlook, diet and lifestyle.

When method 3 fails
This method is not suitable for the weak-willed. It requires a will of iron, and love, compassion and support from the whole family, who must be as strong-minded as the patient and convinced that his or her decision is best.

> *Note:* If you do not have supportive friends or family I would strongly advise against using this method.

Go on a Chang Ming Diet
The Chang Ming Diet is essential if you choose to overcome cancer through self-help. If possible, buy organically grown foods, and select foods suitable to your blood system. If you have difficulty determining the nature of

your blood system, then eat mainly neutral energy foods and always balance cooling energy foods with warming energy ones. Eat a wide variety of food and use different styles of cooking to prevent monotony. Use suitable herbs and spices to activate the salivary glands to aid chewing and digestion. Some people say it is better to avoid using electricity or a microwave oven for cooking. Use glass, enamel, stainless steel or cast-iron pots and pans instead of aluminium.

Scientific evidence has shown that members of the onion and cabbage families, and Shiitake mushrooms, can prevent and help overcome cancer. Macrobiotic teachers say Shiitake mushrooms, *miso* and Job's tears help overcome cancer. Traditional Chinese medicine says garlic is good for preventing and overcoming cancer.

Shiitake mushrooms should be eaten in moderation (once or twice a week, 3 to 4 mushrooms per sitting). Excessive intake may cause arthritis and rheumatism.

Job's tears have cooling energies so they should only be taken by those with overheated blood systems. Boil them with brown rice in the proportion of one table-spoon raw Job's tears to one-third cup raw brown rice.

Exercise

Exercises like *taijiquan* and *qigong* are equally important if you aim to heal yourself with this method. The Chang Ming Diet gives you the necessary complex carbohydrates, proteins, polyunsaturated fatty acids, vitamins and minerals for building up the immune system. *Taijiquan* and *qigong* help improve the flow of *qi* and blood to prevent weakness of *qi*, stagnation of *qi*, obstruction of blood and

phlegm. Some of the best *qigong* masters in China used to be cancer patients. If you cannot find a *taijiquan* or *qigong* master, try yoga, *do-in* or chanting.

Participate in lots of enjoyable activities to help you forget the disease. Live each day to its fullest.

Alternative therapy

It is of the utmost importance that patients adopting this third method of overcoming cancer seek the advice of alternative practitioners who prescribe Bach Flower Remedies (see page 226). It is also good for such patients to get in touch with a cancer healing centre where alternative therapies are practised. Some of these are spiritual healing, crystal healing, creative visualisation, meditation, aromatherapy, reflexology, Bach Flower Remedies and dietary change.

ALTERNATIVE THERAPIES

Bach Flower Remedies

Why are the Bach Flower Remedies so important in this programme of coping with cancer? For the simple reason that they most ably help with emotional problems, and negative emotions do not help the healing process.

We cannot discuss the benefits of the Bach Flower Remedies in detail in a book such as this, but there are two good books on the subject mentioned in Further Reading. Bach Flower Remedies are available in some health food stores and by mail order (See Useful Addresses). A course of treatment may be as follows, but I must emphasise that an open mind is vital to positive result.

Rescue Remedy

This will be the first prescribed because anyone, no matter how strong-willed, tough or prepared, will be bound to be in a state of shock if told he or she has cancer.

Give 4 drops of Rescue Remedy directly on the tongue 6 times a day initially, until you feel that person can cope with the shock or has accepted the fact of cancer, and is ready to fight it. Then slowly decrease the frequency from 6 times daily to 4, to 3, to 2, to once and finally none at all.

When the shock is over, other negative thoughts may arise, so here are some remedies which may be appropriate.

Gentian

For despondency and convalescence

Gorse

For pessimism, chronic depression and despair

Mimulus

For fear of known things, e.g. cancer

Oak

For loss of will to struggle on against illness or adversity

Olive

For exhaustion of mind and energy from overwork or illness, and for convalescence

Rock rose

For sudden illness

Star of Bethlehem

For shock brought on by bad news, or delayed shock

Sweet chestnut

For feelings of hopelessness

White chestnut

For the recurrence of unwanted thoughts

Wild rose

For resignation, loss of will to fight

Note: These are just some examples. There are altogether 38 Bach Flower Remedies.

How to use the Remedies

Five Remedies can be combined at one time. Therefore, if you are already taking Rescue Remedy it is better you do not take any other: Rescue Remedy contains a combination of five (Cherry plum, Clematis, Impatiens, Rock rose and Star of Bethlehem).

Rescue Remedy is the only one you can use directly on the tongue. The other remedies are best diluted in a glass of mineral water. You will need 2 drops for each Remedy. If you require only one Remedy, add 2 drops in a glass of mineral water; if three Remedies are required, you will need a total of 6 drops in the glass of mineral water. You have to take this 4 to 6 times a day until the negative emotions have disappeared, decreasing frequency as this happens.

Aromatherapy

When someone is ill, be it a common ailment or cancer, the smell of something nice always lifts the spirits. So scented flowers like rose, jasmine, freesia, lavender, hyacinth, etc. are important in sickrooms.

The smell of oil of lavender is excellent in relieving stress and tension and if you have a bath to which 4 drops of oil of lavender have

been added just before you step in, it will boost your immune system. Have such a bath 2 to 3 times a week.

In some countries people go to an aromatherapist to have 1 to $1^1/_2$ hours of the most aromatic and uplifting massage in order to remove all their cares and help them heal faster.

Reflexology

It is best you go to a reflexologist once or twice a week for a thorough reflexology session. In this way, you will be able to relax completely, as well as receive healing through the hands of the therapist. In between sessions you can use a wooden foot roller to maintain good health. (See Chapter 16, page 225.)

Creative visualisation

Many cancer patients have found this method of great benefit in helping their cancerous growths decrease in size or just in coping with the disease itself. The patient is taught at Cancer Healing Centres to imagine their immune system 'eating away' their cancer cells or growths.

Crystal healing

This is a very ancient art believed to have been practised by the people of legendary Atlantis centuries ago. Crystals containing powerful electromagnetic energies were used to heal people in a manner similar to acupuncture needles. Details are available at Cancer Healing Centres in some countries.

Spiritual healing

This is available at Cancer Healing Centres. A healer will place his hands over your aura to give you healing energies so that you have greater ability to heal yourself.

Meditation

This is the best, besides *qigong* and *taijiquan*, because in meditation, the body relaxes completely, to allow healing to occur.

APPENDIX A CLASSIFICATION OF FOODS

Whole Cereal Grains

Cooling	Neutral	Warming
Buckwheat	Brown rice	Oat groats
Millet	Red rice	
Pot barley	Rye	
Whole wheat grains	Sweet corn	

Legumes and Pulses

Cooling	Neutral	Warming
Fermented black soyabeans	Aduki beans	Lentils
	Black-eyed beans	
Fermented soyabean cheese (without chillies)	Black soyabeans	
	Broad beans	
	Chick-peas	
Fermented soyabean cheese (red)	Dried bean curd	
	Dried soyabean sheets (fu zhou)	
Miso	Fermented soyabean cheese (with chillies)	
Mung beans		
Shoyu		
Soyabeans	Haricot beans	
Tamari	Hyacinth beans	
Tempeh	Peas	
Tofu	Red kidney beans	

Seeds and Nuts

Cooling	Neutral	Warming
Bitter apricot kernels	Almonds	Chestnuts
Ginkgo nuts	Lotus seeds	Pumpkin seeds
	Peanuts	Sesame seeds (beige and black)
	Pine nuts	Sunflower seeds
	Sweet apricot kernels	Walnuts
		Watermelon seeds

Vegetables

Cooling	Neutral	Warming
Alfalfa sprouts	Beetroot	Carrot
Angled luffa	Broad beans	Chinese chives
Arrowhead tubers	Broccoli	Leek
Asparagus	Brussels sprouts	Onion
Beetroot greens	Cabbage (white, green	Shallot
Bitter gourd	and Savoy cabbage,	Spring onion
Celery	winter and spring	
Chicory	greens and kale)	
Chinese box thorn	Cauliflower	
leaves	Celeriac	
Chinese Peking cabbage	Chinese flowering	
Chinese radish	cabbage	
Chinese spinach	Chinese kale	
Chinese white cabbage	Fennel	
Courgette	Four-angled beans	
Cress	French beans	
Cucumber	Garland chrysanthemum	
Dandelion leaves	Lamb's lettuce	
Endive	Landcress	
Fuzzy melon	Long beans	
Kohlrabi	Parsnip	
Lettuce	Pea shoots	
Lotus root	Pumpkin	
Marrow	Runner beans	
Mung bean sprouts	Snow peas	
Mushrooms	Squash	
Nettles	Swede	
Radicchio rosso	Sweet corn	
Radish	Sweet potato	
Red cabbage	Sweet potato leaves	
Slippery vegetable	Taro	
Soyabean sprouts	Turnip	
Spinach	Yam	
Swatow mustard cabbage		
Swiss chard		
Water chestnut		
Watercress		
Water spinach		
Winter melon		
Yam bean		
Yellow cucumber		

Herbs and Spices

Cooling	Neutral	Warming
Aloe vera	Elderberry	Basil
Borage	Liquorice	Bay leaves
Burdock	Parsley	Caraway seeds
Chamomile	Raspberry	Cardamom
Chickweed	Rosemary	Chives
Chrysanthemum	Sage	Cinnamon
Comfrey	Screwpine leaves	Cloves
Corn silk	Thyme	Coriander leaves
Dandelion		and seeds
Lemon balm		Cumin
Mint, cornmint and		Dill leaves and
peppermint		seeds
Purple sage		Fennel leaves and
Slippery elm		seeds
Tamarind		Fenugreek
Tarragon		Garlic
Turmeric		Ginger
Vervain		Lemongrass
		Mugwort
		Mustard
		Nutmeg
		Oregano
		Pepper
		Savory (summer and
		winter)
		Sichuan pepper
		Spearmint
		Star anise

Dried Ingredients

Cooling	Neutral	Warming
Buddha's fruit	Black wood ear	Chinese black date
Chinese box thorn	Dried abalone	Chinese red date
berries	Dried oyster	Dang gui
Figs	Dried scallop	Dang shen
Golden needles	Dried shrimp	Ginseng
Job's tears	Dried squid	Huang shi
Persimmon	Raisin	Longan (dried)
Snow ear fungus	Shiitake mushroom	Silver fish (dried)
	(dried)	Tangerine peel

Eggs

Cooling	Neutral	Warming
Duck egg		Chicken egg
Fish egg		Quail egg
Preserved duck egg		
Preserved quail egg		
Salted duck egg		

Flesh Foods

Cooling	Neutral	Warming
Abalone (fresh)	Smoked fish*	Beef*
Clam		Black-boned
Cockle		chicken
Crab		Chicken
Duck		Goose
Fish#		Lamb*
Jellyfish		Mutton*
Lobster		Pigeon
Mussel		Pork*
Octopus		Rabbit
Oyster (fresh)		Turkey
Periwinkle		Veal*
Prawn		
Scallop (fresh)		
Shrimp		
Squid		
Whelk		

Although all fish have cooling energies, among that group some fish are more cooling, some neutral and some more warming. See Chapter 10, Fish and Other Seafoods.

* These foods are not recommended.

Fruits

Cooling	Neutral	Warming
Banana	Apple	Apricot
Ciku	Date	Blackberry
Coconut	Fig	Blackcurrant
Custard apple	Grape	Cherry
Grapefruit	Guava	Durian
Jackfruit	Papaya	Longan
Lemon	Plum	Lychee
Malay apple	Raspberry	Mango
Mandarin		*Mata kucing*
Mangosteen		Rambutan
Orange		Strawberry
Pear		
Persimmon		
Pineapple		
Pomelo		
Rose apple		
Sea apple		
Star fruit (Carambola)		
Water apple		
Watermelon		

Dairy Products

Cooling	Neutral	Warming
Buttermilk*	Cottage cheese*	Butter*
Curd cheese*	Milk*	Cheese (hard)*
Ice-cream*	Soft cheese*	Cream*
Kefir*		Cream cheese*
Quark*		Ghee*
Sourmilk*		Powdered milk*
Whey cheese*		
Yogurt*		

* All these are not recommended.

Beverages

Cooling	Neutral	Warming
Naturally fizzy mineral water	Still mineral water	Warmed up still mineral water
Tea*	Tap water	Boiled water
Honey water	Barley malt drink	Alcohol*
Pot barley water	Rice malt drink	Cocoa*
Soyabean milk	Almond milk	Coffee*
Borage tea	Peanut milk	Drinking chocolate*
Burdock tea	Japanese tea	Horlicks*
Chamomile tea	Parsley tea	Milo*
Chrysanthemum tea	Raspberry tea	Ovaltine*
Comfrey tea	Rosemary tea	Sunflower seed milk
Corn silk tea	Sage tea	Walnut milk
Dandelion tea	Thyme tea	Caraway seed tea
Lemon balm tea	Apple juice	Cinnamon tea
Mint, cornmint, peppermint tea	Grape juice (white or red)	Fennel seed tea
Vervain tea	Guava juice	Fenugreek tea
Clementine juice	Papaya juice	Ginger tea
Coconut water	Plum juice	Mu tea
Grapefruit juice	Raspberry juice	Mugwort
Lemon juice	Redcurrant juice	Spearmint tea
Lime juice	Sugar cane juice (from deep red-purple skin varieties	Apricot juice
Pear juice		Blackberry juice
Pineapple juice		Blackcurrant juice
Mandarin juice		Cherry juice
Melon juice		Lychee juice
Orange juice		Longan juice
Star fruit, carambola juice		Nectarinr juice
Sugar cane juice (from pale yellow-green skin varieties)		Strawberry juice
Tangerine juice		
Watermelon juice		

* These are not recommended.

APPENDIX B   CHARTS FOR FEET REFLEXOLOGY

Right Foot (Bottom)

Left Foot (Bottom)

Sinus area — Brain — Sinus area

Side Neck

Atlas/Axis

Pituitary

7th Cervical

Eyes

Throat/Neck/
Thyroid

Eyes

Ears

Lungs/Breasts

Ears

Shoulder

Thymus

Shoulder

Arm

Relative to
thyroid
bronchial
area

Heart

Arm

Solar plexus

Solar plexus

Oesophagus

Liver

Stomach

Gall bladder

Diaphragm

Spleen

Adrenals

Waistline

Pancreas

Waistline

Transverse colon

Kidneys

Transverse colon

Ascending colon

Small intestines

Descending colon

Ileocecal valve
and appendix

Ureter tubes

Bladder

Coccyx
Sacrum

Sigmoid colon

Sciatic

Sciatic

 Spinal column

Right Inside Foot

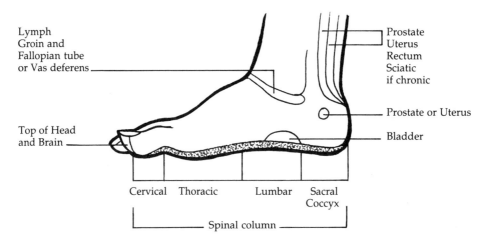

Lymph
Groin and
Fallopian tube
or Vas deferens

Prostate
Uterus
Rectum
Sciatic
if chronic

Prostate or Uterus

Top of Head
and Brain

Bladder

Cervical   Thoracic   Lumbar   Sacral
Coccyx

Spinal column

Top Right Foot

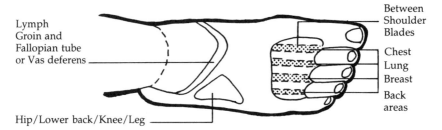

Lymph
Groin and
Fallopian tube
or Vas deferens

Between
Shoulder
Blades

Chest
Lung
Breast

Back
areas

Hip/Lower back/Knee/Leg

Right Outside Foot

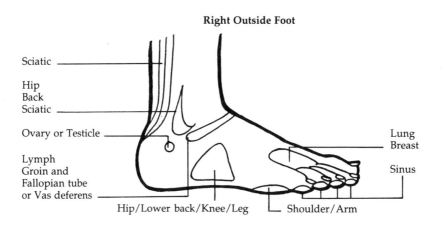

Sciatic

Hip
Back
Sciatic

Ovary or Testicle

Lymph
Groin and
Fallopian tube
or Vas deferens

Lung
Breast

Sinus

Hip/Lower back/Knee/Leg

Shoulder/Arm

Note: All reflex areas must be worked bilaterally, i.e. on both feet.

These diagrams illustrate how to give both feet a general massage from toes to heels before massaging specific reflex areas for specific problems.

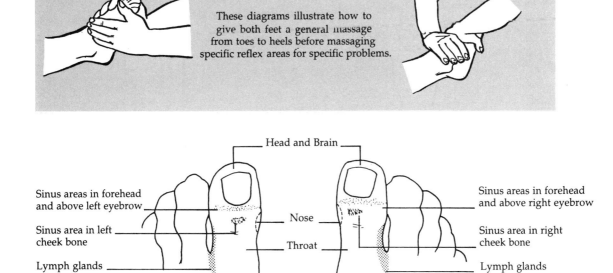

Head and Brain

Sinus areas in forehead and above left eyebrow

Sinus area in left cheek bone

Lymph glands

Nose

Throat

Sinus areas in forehead and above right eyebrow

Sinus area in right cheek bone

Lymph glands

Head and Brain

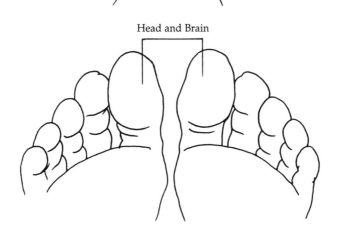

Details of the Big Toe

APPENDIX C ACUPUNCTURE POINTS FOR ACUPRESSURE, MOXIBUSTION AND AROMATHERAPY

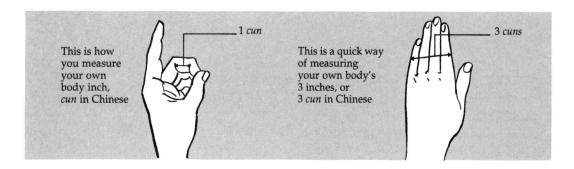

1 *cun*

This is how you measure your own body inch, *cun* in Chinese

This is a quick way of measuring your own body's 3 inches, or 3 *cun* in Chinese

3 *cuns*

FIG 1

Large Intestine 4 (*Hegu*)

Large Intestine 4 (*Hegu*)
See page 229 on how to locate this point.

FIG 2

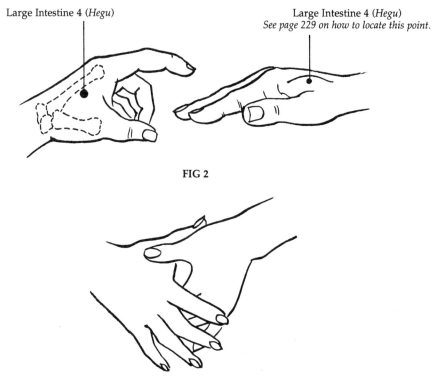

Acupressure on Large Intestine 4 (*Hegu*) on right hand.
Do the same for left hand.

FIG 3

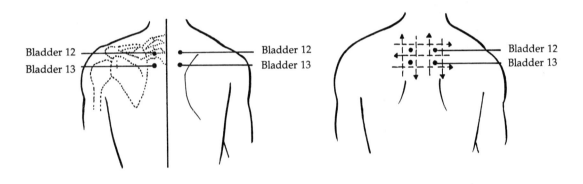

Bladder 12 ——
Bladder 13 ——

—— Bladder 12
—— Bladder 13

Back View

FIG 5

Bladder 12 ——
Bladder 13 ——

—— Bladder 12
—— Bladder 13

Back View
Moxibustion points for wind cold (see Chapter 18)

FIG 4

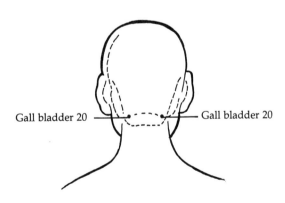

Gall bladder 20 ——

—— Gall bladder 20

Back View

FIG 6

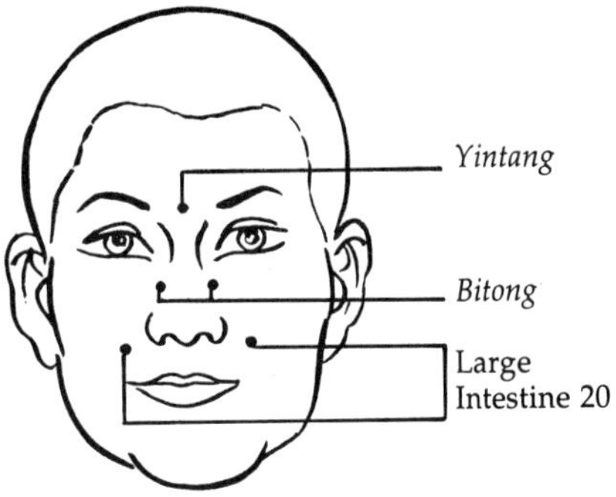

Yintang

Bitong

Large
Intestine 20

FIG 7

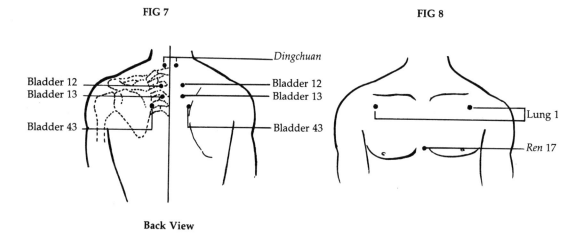

Dingchuan

Bladder 12
Bladder 13

Bladder 43

Bladder 12
Bladder 13

Bladder 43

Back View

FIG 8

Lung 1

Ren 17

FIG 9

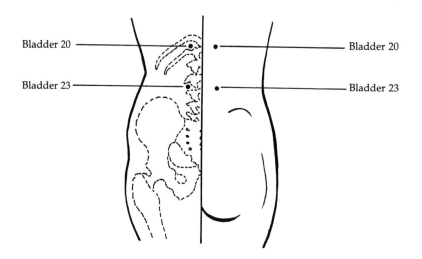

Bladder 20

Bladder 23

Bladder 20

Bladder 23

Back View

FIG 10

FIG 11

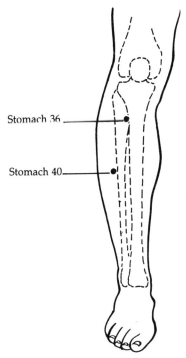

Stomach 36

Stomach 40

Right Leg
Find points Stomach 36 and
Stomach 40 on left leg too.

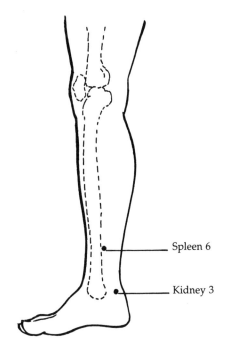

Spleen 6

Kidney 3

Right Leg
Find points Spleen 6 and
Kidney 3 on left leg too.

FIG 12

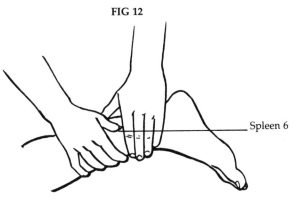

Spleen 6

How to locate Spleen 6
It is 3 *cun* directly above the tip of the medial
malleolus. Do the same for the other leg.

FIG 13

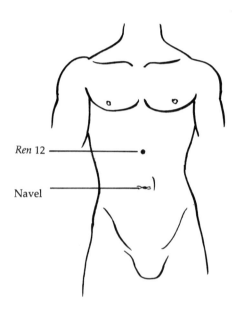

Ren 12

Navel

Ren 12 (*Zhongwan*) is located halfway between the Xiphoid process and the navel.

FIG 14

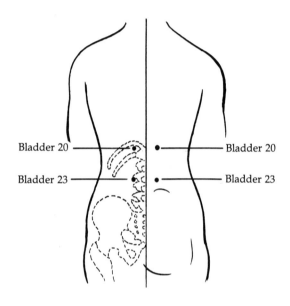

Bladder 20 — — Bladder 20

Bladder 23 — — Bladder 23

Back View

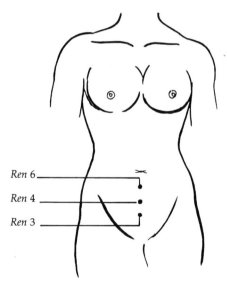

Ren 6

Ren 4

Ren 3

FIG 15

FIG 16   **FIG 17**

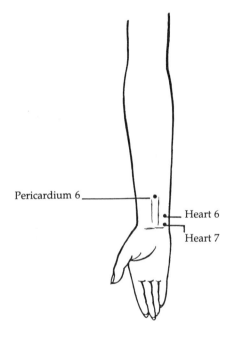

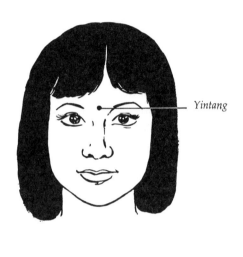

Pericardium 6

Heart 6

Heart 7

Yintang

Right Arm
Find points Pericardium 6, Heart 6 and
Heart 7 on left arm too.

BIBLIOGRAPHY

Belleme, John, 'Shiitake–The Healing Mushroom', *East West Journal*, Dec 1981, Vol. II, No. 12, East West Journal, Inc, Massachusetts, USA.

Brown, Sarah, *Sarah Brown's Vegetarian Cookbook*, Dorling Kindersley Ltd, London, UK.

Byers, Dwight C., *Better Health with Foot Reflexology, The Original Ingham Method, Including Hand Reflexology*, Ingham Publishing, Inc, Florida, USA.

Chaitow, Leon, 'Picture of Health, Fishing for Health, Exercise Against Cancer', *Here's Health*, Aug 1986, Vol. 31, No. 359, Argus Health Publications Ltd, Surrey, UK.

____, 'Picture of Health, Storm in a Coffee Cup', *Here's Health*, June 1986, Vol. 31, No. 357, Argus Health Publications Ltd, Surrey, UK.

Chin, H.F. and Yong, H.S., *Malaysian Fruits in Colour*, Tropical Press Sdn Bhd, Kuala Lumpur, Malaysia.

Deadman, Peter, 'Asthma', *The Journal of Chinese Medicine*, No. 10, May 1982, Sussex, UK.

Derient, Dr W., 'Androgen-Hormonal Curative Influence of a Neglected Plant', *Wonderful Herbal Remedies*, W.D. Walters, MPS Celtic Educational (Services) Ltd, Swansea, UK.

Family Medical Encyclopaedia, An Illustrated Guide, Hamlyn, London.

Flows, Bob and Wolfe, Honora, *Prince Wen Hui's Cook Chinese Dietary Therapy*, Paradigm Publications, Massachusetts, USA.

Harrison, S.G., Masefield, G.B. and Wallis, Michael, *The Oxford Book of Food Plants*, Oxford University Press, Oxford, UK.

Heywood, V.H. (Consultant Editor), *Flowering Plants of the World*, Oxford University Press, Oxford, UK.

Hoffman, David, *The Holistic Herbal, A Herbal Celebrating the Wholeness of Life*, The Findhorn Press, Scotland, UK.

Hyatt, Richard and Feldman, Robert, *Chinese Herbal Medicine, Ancient Art and Modern Science with Therapeutic Repertory*, Wildwood House Ltd, London, UK.

Hyne-Jones, T.W., *Dictionary of the Bach Flower Remedies*, C.W. Daniel Co. Ltd, Essex, UK.

Jeans, Helen, *Grains, Nuts and Seeds, Concentrated Sources of Natural Nutrition*, Thorsons Publishers Ltd, Northamptonshire, UK.

Kaptchuk, Ted J., *The Web that has no Weaver, Understanding Chinese Medicine*, Congdon & Weed, Inc, New York, USA.

Keys, John D., *Chinese Herbs, Their Botany, Chemistry and Pharmaco-dynamics*, Charles E. Tuttle Company, Tokyo, Japan.

Kao, Linda Chih-ling, *Nourishment of Life, Health in Chinese Society*, The Commercial Press, Hong Kong.

Leung, Albert Y., *Chinese Herbal Remedies*, Wildwood House Ltd, Hounslow, UK.

'Diabetes – Trying to live naturally', *Here's Health*, Oct 1983, Vol. 28, No. 325, Newman Turner Publications Ltd, Surrey, UK.

Lucus, Richard, *Secrets of the Chinese Herbalists*, Thorsons Publishers Ltd, Northamptonshire, UK.

Marshall, Janette, 'High IQ Food – Can the food you eat really improve your thinking power?' *Here's Health*, Mar 1985, Vol. 30, No. 342, Newman Turner Publications Ltd, Surrey, UK.

Marshall, Janette, 'Safe Sources of Meat – How to avoid hormones and antibiotics', *Here's Health*, Jan 1985, Vol. 30, No. 340, Newman Turner Publications Ltd, Surrey, UK.

Needles, Joseph, 'Bi Syndrome (Part One)', *The Journal of Chinese Medicine*, No. 10, May 1982, Sussex, UK.

Phillipps, Karen and Dahlen, Martha, *A Guide to Market Fruits of Southeast Asia*, South China Morning Post Ltd, Hong Kong.

Phillipps, Karen and Dahlen, Martha, *A Popular Guide to Chinese Vegetables*, South China Morning Post Ltd, Hong Kong.

Ryman, Danicle, *The Aromatherapy Handbook, The Secret Healing Power of Essential Oils*, Century Publishing Co. Ltd, London, UK.

Scott, Julian, 'The Diagnoses and Treatment of Headaches', *The Journal of Chinese Medicine*, No. 15, May 1984, Sussex, UK.

Shreeve, Dr Cardine, 'Coping with Cystitis', *Here's Health*, Sep 1984, No. 336, Newman Turner Publications Ltd, Surrey, UK.

____, 'How to Control Thrush – Natural ways to combat this persistent problem', *Here's Health*, Feb 1985, Vol. 30, No. 341, Newman Turner Publications Ltd, Surrey, UK.

So Yan-kit, *Yan-kit's Classic Chinese Cookbook*, Dorling Kindersley Ltd, London, UK.

Soo, Chee, *The Tao of Long Life, The Chinese Art of Ch'ang Ming*, Aquarian Press, Northamptonshire, UK.

Tan, Cecelia, *Penang Nonya Cooking, Foods of My Childhood*, Times Books International, Singapore.

Tan, Terry, *Cooking with Chinese Herbs*, Times Books International, Singapore.

Tisserand, Maggie, *Aromatherapy for Women, Beautifying and Healing Essences from Flowers and Herbs*, Thorsons Publishers Ltd, Northamptonshire, UK.

Tisserand, Robert, *The Art of Aromatherapy*, CW Daniel Company Ltd, Essex, UK.

Walters, W.D., M.P.S., *Wonderful Herbal Remedies*, Celtic Educational (Services) Ltd, Wales, UK.

Wollner, David and Seamens, Don, 'Shopper's Guide to Natural Foods – Seaweeds and Beans', *East West Journal*, Sep 1981, Vol. II, No. 9, East West Journal, Inc, Massachusetts, USA.

Chinese Sources

A Barefoot Doctor's Manual, prepared by the Revolutionary Health Committee of Hunan Province, Routledge & Kegan Paul, UK.

Chinese Herbal Medicine Materia Medica, compiled and translated by Don Bensky and Andrew Gamble with Ted Kaptchuk, Eastland Press, Inc, Washington, USA.

Essentials of Chinese Acupuncture, compiled by Beijing College of Traditional Chinese Medicine, Shanghai College of Traditional Chinese Medicine, Nanjing College of Traditional Chinese Medicine, The Acupuncture Institute of the Academy of Traditional Chinese Medicine, Foreign Languages Press, Beijing, China.

FURTHER READING

Besides reading the books listed in the Bibliography, here are more books which are highly recommended to increase your knowledge of self-help.

Bach, Dr Edward, *Heal Thyself: An Explanation of the Real Cause and Cure of Disease*, C.W. Daniel Company Ltd.

_____, *The Twelve Healers*, C.W. Daniel Company Ltd.

Brohn, Penny, *Gentle Giants, The Powerful Story of One Woman's Unconventional Struggle against Breast Cancer*, Century Hutchinson.

Butt, Gary and Bloomfield, Frena, *The Chinese Way of Health through Food; Harmony Rules*, Arrow Books.

Carpenter, Moira, *Curing PMT the Drug-free Way*, Century Arrow.

Carter, Mildred, *Helping Yourself with Foot Reflexology*, Parker Publishing Company, Inc.

Carter, Mildred, *Hand Reflexology: Key to Perfect Health*, Parker Publishing Company, Inc.

Chaitow, Leon, *Candida albicans – Could Yeast be Your Problem? The non-drug approach to the treatment of Candida infection: the proliferation of a parasite yeast that lives inside all of us*, Thorsons Publishing Group.

Davies, Dr Stephen and Stewart, Dr Alan, *Nutritional Medicine, The drug-free guide to better family health*, Pan Books.

Flows, Bob, *Path of Pregnancy*, Paradigm Publications.

Grossman, Richard, *The Other Medicines, The Unique Treat-Yourself Guide to Natural Remedies and Therapies*, Pan Books.

Harrison, Shirley, *New Approaches to Cancer*, Century.

Hoffman, David, *The Holistic Herbal Way to Successful Stress Control*, Thorsons Publishing Group.

Ingham, Eunice D., *Stories the Feet Can Tell Through Reflexology*, Ingham Publishing Inc.

Kushi, Aveline Tomoko, *How to Cook with Miso*, Japan Publications Inc.

Kushi, Michio, *The Book of Macrobiotics, The Universal Way of Health and Happiness*, Japan Publications Inc.

_____, *The Cancer Prevention Diet, Michio Kushi's Nutritional Blueprint for the Relief and Prevention of Disease*, St Martin's Press.

Laver, Mary and Smith, Margaret, *Diet for Life, A Cookbook for Arthritis*, Pan Books.

Lo, Kenneth, *Chinese Cooking and Eating for Health*, Mayflower, Granada Publishing.

Mindell, Earl, *Pills and You, The Revolutionary Guide to Medicine, Nutrition and Health by the World Famous Nutritionist Earl Mindell*, Arlington Books.

_____, *The Vitamin Bible, How the right vitamins and minerals can revolutionise your life*, Arlington Books.

Pietroni, Dr Patrick, *Holistic Living, A Guide to Self-care by a Leading Practitioner*, Dent Paperbacks.

Scheffer, Mechthild, *Bach Flower Therapy, Theory and Practice*, Thorsons Publishers Ltd.

Yudkin, John, *Pure White and Deadly*, Viking.

Diet, Exercise, Massage, The Chinese Way to a Long and Healthy Life, compiled and edited by The People's Medical Publishing House, Beijing, China, Joint Publishing Co. (HK).

East West, The Journal of Natural Health and Living, Kushi Foundation Inc.

Here's Health, Argus Health Publications.

Useful Addresses

Bach Flower Remedies

Australia

Martin and Pleasance
Wholesale Pty Ltd
PO Box 4
Collingwood, Victoria 3066
Tel: 419-9733

Nonesuch Botanicals Pty Ltd
PO Box 68
Mt Evelyn, Victoria 3796
Tel: 762-8577

Austria, Germany, Switzerland

Mechthild Scheffer
Bach Centre – German Office
Eppendorfer Landstrasse 32
2000 Hamburg 20
Tel: 040/46-10-41

Canada, United States of America

Ellon (Bach USA) Inc
PO Box 320
Woodmere, NY 11598
Tel: 516-825-2229

Denmark

Camette, Murerveg
6700 Esbjerg
Tel: 05-155444

Holland

Holland Pharma
Postbus 37
7240 AA Lochem
Tel: 05730-2884

United Kingdom

The Bach Flower Remedies Ltd
The Bach Centre
Mount Vernon, Sotwell
Wallingford
Oxon OX10 0PZ
England, UK
Tel: 0491-39489/34678

Essential Oils

United Kingdom

Aroma-Therapy Supplies
52 St Aubyns Road
Fishergate
Brighton BN4 1PE
Tel: 0273-412139

United States of America

Original Swiss Aromatics
PO Box 606
San Rafael, CA 94915

Moxa Sticks
(Available from most Chinese herbalists)

United Kingdom

P.H. Medical
Acupuncture and Electro-
therapy Equipment
16 Birch Close
New Haw, Weybridge
Surrey KT15 3JT
Tel: 0932-45495

INDEX

For convenience, the following have been incorporated in the index:
- Recipes are listed under one entry, 'Recipes', and refer only to the first mention of the particular recipe with notes on proportions and preparation.
- The various types of any particular ailment are listed under their subject category – for example, 'deficient kidney *yang*' under 'Constipation'.
- Traditional Chinese syndromes such as 'deficient kidney *yang*' will also be listed separately under 'Syndromes'.

Abalone 128
Aches and pains 19
    citrus fruits inadvisable for 168-9
    jackfruit inadvisable for 171
    pineapple inadvisable for 172
    see also Wind
Acidity
    millet for 31
    of foods 20
Acne
    Aloe vera for 113
    apricots inadvisable for 166
    bitter gourd for 89
    chrysanthemum for 114, 180
    coffee in excess causes 177
    lotus root for 94
    mint for 116
    mango inadvisable for 175
    mung bean soup for 53
    rambutans inadvisable for 175
    seaweeds for 85
    water chestnuts for 97
    watermelons for 173
Acne, symptoms and adjustment of imbalances 294-8
Acupressure
    for asthmatic babies 259
    for heart failure 312
    for premenstrual tension 346
    see Acupuncture points
Acupuncture 12, 225,
    for asthma 252, 254-5, 258
    for colds and 'flus 239, 240
    for gout 288
    for headaches 261, 263, 265, 266-8, 270-5
    for multiple sclerosis 325
    for sinusitis 244, 246
Acupuncture (acupressure) points 224
    Appendix C 376-81

Bitong 239, 243
Bladder 12 239, 251, 259
Bladder 13 239, 243, 251, 259
Bladder 20 253, 257, 267
Bladder 23 257
Bladder 43 251
Dingchuan 251, 259
Du 26 312
Gall Bladder 20 239, 263
Heart 1 312
Heart 6 346
Heart 7 346
Heart 9 312
jawline for lymphatic glands 239
Kidney 3 257-8
Large Intestine 4 230, 239, 243, 261, 263, 265-6
Large Intestine 20 239, 243
Lung 1 251
Pericardium 6 346
Ren 17 251
Spleen 6 253, 257, 267, 346
Stomach 36 253, 257, 266-7, 346
Stomach 40 253, 267
Yintang 239, 243, 266-7, 346
Aduki beans 58-60
    diuretic property of 58
Alcohol
    alcoholic beverages 16, 19
    never to be taken with durian 174
Alfalfa sprouts 87
Alkalinity of food 20
    in *miso* 50
Almond 71-2
    almond cream 72
    dry-roasted with *tamari* 72
Almond milk 182
Aloe vera 113, 298, 317
Amenorrhoea 182
Anaemia
    blackberries for 167
    grapes for 169
    hair loss and 332
    longan for 132, 170
    lotus root for 94
    neutral and warming chicken dishes for 158-63
    oysters for 128
    Shiitake mushrooms for 130
    sunflower seed milk for 182
    tonic for 133-4
Angled luffa 87-8
Antibiotics 16-17, 50
Anxiety

    as a nervous disorder 16
    chamomile tea for 180
Apple 165-6
Apple juice 183
Apricot juice 185
Apricot kernels
    bitter 71
    sweet 72
    toxicity of 72
Apricots 166
Arame 82-3
Aromatherapy 223-4
    for arthritis and rheumatism 282
    for cancer 365-6
    for the heart 312
    for multiple sclerosis 325
    for premenstrual tension 343, 346
    for psoriasis 317-18
    see Essential oils
Arrowhead tubers 88
Arthritis 19, 276-84
    bananas inadvisable for 170
    black soyabeans for 61, 62
    celery for 89
    coconut inadvisable for 171
    ginger for 123
    jackfruit inadvisable for 171
    mustard for 124
    pepper for 124
    pineapple inadvisable for 172
    seaweeds for 79
Arthritis and rheumatism, kinds of, their symptoms and adjustment to imbalances
    bony *bi* 277-83
    febrile *bi* where heat predominates 277-83
    fixed *bi* where damp predominates 277-83
    painful *bi* where cold predominates 277-83
    wandering *bi* where wind predominates 276-83
Asparagus 88
Asthma 248-59
    ciku inadvisable for 171
    foods to avoid 258
    ginkgo nuts for 71
Asthma, kinds of, their symptoms and adjustment to imbalances
    accumulation of mucus (cold type) 252-4
    accumulation of mucus (heat type) 254-5

deficient kidney *qi* 255-8
deficient lung *qi* 255
external wind cold entering the
    lungs 248-52
Aubergine 19

Bacang 15
Bach Flower Remedies 226, 265, 288, 325,
    364-6
Backache
    cinnamon for 121
    fenugreek for 122
Balding, causes and adjustment to
    imbalances 330-3
    exercises for 332-3
Bananas 170
Barley 29-30
    barley malt extract 183
    pot and pearl 29
    pot barley water 178
Basil 120
Baths
    avoid bathing in *yin* hours 278
    cinnamon bath 282, 284
    comfrey tea foot bath 288
    for genital area in thrush 353-4
    ginger bath 282, 284
    lavender bath 229, 231, 237, 245,
        246, 325
    mustard foot bath 238
Bay leaves 120
Beetroot 100
Beetroot greens 88-9
Beri-beri
    aduki bean recipe for 59
    peas for 66
Beverages 177-85
    cooling beverages 179-82
    neutral beverages 182-3
    warming beverages 183-5
Bi, definition of 276
Biscuits 16
Bites, insect 15
Bitter gourd 89
Blackberry 167
Blackberry juice 185
Blackcurrant 167
Blackcurrant juice 185
Black-eyed beans 60-1
Black moss
    see *Fat choy*
Black wood ears 128
Bladder
    parsley for 118, 182
Bleeding
    vaginal 73
Blood pressure
    low 80

see also High blood pressure
Blood systems
    cooled 13-15, 19-20, 25, 51, 80,
        129
    diabetes 29
    effects on tongue, urine and stools 14
    natural 15
    overheated 13-15, 19-20, 29, 50,
        128, 142
    symptoms and signs 14-15
    yang constitution 14
Body
    clock 215
    dampness and manifestations 25
    heat 14
Boils 19
    Aloe vera for 113
    apricots inadvisable for 166
    bitter gourd for 89
    chrysanthemum for 114, 180
    coffee in excess causes 177
    mango inadvisable for 175
    mint for 116
    rambutans inadvisable for 175
    water chestnuts for 97
    watermelons for 173
Bone development
    seaweeds for 85
    sesame seeds for 75
Bone structure 13
Borage 113
    borage tea 180
Bowel problems 18
    oat groats for 43
Brain
    diet for 334-7
    fish for 141
    walnuts for 76
Bran 28
    many layers of, in brown rice 37
Breath, bad 14
    Chinese box thorn berries for 126
    chrysanthemum for 114, 180
    coffee in excess causes 177
    pear for 165
Brews, herbal 14
Broad beans 100
Broccoli 100
Bronchitis
    comfrey for 114
    dandelion root for 115, 180
Brown rice
    flakes 40
    relative merits of grain sizes
        36-7
Bruises
    turmeric for 117
Brussels sprouts 101
Buddha's fruit 126

Buckwheat 30
Buckwheat noodles 31
Bulgar 34
Burdock 113
    burdock tea 180
Burns
    Aloe vera for 113

Cabbage 101-2
    varieties 102
Cakes 16
Calories, laden 18
Cancer 10, 26
    alternative therapy 364-6
    causes 355-7
    exercise for 362-3
    linked to coffee intake 178
    meals for nausea 362
    methods for coping with cancer
        357-66
    Shiitake mushrooms for 130
    skin 113
Carambola
    see Star fruit
Caraway 120
Caraway seed tea 184
Carbohydrates
    complex 28
    simple (white sugar) 28
Cardamom 120
Carob 178-9
Carotene 108
Carrageen 84
Carrot 108
Cataracts
    effect of chillies 19
Catarrh
    thyme for 119
Catarrh, mucus, phlegm, sputum
    bananas inadvisable for 170
    ciku inadvisable for 171
    citrus fruits inadvisable for 181
    dates inadvisable for 169
    honey in excess causes 182
    longans inadvisable for 170
    mandarins inadvisable for 168
    peanut milk in excess causes 182
    sweet oranges inadvisable for
        169
    thyme tea for 183
Cauliflower 102
Celeriac 102
Celery 89
Cells
    embryo 11
    growth and repair 16, 18
Central nervous system 18
Chakras 221

Chamomile, German 113-14
  chamomile tea 180
Chang Ming (Tao) Diet *passim*
  cooking method selection in
    187-8
  food selection in 187
  for acne 294-7
  for arthritis and rheumatism 279-
    81
  for asthma 249-50, 252, 253, 254-
    5, 257
  for balding 330-2
  for the brain 334-7
  for cancer 358-62
  for colds and 'flus 237-8, 240
  for constipation 227-9, 230, 231, 232,
    233, 234
  for cystitis 290-1
  for diabetes 300-4
  for dysmenorrhoea 349
  for eyesight 326-7
  for gout 287-8
  for headaches 261-2, 263, 264, 267, 268,
    269
  for high blood pressure 305-11
  for lower back pain 285-6
  for leucorrhoea 352-3
  for migraines 273, 274
  for mittleschmerz 350-1
  for multiple sclerosis 322-4
  for premenstrual tension 342-4, 346
  for prostatitis 293
  for psoriasis 31517
  for sinusitis 242-3, 244-6
  fruits in 164
  legumes and pulses in 15, 47
  reasons for cooking in 186-7
  vegetables in 86, 164
  whole cereal grains in 15, 28-9
Change, law of spirallic 11
Chanting 221-3
Cheese varieties 15-16
Chemicals
  antibiotics, hormones 17
  chemically treated manmade
    containers 20
  insecticides, pesticides 16
Chemotherapy 225
Cherry 167
Cherry juice 185
Chestnuts 73-4
  roasted 73-4
Chicken 154-63
  benefits of 154
  black-boned chicken the most
    nourishing 154
  cooling chicken dishes 155-8
  free-range desirable 154
  neutral chicken dishes 158-60

  old hen more nourishing 154
  warming chicken dishes 160-3
Chick-peas 63-4
Chickweed 114
Chicory 89-90
Children 12-13
Children, foods suitable for 42, 46, 70, 74,
    75, 76, 77-8, 85, 111, 139-40, 143, 145,
    153, 158-60, 163, 175-6, 185
Chillies 19
Chinese black dates 130
Chinese box thorn berries 126-7
Chinese box thorn leaves 90
Chinese chives 108-9
Chinese flowering cabbage 102-3
Chinese kale 103
Chinese Peking cabbage 90
Chinese radish 90
Chinese red dates 130
Chinese spinach 91
Chinese white cabbage 91
Chiropractic help 224-5
Chives 120
Chocolate 15
  see Cocoa
Cholesterol, high blood 16
  bitter gourd for 89
  black wood ears for 128
  cooking eggs for 135
  dried shrimps inadvisable for 129
  fish congee for 144
  fish for 143
  garlic for 122
  oats for 43
  onion for 109
  red kidney-beans for 67
  rosemary tea inadvisable for 183
  seaweeds for 79
  Shiitake mushrooms for 130
Chrysanthemum 114
  chrysanthemum tea 180
Cider 19
Ciku 170-1
Cinnamon 121
Cinnamon tea 184
Classification of foods (from cooling to
    warming) 15, Appendix A, 367-72
Clementine juice 181
Climate
  conditions affect blood system 13
  effect of on blood systems 13
Clots, preventing
  lotus root for 94
  watercress for 98
Cloves 121
Cocoa 178-9
  see Carob
Coconut products 17
Coconut juice 181

Coconuts 171
Coffee 177-8
  substitutes 178
Cold hands and feet
  cinnamon for 121, 184
  fenugreek for 122
  pepper for 124
Colds and 'flus 236-41
  carrot for 108
  cloves for 121
  elderberry for 118
  gargles for 239, 240
  garlic for 123
  ginger for 123, 184
  leek for 109
  mint for 116
  Mu tea not advisable for 184
  mustard for 124
  onion for 109
  Shiitake mushrooms for 130
  spearmint for 125
  spring onion for 110
  vervain tea for 181
Colds and 'flus, kinds of, their
    symptoms and adjustment to
    imbalances
  wind cold 236-9
  wind heat 236-7, 239-40
Cold sores
  Aloe vera for 113
Colitis
  slippery elm for 116
Colouring, artificial 19
Comfrey 114-15
  comfrey tea 180
Complexion
  cabbage for 101
  red 14
  walnuts for 76-7, 183
Conception, time of 13
Conjunctivitis 19
Constipation 227-35
  agar agar for 84
  apple for 165
  bananas for 170
  black sesame seeds for 76
  brown rice for 37
  caused by excess guava 174
  celery for 89
  Chinese spinach for 91
  coffee in excess causes 178
  figs for 127, 169
  gandum for 34
  grapes for 169
  honey for 182
  linseed for 77
  massage for warming lower abdomen
    220
  onion for 109

papaya for 173
persimmon for 127, 169
pomeloes for 172
raisins for 129-30
seaweeds for 79
slippery elm for 116
slippery vegetable for 96
tarragon for 116
types 227
watermelons for 173
Constipation, kinds of, their
  symptoms and adjustment to
  imbalances
    deficient blood 232-3
    deficient kidney *yang* 234-5
    deficient *qi* 231-2
    full heat 227-30
    obstruction of food 230
    stagnation of *qi* 230-1
    when to empty bowels 235
Constitutional make-up 13
Convenience foods 16, 20
Cooking methods
  recommendations 15, 26-7, 186-8
Cooking oils 24-5
  pure roasted sesame seed oil 25
Cooling energy foods 13-15, 20
Coriander 121
Corn silk 115
  corn silk tea 180
Cough
  apricot kernels for 72
  cinnamon for 121
  comfrey for 114, 180
  ginger for 123
  ginkgo nuts for 71
  honey for 182
  liquorice for 118
  pear for 165
  rambutans inadvisable for 175
Courgette 91-2
Cramps
  water spinach believed to cause 98
Cream 16
Cress 92
Crockpots 26-7
Crystal healing 366
Cucumber 92
Cumin 121
Custard apples 171
Cuts
  chickweed for 114
  comfrey for 114
Cystitis 19
  corn silk for 115, 180
  fish congee for 144
  Job's tears for 127
  mango inadvisable for 175
  pot barley for 29-30

rambutans inadvisable for 175
Cystitis, symptoms and adjustment to
  imbalances 289-92

Dairy products 16
Damp heat 14
  apricot kernels for 72
  brown rice congee for 40
  carrageen for 84
  coffee in excess causes 178
  fruit in excess causes 164
  hyacinth beans for 65
  Job's tears for 127
  lychees in excess causes 170
  mandarins in excess causes 168
  mangoes in excess causes 175
  pineapple in excess causes 172
  pot barley water for 179
  rambutans in excess causes 175
  symptoms 164
Dandelion leaves 92-3
Dandelion root 115
  dandelion tea 180-1
Dang gui 130-1
  for women 341
Dang shen 131
Dates 169
Deadly Nightshade
  see *Solanaceae*
Deficient kidney *yang*
  raspberries for bedwetting caused by
    166
Depression
  as a nervous disorder 16-17
  coffee in excess causes 178
  raspberry tea for 182
Diabetes
  bitter gourd for 89
  corn silk for 115, 180
  fish congee for 144
  haricot beans for 64
  millet for 31
  pot barley for 29-30
  red kidney-beans for 64
  Shiitake mushrooms for 130
  whole wheat grains for 33
Diabetes 299-304
Diagnosis
  tongue, stools and urine 14
Diarrhoea 18
  chestnuts for mild cases of 73
  cock's crow diarrhoea 170, 215
  figs inadvisable for 169
  grapes inadvisable for 169
  lychees for 170
  massage for warming lower abdomen
    220
  nutmeg for 123

persimmon for 127
recipe for spleen-deficient diarrhoea
  73
sesame seeds inadvisable for 75
Digestion
  basil for 120
  cardamom for 120
  chicory for 89
  coriander for 121
  cumin for 121
  dill for 121
  durians difficult for 174
  fennel 122, 184
  fish for 141
  garlic for 122-3
  ginger for 123
  lemongrass 123
  linseed for 77
  mandarins for 168
  mint tea for 181
  mustard for 124
  nutmeg for 123
  oregano for 124
  papaya for 173
  pot barley for 29
  rosemary tea for 182
  sage tea for 183
  slippery elm for 116
  spearmint for 125, 185
  thyme for 119, 183
Dill 122
Diuresis
  aduki beans for 61
  black soyabeans for 61
  dandelion leaves for 92
  dandelion root coffee for 178
  grapefruits for 168
  mung beans for 52
  raspberries for 166
  rosemary for 119
  spring onion for 110
  tangerine peel 132
  tarragon for 116
Dizziness
  black soyabeans for 61, 62
Do-in exercises 217-20
Dried ingredients 126
  cooling dried ingredients 126-8
  neutral dried ingredients 128-30
  warming dried ingredients 130-4
Drugs 14, 225
Duck 15
Dulse 80, 84
Durian 174
  paired with mangosteen 174
  never to be eaten with alcohol 174
Dysentery
  persimmon for 127
Dysmenorrhoea, kinds of, their symptoms

and adjustment to imbalances
deficiency of *qi* and blood 349-50
stagnation of blood 347-8
stagnation of liver *qi* 347
stagnation of *qi* and/or blood due to
  cold 348-9

Eczema
  Aloe vera for 113
  apricots inadvisable for 166
  bitter gourd for 89
  burdock for 113, 180
  chickweed for 114
  chrysanthemum for 114, 180
  coffee in excess causes 177
  durian inadvisable for 174
  lotus root for 94
  mango inadvisable for 175
  mint for 116
  rambutans inadvisable for 175
  water chestnuts for 97
Eggs 135-40
  chicken eggs 135-7
  duck eggs 137-8
  fish eggs 138-9
  preserved duck eggs 138
  preserved quail eggs 137
  quail eggs 137
  salted duck eggs 138
  steamed for the young, invalids or
    elderly 136
  when to avoid eggs 135, 138
Elderberry 117-18
Elderly, food for 41, 42, 60, 65, 128, 130,
  135, 143, 145, 158-63
Endive 93
Energy
  cold and hot energy foods 13
  conserving energy 214-5
  cooling, neutral and warming foods
    20
  raw food energy 186
Enteritis
  slippery elm for 116
Epilepsy 15
  coconut inadvisable for 171
  jackfruit inadvisable for 171
Essential and aromatic oils
  how to use them 223-4
Kwon Loong Foong Yau 244
  oil of black pepper 269, 282
  oil of chamomile 317
  oil of cinnamon 282, 284
  oil of clary sage 343, 346-7, 351
  oil of comfrey 282
  oil of cypress 282
  oil of eucalyptus or pine 238, 244
  oil of fennel 232

oil of ginger 238, 265, 270, 282, 284,
  348-9
oil of juniper 282, 285, 333, 343
oil of lavender 282, 312, 317-18, 333,
  343
oil of neroli 343
oil of peppermint 268, 274
oil of rose 312, 317
oil of rosemary 231, 263, 333
oil of safflower 285
Olbas oil 238, 244
see also Baths, lavender
Exercises
  chanting 221-2
  deep breathing 222, 243, 244, 245, 250,
    253, 255, 257, 338-9
  for arthritis and rheumatism 281
  for balding 332-3
  for eyesight 327-9
  for high blood pressure 311
  for multiple sclerosis 324-5
  qigong 220, 225, 231, 232, 233, 235, 243,
    245, 250, 253, 255, 257, 262-7, 269,
    273-5
  taijiquan 220, 231, 232, 233, 235, 243,
    245, 250, 253, 255, 257, 262-7, 269,
    273-5
  yoga 220, 231, 232, 233, 243, 245, 250,
    253, 255, 257, 262-7, 269, 273-5
Eyes
  sore, red 90, 114, 116, 177, 180
  whites of 14
Eyesight
  black sesame seeds for 76
  black soyabeans for 62
  Chinese box thorn berries for 127
  raspberries for 166
Eyesight, failing 326-9
  exercises for 327-9

Fat choy 83-4
Fats
  saturated 16-17
Fennel 103, 122
Fenugreek 122
Fever
  durian inadvisable for 174
Figs 127, 169
Fish and other seafoods 141-53
  cooling fish dishes 143-6
  neutral fish dishes 146-8
  seasoning of 141-2
  temperate water fish 142
  tropical water fish 143
  warming fish dishes 148-51
  when to avoid seafood 151
Flour products 15, 18
Four-angled beans 103

French beans 103
Fruit juices 181
Fruits 164-76
  advantages of local fruit 164
  adverse conditions caused by excess
    164
  Mediterranean fruits 168-70
  temperate fruits 165-8
  tropical fruits 170-5
  when suitable 164
Fuzzy melon 93

Gall bladder problems
  dandelion root for 115, 180
  fish congee for 144
  Job's tears for 127
  mango inadvisable for 175
  oat groats for 43
  parsley for 118, 182
  rambutans inadvisable for 175
  rosemary tea for 182
  vervain for 117, 181
Gallstones, preventing
  Shiitake mushrooms for 130
  turnips for 108
Gargles
  sage and honey gargle 240
  sea-salt gargle 239
Garland chrysanthemum 104
Garlic 122-3
Gastric ulcer
  see Ulcers
Gastritis
  dandelion root for 115, 180
  slippery elm for 116
  thyme for 119, 183
Ginger 123, 184
  ginger compress 304
Ginkgo nuts 71
Goitre
  seaweeds for 79
Golden needles 127
Gomasio 75
  how to make salt-free *gomasio* 75
Gout, symptoms and adjustment to
  imbalances 287-8
Grapefruit 168
  avoid eating with tea 168
Grapefruit juice 181
Grape 169
Grape juice 183
Grey hair
  black sesame seeds for 76
Guava 19, 173
Guava juice 183

Hair
  fat choy for 83, 85
  hiziki for healthy hair 82
  longans for 170
Haricot beans 64-5
Hay fever 247
Headache
  Chinese box thorn berries for 126
  Chinese box thorn leaves for 90
  chrysanthemum for 114, 180
  coffee in excess causes 177
  mint tea for 181
Headaches, kinds of, their symptoms
    and adjustment to imbalances
  back of head (dull, heavy) 271
  back of head (full, bursting) 271
  back of head (tight, boring) 271-2
  back of head (varying from dull and
    sharp) 272
  classification 260
  front of head or forehead (dull, heavy)
    266-7
  front of head or forehead (full,
    bursting) 268
  front of head or forehead (tight,
    boring) 268-9
  front of head or forehead (varying
    between dull and sharp) 269
  sides of head or temples (dull, heavy)
    269-70
  sides of head or temples (full,
    bursting) 270
  sides of head or temples (tight,
    boring) 270
  sides of head or temples (varying
    between dull and sharp) 270
  top of head (dull, heavy) 261-3
  top of head (full, bursting) 264-5
  top of head (tight, boring) 264-5
  top of head (varying between dull and
    sharp) 265
  whole head 273
  see also Migraines
Heart
  linseed for 77
  lotus seeds for 72
  whole wheat grains for 33
Heated blood systems
  pot barley for 30
Heat rash
  coffee in excess causes 177
  mint for 116
  mung bean soup for 53
  seaweeds for 85
Hepatitis
  dandelion root for 115, 180
  mango inadvisable for 175
  rambutans inadvisable for 175
Herbs and spices 112-25

  cooling herbs and spices 113-17
  choosing 188
  herbal infusion 112, 240
  neutral herbs and spices 117-120
  warming herbs and spices 120-25
High blood pressure 19
  bitter gourd for 89
  celery for 67, 89
  cooking eggs for 135
  corn silk for 115, 180
  dried shrimps inadvisable for 129
  fish congee for 144
  garlic for 122
  Mu tea inadvisable for 184
  onion for 109
  persimmon for 169
  rosemary tea for 183
  salted duck eggs inadvisable for 138
  scallops for 128-9
  seaweeds for 79
  shiitake mushrooms for 130
  white fish for 143
High blood pressure, symptoms and
    adjustment to imbalances 305-13
Hiziki 82
Hoi tai
  see *kombu*
Honey 182
Huang shi 132
Hyacinth beans 65

Impotence
  raspberries for 166
Indigestion
  brown rice congee for 40
Insomnia
  chamomile for 114, 180
  coffee in excess causes 177
  lotus seed recipe for 72-3
  walnuts for 76-7
Intestinal worms
  pumpkin seeds for 74
  sunflower seeds for 76
Intestines
  linseed for 77
Invalids
  fish for 143, 145

Jackfruit 171
Japanese tea 183
Jaundice
  rosemary tea for 182
  vervain for 117, 181
Jing, definition of 334
  improving 338-9
Job's tears 127

Kelp
  see *Kombu*
Kidneys
  black-eyed beans for 60
  black sesame seeds for 76
  black soyabeans for 61
  cinnamon for 121
  fenugreek for 122
  linseed for 77
  lotus seeds for 72
  millet for 31
  parsley for 118, 182
  walnuts for 76, 183
  warming up kidneys exercise 220, 286
  whole wheat grains for 33
Knees, weak
  cinnamon for 121
  fenugreek for 122
Kohlrabi 93
Kombu 80-1

Lamb's lettuce 104
Landcress 104
Laverbread
  see *Nori*
Leek 109
Legumes and pulses 47-70
  basic recipes 47-8
  for babies and infants 70
  cooking method to overcome
    flatulence caused by 47-8
  properties 47
Lemon balm 115, 181
Lemongrass 123
Lemon juice 181
Lemons 168
Lentils 68-70
Lettuce 93-4
Leucorrhoea
  ginkgo nuts for 71
  hyacinth beans for 65
  Job's tears for 127
  mango inadvisable for 175
  rambutans inadvisable for 175
  seaweeds for 79
Leucorrhoea, kinds of, their symptoms
    and adjustment to imbalances
  damp heat 352-3
  deficiency of *qi* and blood 351-2
Lime 181
Linseed 77
Liquorice 118
Liver
  black sesame seeds for 76
  Chinese box thorn berries for 126
  dandelion leaves for 92
  linseed for 77
  parsley for 118, 182

plums for 166
rosemary for 119, 182
Longan 132, 170
Longan juice 185
Long bean 104-5
Lotus root 94
Lotus seed 72-3
    when not to use 72
Lower back pain, kinds of, their
    symptoms and adjustment to
    imbalances
      deficiency of kidneys 285
      invasion and retention of wind, cold
        or damp 285
      stagnation of *qi* and blood 286
Lungs
    apricots for 166
    apricots inadvisable for lung heat 166
    Chinese radish for 90
    Chinese spinach recipe for 91
    peaches for 167
    pears for 165
    seaweeds for 79, 84
    snow ear fungus for 127
Lychee 170
Lychee juice 185

Malay apple 171
Mandarin orange 168, 181
Mango 175
Mangosteen 172
    paired with durian 172
Marrow 94
Mastitis
    dandelion root for 115, 180
Mata kucing 174
Meals and menus
    cooling meals for rainy monsoon
      days 191
    cooling meals for summer and hot
      days 189-91
    cooling meals for winter 191
    neutral meals for rainy monsoon
      days 193
    neutral meals for summer and hot
      days 191-3
    neutral meals for winter 193
    warming meals for rainy monsoon
      days 195
    warming meals for summer or hot
      days 193-5
    warming meals for winter 195
Meditation 216, 338-9, 366
Melon 181
Memory, improving 339-40
Men
    ginseng for 130-1
Menopause 351

Menstruation problems
    asthmatic women and 256
    bananas inadvisable for 170
    basil for 120
    caraway seeds for 120
    cinnamon for 121
    coconut inadvisable for 171
    fenugreek for 122
    grapefruits inadvisable for 168
    longan for 132
    Mu tea for 184
    mugwort for 124, 184
    parsley for 118, 182
    pear inadvisable for 165
    persimmon inadvisable for 169
    pineapple inadvisable for 172
    sage for 119, 183
    sweet oranges inadvisable for 169
    tarragon for 117
    see also Premenstrual tension
Mental depression
    brown rice for 37
    whole wheat grain water for 33
Meridians, the twelve 217-19
Migraines
    chamomile for 114, 180
    coffee in excess causes 177
Migraines, kinds of, with their
    symptoms and adjustment to
    imbalances
    deficiency of liver blood 274
    deficiency of *yin* 274-5
    deficiency of *yin* and *yang* 275
    stagnation of liver *qi* 273
    stomach *qi* 273-4
Milk
    cow's 182
    goat's 182
    not to be drunk with watermelon
Millet 31-3
    flakes 33
Mineral water 179
Mint 116, 181
Miso 49-52
    for children 70
    for dry, cracked lips 50
    for nausea 50
    instant packet *miso* 50
    properties 49-50
    shoyu and *tamari* as by-products of
      52
    varieties 50
Mittleschmerz, symptoms and adjustment
    to imbalances 350-1
Motion sickness
    ginger for 123
    strawberries for 167
Moxibustion 224
    for arthritis and rheumatism 282-3

    for asthma 251, 253-4, 258
    for colds and 'flus 239
    for constipation 234
    for dysmenorrhoea 348-50
    for headaches and migraines 269, 272
    for lower back pain 286
    for muscular spasms 288
    for premenstrual tension 345
    for sciatica 284
    how to use the moxa stick 224
Mu tea 184
Muesli, indigestibility of 44
Mugwort 124
Mugwort tea 184
Multiple sclerosis, kinds of, with their
    symptoms and adjustment to
    imbalances 319-25
    deficient liver and kidney 321-2
    deficient spleen and invasion of damp
      in the channels and stomach
      321-2
Mung beans 52-3
    husks as stuffing for pillows 52-3
    properties 52
Mung bean sprouts 94-5
Muscular spasms, adjustment to imbalance
    288
Mushrooms 95
Mustard 124

Nausea
    miso for 50
    sesame seeds for 75
Nectarine juice 185
Nephritis
    corn silk for 115, 180
Nerves
    basil for 120
Nettles 95
Neuralgia
    cloves for 121
Neuralgia, trigeminal, kinds of, their
    symptoms and adjustment to
    imbalances
    deficient kidney *yin* 287
    excessive heat in the liver and
      stomach 286-7
    invasion of wind and heat 286
Nori 83
Nose bleeds
    cinnamon tea in excess causes 184
Nutmeg 123

Oat groats 43-6
Obesity 28
Oedema
    see Water retention

Oils
varieties 25
Onion 109
Orange juice 181
Oregano 124
Osteopathy 224-5
Oysters 128

Pain in joints, muscles and nerves 276-88
see Arthritis and rheumatism, Gout,
Lower back pain, Muscular
spasms, Neuralgia, Sciatica
Panax ginseng 131
Panax ginseng poisoning 131
Pancreas
black soyabeans for 61
brown rice for 37
hyacinth beans for 65
millet good for 31
peas for 66
pumpkin for 64
Papaya 173
Papaya juice 183
Parsley 118
Parsnip 105
Peach 167
Peach juice 185
Peanut 73
advice against over-indulgence in 73
Peanut milk 182
Pear 165
Peas 66-7
varieties 66
Pea shoots 105
Pelvic inflammation 127
mango inadvisable for 175
rambutans inadvisable for 175
Pepper 124
Persimmon 127
Japanese 169
Phlegm
apricot kernels for 72
Buddha's fruit for 126
caused by excess mandarins 168
spring onion for 110
tangerine peel for 132
watercress for 97
Piles
bananas for 170
Pineapple 172
Pineapple juice 181
Pleurisy
borage for 113
Plum 166
Plum juice 183
Poisons
noxious gases of beans 27
Salmonella poisoning 27

Pomeloes 172
Pork 15
Prawns 129, 151-2
Pregnancy and childbirth
asthmatic attacks and 256
black soyabeans during and after
birth 61
coffee inadvisable during 178
dang gui for 130-1
fennel for nursing mothers 122, 184
grapefruits inadvisable for 168
longan for 132
oysters for nursing mothers 128
parsley for smooth delivery 118
pear inadvisable for 165
pineapple inadvisable for pregnant
women 172
raspberry leaf tea for smooth
delivery 182
Premenstrual tension, kinds of, their
symptoms and adjustment of
imbalances
deficiency of blood and *yin* 345-6
deficiency of spleen *yang* and kidney
yang 343-5
stagnation of liver *qi* 342-3
Preservatives 20
Pressure cookers 27
Prickly heat
see Heat rash
Prolapsed uterus, symptoms and
treatment 354
Prostatitis
corn silk for 115, 180
fish congee for 144
Job's tears for 127
pot barley for 30
rambutans inadvisable for 175
Prostate gland problems 292-3
Prostatitis, symptoms and adjustment to
imbalances 293
Psoriasis
Aloe vera for 113, 317
apricots inadvisable for 166
bitter gourd for 89
burdock for 113, 180
chickweed for 114, 317
chrysanthemum for 114, 180
coffee in excess causes 177
durian inadvisable for 174
lotus root for 94
mango inadvisable for 175
mint for 116
rambutans inadvisable for 175
water chestnuts for 97
Psoriasis, symptoms and adjustment of
imbalances 314-18
Pumpkin 105
Pumpkin seeds 74

for prostate gland problems 74, 292
Purple seaweed
see *Nori*

Radiation 225
Radicchio rosso 95
Radish 95-6
Raisins 129-30
Rambutans 175
Rash, heat
chrysanthemum for 114
Raspberry 118, 166
Raspberry juice 183
Raspberry leaf tea 182
Raw food 186
Recipes see also Meals and menus
aduki beans and carrots 58-9
aduki beans with peanuts 59-60
aduki beans with tangerine peel 59
angled luffa soup 87-8
apple and raisin jelly 85
apricot kernel, dried white cabbage
and date tea 72
apricot kernel milk 72
apricot kernel tea 250
Asian vegetarian fried brown rice
39-40
Autumn millet 32
baked fish 149
baked oily fish 150
baked silken *tofu* 56-7
baked white fish with fennel 149
baked white fish with *miso* 149-50
banana couscous 35
barley malt jelly 84-5
basic chicken casserole 160-1
basic chicken congee 157
basic chicken soup 155
black-eyed beans and brown rice 60
black-eyed beans and peanuts 60-1
black soyabean milk 63
black soyabeans and black-boned
chicken soup 61-2
black soyabeans and black sesame
seed stew 62-3
black soyabeans and chicken feet
soup 61
black soyabeans and *kombu* 80-1
black soyabeans and leek stew 62
blood building soup 130
blood building tonic for the old, weak
and anaemic 134
braised chicken 159-60
braised fish with lemongrass 147
braised fish with vegetables 147
brown rice 37
brown rice congee 40, 42
Buddha's fruit decoction 240, 255

Buddha's fruit with cinnamon 250
buckwheat and leeks 31
bulgar 34-5
chestnut and brown rice congee 74
chestnuts and Brussels sprouts
chicken congee 156-7
chicken rice 158-9
chick-peas with fresh coriander leaves
    63-4
cinnamon tea 250
claypot chicken rice 159
cornmeal and *tofu* soup 43
cornmeal polenta 42-3
couscous 35
creamy mushroom soup 45
creamy walnut milk 77
dang gui, longan and egg tonic tea
    344-5
dang gui and longan tonic tea 344
double-boiled *Panax ginseng* and dried
    longan 134
dried Chinese white cabbage and
    unsweetened Iraqi date tea 317
dried scallops and *kombu* soup 129
dried soyabean stick stew 64
dried squid, lotus root and Chinese
    red date soup 129
dried tangerine peel cure 253
dry-roasted sunflower seeds with
    tamari 76
egg drop soup 135-6
fat choy with dried oysters 83
fish congee 144
fish *genmai miso* soup 51-2
fish, *kombu* and *miso* soup 81
fried brown rice 37
fried bulgar 35
frumenty 33-4
gandum 34
ginger and cinnamon tea 238
ginkgo nut and *euryale ferox* sweet
    tea 71
grilled fish 150-1
haricot beans with pumpkin and
    caraway seeds 64-5
jumbo oats muesli 45
kasha 30-1
kombu or *wakame* powder 85
laverbread burgers 83
leg strengthening tea 130
legumes and pulses (basic recipes)
    47-8
leek and carrot *genmai miso* soup 51
lentils and brown rice 69
lentils and thyme 68-9
lentil burgers 69-70
long beans in white fermented
    soyabean cheese 49
lotus seed and brown rice congee 73

lotus seed and egg drop soup 72-3
lotus seed and lotus root tea 73
mangetout (snow peas) with *tofu* 67
millet 31
millet and brown rice 32
millet slice 33
miso soup with brown rice flakes 40
oat groats 44
oat groats muesli 44
onion *miso* sauce 109
poached cod roe 139
popcorn 42
pot barley and brown rice 30
pot barley water 30
red kidney-beans and celery 67-8
roasted sesame seeds
rye and brown rice 41
sautéed fish 148
sautéed leek and herring 148-9
sautéed white fish 148
savoury biscuits with brown rice
    flakes 40-1
savoury jumbo oats 45-6
scrambled eggs 137
slow-cooked *hiziki* with cabbage,
    carrots and long beans 82
snow-ear fungus decoction 255
spring onions for colds and 'flus 110
steamed chicken breast 157-8
steamed eggs 136-7
steamed fish 145
steamed fresh garden peas 66
steamed marinated *tempeh* 58
steamed silken *tofu* 54-5
steamed whole white fish 145
stir-fried *arame*, onion and carrot
    82-3
stir-fried chicken with mung bean
    sprouts 161-2
stir-fried *tofu* with spring onions 56
stir-fried *tofu* with watercress 55
sunflower seed milk or cream 76
Swatow mustard cabbage and sweet
    potato tea 317
sweet corn 41-2
sweet corn and brown rice congee 42
sweet soup with mung beans and
    fresh lotus leaf 53
sweet soup with mung beans and
    Job's tears 53
sweet tea with ginkgo nuts, *fu zhou*
    and apricot kernels 71
tamari braised fish 146
tamari roast chicken 162-3
tea for building up defensive *qi* in
    Autumn, Winter and Spring 133
thick winter pea soup 66
tofu and spinach *mugi miso* soup
    50-1

tofu burger with coriander leaves 57
tofu soup 54
tofu with fermented black soybeans
    48-9
tofu with spinach and black mustard
    seeds 55-6
tonic for building up defensive *qi* in
    the old, weak or exhausted 133
tonic to build blood at the end of a
    menstrual period 133-4
tonifying chicken soup 156
vegan fried brown rice 38
vegetarian fried brown rice 38-9
vitality tea 132-3
wakame, onion and *miso* soup 81
walnut and Chinese red date tea 77
walnuts and brown rice 77
white fish congee 144-5
white fish soup 143-4
whole wheat grains and brown rice
    33
whole wheat grain water 33
wholewheat macaroni with egg 35-6
wholewheat spaghetti with
    mushrooms and *miso* sauce 36
Red cabbage 96
Redcurrant juice 183
Red kidney-beans 67-8
Reflexology 224-5
    Appendix B 373-5
    for acne 298
    for arthritis and rheumatism 282
    for asthma 250-1,
    for the brain 338
    for cancer 366
    for colds and 'flus 238
    for constipation 230, 231, 232, 233
    for cystitis 291
    for diabetes 304
    for headaches 261, 263, 265, 266, 267
    for high blood pressure 311
    for lower back pain 286
    for premenstrual tension 343
    for prostate gland problems 292
    for sciatica 284
    for sinusitis 244, 246
Rheumatism 19
    bananas inadvisable for 170
    black soyabeans for 61, 62
    celery for 89
    cloves for 121
    coconut inadvisable for 171
    ginger for 123
    jackfruit inadvisable for 171
    mustard for 124
    pepper for 124
    pineapple inadvisable for 172
    seaweeds for 79
Rice 36-41

advantages to health 37
red rice 41
see also Brown rice
Rice malt extract 183
Rickets
Shiitake mushrooms for 130
Rose apples 172
Rosemary 119
Rosemary leaf tea 182
Runner beans 105-6
Rye 41

Sage 119
Sage tea 183
Sage, purple 116
Savory 124
Scallops 128-9
Sciatica, kinds of, their symptoms and
adjustment to imbalances
obstruction of wind cold 284
obstruction of wind damp 284-5
stagnation of blood 285
Screwpine leaves 119
Sea apples 173
Sea-salt 24
Seaweeds 79-85
adverse effects of excess 79-80
for babies and teenagers 85
sources of minerals 79
Seeds and nuts 71-8
for babies and infants 77-8
proportion inagers 85
sources of minerals 79
Seeds and nuts 71-8
for babies and infants 77-8
proportion in the Chang Ming Diet
71
Sesame seeds
beige 74-5
black 75-6
in *gomasio* 75
sesame seed milk or cream 75
tahini 75
Shallot 110
Shen
definition of 339
improving 339-40
Shoyu 52
Shiitake mushrooms 130
Sichuan pepper 125
Silver fish 132
Sinusitis, kinds of, their symptoms and
adjustment to imbalances
deficient lung *qi* 242-4
liver and gall bladder damp heat
245-6
stagnation of *qi* and blood 244-5
Skin diseases

burdock tea for 180
pineapple inadvisable for 172
pot barley water for 179
Slippery elm 116
Slippery vegetable 96
Sneezing, persimmon for non-stop 169
Snow ear fungus 127-8
Snow peas 106
Solanaceae 18, 126
Solid fuel cookers 27
Sores
dandelion root for 115, 180
mung bean soup for 53
Sore throat
liquorice for 118
purple sage for 116
sage gargle for 119
Soyabean milk 57, 179-80, 182
Soyabeans 53-8
black 61-3
dried 64
sheets 64
soyabean products 53-4
when not advisable 57
Soyabeans, fermented black 48-9
for fevers 48
Soyabean cheese, fermented 49
Soyabean sprouts 96
Soyasauce
see *Shoyu, Tamari*
Spearmint 125
Spearmint tea 185
Spermatorrhoea
raspberries for 166
Spinach 96-7
Spleen
black soyabeans for 61
brown rice for 37
dang shen for 131
dates for 169
hyacinth beans for 65
lotus seeds for 72
millet for 31
peas for 66
pumpkin for 64
Sprains
comfrey for 114
Spring onion 110
Squash 106
Squid 129, 152-3
Star anise 125
Star fruit 173
Star fruit juice 181
Steroids
borage for 113, 180
liquorice for 118
Stomach
black-eyed beans for 60
dang shen for 131

hyacinth beans for 65
linseed for 77
peas for 66
Stomach ulcer
fish congee for 144
millet for 33
pineapple inadvisable for 172
Shiitake mushrooms for 130
Strawberry 167-8
Strawberry juice 185
Stress
stimulants (e.g. coffee, tea)
inadvisable during 178
sunflower seeds for 76
vervain for 117, 181
Sugar-cane juice 181, 183
Sugar substitutes 25
Sunburn
mung bean soup for 53
Sunflower seed 76
Sunflower seed milk 183
Surgery 225
Swatow mustard cabbage 97
Swede 106
Sweet corn 41-3, 106-7
Sweet oranges 169
Sweet potato 107
Sweet potato leaves 107
Swiss chard 97
Syndromes
absence of *shen* 339-40
accumulation of mucus, cold type 252
accumulation of mucus, heat type 254
attack of cold in bladder channel 272
bi syndromes 272, 276-7
catarrh, mucus or phlegm 267
cold obstruction 264
damp heat 164, 352
deficiency of blood 232-3, 261, 270,
351-2
deficiency of blood and *yin* 345
deficiency of heart 262-3
deficiency of kidneys 285
deficiency of kidney *qi* 255-6
deficiency of kidney *jing* 334, 338, 340
deficiency of kidney *yin* 287
deficiency of kidney *yang* 234
deficiency of liver blood 274
deficiency of lung *qi* 242, 255
deficiency of liver *qi* 231-2, 261
deficiency of *qi* 349, 351-2
deficiency of spleen *yang* and kidney
yang 343
deficiency of stomach blood 266
deficiency of stomach *qi* 266
deficiency of *yin* 274
deficiency of *yang* 275
excessive heat in liver and stomach
286-7

full heat 227
heat in the gall bladder 270
invasion of damp cold or damp 320
invasion of wind and heat 286
invasion of wind, cold or damp 285
liver and gall bladder damp heat 245
liver *yang* rising 264, 270
obstruction of food 230
obstruction of wind cold 284
obstruction of wind damp 284
stagnation of blood 244, 285-6, 347-8
stagnation of liver *qi* 230, 244, 263,
    273, 286, 342, 347-8
stomach cold 269
stomach heat 268, 273
wind cold 236-7
wind heat 236-7

Tahini 75
Tamari 52
Tamarind 116
Tangerine juice 181
Tangerine peel 132
Tao
    definition 11
    levels in adjusting imbalances 216-25
    philosophy of living 214-26
    see Chang Ming Diet
Taro 107
Tarragon 116-17
Tea 177
    addictive, stimulative nature of 177
    effect of tannin on stomach lining 177
    macrobiotics cautioned against 177
Tempeh 57-8
Thirst
    whole wheat grains for 33
Thrush, symptoms and adjustment to
    imbalances 353-4
Thyme 119-20
Thyme tea 183
Thyroid problems and hair loss 333
Tofu 53-4
    for children 70
Tonics 132-4
Tonsilitis
    dandelion root for 115, 180
Toothache
    mint for 116
Turmeric 117
Turnip 107-8

Ulcers
    gastric and duodenal 114, 116, 172,
        180
    mouth and tongue 115, 165
    see also Stomach ulcer

Urinary tract infection
    dandelion root for 115, 180
Urination
    pot barley for 29
    sweet corn for 41
    walnuts for 77

Vaginal infections
    mango inadvisable for 175
    rambutans inadvisable for 175
Varicose veins
    rye for 41
Vegans 19
    not to finish meal with fruit 165
Vegetable juices 185
Vegetables 86-111
    choice of 86
    cooling vegetables 87-99
    in the Chang Ming (Tao) Diet 86
    neutral vegetables 99-108
    warming vegetables 108-11
Vervain 117
Vervain tea 181
Vitamins
    A 79, 108
    B 16-17, 31, 47, 58, 76
    B complex 28, 30-1
    B1 58, 79
    B2 and B3 41
    C 19, 79, 167
    E 28, 47, 77, 79
Vomiting 123
    cherries inadvisable for sufferers 167

Wakame 81-2
Walnut 76-7
Walnut milk 183
Water 179
    boiled water 179
    filtering tap water 179
    mineral water 179
    tap water 179
Water apples 173
Water chestnuts 97
Watercress 97-8
Watermelon 173
    not to be eaten with milk 173
Watermelon juice 181
Water retention
    aduki beans for 58
    black soyabeans for 61, 62
    Job's tears for 127
    parsley tea for 182
    rosemary tea for 182
    seaweeds for 79
    see also Diuresis
Water spinach/convolvulus 98

Wheat 33-6
    benefits of 33
    white flour 33
    wholewheat pasta 35
Whole cereal grains 28-46
    advantages 28
    choosing of 29, 187
    complex carbohydrates in 28
    grain germ and vitality 29
    in Chang Ming Diet 29
    smell 29
    storing 29
Wholegrain milks for babies and infants
    46
Wind in the body
    bananas in excess cause 170
    coconut in excess causes 171
    fruit in excess causes 164
    internal wind 15
    jackfruit in excess causes 171
Winter melon 98-9
Women
    dang gui for 130-1
Women's problems 341-54

Yam 108
Yam bean 99
Yang character 11-14
Yeast 19
Yellow cucumber 99
Yin character 11-14
Yogurt 16